THE
RATIONAL
FAITH

A REVIEW OF THE EVIDENCE
FOR CHRISTIANITY

'Come now, and let us reason together, said the Lord'
Isaiah 1:18

JASON A. CROOK

The Rational Faith: A Review of the Evidence for Christianity

ISBN 9798560825010

The author welcomes correspondence at therationalfaith@gmail.com

Acknowledgments

A book of this kind does not emerge through solitary effort. As the wisest of men once wrote in Proverbs 11:14, 'in the multitude of counsellors there is safety', and I am grateful for the many wise counsellors who generously assisted in the development of what you are about to read. Chief among them is my wife Kirsty, who—in addition to raising our children—devoted countless hours to editing and critiquing its many drafts. Her input, more than anyone else, has helped bring this book to fruition.

I am also grateful for the many experts and readers who took the time to provide comments, answer questions, and offer encouragement. I will not mention them by name out of respect for their privacy, but they include several of the world's top scientists in physics and biology, specialists in philosophy, archaeology, ancient languages and history, theologians and pastors of differing denominations, and published writers from various fields—some twenty figures in all. Just as iron sharpens iron, so did they sharpen this book's arguments. I am indebted for their time and assistance.

I am also indebted to the theologians of old whose works have formed my library. Most of them have been gone for centuries, but the thoughts that once filled their minds now fill my own—thanks to *their* books. Many wrote in times of difficulty and at great personal cost, hoping their words might prove useful someday to even one person. Little could they have known how thankful I would be in the twenty-first century for their efforts. Time has been no barrier to the instruction of their latest student. This book is a tribute to their books.

A final acknowledgment must go to my children, without whom this book would not exist. J.A. James said it best in his 1824 *Christian Father's Present to his Children* that 'Never did I pass a more truly solemn or interesting moment, than that in which my firstborn child was put into my arms, and I felt that I was a father'. With each of their arrivals, I have only become more conscious that, like all children, they are immortal souls with the stamp of eternity upon them. It was for them that I first assembled the library which supplied the initial arguments for this book, and with their encouragement that I have brought it to an end.

Contents

Introduction

In 1797, the English parliamentarian and abolitionist William Wilberforce published a book that shocked British society. Having entered Parliament at twenty-one, Wilberforce was wealthy, socially connected, and one of the country's most eligible bachelors. Praised in Paris as the wittiest man in England and comfortable in the presence of diplomats and kings, it was a great surprise to many when—after years of secret effort—he released a 450-page book examining the state of Christianity within Great Britain.[1] Commenting on the differences between Biblical Christianity and the superficial form practiced by many in the upper class, he warned against the rise of 'infidelity', or atheism, amongst his peers:

> the time is fast approaching when Christianity will be almost as openly disavowed in the language, as in fact it is already supposed to have disappeared from the conduct of men; when infidelity will be held to be the necessary appendage of a man of fashion, and to believe will be deemed the indication of a feeble mind and a contracted understanding.[2]

In view of the state of Christianity today, these words appear to have been all too prophetic. To many, particularly in the West, a belief in Christianity has become synonymous with faith in the absurd, akin to believing in 'fairies at the bottom of the garden'.[3] Far from being seen as the religion of intellectuals—of men like Isaac Newton, Robert Boyle and Blaise Pascal—it is instead now frequently derided as the refuge of the anti-intellectual, the shelter of the 'infantile', and the crutch of those 'who are afraid of the dark'.[4]

The purpose of this book is to counter these impressions by reviewing the evidence for Christianity—to demonstrate that it is rational and, above all else, true. It is a book for sceptics and seekers, and has been organised to examine key aspects of Christian doctrine: *Is there a God? Is the Bible credible? Can we establish that what Christianity teaches is true?* Each chapter contains endnotes to enable the verification of what has been presented, and to facilitate the research of those who wish to explore further. As the quantity of source material will reveal, there is little in this book that could be considered original; most of what follows has been said—and with greater eloquence—by others over the centuries. Its value lies in its compilation, with a multitude of facts and arguments brought together into a single volume. Five years of research have gone into its creation, and it is being distributed at no profit to the author. Having no financial incentive, nor, as an international lawyer, any professional interest in publishing it, my hope is that it will be received as the work of one who has investigated its subject thoroughly and wishes to share the conclusions about its truth.

The structure of this book is like a pyramid, with a broad base rising to a single point. At the top is the ultimate conclusion that Christianity is the one true religion—best summarised by Jesus' words in John 14:6 that 'I am the way, the truth, and the life. No one comes to the Father except through Me'. Beneath this are a series of chapters that build upon one another as the reader climbs to the pinnacle. Care has been taken to present the information in these chapters as comprehensively—yet concisely—as possible, but they may not be of equal interest to all readers. At the base is Chapter 1—a broad historical overview of how the West rejected Christianity and why a book of this kind is necessary. Although different in some respects from the other chapters, it helps set the book's tone—the more one understands the past, the easier it is to make sense of the present. Chapter 2 examines key scientific and logical arguments for the existence of God. For those desiring a thorough grounding in the relevant evidence, it offers much for contemplation. Chapter 3 tests the world's other major religions to show why they cannot, on logical grounds, be true. With Judaism and Christianity the sole survivors of these tests, the remaining chapters then focus on the Bible to distinguish between them. Chapter 4 looks at how the Bible was created, Chapter 5 at how it has been carefully transmitted over the ages, and Chapter 6 at how we may know it to be true using a variety of evidentiary approaches. Chapter 7 then explores what the Bible teaches about man's fall into sin and need of a redeemer, with Chapter 8 examining in detail the prophecies about this redeemer and how Jesus is the sole individual to fulfil them. Chapter 9 concludes with a message of hope in Christ, before giving way to the end-of-chapter notes.

As the eighteenth-century Christian writer and scientist Baron Albrecht von Haller once observed, 'Truth loses nothing by being closely examined', and, 'If we believe more through the influence of custom and example, than from the arguments of reason, or the internal conviction of our own minds, this kind of persuasion is false and groundless, nor is [it] capable of giving confidence or peace'.[5] I pray that this book might serve those who have never been presented with the evidence for Christianity, or who harbour doubts about whether it is really true. I also hope that it will be a resource to those Christians seeking a deeper understanding of their faith and confidence in its truth. God warned in Hosea 4:6 that 'My people are destroyed for lack of knowledge', and we are commanded in 1 Peter 3:15 to 'always be ready to give a defence to everyone who asks you a reason for the hope that is in you'. To this end, I would echo the words of the nineteenth-century theologian Thomas Chalmers:

> In discussing the evidence of Christianity, all that we ask of our reader is to bring along ... the same sober and inductive spirit, that is now deemed so necessary in the prosecution of the other sciences; to abandon every system of theology, that is not supported by evidence, however much it may gratify his taste, or regale his imagination, ... and to maintain, through the whole process of the investigation, that strength and intrepidity of character, which will follow wherever the light of argument may conduct...[6]

If you are ready to examine the evidence for yourself, turn the page.

Soli Deo Gloria.

Jason A. Crook, LL.M.
Attorney & Solicitor

1

The Cult of Reason

As the pale light of an autumn day shone through the medieval glass of Notre-Dame in Paris, visitors to the cathedral on November 10, 1793 witnessed a most unusual spectacle. In place of the traditional service, they instead observed a company of men in Roman attire carrying the 'Goddess of Reason' to her throne atop the high altar.[1] Played by a local opera performer, this living centrepiece of the 'Festival of Reason' then received the adoration of girls in white dresses, members of the National Convention, and assembled supporters of the French Revolution.[2] After a rousing series of patriotic songs, Pierre Gaspard Chaumette, one of the founders of the new 'Cult of Reason', enthusiastically proclaimed:

> Legislators! fanaticism has given way to reason. Her bleared eyes could
> not endure the brilliancy of the light. This day an immense concourse
> has assembled beneath these fretted vaults, which for the first time have
> echoed to the voice of truth. There it is that the French have celebrated
> the only true worship, that of liberty, that of reason.[3]

Ending his address with a flourish, Chaumette then kissed the obliging goddess to cheers of 'The republic forever! Reason forever! Down with fanaticism!'[4] To one approving attendee and self-styled 'personal enemy of Jesus Christ', Anacharsis Cloots, this revolution against religion was only natural, given his belief—shared by many of his compatriots—that 'Humankind is God' and that God's attributes 'really belong[ed] to the political divinity'.[5] Against the light of revolutionary liberty, Christianity was the vanquished fanaticism of a dark and discredited age.

Unknown to those celebrating reason's purported triumph in what had, only hours before, been one of Europe's greatest cathedrals, within months many of them, including Chaumette and Cloots, would lie dead—executed by the very 'political divinity' they had so diligently sought to create.[6] But despite the guillotining of its leadership and official repudiation in 1794 when Maximilien Robespierre's amorphous 'Cult of the Supreme Being' supplanted it as France's civic religion, the Cult of Reason's ethos would ultimately prove long-lasting—advancing the ideas that Christianity is synonymous with fanaticism, reason is opposed to religion, and that God, if He should exist, is the enemy of liberty.[7]

Although very much a product of its time, the Cult of Reason is arguably more relevant today than it was some two centuries ago. Notre-Dame may no longer ring with Chaumette's booming voice, but the sentiments he and others expressed that fateful November Sunday continue to echo across the world. In a time of rising religious scepticism, declining church attendance, and a general sense of spiritual malaise throughout the West, many would perhaps feel justified in asking whether Christianity can 'endure the brilliancy of the light' shone by modern society.[8] Have scientific advancements discredited it intellectually?[9] Have its teachings somehow 'failed humanity'?[10] Must we conclude that it has simply 'had its day and should now be left to die in peace'?[11]

This book, unsurprisingly, rejects such sentiments. But in order to establish the truth of Christianity, we must begin with first principles, or what Aristotle described as 'the first basis from which a thing is known'.[12] For Christianity, this consists of a belief in the existence of God. Indeed, many of the earliest church creeds begin with the confession 'I believe in God...' before progressing to other doctrinal statements.[13] But is it rational to hold such a belief? This is perhaps the most important question facing the human mind, given that one's entire worldview will be shaped by the answer. As with any question of great magnitude, however, we must begin by defining its terms. What do we mean by 'rational' and 'God'? For now, simple dictionary definitions will suffice, with the Oxford English Dictionary defining the former as that which is 'based on or in accordance with reason or logic', and the latter as 'the creator and ruler of the universe; the supreme being'.[14] Phrased accordingly, our inquiry concerns the reasonableness of believing in a deity that created the universe and all within it. But before delving into the arguments for God's existence—set out in Chapter 2—it is useful to examine the events that have made it necessary to present them in the first place. What happened to transform a largely-Christian culture into the one we now see? What gives some arguments for God's existence more power today than others? *Why do those arguments matter?* To understand this, we must first undertake a brief history of belief.

1. Religion in the Ancient and Medieval Eras

At the appointed hour on a certain day in 399 BC, the door to a small Athenian prison cell opened to admit an executioner. In his hands was a bowl of poison hemlock, the drinking of which would cause death by muscular paralysis within minutes. Inside the cell sat his victim—a shabbily-dressed man of seventy years—who, after a brief conversation, drank the poison in the sorrowful company of his few remaining friends.[15] Rebuking them for their immoderate grief, the prisoner paced the confines of his cell until his legs grew heavy. Lying down, he then waited for the rising numbness to reach his heart.[16] When it finally did a few moments later, Socrates, the renowned philosopher, breathed his last.[17]

Although the decision to execute him had undoubtedly been influenced by politics, to say nothing of the gratuitous antagonism he had shown to his accusers, the official reasons for Socrates' condemnation were twofold: corrupting the youth of Athens and for *asebeia*, or 'not acknowledging the gods the city acknowledged'.[18] This was not, to be sure, the same charge as atheism as we would now understand it, for Socrates in fact worshipped gods but in a manner different from what the Athenian authorities regarded as appropriate.[19] Shocking as his punishment might seem to our modern sensibilities, it illustrates the degree to which religion was regarded as a public, rather than private, affair in the ancient world. Belief in the divine was not simply a matter of individual conscience, but a civic duty. Those who shunned the established belief system—like the first-century Christians in Rome—were not only seen as odd, but treasonous, in a time when the well-being of the state was thought to rest upon a proper relationship with the gods.[20]

The fact that we regard such punishments as barbaric today illustrates the extent to which Western thought has changed over the last 2,500 years. But how did we get here? To fully answer this question would require a book much longer than the present volume, and any attempt to do justice to it in a single chapter can only involve the broadest of brushstrokes. Nevertheless, the overall picture is relatively clear. Up until the nineteenth century, religion was a matter of civic concern. Even when the religion changed, as it did when the Roman Empire embraced Christianity, the state's attitude generally did not change with it.[21] When the Council of Nicaea met in 325 to consider the Arian challenge to orthodox Christianity, for instance, the emperor's ultimate response was to banish Arius for his heretical beliefs.[22] Six centuries later when the Danish king Harald Bluetooth converted to Christianity, his subjects were simply ordered to reject paganism.[23] Whatever role individual conscience might have played was often overshadowed by the necessity of adhering to the ruling faith.

Such was the general situation when Martin Luther nailed his theses to the Wittenberg cathedral door in 1517, initiating the Reformation. Although one could devote a lifetime to studying its consequences, two of its outcomes were particularly significant. The first related to the role of authority, especially when it came to interpreting the Bible. At the Diet of Worms in 1521, convened by the Holy Roman Emperor to allow Luther to clarify his position on certain teachings, Luther refused to withdraw his objections and stated that 'Unless I am convinced by the testimony of the Scriptures or by clear reason [that I am wrong] I am bound by the Scriptures I have quoted and my conscience is captive to the Word of God'.[24] Although many of his proposals were not overly objectionable to some within the Church—with the Catholic scholar Desiderius Erasmus noting that 'many of the reforms for which Luther calls are urgently needed'—the issue of interpretive authority was non-negotiable.[25]

Sympathetic as he was to many of Luther's positions, Erasmus—like many others—saw danger in rejecting the Church's authority to interpret the meaning of scripture. In the absence of a sole interpreter, dissension would be the inevitable result.[26] In 1529, Luther experienced this when, at a convocation with the Swiss reformer Ulrich Zwingli to establish unity amongst the leading Protestants, they failed to agree on the nature of the Lord's Supper.[27] Doctrinal disunion soon gave rise to political disunion, with a group of Lutheran princes forming a defensive alliance to guard against attack by Catholic imperial forces.[28] Following a series of battles, the parties agreed to the Peace of Augsburg in 1555, which established the principle of *cujus regio, ejus religio*, or 'whose the rule, his the religion'.[29] The Lutheran 'faith of the Augsburg Confession' was officially recognised, alongside the 'old Catholic faith'.[30] Anything else was still regarded as heretical, and the inhabitants of a prince's dominion were expected to adhere to his religion, whether Catholic or Lutheran.[31] But if they could not do so, they were to be allowed to peacefully depart, 'hindered neither in the sale of their estates after due payment of the local taxes nor injured in their honour' if they chose to leave and settle elsewhere.[32]

2. Early Modern Attitudes

Peace in Europe did not last, and the religious question was soon involved in the Dutch war of independence and the Thirty Years' War between the Catholic Habsburgs and the Protestant states of the Holy Roman Empire.[33] In 1648, the Peace of Westphalia was concluded between the European powers, setting out, amongst other things, that those who 'shall profess and embrace a Religion different from that of the Lord of the Territory' would:

be patiently suffer'd and tolerated ... to attend their Devotions in their Houses and in private, with all Liberty of Conscience, and without any Inquisition or Trouble, and even to assist in their Neighbourhood, as often as they have a mind, at the publick Exercise of their Religion ... provided [they] do their Duty in all other things, and hold themselves in due Obedience and Subjection, without giving occasion to any Disturbance or Commotion.[34]

In a divergence from historical practice, a person could now hold a different faith from a country's rulers, provided it was Catholicism, Lutheranism, or Calvinism.[35] This led to the second consequential outcome of the Reformation, the rise of pluralistic societies. Nowhere was this more evident than in the New World, where a mixture of cultures meant that the old model of a state-mandated religion could not long endure. Although several colonies had state-supported churches and the 'principall Ende' of the Massachusetts Bay colony was declared to be winning 'the Natives ... to the Knowledg and Obedience of the onlie true God and Savior of Mankinde', religious tolerance was a feature of many settlements.[36] A year after the Peace of Westphalia, Maryland enacted 'An Act Concerning Religion' specifying that no person 'professing to beleive in Jesus Christ, shall from henceforth bee any waies troubled, Molested or discountenanced for or in respect of his or her religion nor in the free exercise thereof ... nor any way compelled to the beleife or exercise of any other Religion against his or her consent'.[37] In 1682, William Penn expanded upon this in the Frame of Government of Pennsylvania, extending tolerance to those 'who confess and acknowledge the one Almighty and eternal God, to be the Creator, Upholder and Ruler of the world'.[38]

In comparison with pre-Reformation Europe, these provisions were radical. In 1791, they reached a new height when the First Amendment to the United States Constitution was adopted, stating that 'Congress shall make no law respecting an establishment of religion, or prohibiting the free exercise thereof'. There would be no 'Church of the United States' in the new nation, nor would the federal government seek to prohibit the 'free exercise' of religion. Many in Europe's intellectual circles—including in America's ally, France—felt that this represented the pinnacle of Enlightenment ideals about how government should be structured.[39] But, as others soon recognised, state-sanctioned freedom *of* religion could easily transition into state-mandated 'freedom' *from* religion. Following the declaration of the First French Republic in 1792, a programme of de-Christianisation began across the country.[40] Church property was confiscated to pay off the national debt, the Church's governance was reorganised for political purposes, priests were required to swear allegiance to the state—with those who refused given two weeks to leave the country—and cemeteries were stripped of religious symbols.[41] Following the inauguration of the Cult of Reason in 1793, the order was given to close all churches in Paris.[42] Although legitimate criticism could have been levied at certain aspects of the French Church—which owned more than one-tenth of the land, paid no taxes, and possessed a top-heavy bureaucracy of rich bishops and poor priests—the zeal of the revolutionaries went beyond mere administrative reform.[43] As one French organisation boldly declared, 'A new revolution is underway. ... No softness! No indulgence! Fanaticism must be speedily returned to the hell from which it was devised'.[44]

The Revolution's attack on Christianity was not only institutional, but ideological. The Archbishop of Paris was forced—on pain of death—to publicly resign and declare that 'there should be no more public or national worship but that of Liberty and Holy Equality'.[45] He was later executed anyway.[46] Others were forced to say that 'they no longer wished to acknowledge any cult except that of reason and liberty, a cult destined to conquer the globe and break the chains of all peoples'.[47] Bishops were deported for 'blasphemy against the sovereignty of the people'.[48] Statues of the Virgin Mary were guillotined.[49] Graves were ransacked, with caskets and remains used as footballs.[50] In less than five years, France's 40,000 pre-revolutionary church parishes were violently reduced to only a few hundred.[51] Desecration was both the means and the end.

Officially, there was to be 'tolerance of all religions as long as they do not trouble the new faith of liberty and reason', but, in practice, France had become the first government in history to endorse state-sponsored atheism.[52] In contrast to the United States, which refused to endorse a particular religion under its Constitution, France's revolutionary leaders merely continued the longstanding tradition of government promotion of belief, but with the 'faith of liberty and reason' substituted for Christianity. Although the Cult of Reason ultimately proved short-lived, the 'Reign of Terror' that accompanied it left a lasting mark upon the West. In a single year, 16,594 *official* executions took place across France, including 325 for 'refractory clergy' and those who had concealed them.[53] Far from ushering in a new era of enlightenment, France's secular revolution had exposed the depths of human depravity. It had also 'established what amounted to a permanent party dedicated to using political power, when it could, for the systematic expunging of religious influence from public life'.[54]

3. Scientism and the Death of God

In the years following the French Revolution, the pendulum briefly swung back in favour of religion in society. Many in America had welcomed the French Revolution as a parallel to their own, but the anti-religious ideas and actions of the revolutionaries soon alienated them, to the point that it 'was used in America to discredit the Enlightenment philosophical tradition and to justify a popular denunciation of European intellectual life'.[55] By the late 1790s, America was experiencing a widespread religious revival.[56] In contrast to the 'gloomy, frightening portrait of deistic or atheistic French republicanism and its many sins, American religious writers emphasized that American republicanism rested on Protestant religious traditions and that the nation's future depended on evangelical Christianity'.[57] A similar revival occurred in England with the Oxford Movement, where a small community of gifted and devout thinkers 'banded together in order to seek to restore the Church of their day to what they conceived to be its primitive glory'.[58]

Alongside these developments, other changes occurred across Western society. With the coming of the Industrial Revolution, many patterns of rural life were disrupted as people moved from farms and villages to work in factories in larger cities.[59] While this often brought about a change in their religious habits, it also fostered a growing sense that mankind, acting through technology, could remake the world in its image.[60] This eventually contributed to the development of an ideology known as 'scientism', which held that scientific knowledge was the preeminent source of authority.[61] In the 1840s, the French philosopher Auguste Comte argued that societies progressed through three stages of development—first 'the theological, then the metaphysical or philosophical, and finally the positive or scientific'.[62] Like many reforming minds who would follow him, Comte looked forward to the dawn of the scientific stage, when science and scientific principles 'free from uncertainty and ambiguity would provide a rational and unassailable basis for the reformulation of human society'.[63]

With science increasingly seen by some to be 'the only acceptable system for gaining knowledge', and anything else regarded 'at best a poor second, or simply a delusion', it was unsurprising that religious beliefs came under increased scrutiny.[64] Following Charles Darwin's exposition of natural selection in his 1859 book *On the Origin of Species*, some began to question the Biblical accounts about the origin of life.[65] A more overt attack on religion soon came from the writings of Karl Marx, who regarded faith as a false mode of consciousness that left man a 'degraded, enslaved, rejected, contemptible being'.[66] In order to progress to truly human self-awareness, he insisted, religion had to be abolished. Not only was it 'simply a form of self-deception', he argued, it was 'also a powerful device whereby the ruling class manipulate[d] the working class'.[67] Europe's upper classes were content to hypocritically proclaim 'for us Voltaire; for the people, masses and tithes; for us pious phrases; for the people Christian practice', much as William Wilberforce had criticised the British upper class for, over half a century earlier.[68]

Reflecting upon the decay of religious belief in connection with the Crimean War, Marx wrote that:

> We there see England, professedly Protestant, allied with France, professedly Catholic ('damnably heretical' as they naturally are in each other's eyes, according to the orthodox phraseology of both) for the purpose of defending Turkey, a Mohammedan Power, whose destruction they ought most religiously to desire, against the aggressions of 'holy' Russia, a Power Christian like themselves.[69]

To Marx, such an arrangement was inexplicable if Europe's leaders were truly motivated by religious convictions. Having searched across France and England for any religious criticism of the war, he found only three pamphlets which condemned the involvement of Christian nations in such a conflict.[70] Concluding that Europe's political elite no longer believed in the faith they publicly preached, he wrote:

> From the period of the Protestant Reformation, the upper classes in every European nation, whether it remained Catholic or adopted Protestantism ... began to unfasten themselves individually from all religious belief, and become freethinkers so-called. [... but from] the period of the French Revolution ... the masses, firstly of France, and afterwards of all Western Europe ... began to entertain an ever-growing aversion from religious dogma. The total abolition of Christianity, as a recognised institution of State by the French Republican Convention of 1793, and since then the gradual repeal in Western Europe, wherever the popular voice has had power ... announce the well-known direction of the popular mind in Europe.[71]

In 1882, the German philosopher Friedrich Nietzsche reflected on this 'popular mind' when he wrote 'God is dead. God remains dead. And we have killed him. How shall we comfort ourselves, the murderers of all murderers? What was holiest and mightiest of all that the world has yet owned has bled to death under our knives: who will wipe this blood off us?'[72] Although he was an atheist, Nietzsche saw the implications of a society that was rapidly losing its Christian beliefs. Writing with an uncanny prescience, he predicted as a consequence that 'There will be wars such as have never been waged on earth', and 'I foresee something terrible, Chaos everywhere. Nothing left which is of any value'.[73] Atheism might have been a hedonistic luxury for the elite few in a Christian society, but its implications for the wider population were dire:

When one gives up the Christian faith, one pulls the right to Christian morality out from under one's feet. This morality is by no means self-evident: ... Christianity is a system, a whole view of things thought out together. By breaking one main concept out of it, the faith in God, one breaks the whole: nothing necessary remains in one's hands. Christianity presupposes that man does not know, cannot know, what is good for him, what evil; he believes in God, who alone knows it. Christian morality is a command; its origin is transcendent; it is beyond all criticism, all right to criticism; it has truth only if God is the truth—it stands and falls with faith in God. When [one thinks] that they know 'intuitively' what is good and evil, when they therefore suppose that they no longer require Christianity as the guarantee of morality, we merely witness the effects of the dominion of the Christian value judgment and an expression of the strength and depth of this dominion.[74]

Perceptive as Nietzsche was, his predictions did not immediately come to fruition. As the twentieth century began, many looked to the future with optimism. Comte's theory about the rise of enlightened scientific societies appeared to be on the verge of reality, with one writer declaring in 1909 that 'Children make religions. Grown up people create science. ... Religion is the science of the child. Science is the religion of the matured man'.[75] Five years later, this progressive vision was shaken by the outbreak of World War I, when science was harnessed to produce death and misery on an industrial scale. Nine million men were killed over the course of the war—with a further twenty-eight million wounded—leaving three million widows, six million fatherless children, and tens of millions of grieving parents and relatives.[76] Civilised men who had volunteered for 'God, King and County', often with encouragement from their churches, returned home scarred by trench warfare.[77] As one British private recorded about the breakdown of basic human decency, 'in the trenches during the night, you could hear the groaning of the dying—but you couldn't go out to help them. There were rats feeding on their flesh'.[78] In Britain, 'The established church was part of the old order, rural, aristocratic, hierarchical, which was smashed to pieces at the Battle of the Somme on 1 July 1916. With some brave exceptions it had not much to say to the common soldiers as they fought and died'.[79]

Nietzsche's terrible war had finally come. Writing at a distance of more than a century after the war's conclusion, it is difficult to articulate the collective trauma it inflicted on European society—especially in the sphere of religious belief and deference to religious authorities. As Philip Larkin expressed in the closing stanza of his poem *MCMXIV*:

Never such innocence,
Never before or since,
As changed itself to past
Without a word – the men
Leaving the gardens tidy,
The thousands of marriages,
Lasting a little while longer:
Never such innocence again.[80]

Commemorated across memorials large and small, the great 'War to End All Wars' ended empires, brought new countries into being, and established the United States as a world power.[81] It also saw the overthrow of Tsarist Russia and the implementation of Marx's communist ideology. For the first time since the French Revolution, a government was actively committed to the destruction of religion. Although the Russian Constitution of 1918 officially recognised that 'the right of religious and anti-religious propaganda is accorded to every citizen', it also denied 'monks and clergy of all denominations' the right to vote.[82] Notwithstanding proclamations of religious neutrality, one top-secret document written by the Cheka—or secret police—in 1920 noted how 'Communism and Religion are mutually exclusive', and that religion had to be destroyed.[83]

For many intellectuals, communism's rejection of Christianity was a cause for celebration rather than concern. As the British sociologists Beatrice and Sidney Webb noted with approval, 'It is exactly the explicit denial of the intervention of any God, or indeed of any will other than human will in the universe, that has attracted to Soviet Communism, the sympathies of many intellectuals, and especially of scientists in civilised countries'.[84] In a pamphlet published by *The Left Review* in 1936, they wrote:

> The feature of Soviet Communism that has most scandalised the western world is undoubtedly the widespread 'anti-godism' which is common to the Soviet Government and a large and apparently a steadily increasing proportion of the whole population. An aggressively dogmatic atheism denies the existence, and the possibility of the existence, of anything supernatural behind or beyond what science can apprehend or demonstrate. This sweeping denial has, it is claimed, the merit of a public and persistent repudiation of the equivocal hypocrisy in which the governments and churches of other countries, together with the hosts of merely conventional Christians, are to-day implicated ... One result of this widely spread equivocation is seen in the practical abandonment at the present time by millions of young persons in Europe and America, not only of Christianity, but also,

along with it, of nearly all the commandments by which their parents were guided … All this is noticeably increasing the number of those who think that there is something to be said for the paradoxical claim of Soviet Communism that it is, in morals as well as in economic and political science, actually leading the world.[85]

It would take time for the full measure of communism's failures to become evident, but even in 1936 the idea that the Soviet Union was a world leader in morals was absurd to anyone who looked closely. In 1922 alone, 2,691 priests, 1,962 monks, and 3,447 nuns had been killed on account of their beliefs.[86] In a letter to the Politburo that year, the Soviet leader Vladimir Lenin had written that 'The more representatives from the reactionary clergy and the recalcitrant bourgeoisie we shoot, the better it will be for us. We must teach these people a lesson as quickly as possible, so that the thought of protesting again doesn't occur to them for decades to come'.[87] Such was the Soviet Union's moral leadership.

In one respect, however, the Webbs were right—Christianity was showing signs of cultural decline, even if their estimate of the irreligious was overstated. Thomas Hardy's poem, *God's Funeral*, had captured the mood with its depiction of a cortege bearing the 'man-projected Figure … whom we can no longer keep alive', stating that 'tricked by our own early dream … we grew self-deceived … And what we had imagined we believed'.[88] Practicing Christians were increasingly regarded as eccentrics, if not worse. In a letter to H.L. Mencken, the poet Ezra Pound wrote that 'Christianity has become a sort of Prussianism, and will have to go. … It has its uses and is disarming, but it is too dangerous. Religion is the root of all evil, or damn near all'.[89] Virginia Woolf, Queen of the London literati, wrote to her sister in 1928 about their friend T.S. Eliot, complaining that 'I have had a most shameful and distressing interview with poor dear Tom Eliot, who may be called dead to us all from this day forward. He has become an [Anglican], believes in God and immortality, and goes to church. I was really shocked. A corpse would seem to me more credible than he is. I mean, there's something obscene in a living person sitting by the fire and believing in God'.[90]

4. THE COLD WAR AND SEXUAL REVOLUTION

Obscene as Woolf might have found Eliot's newfound faith, the world soon experienced greater shocks. Five years after her letter, Adolf Hitler became Chancellor of Germany.[91] Embarking on a programme of anti-Semitic nationalism, he soon came into conflict with some of the country's churches. Within a year of him taking office, 139 delegates met in the city of Barmen to declare their opposition to the 'German Christian' movement, which held that Christianity was compatible with Hitler's ideology.[92] Among its provisions, the Barmen Declaration 'reject[ed] the false doctrine, as though the State, over and beyond its special commission, should and could become the single and totalitarian order of human life'.[93] The Catholic Church also declared its opposition to Hitler's policies. In his encyclical *Mit Brennender Sorge*, smuggled into the country in 1937 to be read on Palm Sunday,[94] Pope Pius XI condemned 'leaders [who] pretend to draw from the so-called myth of race and blood':

> None but superficial minds could stumble into concepts of a national God, of a national religion; or attempt to lock within the frontiers of a single people, within the narrow limits of a single race, God, the Creator of the universe … In your country … there is more than one [leader] whose official position is intended to create the impression that this infidelity to Christ the King constitutes a signal and meritorious act of loyalty to the modern State. … The fool who has said in his heart 'there is no God' goes straight to moral corruption (Psalms xiii. 1), and the number of these fools who today are out to sever morality from religion, is legion. … The resulting dereliction of the eternal principles of an objective morality, which educates conscience and ennobles every department and organization of life, is a sin against the destiny of a nation, a sin whose bitter fruit will poison future generations.[95]

Two years later, Germany's invasion of Poland triggered World War II.[96] For the second time in twenty-five years, the great powers were once again engaged in total war. In comparison with the first World War, however, the conflict had grown broader and the weapons far deadlier. On the first day of the destructive Battle of the Somme in 1916, for instance, some 25,000 British and German soldiers had been killed after hours of fighting; at Hiroshima in 1945, over 70,000 people were killed more-or-less instantly with a single bomb.[97] By the end of the conflict, Europe was an exhausted shell of its former self, with the United States and the Soviet Union—wartime allies—left standing as the world's two superpowers.[98]

With the end of the war, the temporary alliance between the two nations started to fray. As the Cold War began, their ideological differences became increasingly evident and impossible to ignore. In addition to the atheistic influences of the Communist Party, the Red Army, and its schools and trade unions, the Soviet Union also contained several million members of the League of the Militant Godless, founded in 1925 to promote atheism.[99] Watching the Soviet Union execute its designs for post-war Europe, many in the United States felt that they were witnessing nothing less than an attack on civilisation. In response, President Truman declared in 1945 that 'I believe honestly that Almighty God intends us to assume the leadership which he intended us to assume in 1920, and which we refused'.[100] In the Senate, Alexander Wiley declared that religious faith would be the central issue in the unfolding Cold War, with his colleague Robert Taft warning that 'the communists have made their beliefs into a crusading religion' which would require an American response.[101]

To secure the world against the evils of communism, the United States would have to fight what amounted to a holy war.[102] An alliance was soon formed with Pope Pius XII, whose 1949 *Decree Against Communism* had declared that it was not possible to be both Catholic and communist.[103] He offered access to the Vatican's worldwide network of intelligence sources, providing a valuable picture of activities behind the Iron Curtain.[104] When President Eisenhower took office in 1953, he continued many of Truman's religious policies. At his inauguration he led the nation in prayer, asking God to 'Give us, we pray, the power to discern clearly from right and wrong'.[105] In a speech to the American Legion, he declared that 'without God, there could be no American form of government, nor an American way of life. Recognition of the Supreme Being is the first—the most basic—expression of Americanism'.[106] He became the first president to be baptised in office, and in 1954 the words 'under God' were added to the Pledge of Allegiance.[107] In signing that law, Eisenhower stated:

> From this day forward, the millions of our school children will daily proclaim in every city and town, every village and rural schoolhouse, the dedication of our nation and our people to the Almighty. To anyone who truly loves America, nothing could be more inspiring than to contemplate this rededication of our youth, on each school morning, to our country's true heritage. Especially is this meaningful as we regard today's world. Over the globe, mankind has been cruelly torn by violence and brutality and, by the millions, deadened in mind and soul by a materialistic philosophy of life. ... in this way we shall constantly strengthen those spiritual weapons which forever will be our country's most powerful resource, in peace or in war.[108]

If the United States viewed itself as engaged in a war for religion, the Soviet Union equally saw itself as engaged in a war for its extermination. Under Nikita Khrushchev, who claimed that he would 'take God by the beard' and boldly predicted that he would show the last Christian on television by 1980, 70% of the Orthodox churches that had existed since 1959 were closed, and a broader campaign of religious persecution ensued.[109] In 1966, Richard Wurmbrand testified before a US Senate subcommittee on the conditions faced by religious believers in Soviet prisons. Recounting his experiences as a Romanian inmate, he described how Christianity was sadistically mocked by the authorities, including an instance in which 'they crucified a cat before ourselves. They beat nails in the feet of the cat and the cat was hanging with the head down, and now you imagine how this cat screamed and the prisoners, mad … [gave] statements against their wives, against their children, against their parents to free the cat'.[110] In response to a question by Senator Thomas Dodd about whether Christians were treated differently because of their beliefs, he recounted how:

> The[y] were tortured in a form which should mock their religion. … One Sunday morning in the prison of Pitesti a young Christian was already the fourth day, day and night, tied to the cross. Twice a day the cross was put on the floor and 100 other cell inmates by beatings, by tortures, were obliged to fulfill their necessities upon his face and upon his body. Then the cross was erected again and the Communists swearing and mocking 'Look your Christ, look your Christ, how beautiful he is, adore him, kneel before him, how fine he smells, your Christ.'[111]

Even for those who escaped the worst excesses of Soviet torture, the penalty for exercising their nominally-protected religious beliefs could be severe. On December 12, 1968, Nadezhda Stepanova Sloboda, a mother of five, was sentenced to four years in a labour camp for 'organising an illegal Baptist congregation'.[112] A court had previously taken her two eldest children by force to a children's home, 'because they had been brought up by their mother in a religious and thus an anti-social manner'.[113] Although they escaped several times, they were forcibly taken back until their mother was locked away.[114] Under the Soviet Family Law, a parent's rights could be terminated if they 'exercise[d] a harmful influence on the children by immoral, anti-social behaviour', which included religious practice.[115] One court ruled in 1969 that the parental rights of Christians could not be recognised because their children would be alienated from 'social life', with Baptist children in particular 'usually recognisable by their appearance; the stamp of religiosity is graven on their faces'.[116]

As the Soviet Union continued its crackdown on religion, a cultural shift occurred in the West that would ultimately weaken religion. In May 1960, the US Food and Drug Administration approved a drug called Enovid, the world's first contraceptive pill.[117] By July 1962, some 150,000 women in Britain were taking it and by 1963 some 2.3 million American women had joined them.[118] A sexual revolution had begun, which quickly led to a moral revolution. As the British psychologist Eustace Chesser argued, contraception promised to remove the problems that arose from sexual activity outside of marriage, since 'people should have the right to choose between being chaste and unchaste as long as society doesn't suffer'.[119] Shocking as many found this statement to be, he was merely the latest figure to link sexual liberation with a change in moral norms. As early as the 1930s, the British philosopher Aldous Huxley had observed that 'The philosopher who finds no meaning in the world is not concerned exclusively with a problem in pure metaphysics. He is concerned to prove that there is no valid reason why he personally should not do as he wants to do ... The voluntary, as opposed to the intellectual, reasons for holding the doctrines of materialism, for example, may be predominantly erotic'.[120] Writing further:

> For myself, as, no doubt, for most of my contemporaries, the philosophy of meaninglessness was essentially an instrument of liberation ... from a certain system of morality. We objected to the morality because it interfered with our sexual freedom ... The supporters of these systems claimed that in some way they embodied the meaning (a Christian meaning, they insisted) of the world. There was one admirably simple method of confuting these people and at the same time justifying ourselves in our political and erotic revolt: we could deny that the world had any meaning whatsoever.[121]

If the world held no meaning, there was no reason one should not do as he wanted. If there was no God there could be no sin, and if there was no sin there could be no ultimate standard to say that one's behaviour was wrong. For Huxley and his contemporaries, the path to sexual freedom lay in atheism. Liberating as this could be, however, he recognised a downside since 'those who, to be liberated from political or sexual restraint, accept the doctrine of absolute meaninglessness tend in a short time to become so much dissatisfied with their philosophy (in spite of the service it renders) that they will exchange it for any dogma, however manifestly nonsensical, which restores meaning if only to a part of the universe'.[122]

By the end of the 1960s, a growing number in the West were rejecting religion to embrace the freedoms of Huxley's 'philosophy of meaninglessness'. In Britain, the proportion of people who regularly attended church dropped significantly to less than 15%, and 'Across the board, the British people started to reduce the role of religion in their lives'.[123] Weekly church attendance in the United States held steadier at around 40%, but posted a decline from the 46-49% it had been in the 1950s.[124] Similar downward trends occurred in Canada and Australia.[125] If the church of the 1960s was regarded as the 'upholder of traditionalism and morality', the swelling ranks of the Baby Boomers—those born between 1946-1964—were increasingly uninterested in what it had to offer, choosing instead to 'tune in, turn on, and drop out' as they engaged in experimentation and rebellion.[126] In the

United States, a portent of the new era occurred at the Woodstock music festival in 1969. In an editorial published on August 18, 1969, the *New York Times* reported with unconcealed disdain that:

> The dreams of marijuana and rock music that drew 300,000 fans and hippies to the Catskills had little more sanity than the impulses that drive the lemmings to march to their deaths in the sea. ... What kind of culture is it that can produce so colossal a mess? One youth dead and at least three others in hospitals from overdoses of drugs; another dead from a mishap while sleeping in an open field. ... Surely the parents, the teachers and indeed all the adults who helped create the society against which these young people are so feverishly rebelling must bear a share of the responsibility for this outrageous episode.[127]

As the Baby Boomers came of age, they began to alter their respective countries. In Britain, abortion—which had generally been illegal under the Offences Against the Person Act 1861—was legalised through the Abortion Act 1967.[128] The US Supreme Court followed suit in 1973 in the *Roe v. Wade* decision, despite Justice White's dissent that there was 'nothing in the language or history of the Constitution to support the Court's judgment'.[129] In France, the government nearly collapsed in 1968 over a series of student protests, which briefly saw the president leave for a military base in Germany.[130] Shortly thereafter, domestic opposition forced the United States to end its war against the communists in Vietnam.[131] As the youth of the emerging 'counterculture' asserted themselves, many of their wartime parents felt bewildered by the changes to their societies. As one essayist noted, 'They see all they stood for challenged and called into question. ... They feel like strangers in the very house they have built, foreigners in a strange land they themselves settled'.[132]

The sense of bewilderment would continue for many as the 1970s saw the introduction of no-fault divorce laws, which led to an increase in divorces and a decrease in the living standards of the divorced.[133] In England and Wales, the annual abortion rate doubled to 111,000 by 1973—dwarfed by the 616,000 in the United States that year—and health officials worldwide began warning against the spread of sexually transmitted diseases, which had begun 'veering sharply upward'.[134] Subscriptions to *Playboy* magazine grew to around 7 million copies a year, whilst church attendance continued to decline.[135] By the end of the decade, only 11% of adults in England regularly attended, with broad declines in 'virtually every European county'.[136] In keeping with Huxley's admonition that some would embrace 'any dogma, however manifestly nonsensical' to restore a sense of order to their lives, the 1970s also saw the emergence of many 'new age' belief systems, replete with healing crystals, incense, and astrology.[137] Even the First Lady of the United States dabbled in it, with Nancy Reagan consulting an astrologer, Joan Quigley, after the assassination attempt on her husband.[138] Unknown to all but select White House staffers, Quigley would develop charts that 'predicted which days would be good ones and which would be bad for the president', with flights and appearances often rescheduled to accommodate them—something that would have been unthinkable only a few years before.[139]

Changed by the sexual revolution that had swept across it, America's holy war against the Soviet Union had morphed into a cultural and economic battle for supremacy. Notwithstanding its struggles in Vietnam, its policy of containing the spread of communism had generally been successful.[140] By the 1980s, the US economy was around three times the size of its rival, with the Soviet economy heavily distorted by military outlays as high as 40% of GDP—eight times the percentage in the United States.[141] America might not have been able to defeat the Soviet Union militarily without risking nuclear war, but it was well-poised to outspend it.[142] In 1988, an essay recognising this appeared in the Communist Party's Central Committee magazine, *Kommunist*. Written by three members of the Academy of Sciences, it 'recognized explicitly that continuing military rivalry with the United States would result in further deterioration of the Soviet economic position', and that reforms were necessary to reverse the decline.[143]

Under any measure one considered, life under communism was abysmal. Annual alcohol consumption was estimated at 14 litres per capita, 75% higher than the amount the World Health Organization considered likely to cause major medical problems.[144] In 1987, some 6.4 million abortions had occurred across its territory—nearly a million more than the number of births that year.[145] A Soviet man could expect to live 6.67 fewer years than his American counterpart, and a Soviet infant was two and a half times more likely to die during its first year than one born in the United States or United Kingdom.[146] Instead of ushering in an atheistic paradise, communism had 'suppressed economic vitality and spontaneity, protected its own inability to be cured, and locked people in a vicious circle of equality in misery'.[147]

Although seventy years might have passed since Lenin had declared war on religion, Christianity had not been eradicated. In a speech given in March 1988, the chairman of the Council for the Affairs of Religions, K.M. Kharchev, noted that 'there is no trend toward a reduction in religiosity in the Soviet Union. Every year, a million church funerals take place; this is 20-30 percent of the deceased, and a church funeral, in my opinion, is the most reliable indicator of religiosity, because while living, people lied, being afraid to lose their jobs'.[148] Coinciding with calls for political and economic reform, 1988 also saw the millennial anniversary of the Christianisation of Kyivan Rus, the Soviet Union's ancestral predecessor.[149] This led to a 'great religious upsurge', as many reconsidered their attitude toward religion, with over 70% of Muscovites surveyed the following year expressing the desire to see clergymen allowed in government.[150]

Change was in the air, and the Soviet leadership was beginning to lose control. Revolutions soon broke out across Eastern Europe, overturning decades of communist rule.[151] On November 9, 1989, the Berlin Wall fell, bringing an end to nearly thirty years of restricted travel between East and West.[152] Two months later in Moscow, McDonald's—one of America's most visible cultural symbols—opened its first Russian restaurant a mere two kilometres from the Kremlin, serving more than 30,000 customers who queued for hours to visit on its first day.[153] Communism was crumbing, and on December 25, 1991, Gorbachev addressed the world on television to resign from the Soviet presidency.[154] As his speech ended, the red hammer-and-sickle flag was lowered over the Kremlin for the last time, marking the end of the Soviet Union.[155]

With the collapse of its rival, the United States stood unchallenged as the world's sole superpower. Following Gorbachev's resignation, President George H.W. Bush delivered an address from the White House acknowledging the Soviet Union's demise. Though careful to speak diplomatically, the Soviet Union's end was a decisive victory for the United States.[156] Only two years earlier, the American political scientist Francis Fukuyama had written an article titled *The End of History?* that ambitiously predicted the triumph of Western culture:

> The triumph of the West, of the Western *idea*, is evident first of all in the total exhaustion of viable systematic alternatives to Western liberalism. … What we may be witnessing is not just the end of the Cold War, or the passing of a particular period of post-war history, but the end of history as such: that is, the end point of mankind's ideological evolution and the universalization of Western liberal democracy as the final form of human government.[157]

With the Soviet Union's dissolution, Fukuyama's thesis appeared to be coming true, with the global order transitioning from decades of bipolar conflict to a unipolar *Pax Americana*. An article in the *Naval War College Review* noted that 'The end of the Cold War left the United States in a position of power unseen since the Roman Empire'.[158] Complementing its military strength and financial dominance, it also possessed an arsenal of 'soft power', or the ability to influence others to act in its interests through cultural attraction.[159] This was partly due to its linguistic dominance, with George Steiner, the President of the English Association, noting that 'so far as it is indeed the world-language, English is, essentially,

American-English'.[160] Many had grown up listening to American music, watching American movies, and buying American brands, to say nothing of their exposure to the images of 'liberty, affluence, and democracy' that had been broadcast to counter Soviet propaganda.[161] To its admirers, America combined the glamour of Hollywood and a spirit of innovation to produce a powerful cultural vision.

To some extent, this was hardly new. Lenin's successor, Joseph Stalin, once purportedly remarked that if he 'could control the medium of the American motion picture, [he] would need nothing else to convert the entire world to communism'.[162] With the development of satellite television and the internet, the United States now possessed—for good or ill—the means to export its culture to the farthest corners of the earth.[163] Much of this was undoubtedly positive, with the 'Voice of America' transmitting programming in over thirty languages to global audiences by the early 1990s, but, with the coarsening of society since the 1960s, a growing percentage of American entertainment was becoming cruder, more violent, and sexualised.[164] In November 1992, *Billboard* magazine reported that Madonna's album *Erotica* appeared in the top five chart slots in Australia, France, Italy, Japan, and the United Kingdom, with its title track topping the Eurochart Hot 100.[165] A year later, more than three million copies of the video game *Mortal Kombat* sold in a matter of months, with players able to experience the two-dimensional gore of ripping an opponent's heart out, or tearing off their head and spinal cord.[166] Four years later in 1997, *GoldenEye 007* was released— eventually selling over eight million copies—with players able to experience a first-person shooter perspective as they killed digital enemies with a wide assortment of weapons.[167] These games quickly paled in comparison, however, to the *Grand Theft Auto* series, which debuted the same year and featured missions ranging from 'stealing cars and rounding up prostitutes to killing competing gangsters and shooting police officers to earn money and rewards'.[168] As one reviewer noted about *Grand Theft Auto III*, released in 2001:

> this is a technically marvelous game that at the same time is absolutely reprehensible. This is a game that rewards you for causing mayhem. This is a game that is about causing mayhem. It's a game that rewards you for killing innocent people by the dozen. ... I can hijack a car, kill the driver, run someone down on the street, commit drive-by shootings, and score points for doing all of it. In some scripted sequences, I'm tasked to kill people at random. In one, the identities of the victims don't even matter. ... we know the game isn't for kids. But who is it really for, anyway? *Is this game appropriate for anyone?*[169]

Notwithstanding such concerns, the following months saw it sell over two million copies in the United States and win 'Game of the Year' at the Game Developers Choice Awards, before selling more than 14.5 million copies globally.[170] A year later, the National Research Council reported that adult online content had become a billion-dollar industry in the United States, with over 70 million people worldwide viewing at least one pornographic website each week—20 million of whom viewed pages hosted in America and Canada.[171]

Beyond the changes to entertainment, the decline of religion and sexual norms were breaking down the bonds of society. Writing in the *Quarterly Journal of Economics* in 1996, three economists—including Janet Yellen, the future Chair of the US Federal Reserve—modelled the impact of the sexual revolution on 'female immiseration'. Noting that 'Rising out-of-wedlock birthrates are of social policy concern because children reared in single-parent households are more likely to be impoverished and to experience difficulties in later life', they observed that sexual activity without commitment was:

> immiserizing at least some women, since their male partners do not have to assume parental responsibility in order to engage in sexual relations. ... The sexual revolution, by making the birth of the child the *physical* choice of the mother, makes marriage and child support a *social* choice of the father [... as] potential male partners can easily obtain sexual satisfaction [outside of marriage] ... Thus, women who, in the absence of contraception and abortion, would not engage in premarital sexual activity without assurance of marriage will feel pressured to participate in uncommitted relationships once contraception and abortion become available. ... *A move to this no-commitment trap is likely to reduce welfare for all women.* In this example the gains from the advent of abortion and contraception accrue totally to the men. ... Nowadays women are freer to choose, but [under this model] the man reasons: 'If she is not willing to obtain an abortion or use contraception, why should I sacrifice myself to get married?'[172]

The shift in views on marriage might have been a recent development, but the 'general lowering of moral standards' had been predicted decades earlier, with Pope Paul VI warning in his 1968 encyclical *Humanae Vitae* that men might 'forget the reverence due to a woman, and, disregarding her physical and emotional equilibrium, reduce her to being a mere instrument for the satisfaction of his own desires'.[173] The rising impact of men abandoning their families to pursue other relationships was equally bleak, with the British institute Civitas noting that 'For many mothers, fathers and children, the "fatherless family" has meant poverty, emotional heartache, ill health, lost opportunities, and a lack of stability. The social fabric—once considered flexible enough to incorporate all types of lifestyles—has been stretched and strained'.[174]

5. The Cult of Reason Reborn

Although the United States was by no means the sole cause of—or contributor to—these trends, its position of dominance meant that it was able to give them greater prominence as its society changed than they otherwise would have enjoyed. By the beginning of the twenty-first century, Western culture was radically different from what it had been only 100 years before. Two measures in particular demonstrated the sexual revolution's impact on social norms:

Divorces (per 100,000 population)	1900 [175]	2000 [176]
Britain†	2	400
France	23	300
Germany	15	350
Netherlands	10	320
United States	73	620

Illegitimate Births (per 1,000 births)	1900 [177]	2000 [178]
Britain†	40	395
France	88	436
Germany	84	234
Netherlands	23	249
United States	*	332

† Data reported for England and Wales.
* Official records for this category were not kept in the United States in 1900. Statistics for 1920 show an illegitimacy rate of 22.7 per 1,000 births.[179]

Alongside these changes, the percentage identifying as having 'no religion' was on the rise, increasing to 14.2% in the United States and 14.8% in the United Kingdom by 2001, and 17.5% and 25.1% respectively by 2011.[180] Aiding this shift were a series of authors with provocative bestsellers such as Richard Dawkins' *The God Delusion*, Christopher Hitchens' *God is Not Great*, and Sam Harris' *The End of Faith*. In 2006, the journalist Gary Wolf coined the term 'New Atheism' to describe the belief that atheism should 'condemn not just belief in God but respect for belief in God'.[181] Old Atheism might have rejected faith, but New Atheism declared war on it, from Dawkins' idea that there was 'something to be said for society stepping in' to prevent children being raised 'to believe manifest falsehoods' to Harris' call for 'a religion of reason' that 'would have prayer without bullshit'.[182] Even children's author Philip Pullman admitted to 'trying to undermine the basis of Christian belief' through his stories.[183]

The zeal of the New Atheists might have lacked the violence of their Soviet and French predecessors, but in other respects the resemblance was striking. When one considers Richard Dawkins' remark in *The God Delusion* that 'the phrase "child abuse" is no exaggeration when used to describe what teachers and priests are doing to children' whom they encourage to believe in God, it recalls Nadezhda Sloboda's children being taken 'because they had been brought up … in a religious and thus an anti-social manner'.[184] Sam Harris' denunciation of religion's 'patently absurd and increasingly maladaptive' ideas echoes the French revolutionaries' belief that 'Religion is the only obstacle to universal happiness. It is high time to destroy it'.[185] Then there is Christopher Hitchens' view that 'Religion poisons everything. As well as a menace to civilisation, it has become a threat to human survival', a sentiment not far removed from those who wished religion to be 'speedily returned to the hell from which it was devised'.[186]

Though lacking the pageantry and guillotines of its eighteenth-century forerunner, a new Cult of Reason has emerged in Western thought. Possessing the same dictatorial impulses that motivated its original movement, it seeks to advance the 'faith of liberty and reason' by undermining Christianity's intellectual and moral foundations and by making it 'too embarrassing to believe in God'.[187] In much of Europe it appears to have succeeded, with a study of data from the 2016 European Social Survey showing that in twelve out of the twenty-two nations analysed, more than half of those aged 16-29 had no religious identity—with 70% in the United Kingdom and a staggering 91% in the Czech Republic responding accordingly.[188] From these findings, the study's author concluded that 'Christianity as a default, as a norm, is gone, and probably gone for good—or at least for the next 100 years' and that, 'With some notable exceptions, young adults increasingly are not identifying with or practising religion'.[189]

Taking these facts to be so, what do they hold for the future? Under any realistic assessment, it must be recognised that in many locations 'The new default setting is "no religion", and the few who are religious [will be] swimming against the tide'.[190] Importantly, however, the study also suggested an explanation: many young Europeans 'will have been baptised and then never darken the door of a church again. Cultural religious identities just aren't being passed on from parents to children'.[191] But why did those who came of age in the twentieth century collectively fail to pass on their beliefs to those in the twenty-first? Thus far, we have considered the history of *what* happened to cause Christianity's decline, but the equally important question is *why* it happened. Demographically, Christianity undoubtedly suffered a grievous wound with the outbreak of World War I—an event that defined the course of the twentieth century and continues to shape the modern era. As the author Peter Hitchens eloquently noted from a British perspective about the men who died:

> They were the faithful, the best, self-selected for early childless death in the mud. We could not afford to lose them. Their names, listed intolerably outside Oxford and Cambridge Colleges, in the chapels of the great schools, and on granite memorials in every city, town, and village, are the names of those who would have maintained our traditions of Christian liberty and justice in every calling, profession, and trade, and who now lie, far from home, dead before they could get children and pass on their virtues.[192]

The destruction of so many of the West's youth clearly took its toll on the societies they left behind, but this can only tell part of the story. Even before the first shots of 1914 were fired, Christianity was facing challenges. Sixty years earlier in the context of the Crimean War, Karl Marx had perceived that many in the cultural elite had abandoned religion, even as they publicly affirmed it to their still-believing countrymen. Faced by what he regarded as hypocrisy, it was perhaps too easy for him to conclude that religion was merely a tool of the rich for the manipulation of others. But why had Europe's elite abandoned Christianity? Pierre Chaumette gave an important clue when he praised 'the only true worship' of liberty and reason at the Festival of Reason in 1793, but 'reason' appears to have had little to do with it.[193] The Enlightenment that had begun in the seventeenth century had changed Western concepts of philosophy and science, but Christianity had remained largely unscathed—with the Church still retaining much of the unshaken certitude it had possessed in the Middle Ages.[194] Even when Deism raised the idea of a non-interfering God who created the world and left mankind to its own devices, there were no shortage of authors ready to forcefully denounce it.[195] The challenges posed by nineteenth-century scientism were also not yet present; Darwin did not publish his theory of evolution until 1859, and James Hutton's theories about geologic time were not published until 1788, and then only to a limited readership.[196] 'Reason', such as it was, cannot account for the aristocratic abandonment of belief.

One theory regarding 'liberty' can, however. 300 years before hormonal birth control and its transformation of Western society, Europe's nobility had their own sexual revolution—with equally devastating consequences for their religious beliefs. At the French royal court, a libertine culture emerged where the nobility increasingly 'took sexual pleasure however they wanted'.[197] Two sexual scandals involving organised groups of nobles erupted at Versailles in 1682 and 1722, with the participants all possessing 'formidable connections or at least positions in the court'.[198] An 'ethos of sexual morality completely divorced from Church tradition' was spreading, with observers noting that 'extramarital relationships had become normalised among noblemen and noblewomen alike', vindicating libertine attitudes toward marriage and religion.[199] What had previously been done furtively soon began to be flaunted in high society.

Across the English Channel conditions were hardly better, with Charles II ecumenically having both a Catholic and Protestant mistress. When the latter's coach was greeted in 1681 by an angry mob who believed it to be carrying the 'hated' Catholic mistress, the occupant defused the situation by stating 'Pray, good people, be civil: I am the *protestant* whore'.[200] By one account, the English court consisted of 'a motley collection of rakes, debauchees, drunkards and whores' whose 'sexual proclivities rapidly became widely known'.[201] When George Morley rebuked them in a sermon on Christmas Day 1662, the diarist Samuel Pepys observed 'how far they are come from taking the reprehensions of a bishop seriously … they all laugh[ed] in the chapel when he reflected on their ill courses and actions'.[202] Thomas D'Urfey, a poet who attended court from 1676, perhaps captured the mood of their libertine rebellion best:

> Whilst Love Predominates over our Souls,
> A Pox on Counsel from tedious Old Fools;
> Reproofs of the Church-men but whet us the more,
>   Whilst liberty Teaches,
>   And appetite Preaches,
> No wealth like a Bottle, no joy like a Whore.
>
> Long Tales of Heav'n to Fools are given,
> But we put pleasure in making the Scale even;
> Thus kissing, and Wenching, and Drinking brave Boys,
>   We drive out Collicks
>   By nightly Frolicks,
> And drown short Life in a Deluge of Joys.[203]

Rather than the nobility's rejection of Christianity arising from a balanced consideration of the evidence, they appear to have abandoned it merely because—long before Huxley—they objected to its interference with their personal freedom.[204] Although they did not publicly espouse atheism, they had indeed, as a class, 'unfasten[ed] themselves … from all religious belief' as Marx later recognised.[205]

Christianity was rejected because it spoke of 'self-denial and the cross, those terrible blows to flesh and blood', which were necessary to appease a divine justice that would otherwise 'prey upon the sinner forever'.[206] To effectively banish the guilt of sin, one first had to banish the belief in God. By the time Marx searched for evidence of faith amongst the aristocracy as a class, he was generally about 200 years too late to find it.

Many places throughout the West have become post-Christian and it is important to understand how that happened. Although the original Cult of Reason was short-lived, its influence has been significant as the last few hundred years have shown. To its adherents, religion was seen to be incompatible with reason and a threat to liberty—themes that would resonate with many today. These two challenges should—*and can*—be addressed. Of the two, 'liberty' is perhaps the greater challenge because its passions run deeper. But as the Anglican minister Robert South recognised in one of his sermons in 1665, Christianity 'intrenches upon none of our privileges, invades none of our pleasures; it may indeed sometimes command us to change, but never totally to abjure them'.[207]

Sixty years after the promise of free love, the idea, as Eustace Chesser put it, that one could be 'unchaste as long as society doesn't suffer' has foundered on the shoals of experience.[208] It's very 'success' has brought about its failure. In the United States and United Kingdom alone, since its legalisation over 54,000,000 abortions have taken place, equivalent to losing the entire population of Kenya.[209] Over 5,000,000 rapes have been recorded since 1960,[210] and between 2006-2016 over 14,000 people were murdered by their intimate partners—with one such killing occurring roughly every six hours.[211] Every year, some $17 billion is spent treating sexually transmitted infections,[212] with approximately forty new diagnoses made every minute.[213] One divorce is finalised every thirty seconds, forever altering the lives of those involved.[214] Even if one discounts the physical harm, emotional turmoil and financial ruin behind these figures—drawn from only *two* countries—it is clear that the sexual revolution has not increased the sum of human happiness. In this light, we can better understand how Christianity offers an alternative moral framework that is not only compatible with liberty and beneficial to our earthly well-being, but, more importantly, crucial to our eternal happiness.

We can address the second challenge—that Christianity is opposed to reason—by demonstrating that Christianity is, in fact, *true*. To some, the belief in a God who made the world and then sent His Son to save its inhabitants from hell is not only irrational, but childish—the sort of folklore that made sense before science could explain the mysteries of nature. In a world shaped by scientism, secularism, and the sexual revolution, how do we respond? As Mark Noll observed in *The Scandal of the Evangelical Mind*, one challenge is that, for several generations,

Christianity in the West has intellectually disengaged.[215] The reasons for this are many and do not apply equally across all denominations, but the general impact of Christian thinking on culture as a whole has been slight.[216] This failure of the modern church to collectively embrace its intellectual responsibilities has led to significant consequences.[217] How many have left churches, possibly never to return, because they felt that Christianity lacked substance or that their legitimate questions about historical or scientific matters were ignored or dismissed?

The Christian is taught in 1 Peter 3:15 to 'always be ready to give a defence to everyone who asks' about the reason for our beliefs, but how often do we rise to the occasion? In a world that prizes authenticity ever more highly, we must engage with the hard questions. We must also rediscover the riches of our theological heritage. The arguments for Christianity possess an ancient strength, and although a modern Cult of Reason has arisen to challenge it, its challenges are not new. There is much in the wisdom of the past that can re-introduce Christianity to a post-Christian generation, beginning with the evidence in Chapter 2 for the existence of God.

2

This We Call God

At a small monastery in northern France in 1076, a monk named Anselm once wrote that 'There is a being which is best, and greatest, and highest of all existing beings'.[1] So began his *Monologion*, in which he noted that a person could come to recognise God's existence 'even if his mental powers are very ordinary, by the force of reason alone'.[2] Developing what would become known as the ontological argument for the existence of God, Anselm posited that nothing greater can be conceived to be, and God as a concept cannot be conceived *not* to be, even in the minds of those who would deny His existence.[3]

Although his basic argument remains sound after nearly 1,000 years, it is perhaps not as persuasive to modern audiences as it once was. Having come through the Enlightenment and scientific revolution, we have all been influenced to varying degrees by the Comtean view of social development, in which knowledge was seen to progress from 'the theological, then the metaphysical or philosophical, and finally [to] the positive or scientific' stage, with scientific knowledge regarded as the pinnacle of wisdom.[4] Whilst there may have been a partial retreat from the nineteenth-century scientism that regarded every other system for acquiring knowledge as 'at best a poor second, or simply a delusion', the fact remains that we live in an age that prizes scientific knowledge.[5] This is not a problem for Christianity—science has enriched our understanding of the world immeasurably—but it does mean that any discussion about the evidence for God will demand more cognisance of scientific developments than it once did.

How, then, can one argue in the modern, scientific era for the existence of a being that cannot be seen? As Chapter 1 noted, the belief in God is the foundational element of Christianity—without it, everything else necessarily falls. But what makes God any more real than an imaginary childhood friend? What evidence can be adduced to demonstrate His reality? As the astronomer Carl Sagan once noted, 'Extraordinary claims require extraordinary evidence'.[6] Can such evidence be put forward for God?

A number of arguments can be made for the existence of God, but two are especially powerful in the current scientifically-minded climate. Each, in a sense, is a sub-species of the Biblical statement in Romans 1:20 that 'since the creation of the world [God's] invisible attributes are clearly seen, being understood by the things that are made, even His eternal power'. Even if God cannot directly be seen, His existence can be rationally inferred from a study of creation. But with so many of the world's attributes capable of explanation via natural processes, what room is left for the divine? As scientific knowledge advances, have we reduced God to merely being a 'God of the Gaps' who operates only where our knowledge falls short?[7]

The arguments in this chapter reject that approach. One can find evidence for God within natural processes, but the following arguments go further by asserting that God's existence is not only a possible inference, but a *necessary* one, for the conditions they describe to exist.[8] These are, namely, the arguments from cosmology and abiogenesis. Considered in more detail, they illustrate not only the difficulty, but the *impossibility*, of a purely natural explanation for their occurrence.

1. THE COSMOLOGICAL ARGUMENT

The field of cosmology, or the study of the universe, is best approached with a strong sense of humility. Apart from the intricacies of the laws that govern it, its magnitude quickly overwhelms the mind. At present estimates, there are believed to be some two trillion galaxies in the observable universe, each of which may contain, like our own galaxy, several hundred billion stars.[9] At the opposite end of the spectrum, more than a trillion atoms could sit atop the dot at the end of this sentence, to say nothing of the even smaller subatomic particles that would comprise them.[10] As you read this you are, depending on your latitude, rotating with the earth at up to 1,660 kilometres per hour, orbiting the sun at over 107,000 kilometres per hour, and travelling around the centre of the galaxy at over 828,000 kilometres per hour—all without any sensation of movement.[11] In comparison with the universe, we are but very small indeed.

Small though we might be, mankind has always had an interest in understanding our surroundings. For the ancient Hindus, the universe was believed to be merely the latest iteration of universes that had emerged from a repetitive cycle of creation and destruction—sometimes symbolised by a hatching golden egg—without beginning or end.[12] For the Egyptians and Mesopotamians, it was thought to have evolved from a 'watery, motionless, limitless, and eternal uniformity'.[13] For the Greek philosopher Democritus, the universe was infinite and full of eternal atoms that combined to form innumerable worlds.[14] For his fellow countryman and philosophical opponent, Aristotle, the universe was eternal but finite, with the earth at its centre.[15]

Amidst these viewpoints, one culture put forward a different explanation for the universe's existence. In the first chapter of the Book of Genesis, the Hebrew writer Moses declared that 'In the beginning God created the heavens and the earth'. Simple though this might have seemed, it revealed two logically distinct concepts—first, that the universe was *created* by God, and secondly, that it had a *beginning* in time. 'Created' and 'beginning' were neither synonymous nor redundant; the former referred to the fact that God was the source of the universe's being, and the latter to the universe having had a starting point, rather than stretching infinitely into the past. In contrast to those who claimed the universe was eternal, Genesis declared that it was not, and in fact had begun through the creative act of a single deity.

Although this view was not widely held at the time, questions about the universe's origin were soon overtaken by disputes about its arrangement.[16] In the third century BC, Aristarchus of Samos questioned the Aristotelian geocentric model by arguing that the earth revolved around the sun and rotated on its axis—views that proved so controversial that the stoic philosopher Cleanthes denounced them as impious.[17] As recorded by Plutarch:

> Cleanthes thought that the Greeks ought to have called Aristarchus the Samian into question and condemned him of blasphemy against the Gods, as shaking the very foundations of the world, because this man, endeavoring to save the appearances, supposed that the heavens remained immovable, and that the earth moved through an oblique circle, at the same time turning about its own axis.[18]

With Aristarchus' heliocentric model condemned to obscurity, Aristotle's ideas dominated scientific discourse. Building upon his work, the Alexandrian astronomer Ptolemy argued in the second century AD that the earth was at the centre of the universe, with the sun, moon, planets and stars all orbiting it on curves called epicycles.[19] Although this would become the standard cosmological model for the next 1,500 years, the notion of an eternal universe eventually came under criticism.[20] Writing in the 500s, the Christian scholar John Philoponus argued that it was logically necessary for the world to have had a beginning, with the scriptural accounts of a God-created universe aligning with science or 'natural philosophy'.[21] To Philoponus, God, who transcends nature, created matter with the capacity to develop from chaos to an organised state.[22] Aristotle's arguments for an eternal universe were not only defective, but could be disproven. Since, logically, one could neither travel to the beginning of an infinite series or add to it, the fact that generations were increasing on earth proved to him that the universe was not eternal:

1. If the universe were eternal, then the generation of any non-eternal object would be preceded by an infinite series of generations of non-eternal objects.

2. An infinite series cannot be traversed.

3. (Hence) The Universe is not eternal.

And secondly:

1. If the universe is eternal, then there has been an infinite number of past generations.

2. The number of generations is increasing.

3. An infinite number cannot be added to.

4. (Hence) The Universe is not eternal.[23]

Innovative as his arguments were, Philoponus would prove more influential to medieval Islam than to Christianity, since his condemnation at the Third Council of Constantinople in 680 led to him being forgotten in the West.[24] Drawing upon them 400 years later, the Islamic philosopher Al-Ghazāli wrote in his *Jerusalem Tract* that 'It is self-evident to human reason that there must be a cause for the origination of anything originated. Since the universe is originated it follows that there was a cause for its origination'.[25] As proof, he observed that objects in the universe were either at rest or in motion, and since both rest and motion are originated, 'it follows that what is subject to the originated is itself originated'. Concluding what would become known as the Kalām Cosmological Argument, Al-Ghazāli stated that 'The sum of all this is that the universe is subject to origination, that it is therefore originated, that its actual origination is proved, and that its dependence upon the Creator is *ipso facto* comprehensible'.[26]

With the Christianisation of Europe, the view of a divinely-created non-eternal universe became predominant. In the thirteenth century, however, Christianity found itself facing challenges from both Islam and 'the naturalism of secular culture', brought about in part by a rediscovery of Aristotle's works.[27] In response, a young priest in Paris named Thomas Aquinas began writing a massive work in the 1250s that would become known as the *Summa Contra Gentiles*.[28] Written for a non-Christian audience, it attempted to demonstrate the truth of Christianity based upon the light of natural reasoning.[29] With respect to the eternity of the universe, Aquinas acknowledged Philoponus' arguments about how an infinite number could not be traversed or increased, but felt that 'these arguments, though not devoid of probability, lack absolute and necessary conclusiveness. … a more effective approach toward proving the non-eternity of the world can be made'.[30] Despite disagreeing with Aristotle's belief in an eternal universe, Aquinas drew upon his logical arguments for the existence of God—seen as both the universe's unmoved mover and first cause—to prove the universe's origination:

> Everything that is moved is moved by another. That some things are in motion … is evident from sense. Therefore, it is moved by something else that moves it. This mover is itself either moved or not moved. If it is not, we have reached our conclusion—namely, that we must posit some unmoved mover. This we call God. If it is moved, it is moved by another mover. We must, consequently, either proceed to infinity, or we must arrive at some unmoved mover. Now, it is not possible to proceed to infinity. Hence, we must posit some prime unmoved mover.[31]

> In all ordered efficient causes, the first is the cause of the intermediate cause, whether one or many, and this is the cause of the last cause. But, when you suppress a cause, you suppress its effect. Therefore, if you suppress the first cause, the intermediate cause cannot be a cause. Now, if there were an infinite regress among efficient causes, no cause would be first. Therefore, all the other causes, which are intermediate, will be suppressed. But this is manifestly false. We must, therefore, posit that there exists a first efficient cause. This is God.[32]

Putting this together, he argued that 'creation is the act of an infinite power alone',[33] and 'our assertion stands, namely, that God produces some effect from nothing pre-existing. If something exists before it … we must either go on to infinity, which is impossible in natural causes, as Aristotle proves … or we must arrive at a first being which presupposes no other. And this being can be none other than God Himself'.[34] Since an infinite regress of events was impossible, there had to be a *first* event whose cause was precipitated by something uncaused—just as someone had to touch the first domino before the second and subsequent dominos could fall. As powerful as this argument was, however, it did not earn him universal admiration. Writing against his work a century later, the Orthodox monk Kallistos Angelikoudes produced a lengthy polemic 'Against that which Thomas the Latin writes in heretical fashion and outside the chorus of the holy Church, [being] a clear refutation of his arrogant disregard for holy scripture'.[35] To Angelikoudes, Aquinas' appreciation of classical knowledge showed that he had 'fallen prey to the demons', and that his arguments were 'so utterly beholden to empty profane wisdom, that it should be recognized as directed not against the pagans but against God's holy Church'.[36] In contrast to the view that faith and reason were compatible, Angelikoudes argued that human reason had nothing of real value to contribute to theology and that external learning itself possessed an 'utter futility'.[37]

Rejecting Angelikoudes' anti-intellectualism, Western Europe instead embraced the emerging developments of the Renaissance. Universities were founded in several of the continent's principal cities, and many within the Church took a keen interest in promoting the revival of learning.[38] One such individual was Lucas Watzenrode, the Bishop of Warmia.[39] Counting many of the Renaissance's leading figures amongst his friends, his life changed in 1483 when his sister's children came under his guardianship.[40] The youngest of them, a boy named Nicholas, was especially clever, and he took care to ensure that his nephew was well-educated.[41] By 1503, he had paved the way for him to study law, medicine, and to serve as an apprentice to the Roman Curia at the Vatican.[42]

It would be in astronomy, however, that his nephew, Nicholas Copernicus, would leave his mark. By 1514, Copernicus had produced a short work for his friends and colleagues known as the *Commentariolus*, 'maintaining that the earth moves while the sun is at rest'.[43] Although not intended for a wider audience, his theory soon spread across Europe. In 1533, Pope Clement VII was informed of it during a lecture given in the Vatican gardens.[44] Impressed by what he heard, he presented the lecturer with a book as a reward.[45] With many in the Church's upper echelons intrigued by Copernicus' theory, the Archbishop of Capua, Nikolaus von Schönberg, wrote to him from Rome on November 1, 1536:

> Some years ago ... I began to have a very high regard for you, ... [f]or I had learned that you had not merely mastered the discoveries of the ancient astronomers uncommonly well but had also formulated a new cosmology. In it you maintain that the earth moves; that the sun occupies the lowest, and thus the central, place in the universe ... with the utmost earnestness I entreat you, most learned sir, unless I inconvenience you, to communicate this discovery of yours to scholars, and at the earliest possible moment to send me your writings on the

sphere of the universe together with the tables and whatever else you have that is relevant to this subject. Moreover, I have instructed Theodoric of Reden to have everything copied in your quarters at my expense and dispatched to me. If you gratify my desire in this matter, you will see that you are dealing with a man who is zealous for your reputation and eager to do justice to so fine a talent.[46]

Six years later, Copernicus included this letter in the preface to his six-volume work *On the Revolutions of the Heavenly Spheres*.[47] Setting out evidence for the earth's rotation and revolution around the sun, he noted that 'Although there are so many authorities for saying that the Earth rests in the centre of the world that people think the contrary supposition inopinable and even ridiculous ... the question has not yet been decided and accordingly is by no means to be scorned'.[48] Supporting his argument with tables and charts, he wrote:

> the heavens are immense in comparison with the Earth ... and it does not follow that the Earth must rest at the centre of the world. And we should be even more surprised if such a vast world should wheel completely around us during the space of twenty-four hours rather than that its least part, the Earth, should. ... [T]his movement ... would necessarily be very headlong and of an unsurpassable velocity. ... why not admit that the *appearance* of daily revolution belongs to the heavens but the *reality* belongs to the Earth?[49]

Transformative as his model was, it required refinement to explain existing astronomical data. In 1609, Johannes Kepler demonstrated that the planets moved around the sun in elliptical, rather than circular, orbits.[50] Believing that scientific laws were 'within the grasp of the human mind' and that 'God wanted us to recognize them by creating us after his own image so that we could share in his own thoughts', Kepler developed three laws of planetary motion, with the goal of showing that 'the heavenly machine is ... similar to clockwork in so far as almost all of the manifold motions are taken care of by one single absolutely simple magnetic bodily force'.[51] Seventy-eight years later, Isaac Newton demonstrated that this force was gravity.[52] In his *Mathematical Principles of Natural Philosophy*, Newton formulated his law of universal gravitation—every particle of matter, however small, exerted an attractive force on all other particles, with the magnitude of this force dependent upon their mass and distance.[53] The sun pulled the earth and other planets towards itself at the same time that they exerted a similar, if much smaller, force on it and each other.[54] But to Newton:

these bodies may, indeed, persevere in their orbits by the mere laws of gravity, yet they could by no means have at first derived the regular position of the orbits themselves from those laws. ... This most beautiful system of the sun, planets, and comets, could only proceed from the counsel and dominion of an intelligent and powerful Being. ... This Being governs all things, not as the soul of the world, but as Lord over all; and on account of his dominion he is wont to be called Lord God ... or Universal Ruler ... He is not eternity or infinity, but eternal and infinite; he is not duration or space, but he endures and is present. He endures for ever, and is everywhere present; and by existing always and everywhere, he constitutes duration and space. Since every particle of space is *always*, and every indivisible moment of duration is *everywhere*, certainly the Maker and Lord of all things cannot be *never* and *nowhere*. ... the Supreme God exists necessarily; and by the same necessity he exists *always* and *everywhere*.[55]

Yet if gravity applied to all matter throughout the universe, why had it not collapsed in on itself? Addressing this in a letter to his colleague Richard Bentley, Newton wrote that if matter 'was evenly disposed throughout an infinite space, it could never convene into one mass; but some of it would convene into one mass and some into another, so as to make an infinite number of great masses scattered at great distances from one another throughout all that infinite space'.[56] By implication, the universe had to be incredibly vast, extending far beyond the sun and planets. It was therefore likely that other stars and planets existed beyond the limits of human detection.

In 1750, the British astronomer Thomas Wright acknowledged this when, describing what would one day become known as galaxies, he wrote that 'the many cloudy Spots, just perceivable' in the night sky may 'be external creation, bordering upon the known one; too remote for even our telescopes to reach'.[57] With respect to the Milky Way, which appeared to be a 'vast ring of stars, scattered ... in the direction of a perfect circle', Wright argued that its existence refuted the atheistic notion—then beginning to gain ground—that mankind was alone in the universe and that 'a more exalted state cannot be hoped for':

This is the fatal Rock upon which all weak Heads and narrow Minds are lost and split upon ... I have often wonder'd how thinking Men could possibly fall into so gross an Error, as that of a Spirit's Annihilation [at death] ... Chance can only effect Disorder, Discord, and Confusion; *ergo*, the visible Harmony and Beauty of the Creation declare for a Direction; and this must of Consequence ... proceed from the Wisdom and Power of an eternal being, *God of Infinity*, the Author of all Ideas:

And if this primitive Power produced us his Creatures from nothing, nothing can be wanting to revive our Frames again ... how absurd it is to suppose one Part of the Creation regular, and the other irregular ... consequently we may reasonably expect, that the [Milky Way], which is a manifest Circle amongst the Stars ... will prove at last the Whole to be together a vast and glorious regular Production of Beings...[58]

Fifty years after Wright's hypothesis about galaxies, a separate development occurred that would have important consequences for astronomical research. In a paper presented to the Royal Society in 1801, a twenty-eight year old doctor named Thomas Young put forward the idea that light consisted of waves, with 'the sensation of different colours depend[ing] on the different frequency of vibrations'.[59] In his lecture *On the Nature of Light and Colours*, he noted that 'From a comparison of various experiments, it appears that the breadth of the undulations constituting the extreme red light must be supposed to be, in air, about one 36 thousandth of an inch, and those of the extreme violet about one 60 thousandth'.[60] The rainbow of colour that appeared when light passed through a prism therefore reflected different wavelengths, with red having the longest wavelength and violet the shortest.[61] Although Newton and others had worked with prisms and light, this was the first time the wavelengths of colours had been proposed and measured.

The implications of this discovery became clearer in 1842 when the Austrian physicist Christian Doppler put forward what would become known as the 'Doppler Effect'. Recognising that a ship steering towards oncoming waves 'has to receive, in the same amount of time, more waves with a greater impact compared with a ship that is not moving', he examined whether this held true for other waves.[62] With respect to light, if the source of the light and the observer were 'both at rest, then the observed and emitted frequency are the same. If the observer moves towards the source, however, the frequency will increase, and if he moves away it will decrease. Movement of the source will produce similar effects'.[63] To an observer, the light of a distant object would appear to change colour as it moved closer or farther away.[64] Building upon this, the French physicist Armand-Hippolyte-Louis Fizeau observed in 1848 that it could explain a shift in the spectral lines of stars, and by 1868 a British astronomer, William Huggins, had used it to find the speed of a star moving away from the earth.[65]

In 1912, a more profound application occurred when Vesto Slipher, an astronomer in the United States, discovered that, based upon 'the shift at the violet end of the spectrum', the Andromeda galaxy was approaching the solar system at nearly 300 kilometres per second.[66] Although 'the faintness of the spectra ma[de] the work heavy and the accumulation of results slow', he felt that it 'might not be fruitless to observe some of the more promising spirals for proper motion'.[67] Three years later, he produced a more detailed report into the velocity of fifteen galaxies, twelve of which appeared to be moving away from the solar system at an average rate of 400 kilometres per second.[68] But why were they moving? It was one thing for a single star to move as Huggins had observed, but why would trillions of them move in a particular direction?[69] Newton had posited that gravity could cause matter to group into 'an infinite number of great masses', but what could explain the fact that the majority of galaxies seemed to be moving away from, rather than towards, the solar system?[70] This was especially puzzling since it appeared to clash with Albert Einstein's latest work on relativity, in which the attractive force of gravity was counterbalanced by the repulsive force of his cosmological constant to produce a static universe.[71] Under a balanced cosmological model, how was such movement even possible?

In 1927, a solution was put forward by a Belgian priest named Georges Lemaître. Having studied under some of the world's preeminent scientists at Cambridge and the Massachusetts Institute of Technology, he argued in his paper, *A Homogeneous Universe of Constant Mass and Growing Radius Accounting for the Radial Velocity of Extragalactic Nebulae* that the movement of galaxies could be explained by an expanding universe.[72] As novel as this theory was, however, the initial reaction from the scientific community was underwhelming. When he attempted to tell Einstein about his work at a conference in Brussels, the German physicist dismissively remarked 'Your calculations are correct, but your physics is abominable'.[73] Discouraged, Lemaître then temporarily abandoned any attempt to promote his theory.[74] Two years later, though, Edwin Hubble used a sample of thirty galaxies with known redshifts to present a redshift-distance relation.[75] From data gathered at the Mount Wilson observatory, it appeared that the galaxies were indeed moving apart, providing evidence for Lemaître's theory.[76] After seeing the data for himself, Einstein publicly renounced his static model of the universe and endorsed Lemaître's work.[77] But if the universe was expanding as the data suggested, why was it doing so? Once again, Lemaître had an answer. Writing in the journal *Nature* in 1931, he argued that:

> quantum theory suggests a beginning of the world very different from the present order … in atomic processes, the notions of space and time are no more than statistical notions; … If the world has begun with a single quantum, the notions of space and time would altogether fail to have any meaning at the beginning; … we could conceive the beginning of the universe in the form of a unique atom, the atomic weight of which is the total mass of the universe.[78]

Under this approach, 'The radius of space began at zero', followed by 'a rapid expansion determined by the mass of the initial atom, almost equal to the present mass of the universe'.[79] The movement of distant galaxies—observed through their redshifts—was merely a continuance of this expansion.

Although a growing body of data seemed to confirm Lemaître's theories, not all were convinced. In an interview with the BBC in 1949, the British astronomer Fred Hoyle dismissed what he called the 'big bang' theory that the universe had begun with an explosion.[80] To Hoyle, a proponent of the 'steady-state' theory of an eternal universe that replenished itself with newly created matter, 'The reason why scientists like the "big bang" is because they are overshadowed by the Book of Genesis. It is deep within the psyche of most scientists to believe in the first page of Genesis'.[81] Ten years earlier, a similar criticism had been voiced by the Swedish physicist Hannes Alfvén, who felt that Lemaître's theory had been motivated by a 'need to reconcile his physics with the Church's doctrine of creation'.[82] To Lemaître, however, his theories about the universe remained outside any metaphysical or religious question.[83] In the tradition of Aquinas, he felt that religion and science were two roads leading to the same ultimate truth:

> Nothing in my working life, nothing I have ever learned in my studies
> of either science or religion has ever caused me to change that opinion.
> I have no conflict to reconcile. Science has not shaken my faith in
> religion and religion has never caused me to question the conclusions
> I reached by scientific methods.[84]

Notwithstanding scientists' alleged preference for Genesis, another argument had to be addressed. If the universe had begun from a 'radius of zero' and expanded to its present size, the forces involved would have been immense, involving temperatures theoretically as high as 10^{32} degrees kelvin in its early stages.[85] Surely such a 'bang' would have left some trace. As Hoyle asked in his book, *Frontiers of Astronomy*, 'Was there ever a superdense state? It is a suspicious feature of the explosion [big bang] theory that no obvious relics of a superdense state of the Universe can be found'.[86] In the late 1940s, however, scientists predicted that such a 'relic' could be found in the form of background radiation.[87]

In 1964, two scientists at Bell Labs in New Jersey—Arno Penzias and Robert Wilson—were using a sensitive antenna to detect radio waves when they noticed a persistent weak signal.[88] Despite their efforts to remove all sources of interference, the signal remained—regardless of the direction in which it was pointed.[89] Frustrated by their inability to remove the excess signal noise, they contacted Robert Dicke at Princeton University, who happened to be designing a device to test for cosmic radiation from the early universe.[90] Surprised to hear that his work had been 'scooped', Dicke and his team inspected the antenna and affirmed that it had detected the radiation they were looking for.[91] Fourteen years later, Penzias and Wilson received the Nobel Prize in Physics for their discovery of cosmic microwave background radiation, offering evidence of the remnant heat left over from the universe's initial explosion.[92]

Colour image of cosmic background radiation, NASA/WMAP (2012)

With the discovery of the cosmic microwave background, support for the 'steady state' theory of the universe became unsustainable.[93] But although the expansionary or 'big bang' theory had become the standard cosmological model, questions remained about its operation. From an examination of the data, it appeared that the temperature of the background radiation was essentially uniform throughout the universe, notwithstanding the tremendous variations that would have existed at its formation.[94] But this presented a challenge. How could such a high degree of uniformity have arisen when the exchanges of energy necessary to achieve it could not have occurred over the universe's observable distance? A bucket of ice cubes and a bucket of boiling water set beside one another will eventually reach the same temperature, but what if they were 100 trillion kilometres apart? Simply put, the universe seemed too big; energy cannot be transferred farther than the maximum distance that light could have travelled since the beginning of the universe, and yet the cosmic background radiation showed uniformity over a *much* greater distance than this.[95]

In 1980, an American physicist named Alan Guth put forward a possible explanation. From his interpretation of the data, it appeared that the universe had undergone a tremendous expansion—at a rate far greater than the speed of light—between 10^{-35} and 10^{-33} seconds after the explosion, growing from a 'small subnuclear-sized dot to a region about 3 meters across'.[96] Although this might not seem especially explosive, it was equivalent to a grain of sand growing to the size of the observable universe in one billionth of the time it would have taken light to cross the nucleus of an atom.[97] To achieve such a level of cosmic background uniformity in the time allotted, the early universe would have had to have expanded at more than *ninety* times the speed of light.[98] This growth, moreover, was not an expansion *into* space, but an expansion *of* space.[99] From an infinitely-dense point with a size of zero, space itself—containing all matter and energy in the universe—had exploded outward with unimaginable force.[100]

But what did this mean? How could energy move faster than the speed of light, the theoretical maximum speed in the universe? Was the universe expanding into *nothing*, or was there something beyond the 'edge' of the expansion? Ultimately, it was impossible to say, since the expansion of the universe relative to the speed of light meant that there would eventually come a point, or cosmological horizon, past which even the most powerful telescopes would never be able to peer.[101] This also meant that past a certain stage of its development, it would be impossible to obtain definitive answers about what happened in the earliest moments of the universe. One could recognise that a 'big bang' had occurred, but, as Stephen Hawking noted, questions about the 'conditions for the big bang are not questions that science addresses'.[102]

Granting all this to be true, where does it leave the search for God? A cautious approach might suggest that there is nothing in the findings of cosmology to disprove God's existence, and that a belief in a divine creator cannot consequently be dismissed as irrational. The astronomer Carl Sagan appeared to recognise this when he wrote that 'the one conceivable finding of science that could disprove a Creator' would be 'an infinitely old universe' since it would never have been created or, ostensibly, required a creator.[103] With the evidence pointing to a universe with a clear beginning, however, this argument was foreclosed. Sagan himself could only go as far as agnosticism, noting that:

> An atheist is someone who is certain that God does not exist, someone who has compelling evidence against the existence of God. I know of no such compelling evidence. Because God can be relegated to remote times and places and to ultimate causes, we would have to know a great deal more about the universe than we do now to be sure that no such God exists. To be certain of the existence of God and to be certain of the nonexistence of God seem to me to be the confident extremes in a subject so riddled with doubt and uncertainty as to inspire very little confidence indeed.[104]

Notwithstanding Sagan's lack of confidence, this book could hardly rest on the premise—however irrefutable—that God cannot be shown to *not* exist, especially when the evidence supports a bolder conclusion. Even if evidence were to emerge to support the 'infinitely old universe' in his argument, it would still not disprove the existence of God, given that it wrongly conflates a lack of *beginning* with a lack of *creation*. As the physicist Stephen Barr has noted:

> a novel has an internal sequence of words. The 'beginning' of a novel consists of the first words in that sequence, whereas the novel's 'creation' takes place in the mind of the novelist. In other words, one can distinguish between the 'beginning' or 'opening' of something, which has to do with its *internal* sequential structure, and its 'origin' in the sense of the *ultimate cause* of its existence. If someone were to ask why a certain novel exists, it would be silly to point to its first words. Rather, one would point to the author. Indeed, there could be a novel whose plot went around in a circle and which was even printed on a scroll that looped around: it would *have* no 'first words,' and yet *would* have an author.[105]

With the evidence pointing to a universe with a beginning, however, Sagan's argument about an infinitely-old universe can be abandoned where he left it. Returning to the current understanding, if the entire universe were contained within a radius of zero, what, by definition, could have remained outside it? Moreover, to the extent something could have been found outside it, how could it have resisted the gravitational force of *infinite* density? If a black hole, formed by a single collapsed star, can exert enough gravity that even light cannot escape, what could possibly escape the gravitational pull of *every* star in an entire universe, assuming there was anything outside the universe to be found?[106] What, for that matter, does a 'radius of zero' even mean? If we imagine a car in a scrapyard, we can envision it being compressed into a smaller block of material. With enough force, we could theoretically crush it down to its most minimal essence. In such a densely-compacted state, it would still occupy some amount of space, however small. But with respect to the universe, the data suggests that the building blocks of every galaxy, planet, animal, and human were once compressed into an infinitely-dense state with a radius of zero, occupying no space at all. This then exploded with unimaginable, greater-than-lightspeed force to produce a region of space with an observable diameter of more than ninety billion light years.[107]

If this is not *creatio ex nihilo*, or 'creation out of nothing', it is difficult to imagine how else to characterise it. A point with a radius of zero might be a valid mathematical construct, but in a physical realm defined by the four dimensions of length, width, height, and time, such a point is no point at all. Even if we grant that concepts such as volume cease to have meaning without space, the end result is still 'something' emerging out of 'nothing'—infinity from a radius of zero. Logically, this should be impossible. As the Greek philosopher Parmenides recognised in the sixth century BC, *ex nihilo nihil fit*, or 'nothing comes from nothing'.[108] And yet, the universe's existence suggests that something did indeed come from nothing. How are we to account for this? Some have suggested that the universe's beginning can be explained by unknown forces acting in natural, albeit unknown, ways, and that there must always have been a 'something' for the universe to have emerged from. Two proposals in this respect are string theory and the multiverse concept. With string theory, the basic argument is that the universe could have been created by the collision of two or more theoretical membranes or 'branes' which in turn are connected to a series of one-dimensional 'strings' that affect all particles in the universe.[109]

But in order for string theory to work, it would have to operate across ten mathematical dimensions rather than our actual four.[110] A key problem, however, is that no one can find these extra dimensions. Some have theorised that they 'may hide from plain view if they curl up into a space that is small enough to escape detection', but this is more of a faith position than demonstrable science.[111] Another critical problem noted by Martin Rees, Astronomer Royal and a former president of Britain's Royal Society, is that the number of spatial dimensions in the universe—length, width, and height—have to be exactly three in order for life to exist; the addition of a fourth spatial dimension would render life impossible.[112] Although string theory has been described by its proponents as a theory that is 'too good to be false', the fact remains that physicists 'haven't even found any indirect empirical corroboration' of it after several decades of research.[113] As for the multiverse, this theory arose from a need to explain why the universe appears fine-tuned for life. Quoting Hawking:

> The laws of science, as we know them at present, contain many fundamental numbers, like the size of the electric charge of the electron and the ratio of the masses of the proton and electron. ... The remarkable fact is that the values of these numbers seem to have been very finely adjusted to make possible the development of life. For example, if the electric charge of the electron had been only slightly different, stars either would have been unable to burn hydrogen and helium, or else they would not have exploded.[114]

Other parameters support this point. With respect to hydrogen, if the strength of the nuclear force had changed the nuclear efficiency value to a mere .006 instead of its actual .007, helium formation could not have occurred and stars would have lacked fuel. If it had been .008, no hydrogen would have remained beyond the earliest stages of the universe, and water formation would have been impossible.[115] For life as we know it to exist, the value had to be exactly .007. As the aforementioned Rees identified in his book, *Just Six Numbers*, this variable, along with five others, 'constitute a recipe for the universe', such that, if any one of them were different 'even to the tiniest degree, there would be no stars, no complex elements, no life'.[116] By American physicist Lee Smolin's estimate, the probability of a universe with fine-tuned parameters like ours randomly occurring is about one chance in 10^{229}, effectively an impossibility.[117]

The response of some to such odds was to suggest that the universe was simply one of many—possibly infinite—universes in a larger 'multiverse', and that there was nothing inherently special about the fact that our universe was fine-tuned to support life.[118] Much like the hypothetical monkeys with infinite time producing the works of Shakespeare on typewriters, they argued that, with enough possible universes, one could be expected to emerge with life-supporting parameters.[119] But as British physicist Paul Davies noted:

> there are some regions of the universe that lie beyond the reach of our telescopes, but somewhere on the slippery slope between that and the idea that there are an infinite number of universes, credibility reaches a limit. ... more and more must be accepted on faith, and less and less is open to scientific verification. Extreme multiverse explanations are therefore reminiscent of theological discussions. Indeed, invoking an infinity of unseen universes to explain the unusual features of the one we do see is just as ad hoc as invoking an unseen Creator. The multiverse theory may be dressed up in scientific language, but in essence it requires the same leap of faith.[120]

A second problem with the multiverse argument is that it would require the fundamental laws of physics to be able to vary from one place to another in order to produce differently 'tuned' universes. Apart from a lack of evidence that this is even possible—could the nuclear force of hydrogen actually be *capable* of changing in another universe? *What* would change it, for instance?—it asks us to accept that which cannot, by definition, be demonstrated. As a number of physicists have noted, 'The multiverse proposal is not provable either by observation, or as an implication of well-established physics. It is under-determined by the data; in particular theories proposing how different physical parameters will necessarily occur in different [universes ...] are untested and untestable'.[121] But even if these theories could be proven to explain the universe's origin, we would still have to consider how the principles that would have made them possible came to be. A force outside of time and space, working from a radius of zero, would still have given rise to time and space.

From current observations of the universe and our understanding of physics, it appears that, at a specific moment in the past, infinite energy exploded from an infinitely-dense point, occupying no space at all, at an exponentially-faster-than-light speed to produce an incomprehensively vast universe uniquely tuned to support our existence. Although some have sought to explain this through naturalistic means such as string theory or the multiverse, neither concept has ever shown corroborative evidence in its favour—to say nothing of the internal challenges each would have to overcome in order to account for the present cosmological state. Difficult as it might seem to accept, *creatio ex nihilo* gives the best account for why there is 'something' rather than 'nothing'.

The inability to ascribe a natural origin to the universe provides strong evidence for the existence of a creative deity. To be clear, however, this is not an attempt to relegate such a deity to being a 'God of the Gaps', who only appears when scientific explanations fail. There have been many phenomena throughout history which, though unexplained at the time, eventually became explainable, and—as Dietrich Bonhoeffer wrote from a Nazi prison cell in 1944—'how wrong it is to use God as a stop-gap for the incompleteness of our knowledge'.[122] But here we are dealing with something entirely different, namely the logical *impossibility* of the universe emerging on its own accord. Although one might argue that we do not know enough about the universe (let alone any hypothetical others) to make such a sweeping statement, we do know enough about logic to recognise that 'something' cannot emerge from 'nothing'. Moreover, the fact that the universe had a beginning allows certain inferences to be made. As the American philosopher William Lane Craig noted:

1. Everything that begins to exist has a cause of its existence.
2. The universe began to exist.
3. Therefore the universe has a cause of its existence.[123]

By itself, this is little different from the argument Al-Ghazāli advanced nearly 1,000 years ago. But Craig took it further. With respect to the second point, why did the universe begin when it did? Why did it not begin ten minutes later or a trillion years earlier? Referring to the principle of determination, he noted that 'when two different states of affairs are equally possible and one results, this realisation of one rather than the other must be the result of the action of a personal agent who freely chooses one rather than the other'.[124] By implication, 'if the universe began to exist, and if the universe is caused, then the cause of the universe must be a personal being who freely cho[se] to create the world'.[125]

Strong as the evidence and logic for this might be, two objections are often made—one scientific, the other philosophical. With respect to the scientific objection, some contend that the creation of the universe *ex nihilo* would violate the laws of physics. As the atheist writer David Mills has argued:

> the universe—which is the sum of all mass-energy—could not, according to the mass-energy conservation law, come into existence *ex nihilo* in the way demanded by creationism. According to this well-confirmed scientific principle, our universe of mass-energy was never created, and cannot be annihilated. To believe in 'scientific' creationism, therefore, is to overlook or dismiss the law of conservation of mass-energy.[126]

It is, of course, correct that under the first law of thermodynamics energy cannot be created or destroyed, but only changed.[127] A fundamental caveat, however, is that it only applies to energy *within an isolated system*.[128] Thus, whilst energy cannot be created or destroyed *within* the universe, the law of conservation of mass-energy really has nothing to say about how the universe acquired that energy in the first place. Moreover, the closer one gets to the earliest moments of the big bang, the more the laws of physics begin to break down. It is true that infinite energy does not normally emerge *ex nihilo*, but it also does not generally travel exponentially faster than light either, as it appears to have once done.

The second objection raises a more interesting philosophical point. If God created the universe, who created God? As Richard Dawkins noted in *The God Delusion*, 'the designer hypothesis immediately raises the larger problem of who designed the designer. The whole problem we started out with was the problem of explaining statistical improbability. It is obviously no solution to postulate something even more improbable'.[129] But is the concept of an uncreated deity really that improbable? Both atheism and Christianity depend upon an uncaused first cause—the disagreement merely arises over its identity. To illustrate this, consider the 'infinite regress' problem. A story is told of a lecturer who, after giving a presentation on the solar system, was accosted by a lady who felt that she had a better theory to explain the position of the earth. When the lecturer asked what it was, she stated that the earth rested on the back of a turtle, which in turn stood on the back of a second turtle. When the lecturer asked what the second turtle stood on, she triumphantly said, 'it's turtles all the way down'.[130] Quaint as such an argument might seem, it is precisely the sort of problem Philoponus had in mind when he argued against Aristotle's eternal universe in the sixth century—noting that 'an infinite series cannot be traversed'.[131] 700 years later, Aquinas expanded upon this with his 'first cause' argument, observing that 'if there were an infinite regress among efficient causes, no cause would be first. Therefore, all the other causes, which are intermediate, will be suppressed'. But, as he recognised, 'this is manifestly false. We must, therefore, posit that there exists a first efficient cause'.[132]

Can anyone rationally argue otherwise? Given the impossibility of an infinite regress, Dawkins' 'larger problem of who designed the designer' is no problem at all—such a designer would simply 'be', in the same way that any impersonal force that gave rise to the universe would, under an atheistic approach, simply 'be'. Under any cosmological scenario one might choose, there must, by definition, be a first, uncaused cause, even if it defies our capabilities to understand how this can be so. But with the atheistic approach, there are larger problems. If one is prepared to accept the virgin birth of the universe—out of nothing at all, by nothing at all—the atheist must not only accept this on faith but still account for why it emerged when it did. Given that the universe has a specific age, what would have caused an impersonal, atheistic first cause to manifest at *that* moment, and not at another? The mere fact that the universe is not infinitely old proves that it did not always have to exist, so something necessarily determined when its beginning would occur. This determining agent then caused, at a specific moment, an infinitely-dense point with a radius of zero to explode with unimaginable force to form the finely-tuned universe we now see. For the atheist, this must forever remain a mystery. For the theist—to quote Aquinas—'this we call God'.[133]

2. THE ABIOGENESIS ARGUMENT

The second scientific argument for the existence of God relates to abiogenesis, or the process through which life arose from non-living matter.[134] Given that there was once no life on earth and today it is found in abundance, such an event undoubtedly occurred. But *how* did it occur? What led to a collection of elements becoming a living organism? How did chemical compounds develop the power to acquire energy, encode information, and reproduce? What turned a desolate world into the rich environment we now see?

Throughout history, there have been various theories as to how life began. One of the earliest and most prominent ideas was the notion of spontaneous generation—a theory advanced by Aristotle in the fourth century BC. In his *History of Animals*, he wrote:

> The nature of animals and vegetables is similar, for some are produced
> from the seed of other plants, and others are of spontaneous growth ...
> So also some animals are produced from animals of a similar form, the
> origin of others is spontaneous, and not from similar forms; from these
> and from plants are divided those which spring from putrid matter,
> this is the case with many insects...[135]

It was clear to Aristotle that some animals gave birth to their own kind, whilst others seemed to spontaneously emerge from 'putrid matter'. In a time with minimal sanitation, it was perhaps unsurprising that many of the more undesirable creatures—insects, snakes, and rats—were believed to spring from society's accumulated filth.[136] Spontaneous generation was also feared to be able to strike in cleaner settings, however, as the Roman architect Vitruvius warned when he advised that libraries be built facing the east, as 'those that are towards the south and west are injured by the worm'.[137] Even Shakespeare acknowledged the role of spontaneous generation when he wrote in *Antony and Cleopatra* that 'Your serpent of Egypt is bred now of your mud by the operation of the sun, so is your crocodile'.[138]

The view that waste could produce rats, books could produce bookworms, and mud could produce crocodiles took a severe hit in 1668 when the Italian scientist Francesco Redi established that rotting meat could not spontaneously produce maggots.[139] In his *Experiments on the Generation of Insects*, Redi wrote:

> I began to believe that all worms found in meat were derived directly from the droppings of flies, and not from the putrefaction of the meat [hence ...] I put a snake, some fish, some eels of the Arno, and a slice of milk-fed veal in four large, wide-mouthed flasks; having well closed and sealed them, I then filled the same number of flasks in the same way, only leaving these open. It was not long before the meat and the fish, in these second vessels, became wormy and flies were seen entering and leaving at will; but in the closed flasks I did not see a worm, though many days had passed since the dead flesh had been put in them.[140]

Two centuries later, the French biologist Louis Pasteur ended the debate by demonstrating that microorganisms could not develop in sterilised environments that had been sealed.[141] After boiling a nutrient broth, Pasteur divided it into portions and exposed them to different controlled conditions.[142] While the flasks that were open to the air and dust soon developed signs of life, the ones that had prevented dust from entering or were sealed did not.[143] After studying the findings, the French Academy of Sciences awarded Pasteur the prestigious Alhumbert Prize.[144] Spontaneous generation as a scientific explanation was now discredited, with its remaining adherents increasingly marginalised.[145] Following Pasteur's experiment, one of his sealed flasks eventually became part of the Science Museum's collection in London, where it remains sterile.[146]

Contemporaneous with Pasteur's research was the work of a British naturalist, Charles Darwin. Following his observations of plants and animals on a survey mission to South America, he published his landmark book *On the Origin of Species by Means of Natural Selection* in 1859, setting out his judgment 'that species are not immutable; but that those belonging to what are called the same genera are lineal descendants of some other and generally extinct species [...and] that Natural Selection has been the main but not exclusive means of modification'.[147] Although his theory would have a transformative impact on the study of biology, he specifically declined to address how life began—even writing in a letter to his friend, Joseph Dalton Hooker, that 'It is mere rubbish, thinking at present of the origin of life; one might as well think of the origin of matter'.[148] Expanding upon this, his colleague Thomas Huxley noted that:

> the causes of the phenomena of organic nature resolves itself into two problems—the first being the question of the origination of living or organic beings; and the second being the totally distinct problem of the modification and perpetuation of organic beings when they have already come into existence. *The first question Mr. Darwin does not touch; he does not deal with it at all*; but he says—given the origin of organic matter—supposing its creation to have already taken place, my object is to show [... how] such states of organic matter as those with which we are acquainted must have come about.[149]

For some, Darwin's failure to address 'the first question' was a glaring omission. The German zoologist Ernst Haeckel wrote that 'The chief defect of the Darwinian theory is that it throws no light on the origin of the primitive organism—probably a simple cell—from which all the others have descended. When Darwin assumes a special creative act for this first species, he is not consistent and, I think, not quite sincere'.[150] Evolution via natural selection was, as another put it, 'the outcome of life from life, and leaves us without an approach to a solution of the mighty question of the origin of life. ... How then are we to conceive the origination of organized creatures?'[151] Even John Tyndall, one of Darwin's supporters, conceded the 'inability to point to any satisfactory experimental proof that life can be developed save from demonstrable antecedent life'.[152]

In 1871, however, Darwin anticipated the future direction of biological research when he wrote that 'It is often said that all the conditions for the first production of a living organism are now present, which could ever have been present. But if (and oh! what a big if!) we could conceive in some warm little pond, with all sorts of ammonia and phosphoric salts, light, heat, electricity, etc, present, that a proteine compound was chemically formed ready to undergo still more complex changes, at the present day such matter would be instantly devoured or absorbed, which would not have been the case before living creatures were formed'.[153] Sixty-five years later, a Soviet biochemist named Alexander Oparin published *The Origin of Life*, setting out his theory that life could have arisen in such a 'pond' from basic molecules that developed in the Earth's primitive atmosphere. Assuming, based upon spectroscopic discoveries of ammonia and methane in Jupiter's atmosphere, that the Earth's early atmosphere was similarly reducing—meaning any traces of oxygen would have been rapidly removed via reactions with other gases—he asserted that:

> It is beyond doubt that ... the physical conditions on the Earth's surface were different than now: the temperature was much higher, the atmosphere had a different composition, light conditions were different, etc., but in this there is nothing unusual or mysterious. Quite the contrary, these conditions are more or less well known to us and we can not only easily picture them to ourselves but we can even reproduce them, to a large extent, in our own laboratories.[154]

Suggesting that the atmosphere was originally composed of methane, ammonia, hydrogen, and water vapour, he theorised that, as the Earth cooled, 'torrents of boiling water must have poured down upon the Earth's surface and flooded it, thus forming the primitive ebullient oceans' which would have then contained 'the simplest organic compounds in solution'.[155] Under such an approach, Darwin's 'warm little pond' could have begun through the atmospheric synthesis of chemical compounds which accumulated on the ground via rain. By themselves, however, Oparin acknowledged that these conditions did 'not furnish an explanation of how life had arisen on our Earth', but merely posited how certain compounds might have been synthesised.[156]

Intrigued by Oparin's ideas, an American student named Stanley Miller approached his advisor, Harold Urey, in the 1950s to see about testing whether organic molecules could be produced from the gases Oparin had assumed were part of the prebiotic atmosphere.[157] After sealing methane, hydrogen, and ammonia in a flask connected to a flask of water, he heated the water to induce evaporation and fired electrical sparks into the mixing chemicals to simulate lightning. Several days later, he discovered that a number of amino acids—the building blocks of proteins—had formed in the solution, providing experimental support for Oparin's belief that simple compounds could have arisen from such a mixture.[158] A few years later, a Spanish researcher named Joan Oró found that adenine and other nucleobases necessary for deoxyribonucleic acid (DNA) and ribonucleic acid (RNA) could develop via a similar process using water, hydrogen cyanide, and ammonia.[159]

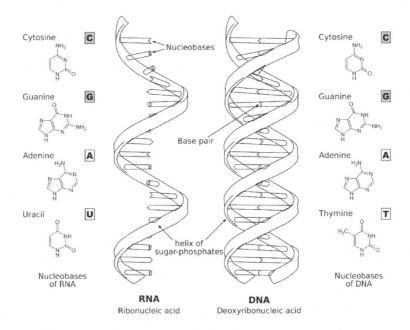

Given the pace of such discoveries, Colin Pittendrigh—professor of biology at Princeton University—boldly predicted in 1967 that 'laboratories will be creating a living cell within ten years'.[160] His zeal would prove premature, however, and in 2011 a critical problem emerged with the Oparin-Miller-Urey-Oró model. In an article published in *Nature* on the oxidation state of Hadean magmas, researchers at Rensselaer's NASA Astrobiology Institute showed that the oxidation levels of cerium in some of the world's oldest zircon crystals possessed an oxidation state 'similar to present-day conditions'.[161] As one of them noted, this meant that 'We can now say with some certainty that many scientists studying the origins of life on Earth simply picked the wrong atmosphere', with their findings proving that 'the conditions on early Earth were simply not conducive to the formation of this type of atmosphere, but rather to an atmosphere dominated by the more oxygen-rich compounds found within our current atmosphere'.[162] Oparin's confident belief that early atmospheric conditions were 'more or less well known', had been misplaced, with the consequence that Miller's experiment had used the wrong ingredients.

But what did this mean? Earlier research with experimental atmospheres had shown that when they became less reducing, their yields of organic compounds 'decreased drastically'.[163] When researchers ran the Miller-Urey experiment again using an updated atmospheric model, they discovered that reactions between carbon dioxide and nitrogen produced nitrites, which destroyed the few amino acids that appeared as fast as they formed.[164] Although 'modest' yields of amino acids could still be produced if iron and calcium carbonate were added to remove the nitrites, it was clear that the Earth's early atmosphere would have been far less hospitable for the production of biologically-necessary compounds than scientists had previously believed.[165] Assuming such compounds could have been synthesised under an oxygenated atmosphere, however, another—and more challenging—problem presented itself. With all life possessing a genetic code based upon DNA or RNA, the origin of this code posed new difficulties for researchers.[166] As Karl Popper, a philosopher of science and self-proclaimed agnostic, noted:

> What makes the origin of life and of the genetic code a disturbing riddle is this: the genetic code is without any biological function unless it is translated; that is, unless it leads to the synthesis of the proteins whose structure is laid down by the code. But ... the machinery by which the cell ... translates the code consists of at least fifty macromolecular components *which are themselves coded in DNA*. Thus the code cannot be translated except by using certain products of its translation. This constitutes a really baffling circle: a vicious circle, it seems, for any attempt to form a model, or a theory, of the genesis of the genetic code. Thus we may be faced with the possibility that the origin of life (like the origin of the universe) becomes an impenetrable barrier to science, and a residue to all attempts to reduce biology to chemistry and physics. ... At any rate we can say that the undreamt-of breakthrough of molecular biology has made the problem of the origin of life a greater riddle than it was before: we have acquired new and deeper problems.[167]

What Popper recognised was a fundamental chicken-and-egg issue for the origin of life—genetic mechanisms could not operate without protein enzymes, and yet those same proteins could not appear without a genetic mechanism.[168] Each was useless, and could not exist, without the prior existence of the other. Moreover, the conditions that would have allowed genetic nucleobases like adenine, cytosine, guanine, thymine, and uracil to accumulate in sufficient quantities for DNA and RNA to form likely never existed on the Earth—Darwin's 'warm little pond' would effectively have had to have been frozen for them to have been stable long enough to group together. As Matthew Levy and Stanley Miller noted in an article published in the *Proceedings of the National Academy of Sciences*, at a temperature of 350°C, found amongst many hydrothermal vents, the half-lives of these nucleobases were between two and fifteen seconds, decaying 'so fast that it would be impossible for [them] to accumulate to significant levels'.[169] Even at 100°C, the half-life of cytosine was a mere nineteen days, with the half-lives of the other compounds ranging from months to years.[170] Calculations of the rates of decomposition of the nucleobases 'clearly shows that these compounds are not stable on a geologic time scale at temperatures much above 0°C', effectively a frozen earth.[171] In order for enough of them to exist for genetic formation:

> the temperature of most of the Earth could not have been much above 0°C. However, even small portions of the Earth at high temperatures can lead to the rapid overall decomposition of organic compounds. For example, if 5% of the ocean is at 100°C and the remainder at 0°C, then assuming rapid mixing, the overall half-life for the decomposition of [adenine] will be ≈ 20 [years] instead of the $\approx 10^6$ [years] at 0°C.[172]

As Levy and Miller concluded, 'the rapid rates of hydrolysis of the nucleobases … at temperatures much above 0°C would present a major problem in the accumulation of these presumed essential compounds on the early Earth. A high-temperature origin of life involving these compounds therefore is unlikely'.[173] Under their scenario of the mixing ocean, for instance—assuming that adenine could be synthesised under plausible atmospheric conditions—a quantity with a half-life of twenty years would be reduced by 97% within a century, greatly limiting the availability of a key genetic component.

Significant as their findings were, there is one major problem with the hypothesis of a frozen Earth. As L. Paul Knauth's research on Precambrian ocean temperatures suggested, temperatures were likely stable for most of this period between 55-85°C, far higher than their data showed that nucleobases could survive at in meaningful quantities.[174] For much of geologic history, Darwin's pond would not have been frozen but practically boiling, which would have greatly accelerated the rate of half-life decay. Assuming that enough of them were synthesised and then survived, they would then have had the secondary problem of combining with ribose, a sugar that helps form the backbone of RNA. As Rosa Larralde and other researchers noted, with a half-life of a mere seventy-three minutes at 100°C, and a few weeks at plausible oceanic temperatures, 'it is difficult to see how ribose could have been available for prebiotic use, even at low temperatures'.[175] Even if the oceans were 'devoid of catalysis by general bases, ribose still decomposes so rapidly that it is difficult to see how it could have played a role in any high-temperature origin-of-life scenario unless it was utilized *immediately* after its prebiotic synthesis'.[176] Deoxyribose, the backbone of DNA, was also found to decompose rapidly, with differences so minor that 'the same considerations apply to [it] as to ribose itself'.[177]

What these studies showed was that, under the Earth's assumed prebiotic conditions, it would have been highly unlikely—if not impossible—for the key genetic components to form through atmospheric synthesis, much less survive long enough in water to combine into DNA or RNA. But even if they managed to do so, they would still face a third problem relating to bonding. Both the horizontal bonds between the four nucleobases and ribose/deoxyribose, and the vertical phosphodiester bonds that join them into a chain of nucleotides, are thermodynamically unstable in water. As Steven Benner and his colleagues at the University of Florida observed, 'Water, for all of its virtues, is bad for RNA':

> water is a nearly unique environment for RNA to function. … RNA can base-pair effectively only in water, as far as we know. On the other hand, water is a problematic solvent for forming RNA from its components. Every nucleotide unit contains at least either three or four bonds that are unstable with respect to hydrolysis. Let us assume (generously) that Darwinian evolution can be supported by an RNA molecule containing only 100 nucleotides. Given that such a molecule contains about 375 bonds that are thermodynamically unstable in water … the chance that they will all be present at the same time in water seems to be vanishingly small.[178]

'Vanishingly small' as these odds might be, a fourth problem emerges relating to the chirality, or 'handedness', of the components. Just as our left and right hands are mirror images of one another, biological molecules also possess mirror forms with identical physical and chemical properties, but 'the manner in which each interacts with other chiral molecules may be different, just as a left hand interacts differently with left- and right-hand gloves'.[179] Although left and right-handed molecules of a compound will, in the absence of a directing template, 'form in equal amounts' when synthesised in labs, DNA and RNA are homochiral—using *only* right-handed nucleotides.[180] Moreover, the enzymes they interact with are also homochiral—using *only* left-handed amino acids.[181] Any components with the 'wrong' chirality will simply not bond into viable nucleotide chains. As Vladik Avetisov of the Russian Academy of Sciences has noted, 'The reproduction of "chiral mutations" … is impossible due to [the] complete loss of the template profile around [the] chiral defect'.[182] Not only would all the necessary components of Benner's 100-nucleotide example have needed to be present at once, they *all* would have needed to possess the same chiral 'handedness'—despite such homochirality not arising in random samples. A nucleotide of that length is, statistically, 'certain to be "unique" [given that] the overwhelming majority of sequences cannot be realized in principle, simply because even the whole Universe is too small for that'.[183] A pre-existing template or mechanism would have been necessary for homochirality to emerge, especially since a racemic—or equal parts—mixture of nucleotides 'will strongly inhibit the synthesis of RNA polymers' in the first place.[184] But as Gyula Pályi and others have noted, the search for a natural mechanism presents its own difficulties:

> Since the formation energies ... [for these molecules] are strictly equal (within limits of measurement), this important particularity of life appears to be in contradiction with the laws of classical thermodynamics. Even if the modern thermodynamical description of open systems would allow mechanisms supposedly leading to the origin and maintenance of life, which includes homochirality as one of its most characteristic and inherent features, these problems represent still a high-level research challenge. At present, highly intellectual theoretical solutions of the problems connected with the so-called biological homochirality are available. However ... some are contradictory to each other and all are characterised by a certain scarcity of experimental verification.[185]

Even if, in spite of such impossibly-small odds—and overlooking any thermodynamic contradictions—a nucleotide chain with the correct chirality managed to form, there is a fifth problem since it would almost immediately start to undergo hydrolytic deterioration. In a living organism, this decay, or hydrolysis, is continuously offset by repairs carried out by its enzymes, but without a pre-existing genetic code to cause their production there would have been no means of repairing the damage caused by the deteriorating chemical bonds.[186] As Karl Popper recognised, the enzymes responsible for repairing the genetic structure first had to be produced by that genetic structure.

In addition to these difficulties, however, there is a sixth problem. Even if one were to assume, in spite of the evidence, that (i) the necessary compounds were able to synthesise via an Oparin/Miller-Urey like process, (ii) they were able to give rise to the genetic nucleobases, (iii) these nucleobases were able to avoid half-life decay, (iv) sufficient quantities of ribose were stable and available for immediate bonding with the nucleobases to form nucleotides, (v) such nucleotides possessed the correct chirality, and (vi) they did not immediately begin to deteriorate, there is still the fundamental question of how genetic *information* appeared. The gene is a package of information, not an object—a DNA or RNA molecule might be the *medium* for genetic material, but it is not the *message*.[187] In the absence of any form of natural selection, what could cause such molecules to arrange themselves into productive genetic sequences? It would be a tremendous leap to jump from such basic molecules to a living, self-sustaining organism capable of acquiring energy and reproducing.

To illustrate the improbability of this occurring on its own accord, consider a simple RNA chain of seventy nucleotides, even smaller than the previous chiral example. With four possible choices for each of the seventy positions—adenine, guanine, uracil, or cytosine—there would be a total of 4^{70} potential arrangements, or 1,393,796,574,908,163,946,345,982,392,040,522,594,123,776 possibilities, with only *one* such arrangement corresponding to our unique chain.[188] Assuming the four nucleobases were able to randomly combine at an incredibly-generous rate of *100 quintillion permutations every second*, it would take over *441 trillion years* to cycle through all possibilities. The probability of such an event randomly occurring during the time the earth has existed is functionally zero. But even this understates the complexity of life. With the smallest genomes found in viruses and symbiotic bacteria that cannot independently reproduce, it is notable that the genome of the *porcine circovirus*, the smallest virus known to infect vertebrates, is 1,759 nucleotides long, more than twenty-five times larger than our hypothetical example.[189] The *bacteriophage MS2*, an RNA virus that infects the *Escherichia coli* bacterium, contains 3,569 nucleotides, making it some fifty-one times larger.[190] These pale in comparison, however, to the *mycoplasma genitalium*, an organism believed to possess the smallest genome capable of sustaining metabolism and replication—with its 580,076 nucleotides, over 8,200 times larger.[191] Faced with such daunting odds, one might well conclude with the atheist Richard Dawkins that 'The essence of life is statistical improbability on a colossal scale. Whatever is the explanation for life, it cannot be chance. The true explanation for the existence of life must embody the very antithesis of chance'.[192]

If we have ruled out chance as an explanation for the origin of life, what is left? We know from the experiments of Redi and Pasteur that spontaneous generation cannot occur, so if life could not have spontaneously or randomly appeared, its emergence must necessarily have been *non*-random. Such was the conclusion of the atheist astronomer Fred Hoyle—mentioned previously—who, reflecting upon his research into interstellar organic compounds, noted that:

> I was constantly plagued by the thought that the number of ways in which even a single enzyme could be wrongly constructed was greater than the number of all the atoms in the universe. So try as I would, I couldn't convince myself that even the whole universe would be sufficient to find life by random processes—by what are called the blind forces of nature. ... Rather than accept the fantastically small probability of life having arisen through the blind forces of nature, it seemed better to suppose that the origin of life was a deliberate intellectual act. ... Taking the view ... unpalatable to scientists, that there is an enormous intelligence abroad in the universe, it becomes

necessary to write blind forces out of astronomy. ... A common sense interpretation of the facts suggests that a superintellect has monkeyed with physics, as well as with chemistry and biology, and that there are no blind forces worth speaking about in nature. The numbers one calculates from the facts seem to me so overwhelming as to put this conclusion almost beyond question.[193]

Two centuries before Hoyle, the French philosopher Voltaire—no admirer of religion—came to a similar conclusion, writing in his *Philosophical Dictionary* that 'It is perfectly evident to my mind that there exists a necessary, eternal, supreme and intelligent being. This is no matter of faith, but of reason'.[194] Although he could not comprehend such a being creating the universe out of nothing, Voltaire nevertheless recognised creation as an intellectual act:

when I see the springs of the human body, I conclude that an intelligent being has arranged these organs in order ... but from this sole argument I cannot conclude anything further than that it is probable that an intelligent and superior being has skilfully prepared and fashioned the matter. I cannot conclude from that alone that this being has made matter out of nothing and that he is infinite in every sense. In vain do I seek in my mind the connection of these ideas: *it is probable that I am the work of a being more powerful than I*; therefore, this being has existed from all eternity; has created everything, is infinite, etc. ... I only see that there is something more powerful than I ...[195]

Despite being limited by an eighteenth-century cosmology that had not yet discovered galaxies, it was clear to Voltaire that some 'intelligent being' more powerful than himself had been involved in ordering biological materials. Faced with the same essential dilemma, albeit on a larger scale, Hoyle similarly concluded that the 'amazing measure of order [of biomaterials] must be the outcome of intelligent design', even as he retained his atheism.[196] The same could not be said, however, for one of the twentieth century's most formidable atheists, Antony Flew. Having written a number of books expounding atheism over several decades—even arguing that the idea of God was philosophically meaningless—Flew acknowledged in 2004 his 'belated' belief in a God who was 'the first initiating and sustaining cause of the universe'.[197] In support, he cited 'the impossibility of providing a naturalistic account of the origin of the first reproducing organisms', and noted in a later book that 'the age of the universe gives too little time for these theories of abiogenesis to get the job done. ... How can a universe of mindless matter produce beings with intrinsic ends, self-replication capabilities, and "coded chemistry"? Here we are not dealing with biology, but an entirely different category of problem'.[198]

Two aspects of this 'different category of problem' were recognised by the Russian-American biologist Eugene Koonin, who wrote in *Biology Direct* that there were two paradoxes at the heart of the process of genetic replication:

> In even the simplest modern systems ... replication is catalyzed by a complex protein replicase ... produced by translation of the respective mRNA which is mediated by a tremendously complex molecular machinery. Hence the first paradox[:] to attain the minimal complexity required for a biological system to start on the path of biological evolution, a system of a far greater complexity, i.e., a highly evolved one, appears to be required. How such a system could evolve, is a puzzle that defeats conventional evolutionary thinking. ... The second paradox ... pertains to the origin of the translation system ... until the translation system produces functional proteins, there is no obvious selective advantage to the evolution of any parts of this elaborate (even in its most primitive form) molecular machine. ... Primitive translation in a protein-free system is conceivable as an intermediate stage of evolution ... but this does not resolve the paradox because, even for that form of translation to function, the core components must have been in place already. ... it is clear that [this origin] is not just the hardest problem in all of evolutionary biology but one that is qualitatively distinct from the rest.[199]

As Koonin concluded, 'Despite considerable experimental and theoretical effort, no compelling scenarios currently exist for the origin of replication and translation, the key processes that together comprise the core of biological systems'.[200] Natural selection cannot account for it, since—until the genetic code reached a point where it could produce proteins—there would have been no selective advantage to one random arrangement over another. Faced with this, he then pivoted to cosmology, stating that the history of life 'include[d] a crucial transition from *chance*', and that the 'spontaneous emergence of complex systems that would have to be considered virtually impossible in a finite universe becomes not only possible but inevitable' under the 'many worlds' hypothesis.[201]

Apart from the fact that, as shown in the last section, no evidence for a 'many worlds' or multiverse arrangement has ever been found, the reference to 'spontaneous emergence' is highly significant. Coming on the heels of the observation that 'no compelling scenarios currently exist for the origin of replication and translation', it is essentially a concession that the origin of life cannot be accounted for by natural means. In the absence of an infinite number of universes in which infinite possibilities can conveniently occur, we are stuck with our single universe in which the emergence of life 'would have to be considered virtually impossible'. Once the unfounded belief in the multiverse is discarded, all that is left is an Aristotelian hope in spontaneous generation—the very concept Redi and Pasteur proved to be impossible. In this respect Koonin is not alone, however, as the following quotations from other authors illustrate:

> If life arose spontaneously from inorganic materials, then it could exist wherever there is the same set of conditions.[202]

> Virtually all biochemists agree that life on earth arose spontaneously from nonliving matter[203]

> Scientific opinion is clearly on the side that believes that life arose spontaneously out of inanimate matter over a long period of time[204]

> The only thing that happens 'by chance' according to the theory of natural selection is mutation, apart from the spontaneous creation of the first living organism from which descended all the rest[205]

Is this not special pleading? We would question the faculties of someone who claimed that insects arose spontaneously from dust, but many appear all-too ready to assert that 'tremendously complex molecular machinery'—with encoded information and the powers to acquire energy, reproduce, and synthesise compounds to repair itself—spontaneously arose from an environment hostile to its existence before arranging itself perfectly against astronomical odds. At its core, this appears to be little better than hypocritically saying 'spontaneous generation cannot happen, except for the one time it *must* have happened because we have no other theory'.

This was the view taken by Ernst Haeckel, who argued that spontaneous generation was no longer possible, but that it might have once been possible 'during the dim past of the Earth's history'.[206] Charles Darwin seemed to endorse a version of this theory with his 'warm little pond' remark that 'at *the present day* such matter would be instantly devoured or absorbed, which would not have been the case before living creatures were formed', though he still regarded it as 'matter' rather than a living organism.[207] But as Alexander Oparin noted in 1957:

> as the methods of scientific investigation of living nature became more and more precise, spontaneous generation was gradually relegated to simpler and simpler organisms. Finally the sudden appearance of even the most primitive organisms from inanimate material was shown to be impossible. Thus, today, the theory of spontaneous generation has no more than a historical interest and cannot serve as an approach to the problem with which we are concerned.[208]

Although writing in the twentieth century, his observation still stands—spontaneous generation has been repeatedly shown to be impossible. Pasteur's findings have not been overturned, flies have not flown from Redi's jars, and scientists have still not created a living cell from scratch. The limitations of the Miller-Urey experiment have become evident, the rapidity of nucleobase half-life decay has been established, the difficulties of ribose synthesis and chemical bonding have been documented, and the probabilities of even the simplest genetic chains forming into correct sequences have been shown to be impossibly small. The chicken-and-egg problem of genetic mechanisms and their translating enzymes has not been solved, nor are there any 'compelling scenarios' for the origin of replication and translation. For all the advancements that have occurred in biology since the 1800s, we remain stuck with John Tyndall's observation that there is no 'satisfactory experimental proof that life can be developed save from demonstrable antecedent life'.[209] If anything, the weight of research has only exposed 'new and deeper problems', as Popper put it.[210]

In light of this, we must recognise the modern belief in spontaneous generation for what it is—a faith position devoid of evidence. This is particularly apparent when it is combined with the theoretical view that the 'spontaneous emergence of complex systems … becomes not only possible but *inevitable*' in a multiverse construct.[211] To quote the physicist Paul Davies once more, 'invoking an infinity of unseen universes to explain the unusual features of the one we do see is just as ad hoc as invoking an unseen Creator'.[212] But why would highly intelligent people place their faith in a theory that was discredited in the nineteenth century? With the difficulties that have emerged in origin-of-life studies, they appear to face a choice between the unprovable and the unpalatable. It cannot be proven that there is more than one universe, let alone that it would be 'inevitable' for spontaneous generation to hypothetically occur in any of them. It also cannot be explained with any degree of confidence how DNA, RNA, or any primitive precursor might have arisen from—and survived in—the prebiotic environment, much less how the enzymes that would have been necessary for their operation could have arisen without their prior existence. Science advances by confronting the unknown, but here, as Antony Flew noted, we face an entirely different category of problem.

Unprovable as spontaneous generation, the multiverse, and a natural origin of life therefore are, the alternative is much harder for some to embrace. If spontaneous generation is truly impossible—as every modern experiment on the subject has shown it to be—then we are left with Fred Hoyle's conclusion that there must exist throughout the universe an agent of incomprehensible intelligence, capable of causing the components of life, and their necessary repair mechanisms, to form and align themselves—without the use of natural selection—into productive genetic sequences. As he recognised, 'the number of ways in which even a single enzyme could be wrongly constructed [are] greater than the number of all the atoms in the universe', which led him, as an atheist, to conclude that 'the origin of life was a deliberate intellectual act'.[213] This view was 'unpalatable', he recognised, but 'The numbers one calculates from the facts seem ... so overwhelming as to put this conclusion almost beyond question'.[214]

One reason some might find such a conclusion unpalatable relates to the limitations of scientific inquiry. Science, as Angus Woodburne once put it, 'deals with the physical and demonstrable', so that some questions might forever lie beyond the realm of experimentation.[215] More discomforting, however, is that the existence of Hoyle's 'superintellect' radically alters our place in the universe. Rather than humanity standing at the pinnacle of cognitive ability, the existence of such an entity—with an intelligence terrifyingly greater than our own—would force us to recognise that we are not alone in the universe, nor are we by any means its most powerful inhabitants. Greater still, if such an entity brought about the origin of life, what relationship might it have to us—and we to it—as our creator? We would have no choice but to recognise its complete supremacy.

This, perhaps, is the crux of the matter. It is far easier for some to place their faith in the impossibilities of spontaneous generation and the multiverse than to acknowledge that the evidence points to a creator to whom we might possibly owe some obligation and deference. As with the origin of the universe, this is not a case in which science has merely failed to uncover the necessary facts, but rather, after centuries of inquiry, *there is no compelling scenario* by which life could naturally arise, and an abundance of evidence illustrating the difficulties of why it could not. One could excuse the ignorance of earlier ages when bookworms were thought to spring from books and crocodiles from mud, but there remains no reason—other than ideological choice—in light of the present evidence, to hold to a theory that has been repeatedly shown to be erroneous. The available information points to a single conclusion, that the origin of life from non-living matter could only have occurred through the supervening act of an intelligent power. Quoting Aquinas once more, 'this we call God'.[216]

3. THE ASTRONOMER AND THE ARCHBISHOP

Thus far, we have considered two logical, naturalistic arguments for the existence of God. But before proceeding any further, we shall return to the two figures mentioned at the beginning of the chapter, Carl Sagan and Anselm of Canterbury. In their respective eras, both were men of incredible gifts who sought a deeper understanding of things. One argued with respect to God that 'Extraordinary claims require extraordinary evidence', whilst the other asserted that God's existence could be recognised even by those whose 'mental powers are very ordinary, by the force of reason alone'.[217]

For Anselm, the claim that God exists would hardly have been 'extraordinary', but something reason could readily affirm. For Sagan, having come of age in the aftermath of scientism and the philosophical 'death of God', it was a more open question. But through the use of reason, applied to the evidence we have, we can establish that an entity of incomparable power and intelligence—whom we call God—brought about the universe and all life within it. Far from discrediting the existence of God, scientific knowledge—properly understood—boldly proclaims it.

We have already considered the impossibility of an infinite regress, so that, whether one is an atheist or a theist, the existence of an eternal, uncreated God is not conceptually problematic. Even if we were to accept Sagan's premise that this is an 'extraordinary claim' requiring 'extraordinary evidence', the burden of proof is still met. By definition, there *has* to be an uncaused first cause in order for anything to exist—it simply cannot be 'turtles all the way down' *ad infinitum*. Is it really any more extraordinary to claim that God exists than to posit that an impersonal first cause manifested at a specific moment—for no apparent reason—to cause infinite energy to explode from an infinitely-dense point to form a finely-tuned universe billions of light-years wide? Not only was this 'cause' able to manifest incalculable power, it also brought about an ordered result with complex life that, by all accounts, could not have arisen in a prebiotic environment. Although some might say that the universe only *appears* finely-tuned because we live in the one version that can support life as we know it, the fact remains that there is no evidence for any other universes beyond our own.

The fact that the universe has an age shows an element of choice in determining when its beginning would occur. Attempts to circumvent the issue by arguing that, since time only began when the universe began, 'what happened before the beginning of the universe is rendered meaningless', misses the point—*why did time begin when it did?*[218] The fact that the universe is not infinitely old proves its existence was not a necessary condition, so why did it begin at all? We also have the impossibility of spontaneous generation and the 'vicious circle' of the genetic code only operating via products that first had to be produced by that very code. We then have the 'fantastically small' probability of even the most basic genetic compounds being randomly assembled, particularly when natural selection could have played no part in it before protein synthesis could occur and variations be selected for. As our nucleotide example showed, there is simply not enough time in the history of the universe for even the most primitive genetic structures to randomly arrange into basic viable sequences reflecting complex information, even if we were to generously hypothesise that their necessary components were able to form, survive, bond together, and avoid hydrolysis.

Ultimately, this is where a choice must be made. But this is not a case where we must decide between two claims of equal strength. The evidence for a creator is far stronger. However unpalatable one might regard the existence of God to be, a spontaneous virgin birth of the universe, to say nothing about the origin of life, raises insurmountable problems for the atheist position. Faced with the observations of this chapter, the atheist must overlook a series of impossibilities in order for their belief system to hold together. It is logically impossible for something to emerge from nothing. It is physically impossible for energy to travel faster than the speed of light. It is biologically impossible for life to spontaneously emerge from non-living matter. And yet, we see evidence of infinite energy exploding from a radius of zero, universal inflation at a rate much greater than the speed of light, and an environment in which even the most primitive ancient life forms are genetically more complex—by orders of magnitude—than could ever randomly assemble in the time the universe has existed. Where, then—to turn Sagan's quote around—is the extraordinary evidence to support the extraordinary claim of a naturalistic origin of life and the universe? Where is the evidence that spontaneous generation can occur? What is the atheist's uncaused first cause, and how does it differ, in any meaningful sense, from an omnipotent deity? To these questions, no compelling answers can be given. In their absence, we assert that a rational consideration of the evidence points to an eternal, uncaused creator who, with infinite power and intelligence, brought about the universe and all life within it.

This we call God.

3

True Religion

Rational as the belief in a divine creator has been shown to be, it will not automatically lead one to Christianity. Although certain characteristics about God can be inferred from creation—such as power, intelligence, and order—an examination of the natural world can only take one so far. It cannot reveal, for instance, what such a being might want with us or why we are here. How are we to interact with something so incomprehensibly greater than ourselves? Nature affirms that there is a God, but a divine revelation is required for us to know anything more.

To suppose that such a revelation has been given for our benefit is not only a reasonable expectation, but a rational one. When we consider the intelligence behind the tremendously complex molecular machinery required for a biological system to even exist—to say nothing about the one-in-10^{229} probability that a universe would randomly have the finely-tuned parameters that ours does—it would be surprising for a being that took such exacting pains in designing its creation to leave us without a means of comprehending it.[1] But here we face a difficulty: where are we to find such a revelation, or—to put the question differently—how are we to distinguish between the multitude of apparent revelations put forward by the world's major religions? Nearly all would regard themselves as being the true religion, yet with each one proclaiming different and contradictory teachings, the divergence of their beliefs establishes that there can only logically be *one true* religion, even if they may all individually possess some elements of truth. The question for this chapter is how are we to evaluate, in as neutral a manner as possible, their competing claims?

Putting aside for the moment why there would be different religions if there was but a single creator, we must first consider the basis for religious belief. In the seventeenth century, the French mathematician and Christian apologist Blaise Pascal wrote that there were three grounds upon which religious belief could be justified—by inspiration, reason, and custom.[2] Of the three, custom is undoubtedly the most prevalent, with many belonging to one religion over another simply because it is all they have ever known. Common though this might be, however, it rests upon a fragile foundation and can easily fall if challenged by logic or contrary evidence. Reason—with its reliance upon arguments rather than habit—offers a stronger basis for belief, but it too is subject to limitations; one may be logically convinced that a deity exists, and yet have no proper conception of it. Inspiration—if true—stands highest of all, offering a link between the creator and the created. But how are we to determine if a claim of inspiration is genuine? For this, we need an objective means of evaluation.

Here we must proceed in a spirit of charity. Most religions will have some teachings which, if interpreted inappropriately, will seem questionable if not erroneous. Our concern is not with passages that are capable of multiple meanings, or that relate to matters that cannot be proven or disproven. Rather, we must consider those claims that are, under the most favourable interpretation possible, simply incorrect. In doing so, our motivation is to enlighten rather than disparage, reflecting a desire to build up the knowledge of the truth even as we must challenge that which is false. No aspersions are cast upon the goodwill of those who hold to these religions, since it is possible to believe in something sincerely, and yet be sincerely mistaken—especially when the circumstances of life have prevented an alternative consideration. Although many will be content with the comfortable, if unexamined, familiarity of their traditional beliefs, the enquiring mind cannot rest until it has searched them thoroughly. In doing so, it must be prepared, quoting Thomas Chalmers, to 'abandon every system of theology, that is not supported by evidence, however much it may gratify his taste', even if it risks a change of faith.[3] Painful as this might be, however, one stands to gain something far more valuable at the end of the endeavour—an unshakeable confidence in the knowledge of the truth.

1. THE FIRST TEST: NATURAL HARMONY

One preliminary test that can determine whether a religion is divinely inspired concerns the harmony of its supposedly-inspired claims with the natural world. If we regard God, the uncaused first cause, to be the author of all creation, He must also be the author of all truth. This means that any divinely-inspired teaching should not be in obvious conflict with what can be demonstrated as true. As the nineteenth-century professor and bishop Renn Hampden noted, 'The same plan of divine providence will be found pervading both the miraculous and natural admonitions of God to man, ... proclaiming the same ultimate origin'.[4] This is not to suggest that all religious claims are to be held up to the light of empirical literalism—some figurative licence must be granted where the interpretation of a passage clearly calls for it. But where an allegedly-inspired teaching concerns a factual claim about the natural world that can be verified with confidence, we may legitimately expect it to align with what science and logic teach if it is, in fact, truly inspired.

Let us consider, by way of example, that an isolated tribe worships horses and believes as a core religious tenet that, from the dawn of creation, only brown horses have existed or could exist. So long as they remain surrounded by brown horses, there is no reason to question this belief, which custom and reason both affirm. But suppose they discover a team of black and white horses—how is their religion to handle this? They might initially dismiss the new horses as trickery or a test of faith—perhaps they are brown horses that have been painted?—but what are they to do when they find that they are indisputably black and white? Can their religion be true if one of its core beliefs is false? Can it credibly claim divine inspiration when the 'inspired' teaching is factually, and unambiguously, wrong?

Surveying the religions of antiquity, it is easy to observe their shortcomings in this regard. It should be obvious to all that the winds are not caused by the flapping of a giant eagle at the top of the Norse tree *Yggdrasil*, which was believed to support the universe, nor do we find the sun lazily traversing the sky on a barge as the Egyptians taught.[5] We find no evidence for a flat earth as Homer and the ancient Greeks initially conceived, nor does it float upon a freshwater ocean called the *abzu* as the Sumerians imagined.[6] Had these beliefs persisted into the modern era, scientific discoveries would have soon nullified them or forced the adoption of radical reinterpretations. Since few, if any, would sincerely hold to such teachings today, we need not concern ourselves with evaluating their claims in detail. Much as the US Supreme Court remarked on a different matter in *Howard v Illinois Central Railroad Co.*, 'To state the proposition is to refute it'.[7] But what of the religions that presently do exist, and which command significant numbers of adherents?

Putting this test into practice, we first turn our attention to Hinduism. From a Western perspective—used to monotheistic religions like Judaism, Christianity, and Islam—the dizzying array of colourful, and often contradictory, beliefs that comprise Hinduism can lead one to question whether it is actually a religion at all. Even amongst Hindus, the answer to this is not always clear. As the Indian Supreme Court noted in the 1995 case *Bramchari Sidheswar Shai & Ors. v State of West Bengal*:

> When we think of the Hindu religion, we find it difficult, if not impossible, to define Hindu religion or even adequately describe it. Unlike other religions in the world, the Hindu religion does not claim any one prophet; it does not worship any one God; it does not subscribe to any one dogma; it does not believe in any one philosophic concept; it does not follow any one set of religious rites or performances; in fact, it does not appear to satisfy the narrow traditional features of any religion or creed. It may broadly be described as a way of life and nothing more.[8]

Whether one characterises it as a religion or simply 'a way of life and nothing more', the various schools of Hinduism do share certain key beliefs, with the Court noting that 'all of them accept the view of the great world rhyme. Vast periods of creation, maintenance and dissolution follow each other in endless succession. … This interminable succession of world ages has no beginning'.[9] Even if one cannot agree on the number of gods in the Hindu pantheon or the specific contours of their beliefs, this view, at least, appears common to all.[10]

But how are we to reconcile the belief in an 'endless succession' of 'world ages', without beginning, with the observations of nature? As the cosmological discussion in the previous chapter demonstrated, evidence obtained over the last century reveals a universe with a clear beginning. Whimsical as the notion of an 'endless succession' of universes might be, there is simply no evidence that this has occurred, and strong evidence that it is incapable of occurring. Although some have posited a 'cyclic' or 'oscillating' cosmological model in which the universe repeatedly expands and contracts, 'the basis of the oscillating universe relies solely on speculation', as the American physicist Alan Guth noted, and 'The idea of an oscillating universe gained currency merely because it avoided the issue of creation—not because there was the slightest evidence for it'.[11]

Beyond the lack of evidence for such cosmological beliefs, two other problems undermine the Hindu notion of an 'endless succession' of universes. First, estimates of the redshifts of distant galaxies suggest that the universe's expansion is accelerating and that, rather than contracting, the universe will continue to expand forever.[12] Secondly, under the second law of thermodynamics, entropy—or the measure of disorder in a system—can never decrease, meaning the universe can never return to its initial state.[13] Even if one were to try to overcome this by invoking some unknown means by which it could contract before expanding again, the entropy of *each cycle* would still increase, meaning the universe cannot have lived through an infinite number of cycles.[14] One could theoretically assume, against the weight of evidence, that a 'succession of world ages' might still be able to occur if the entropy increases were small enough, but such a succession would hardly be 'interminable', and would still have required a beginning.

Buddhism suffers from a similar problem. In the *Aggañña Sutta*, the Buddha instructed his monks that 'Eventually, after a long time ... it comes to pass that the world contracts', before evolving again.[15] Included as part of a longer sermon criticising the Hindu caste system, his teaching reflected ancient India's prevailing astronomical views.[16] But apart from the scientific objections to a cyclic universe, Buddhist cosmology also suffers from a logical problem:

> Buddhism insists [that] there could never have been a time when ... a physical universe in some form or another did not exist. ... The universe of space and time ... is a closed circle of conceptuality in which there is no first cause.[17]

By spurning a first cause as the agent of creation, Buddhism commits itself to an infinite regression. But as the previous chapter noted, this is impossible; it cannot be 'turtles all the way down' with the universe expanding and contracting *ad infinitum*. As Aquinas wrote, 'when you suppress a cause, you suppress its effect' with the result that in 'an infinite regress among efficient causes, no cause would be first. Therefore all the other causes, which are intermediate, will be suppressed'.[18] Around the year 1000 some Buddhists appeared to recognise this weakness, with the Buddhist scholar Edward Conze writing:

> There has never been any interest in the origin of the Universe [in Buddhism]—with only one exception. Around 1000 A.D. Buddhists in the North-West of India came into contact with the victorious forces of Islam. In their desire to be all things to all men, some Buddhists in that district rounded off their theology with the notion of an *Adibuddha*, a kind of omnipotent and omniscient primeval Buddha, who through his meditation originated the Universe.[19]

Although adopted by a few sects in Nepal and Tibet, this idea did not gain traction within Buddhism as a whole, with the result that, today, 'Modern geography and astronomy have invalidated the view of the universe drawn in traditional Buddhist works'.[20] By proclaiming the eternal cyclic creation and destruction of the universe as a revealed truth, Buddhism and Hinduism fail as inspired religions and cannot be the true faith. But it is not only ancient eastern religions which fall at this hurdle—consider too the application of this test to Mormonism. In the nineteenth century, the religion's founder, Joseph Smith, proclaimed that 'truth is knowledge of things as they are, and as they were, and as they are to come; And whatsoever is more or less than this is the spirit of that wicked one who was a liar from the beginning'.[21] As part of this teaching, Smith then proclaimed 'The elements are eternal', and in a separate sermon that 'Earth, water etc.—all these had their existence in an elementary State from Eternity'.[22]

Here, Smith—and by extension, Mormonism—runs into difficulty. When one considers the evidence of a universe with a clear beginning, the inaccuracy of his claims about an eternal universe become obvious. Even if Mormonism were to reject these findings, however, it cannot escape the laws of thermodynamics. As the German physicist Hermann von Helmholtz once noted, 'all force [in the universe] will finally pass into the form of heat, and all heat come to a state of equilibrium. Then ... the universe from that time forward would be condemned to a state of eternal rest'.[23] In light of this, we must ask why, if the universe were truly eternal, thermal equilibrium has not yet been achieved? As the Mormon author Keith Norman recognised, 'Mormonism's insistence that matter ... is eternally existent, without beginning or end, would be met with considerable skepticism in the scientific community', and that:

> Not only does [the modern] scientific cosmology pose a serious challenge to the Mormon version of the universe, but some of its main features seem remarkably congruent to the orthodox Christian doctrine of creation opposed by Mormonism. ... In contrast to the apparent harmony between modern physics and traditional Christianity on the subject of creation and the substantiality of material being, Mormon doctrine now seems to be a relic of the nineteenth century. ... Rather than trying to explain away or simply ignore the implications of a Big Bang cosmology, perhaps Mormons should recognize the need to update their theology.[24]

But this presents an inescapable problem—if one must 'update their theology' to align with the natural world, how can such a religion credibly claim to have been derived from divine inspiration? The teaching on the eternity of the elements is formally regarded by Mormonism as part of the 'Revelation given through Joseph Smith the Prophet, at Kirtland, Ohio, May 6, 1833', so given that it contains an incorrect revelation intended to be regarded as a literal, rather than figurative, truth, how are we to account for its 'revealed' nature? We must either charge God with ignorance or deceit, or recognise that Smith demonstrated—to use his own words—'the spirit of that wicked one who was a liar from the beginning' in proclaiming a 'revealed' truth about nature that was fundamentally untrue. Smith's claim to inspiration—and with it, Mormonism—therefore fails.

Although some might argue that it is inappropriate to hold ancient—or, in Mormonism's case, nineteenth-century—beliefs to the standards of modern physics, the fundamental importance of these claims to their religious worldviews are such that their errors cannot be ignored. Unlike more speculative theological questions, these teachings involve hard claims that can be evaluated: evidence either exists for the universe's eternity, or it does not. Given that the evidence does not support an eternal universe, any religion that proclaims one is fundamentally mistaken. Returning to Renn Hampden's point, a revealed teaching should not clash with our perceptions if it has, in fact, been truly inspired by God. Although there is much that we do not know—and likely never *can* know—about the universe, there is sufficient evidence to establish that it had a beginning. By asserting otherwise, Hinduism, Buddhism, Jainism, and Mormonism, to list but four such religions, prove themselves false.[25]

2. The Second Test: The Nature of Evil

Powerful as this first test is at exposing error, it is less adept at revealing truth. Christianity is not alone in its belief in a non-eternal universe, and if we are to discover the one true religion we must go further than mere cosmology. This requires a second test. Just as the true religion will be able to explain the origin of the universe, it must also give a satisfactory explanation for the existence and nature of evil. How do the world's key religions that survived the first test account for those misfortunes—death, disease, and disaster—that seem to threaten us with impunity?

We need not put forward a theodicy, or a logical consideration of how God could permit evil to exist, at this stage (for this, see Chapter 7). Rather, our present concern involves exploring what various religions have taught about the origin and nature of evil itself. Given that they do not all agree, we will again posit that only the one true religion can give a cohesive account. First, however, we must establish a definition of the term. Traditionally, the concept of evil has been divided into two sub-groups—moral and natural. Moral evil consists of those negative actions that are the products of human agency, such as theft, rape, or murder. Natural evil, by contrast, involves phenomena which are not generally attributable to human agency but nevertheless cause suffering, such as earthquakes, hurricanes, and disease.[26] The true religion must consequently be able to address both components.

Turning first to Sikhism, this religion began in the late 1400s in what is now Pakistan.[27] Under the teachings of Guru Nanak and his successors, it generally asserts that evil and suffering are the consequences of *maya*, or the delusion one experiences when the world's impermanence is misinterpreted.[28] If one becomes attached to the world rather than to its creator, 'the consequence is the disaster of rebirth', or reincarnation.[29] To the extent someone experiences misfortune, it is purportedly attributable to their actions or *karma*, with suffering—even if caused by natural phenomena—ultimately the result of previous moral evils.[30] As noted in the Sikh scripture *Guru Granth Sahib*, 'Weal and woe are the fruit of the deeds of past births. The beneficent Lord, who blesses us with these, alone knows their mystery. Whom canst thou blame, O mortal man? Thou art undergoing hard misery for thy own deeds'.[31]

But to what extent are individuals actually responsible for their actions under Sikhism? In addition to the aforementioned verses, the *Guru Granth Sahib* also declares that 'According to the past writ, which the creator himself wrote, man must act' and 'The Lord himself makes man do good deeds and evil ones'.[32] Under such a theological framework—particularly when reincarnation is factored in—it is difficult to see how any action could truly be regarded as good or evil, given that moral agency would be lacking. If God compels mankind to 'do good deeds and evil ones', what justification could there be for punishing vice or rewarding virtue? If man is merely a robot who 'must act' according to 'the past writ', how could it be claimed that 'Thou art undergoing hard misery for thy own deeds' since he would have had no choice in the matter? Taken to their logical conclusions, such beliefs quickly become *illogical*. Is the murderer following the command of God? Should the child who steals be rebuked? Can the spouse who commits adultery do otherwise? On what basis, if any, can a government punish those who violate its ordinances? If 'The Lord himself makes man do good deeds and evil ones', all actions—no matter how monstrous or meritorious—are ultimately of divine origin and equal worth, a position utterly corrosive to government, family life, and morality.

There is a further problem with the Sikh conception of evil, however. To the Sikh, those 'hard miseries' of life which we would typically regard as natural evils are merely the consequences of those 'deeds' or *moral* evils committed in a previous life. Apart from the question of how satisfactory evidence for reincarnation could ever be demonstrated, this notion of evil suffers from a causative problem. Even if one were to accept, for instance, that the appropriate punishment for a person's theft in the seventeenth century was death by hurricane in the twenty-first, it fails to offer a suitable explanation for why the hurricane occurred. By what mechanism could a person's wickedness—perhaps committed centuries earlier—be able to cause a storm to arise over the ocean? How could it cause a disease or famine? What justice would there be in punishing the evil deeds of a soul that could not remember committing them in a previous life, especially when they were done at the command of the Sikh deity? The Sikh scriptures appear to simply attribute the source of evil to an all-controlling divine force, without addressing these issues.

In contrast to Sikhism's sole deity, the traditional Chinese religion of Taoism contains a pantheon of beings capable of affecting humanity, from the 'Stove God', 'Door God', and 'Goddess of the Latrine' to drought demons, mountain spirits, and 'spirits of the unhappy dead'.[33] In its earliest incarnation, evil was seen as anything that could undermine or was antipathetic to life, although it later took on a moral dimension. In conjunction with the rise of the Chinese imperial state, Taoism's deities eventually developed into an immense spiritual bureaucracy believed to spy on humans and report their acts to a central heavenly archive.[34] Important celestial figures, including the gods of literature, wealth, epidemics, medicine, and exorcism, were seen to have their own ministerial departments, complete with presiding officers, assistants, and an army of subordinates.[35] Any relationship one might have had with these gods was essentially contractual, involving 'regular sacrifices in exchange for regular protection and extraordinary sacrifices in time of illness or other misfortune. Performing one's social and religious duties alone kept one's slate clean of debt'.[36]

Today, Taoism is best understood less as a religion and more as a philosophy or lifestyle. Like Confucianism and Shinto, it contains 'no meaningful eschatology that can answer the eternal and ultimate destiny of man and the world', although it 'vaguely imagine[s] and project[s] a peaceful world through man's collective self-effort'.[37] With respect to the problem of evil, its purported founder, Lao Tzu, regarded 'all evil and suffering as resulting from human actions and from getting out of the natural way', but failed to address why this might have occurred.[38] Suggesting that there were no natural sufferings and that 'there cannot be any physical or mental pains in the universe where the assertive will is not operative', he wrote in the *Tao Te Ching* that 'all things will take their proper places spontaneously' if people followed Tao, or 'the way'.[39] Under this interpretation, evil is merely the result of an assertive use of one's will.[40]

But as with Sikhism, the attribution of all evil to one's will or moral acts, even if not commanded by an all-controlling deity, raises causative problems. If a woman is killed by a falling tree whilst walking through a forest, whose assertion of will caused the tree to fall? Are we to blame the infant struggling against cholera for an inappropriate use of will, or should we condemn the Latrine Goddess? What about the Greek tragedian Aeschylus, who purportedly died when an eagle dropped a tortoise onto his head—are we to attribute this to the will of the eagle, the tortoise, or Aeschylus?[41] What of the fawn burning in a forest fire caused by lightning—whose exercise of will is responsible for its suffering? As our experiences illustrate, any number of natural evils can occur which involve no discernible moral act or exercise of will. By failing to appropriately consider natural evil, Taoism also falls short.

In Shinto, the traditional religion of Japan, the concept of evil is even more amorphous. Lacking any recognised founder, inspired text, or notions of a supreme deity, heaven, or hell, Shinto historically emphasised obedience to family, the customs of society, and the requirements of the state.[42] The worship of the dead took on particular significance since they were regarded as intrinsically connected to the living—the happiness of the departed depended upon the worship received from their descendants, who in turn experienced prosperity based upon the degree of reverence shown to their ancestors.[43] Appeasing the spirit world was of the utmost importance since, as the Shinto scholar Motowori explained:

> Whenever anything goes wrong in the world, it is to be attributed to the action of the evil gods called the Gods of Crookedness, whose power is so great that the Sun-Goddess and the Creator-God are sometimes powerless to restrain them; much less are human beings always able to resist their influence.[44]

Over the centuries, Shinto evolved from seeing 'all evil acts [as] the results of evil influences' to an eventual bifurcation or division into natural and moral evil.[45] Natural evils 'including disasters, pollution, and even the abnormal' were still regarded as being caused by evil spirits, but moral evil was eventually reduced to a matter of relativity:

> In modern Shinto there is no fixed and unalterable moral code. Good and evil are relative. The meaning and value of an action depends on its circumstances, motives, purpose, time, place, etc. ... That which disturbs the social order, causes misfortune, and obstructs worship of the [spirits] and the peaceful development of this world ... is evil.[46]

The emphasis on avoiding disturbances undoubtedly gave rise to a stable society, but the lack of any fixed conception of behaviour—in which some actions are *unconditionally* wrong, no matter the circumstances—shows an under-developed sense of moral evil.[47] Modern Shinto might have reduced moral evil to 'a lack of harmony and beauty' as one author put it, but this fails to explain the depths of human wickedness, much less the reason for its all-too frequent expression.[48] What caused humanity to first experience a lack of harmony, for instance? At what point does disharmony, such as a disagreement or difference of opinion, cross the line into being 'evil'? The view of natural evil as the work of unappeased spirits also fails to account for their existence vis-à-vis the uncaused first cause—how did these 'Gods of Crookedness' come to be, if they were not necessary for the emergence of the universe? Moreover, how could they be more powerful than the one who made them? Important questions about the origin and nature of evil ultimately remain unanswered.[49]

One belief system that fails both the natural harmony and nature of evil tests is the 'Mind, Body, Spirit' or 'New Age' movement, which emerged in the United States and Europe in the 1970s.[50] Although possessing a wide range of beliefs that not all of its adherents equally share, it can be recognised by its emphasis on esoteric or 'hidden' insight. As one New Age historian wrote:

> At an intuitive level, many ... would claim to recognise the 'New Age' when they see it. It manifests itself in shops that specialise in Tarot cards, crystals, incense, alternative remedies and books on ley lines, the paranormal, astrology, and eastern and esoteric spirituality. It appears in the ... services of Reiki healers, yoga teachers and various psychic consultants. ... There are also characteristic events, such as Mind-Body-Spirit festivals and psychic fairs.[51]

Notwithstanding the refusal of some to regard it as a religion at all, the New Age movement draws from many religious traditions—such as Buddhism, Hinduism, and Taoism—even as it 'tends to reject Christianity'.[52] It also builds upon earlier movements that syncretised in the 1960s 'counterculture', from Theosophy and Spiritualism to the Human Potential Movement.[53] Theosophy in particular 'significantly contributed to the development of the New Age phenomenon' with its eclectic ideas.[54] One illustration of its beliefs comes from a report on a lecture delivered in 1894 by Annie Besant, later to become the president of the Theosophical Society, that spoke of how its teachings were first given to 'the Aryan race in its cradle in the north of India':

> The first living intelligences breathed out by the Divine life were the mighty spiritual intelligences which had gradually evolved and developed in past universes. ... Man also was a spiritual intelligence in process of evolution ... which in their turn would come forth ... to rule when a new universe was to be built up.[55]

The belief in past universes runs afoul of the cosmological errors noted in Hinduism—with one commentator describing it in 1905 as 'only Hinduism in a modern dress'—but Theosophy also bequeathed the New Age a struggle with the nature of evil.[56] As Charles W. Leadbeater, one of the Theosophical Society's most prominent members, wrote, 'the idea of evil imposed upon us [externally] is an absurdity, since every man makes his own good and evil destiny for himself; so they say there is in truth no evil but that which we make—all is subjective'.[57] To the extent one experienced 'evil', it was due to actions in a previous life:

every pain that comes to us is not only the payment of a long-past debt, but is also a great opportunity for us now. Out of the evil of long ago we may make a present good, because ... in bearing them we may develop many of the qualities that go to make up the divine man ... we ourselves are sparks of that same Divine flame.[58]

As with Sikhism and Taoism, the attribution of natural evil to one's will or moral acts in a previous life creates a causative problem—to say nothing about the justice of being punished for something one could not remember. Theosophy simply glosses over this as the 'Lords of Karma' decreeing that 'there is only a little more of his debt outstanding; let him have an opportunity of paying that here and now'.[59] Other strands of New Age thought reject this in favour of an even more tenuous belief that evil is simply 'an aberrational product of the mind alone', with this 'fictional negativity includ[ing] illness and poverty as well'.[60] Evil is just an illusion that can be overcome by 'positive thinking' to attain 'the worldly goals of success, health, wealth, happiness, and self-realisation'.[61] It is a self-focused philosophy—placing the burden on the individual to avoid attracting 'negative energy', but unable to account for tribulations such as war, famine, disability, or disease. Rather than address the problem of evil, much of New Age thought simply chooses to reject its existence.

One final belief system to consider is atheism. Although the previous chapter demonstrated the challenges it faces on scientific grounds, it also struggles philosophically. This struggle differs, however, from those faced by the religions noted above. For atheism, the existence of evil at first appears to be no problem at all—rather, as Hans Küng observed, it is in fact 'the rock of atheism' and its most formidable objection to the existence of God.[62] Chapter 7 will deal with this objection directly, but this chapter would be incomplete if it did not recognise that atheism's problem of evil runs far deeper.

Just as the religions above cannot adequately account for moral and natural evil, atheism cannot account for morality. This is not to suggest that 'one can't be good without belief in God', a charge the humanist Greg Epstein felt he had to defend atheism against, but rather that atheism cannot account for good and evil in the first place.[63] In a godless universe of mindless matter and unguided chance, what gives atoms acting in one way the designation of 'good' and atoms acting in another way the designation of 'evil'? Where do the values that make such comparisons possible come from? In an atheistic universe, can any action ever be regarded as objectively wrong? Taken to its logical conclusion, the answer must be no. As the atheist philosopher Richard Rorty understood, for atheism 'there is no answer to the question "Why not be cruel?"'—no noncircular theoretical backup for the belief that cruelty is horrible'.[64] Furthermore:

> Anybody who thinks that there are well grounded theoretical answers to
> this sort of question—algorithms for resolving moral dilemmas of this
> sort—is still, in his heart, a theologian or metaphysician. He believes
> in an order beyond time and change which both determines the point
> of human existence and establishes a hierarchy of responsibilities.[65]

Under an atheistic conception of the universe, however, such an 'order beyond
time and change' is impossible, much less one which 'determines the point of
human existence and establishes a hierarchy of responsibilities'. The atheist who
understood this best was Friedrich Nietzsche, who saw in the 'death of God' the
end of universal moral norms and objective truth.[66] Nothing remained in their
absence but for the *übermensch*, or superior man, to impose his will through power
and circumstance.[67] To such a figure, no action could ever be objectively wrong
because there was no objective source or standard of morality to condemn it. As
the atheist philosopher J.L. Mackie noted, 'objective values' themselves require a
supernatural explanation, something he regarded as 'false' in an atheistic universe:

> If there were objective values, then they would be entities or qualities
> or relations of a very strange sort, utterly different from anything else
> in the universe. … Of course the suggestion that moral judgments are
> made or moral problems solved by just sitting down and having an
> ethical intuition is a travesty of actual moral thinking. But, however
> complex the real process, it will require (if it is to yield authoritatively
> prescriptive conclusions) some input of this distinctive sort … When
> we ask the awkward question, how we can be aware of this authoritative
> prescriptivity, of the truth of these distinctively ethical premises …
> none of our ordinary accounts of sensory perception or introspection
> or the framing and confirming of explanatory hypotheses or inference
> or logical construction or conceptual analysis, or any combination of
> these, will provide a satisfactory answer; 'a special sort of intuition' is
> a lame answer, but it is the one to which the clear-headed objectivist
> is compelled to resort. … The assertion that there are objective
> values … which ordinary moral judgments presuppose, is, I hold, not
> meaningless but false.[68]

Notwithstanding the 'awkward question' about where moral truth might
come from for the atheist—even if one were to accept the 'lame answer' of 'a
special sort of intuition'—a practical problem is that atheists themselves generally
do not act in accordance with these beliefs. In *Darwinism Defended*, Michael Ruse
accepted the existence of objective morality when he wrote that 'The man who
says that it is morally acceptable to rape little children, is just as mistaken as the

man who says that 2+2=5'.[69] Similarly, the Atheist Alliance International, or AAI, acknowledged that 'It would be perverse to argue that bathing your baby daughter in battery acid is morally right. No doubt, we could think of a long list of actions that are equally wrong'.[70] But where does this wrongness come from in a cold, indifferent, atheistic universe? Herein lies atheism's insurmountable philosophical challenge: objective morality is impossible in a godless universe, *and yet objective morality exists in the heart of the atheist.*

Some atheists have tried to explain this by appealing to a humanistic standard of behaviour in lieu of a universal norm. As the AAI wrote on whether atheists can be moral:

> The first point is, behavior can only be moral or immoral if it affects other humans. No matter how you treat a rock, your actions are neither morally right or wrong. Actions have a moral dimension only when they affect other humans (or other sentient beings). Nor is a moral dimension attached to actions that are the result of chance or the natural world. For example, if lightning or a tsunami kills people, we do not say these events are morally wrong.[71]

From there, it was a short assumption for the AAI to conclude that 'Actions that unnecessarily cause suffering or harm to humans are morally wrong, and actions that contribute to human wellbeing are morally right'.[72] Although the theist would agree that lightning and tsunamis are natural instead of moral evils, the AAI's argument suffers from poor reasoning under atheism's own terms. With respect to the first sentence, the notion that behaviour 'can only be moral or immoral if it affects other humans' ignores the issue of animal cruelty, and is itself a value judgment; Nietzsche's *übermensch* might well ask, 'where does this *can only* come from—what authority makes it true?' As he noted in Chapter 1:

> When [one thinks] that they know 'intuitively' what is good and evil, when they therefore suppose that they no longer require Christianity as the guarantee of morality, we merely witness the effects of the dominion of the Christian value judgment and an expression of the strength and depth of this dominion.[73]

In the absence of an objective standard, the first sentence's claim is subjective and unsupported. As for the second sentence, experience does not bear this out. As the outcry over the Taliban's destruction of the Bamiyan Buddhas in 2001 demonstrated, how one treats a rock can matter greatly—even warranting condemnation by the United Nations.[74] As for the third sentence, 'Actions have a moral dimension only when they affect other humans (or other sentient beings)', this again raises the question of *why*? On what basis? According to whom? If 'man is simply an animal', and—as the eighteenth-century atheist David Hume argued, animals are not subject to moral sentiments—how can morality be explained under evolutionary terms?[75] The average atheist would recoil in horror at the man who murders his stepchildren, but the male barn swallow that kills a rival's nestlings to mate with the female has not committed a moral act. Sentience alone cannot explain why, in an atheistic universe, a set of atoms in human form committing such an act is *immoral* whilst another set of atoms committing the very same act in avian form is only *amoral*.

As these examples illustrate, the existence of evil is ultimately a far greater problem for atheism than for theism—religion has to explain why God would *allow* evil to exist, but atheism has to explain *why* it exists. This, however, is something it simply cannot do. In the absence of an objective moral standard, concepts such as good and evil are meaningless. Notwithstanding the arguments of Greg Epstein and others that one can be good without believing in God, Richard Rorty's observation still remains: 'there is no answer to the question "Why not be cruel?"—no noncircular theoretical backup for the belief that cruelty is horrible'.[76] Objective morality should not exist in a godless universe, and yet the atheist clearly perceives its existence—thereby offering a further argument for the existence of God. By denying this and failing to provide a foundation for the objective moral reality we experience each day, atheism can also be regarded as failing this chapter's second neutral test.

3. REVEALED RELIGION

Notwithstanding the number of their adherents or devotional fervency, the majority of the world's religions fail as inspired belief systems due to their cosmological deficiencies and flawed conceptions of evil. Although all religions may contain some elements that cannot objectively be evaluated, we may reject those that proclaim obvious untruths—uninterpretable in any other way—as inspired realities. Whilst this chapter has not addressed all of the world's religions, it has explored some of the key errors of the most prevalent non-Abrahamic ones—comprising more than a quarter of the world's population.[77]

But what of the three Abrahamic religions—Judaism, Christianity, and Islam? Grouped together due to their respective ties to Abraham, the Mesopotamian who left his homeland at God's instruction, they share elements of a common history and monotheistic outlook.[78] The oldest of the three is Judaism. In contrast to the creation accounts of every other culture that could have influenced it, from the Babylonian *Enûma Eliš* to the varying strands of Hindu, Chinese, Egyptian and Graeco-Roman mythology, it alone proclaimed the creation of a non-eternal universe by an eternal God—a position congruent with science and logic. This departure from the cosmologies of the ancient world was then followed by an explanation for evil that accounts for its moral and natural aspects—man and creation were initially good, but became marred through sinful rebellion. In further contrast to the religions of its neighbours, it then imposed upon its adherents the divine command to 'be holy, as I am holy', an edict utterly foreign to the debauchery of ancient mythology.[79] Above all, it promises that humanity's rebellious condition will one day be put right.

In addition to its satisfaction of the tests employed by this chapter, there is also the providential survival of those to whom the revelation was initially committed. For nearly 3,500 years, the Jewish people have endured every hardship imaginable, from war, conquest, desolation, and genocide to the loss of their ancestral homeland and dispersion across the earth. Through it all, they have survived as a distinctive culture. The peoples that once surrounded them, from the Moabites and Hittites to the Tyrians and Sidonians, have vanished into obscurity whilst they have remained. Every empire that has sought their destruction or subjugation has fallen, from the ancient Egyptians, Assyrians, Babylonians, and Romans to the more recent Ottomans and Nazis. In the annals of history, they are without parallel—a fitting status for those to whom God first revealed Himself and called His chosen people.[80]

But in addition to Judaism, two other religions recognise the Hebrew scriptures—or portions of them—as inspired writings, with Christianity regarding them as the Old Testament and Islam affording respect to the Torah and Psalms.[81] Given their commonalities, we cannot simply employ another neutral test to determine which of them is the true religion—our analysis must now take a more textual approach. It is at this juncture that Islam, the youngest of the three, stumbles. Putting aside passages in its religious text, the Quran, that could be open to figurative interpretation—such as when Alexander the Great or *Dhul-Qarnayn* 'reached the setting of the sun, he found it setting in a spring of dark mud'—it possesses two fundamental weaknesses which fatally undermine its claims to be of divine origin.[82]

First, it affirms the truth of texts that contradict it. This is illustrated most clearly with regard to its treatment of the Torah. If the Islamic deity Allah revealed both the Quran (written over 500 years after the Bible was completed) and the books of Genesis, Exodus, Leviticus, Numbers, and Deuteronomy, the revelations contained within each should match, having come from the same source. The Quran expressly claims this position in multiple verses—or surahs—with Surah 3:3 declaring that Allah 'revealed the Torah', and Surah 2:87 affirming that 'We did certainly give Moses the Torah'. That this Torah is the same as the one existing in Muhammed's era (c. 600) is evident from Surah 5:43-44, in which Allah addressed him about Jews who came to him for judgment:

> But how is it that they come to you for judgement while they have the Torah, in which is the judgement of Allah? ... Indeed, We sent down the Torah, in which was guidance and light. The prophets who submitted judged by it for the Jews, as did the rabbis and scholars by that with which they were entrusted of the Scripture of Allah, and they were witnesses thereto.

Unfortunately for the Quran, the Torah—which it is keen to praise—repeatedly contradicts it in ways that prove it cannot have come from the same source. Listed below are ten instances involving direct factual contradictions between the two texts:

- In Surah 11:42-43, one of Noah's sons drowns after refusing to board the ark, whilst Genesis 6:10 records Noah only having three sons—all of whom boarded the ark.

- In Surah 6:74, Abraham's father is named as Azar, whilst Genesis 11:27 names him as Terah.

- In Surah 11:81, angels tell Abraham's nephew Lot to 'let not any among you look back - except your wife', whilst Genesis 19:17 records an angel telling Lot *and* his wife to 'Escape for your life! Do not look behind you nor stay anywhere in the plain. Escape to the mountains, lest you be destroyed'.

- In Surah 12:29, when the Egyptian master catches his wife holding a part of Joseph's clothing—suggesting attempted rape—he says 'Joseph, ignore this' before ordering his wife to 'ask forgiveness for your sin. Indeed, you were of the sinful' in trying to seduce him, in contrast to Genesis 39:19-20 which records that he immediately 'put him into the prison'.

- In Surah 12:100, Joseph is said to have 'raised his parents upon the throne, and they bowed to him in prostration' upon arriving in Egypt, whilst Genesis 35:19 records that his mother died years earlier after giving birth to Benjamin.

- In Surah 28:9, Pharaoh and his wife adopt Moses after his rescue from the river, whilst in Exodus 2:10 this is only done by Pharaoh's daughter.

- In Surah 27:7, Moses tells his family about the burning bush before he goes to see it, whilst in Exodus 3:1-3 he comes across it alone as he tends his father-in-law's sheep in the desert.

- In Surah 40:36-37, Pharaoh tells his advisor Haman to build a Tower-of-Babel-like structure so that he 'might reach the ways … into the heavens' to 'look at the deity of Moses', in contrast to Esther 3 which records Haman as the official of King Ahasuerus of Persia, who reigned nearly 800 years after Moses.

- Surah 7:150-54 states that, after discovering the idolatrous calf, Moses 'threw down the tablets' containing the divine commandments before taking them up again undamaged, whilst Exodus 32:19 states that when Moses 'saw the calf and the dancing', his 'anger became hot, and he cast the tablets out of his hands and broke them at the foot of the mountain'.

- In Surah 20:85-97, a Samaritan leads the Israelites astray through the worship of the aforementioned calf, despite (i) Samaria not being founded until at least 400 years after the Exodus, and (ii) the Samaritans not existing as a separate people from the Israelites until the resettlement of the Assyrian king Sargon II—a further 180 years after its establishment.[83]

The Islamic apologist might claim at this point that it is the Torah, rather than the Quran, which stands in error on these matters, having been corrupted over the centuries.[84] But this raises a theological problem—per Surah 6:115, 'None can alter [Allah's] words', making the Torah not only inerrant, but incorruptible. Given that Surah 5:43-44 confirms that the Torah in Muhammed's day was the same as the one given to Moses—which Chapter 5 will show is effectively identical to the modern text—Islam faces the problem of having to reconcile the irreconcilable. Furthermore, the catch-all provision in Surah 2:106, in which Allah declares that 'We do not abrogate a verse or cause it to be forgotten except that We bring forth [one] better than it or similar to it', cannot help. Islam might be able to change the direction one is required to face when praying from Jerusalem to Mecca—as it did in Surah 2:142-50—but it is a different matter entirely to change the identity of Abraham's father or anything else noted above. All too frequently, the Quran leaves out details about key events or clashes with the Old Testament and historical record, proving a lack of inspiration even as it claims divine inerrancy for the very text that contradicts it.

Islam's second fundamental problem arises from its depiction of God as a deceiver, in contrast to the declaration in Numbers 23:19 that 'God is not a man, that He should lie'. One example of this is found in Surah 3:54. Although modern Quranic texts have softened it to read 'And the disbelievers planned, but Allah planned. And Allah is the best of planners', other translations have rendered 'the best of planners' as 'the best of devisers' or 'the best of schemers'.[85] The true meaning becomes clear, however, when the Arabic is transliterated: *wa-makarū wa-makara llāhu wa-llāhu khayru l-mākirīn.*[86] As Edward Lane's *Arabic-English Lexicon*—one of the earliest and most influential works on the language—shows, *makara* and its associated forms almost never appear in a positive light, but refer to practising:

> deceit, guile, or circumvention, desiring to do to another a foul, an abominable, or an evil, action, clandestinely, or without his knowing whence it proceeded; ... *he practiced an evasion or elusion, a shift, an artifice, or artful contrivance or device, a machination, a trick, a plot ...* or *he exercised art, craft, cunning...*[87]

Lane also referenced a description from the medieval Islamic scholar Abu Hilal al-Askeri that went even further, with it signifying 'as above with the addition of *feigning the contrary of his real intentions*'.[88] However charitably one might render Surah 3:54, it differs significantly from the picture of God in Numbers 23:19.

Even without this verse, the problem of a deceptive deity remains. This becomes apparent when attempting to reconcile Allah's approval of Jesus' disciples with his wrathful condemnation of their teachings on His deity and crucifixion. In Surah 3:55, they are described positively as being 'superior to those who disbelieve' until the day of resurrection, and in Surah 61:14 as being Allah's 'helpers' who were favoured as 'the dominant ones' over unbelievers. Surah 5:72 declares a contradiction, however, that 'They have certainly disbelieved who say, "Allah is the Messiah, the son of Mary" ... Indeed, he who associates others with Allah - Allah has forbidden him Paradise, and his refuge is the Fire', with Surah 4:48 making it the unforgiveable sin.[89] Surah 4:157 then states that Jesus' crucifixion did not happen, but only *appeared* to happen:

> And [for] their saying, 'Indeed, we have killed the Messiah, Jesus, the son of Mary, the messenger of Allah.' And they did not kill him, nor did they crucify him; but [another] was made to resemble him to them. And indeed, those who differ over it are in doubt about it. They have no knowledge of it except the following of assumption. And they did not kill him, for certain.

Notwithstanding the question of who was substituted to look like Jesus or the motivation for the deception, Islam cannot escape the fact that Jesus' deity, crucifixion, and resurrection were the central doctrines preached by His disciples, preserved in both the scriptures and ancient historical records. Why would Allah declare them—who were guilty of Islam's unpardonable sin—to be 'superior' to disbelievers and the beneficiaries of his favour? Why trick them into preaching a false doctrine that would result in the damnation of billions? Numbers 23:19 declares that 'God is not a man, that He should lie', but Surah 4:157 reveals a deliberate lie that would make Allah the indirect founder of Christianity.[90] Moreover, for Allah to be 'of all things, Knowing' as Surah 33:40 declares, his grasp of Christian theology is poor. Instead of attacking the orthodox understanding of the Trinity expressed in Matthew 28:19—Father, Son, and Holy Spirit—Surah 5:116 instead attacks a 'Father-Mother-Son' trinity that no Christian source ever described:

> And [beware the Day] when Allah will say, 'O Jesus, Son of Mary, did you say to the people, "Take me and my mother as deities besides Allah?"' He will say, 'Exalted are You! It was not for me to say that to which I have no right. If I had said it, You would have known it. You know what is within myself, and I do not know what is within Yourself. Indeed, it is You who is Knower of the unseen.'

Putting aside Allah's confusion about a key Christian doctrine, his proclaimed deception of the disciples and wider world concerning Jesus' crucifixion presents an irreconcilable clash with the character of God revealed in Numbers 23:19. When combined with the Quran's contradictions of the Torah noted on the previous pages—despite Surahs 3:3 and 6:115 claiming Allah's authorship of both and their incorruptibility—Islam's lack of divine inspiration becomes apparent.

The exclusion of Islam therefore narrows the field to two—Judaism and Christianity. Given that both draw upon the same scriptures, our discernment between them must be based upon an analysis of the Bible. To remove all doubt about its inspiration and uncorrupted transmission, however, the following three chapters will address two issues—whether we can be confident that the revelation we have today is the same as the original, and whether we can be confident that the original was truthful in what it asserted. Chapter 4 begins with an overview of the Bible's creation, Chapter 5 recounts the history of its preservation, and Chapter 6 examines the evidence for its authenticity or truthfulness. With these matters established, the remaining chapters will then distinguish between Judaism and Christianity to prove that Christianity is, in fact, the one true religion, with a consideration of its teachings and their impact on humanity.

4

The Creation of the Bible

Thus far, we have considered the evidence for God—the uncaused first cause—who brought about the creation of the universe and all within it. We have also seen how the cosmological, moral, and textual shortcomings of religions ancient and modern have disqualified them from being the one true religion, with only the Hebrew revelation of God and creation surviving these tests. But if we are to go further and distinguish between Judaism and Christianity, we must first become properly acquainted with their scriptural sources.

The English word 'Bible' comes from the Greek words τὰ βιβλία, or 'the books'.[1] In its Latin form, these words are expressed as *biblia*, from which the term 'Bible' is derived.[2] Although we often speak of the Bible as if it were a single book, it is actually, as these terms indicate, a collection of many books. The Jewish scriptures contain twenty-four of them—later divided into thirty-nine under Christianity—that are known in Hebrew as the Tanakh after the three sections that comprise it: the Torah, Nevi'im, and Ketuvim, or the 'Teaching', 'Prophets', and 'Writings'.[3] The Torah, or the first five books from Genesis to Deuteronomy, gives an account of the world's creation up to Israel's entry into the land of Canaan. The Nevi'im or 'Prophetic' books include Joshua, Judges, 1-2 Samuel, 1-2 Kings, Isaiah, Jeremiah, and Ezekiel, along with a single book containing the twelve minor prophets known as the Tere Asar.[4] Rounding out the list is the Ketuvim, or 'Writings', containing Psalms, Proverbs, Job, Song of Solomon, Ruth, Lamentations, Ecclesiastes, Esther, Daniel, Ezra, Nehemiah, and 1-2 Chronicles.[5] Of the many subjects appearing throughout their passages, a central theme concerns the promise of a coming deliverer, or Messiah.[6]

1. The Development of the Tanakh

Because of its antiquity, it is difficult to provide specific dates for when all of these books were written, although the process occurred over roughly 1,000 years and was effectively complete by about 300 BC.[7] The Torah, or the first five books of the Tanakh, are attributed to Moses, even though others likely helped shape its final format after his death.[8] Although some have argued that he was not their author—claiming that they were not composed until after the Jewish exile to Babylon in the 500s BC or even that he did not exist—a significant amount of evidence supports a Mosaic date of authorship.[9] At a minimum, the discovery of silver amulets at Ketef Hinnom dating from the seventh century BC and inscribed with the blessing in Numbers 6:24-26 indicates the high regard those verses had achieved in the pre-exilic era, demolishing the claim that the Torah was a post-exilic fiction.[10] Many details in the books themselves also support them having been written by someone with an intimate knowledge of Egypt and the Sinai peninsula as they were around the fourteenth or fifteenth-centuries BC—details that would have been difficult for individuals writing at a distance centuries later to recreate.[11]

Scripturally, the Torah introduces a number of important teachings. As noted in Chapter 2, its beginning declares that God created the heavens and the earth. In contrast to the contemporary religions in the ancient Middle East, it then states that the sun, moon, and stars are not deities or objects of worship, but material substances created by God.[12] This is a singular testament to its divine inspiration; in a time of astrological superstition—when the Egyptians worshipped the sun and the Mesopotamians the moon and planets—it would have been extraordinary for a people influenced by both cultures to reject the prevailing worldview of their neighbours in favour of an unheard-of monotheistic concept of creation.[13] That they not only did so, but placed their faith in the one version of creation that science and logic both continue to uphold, is too fortuitous to have occurred by chance. More important than the Torah's cosmology, however, is the divine promise of a deliverer to crush the power of evil after the rebellion of our first parents.[14] The Torah then records a similar promise made centuries later to Abraham—a Mesopotamian who left his home for a land God would give to his descendants—that all mankind would be blessed through him, a foreshadowing of the Messiah.[15] Its remaining books then record how one branch of these descendants, the Israelites, later left their slavery in Egypt under the leadership of Moses and received a series of divine commandments to regulate their conduct and dedicate them to the worship of the one true God.

As for the Nevi'im and Ketuvim, they collectively contain many books with prophetic passages and historical accounts relating to Israel's conquest of Canaan, the rise and eventual disunion of the Kingdom of Israel, and the forced exile of the Jews to Babylon. Additionally, they warn of the consequences of Israel's spiritual disobedience and provide further prophetic detail about the promised Messiah who would come to deliver them.

Over time, a process of canonisation occurred in which these books were recognised as scripture. Although other texts with religious themes were produced by Hebrew writers—such as the apocryphal books of Tobit and Judith, for instance—they were never recognised as forming part of the Jewish scriptural canon.[16] While there are different theories as to when, where, and how canonisation took place, we can occasionally see evidence of the process in the books themselves. In 2 Kings 22:8, we read how Hilkiah the high priest discovered 'the Book of the Law in the house of the Lord' during the reign of Josiah (639 - 609 BC).[17] Whether this was simply a portion of the Law of Moses or the entire Torah is unclear, but the king was sufficiently alarmed at its warnings about the consequences of Israel's spiritual disobedience that he instituted a programme of religious reform.[18] 2 Kings 23:3 records how:

> the king stood by a pillar and made a covenant before the Lord, to follow the Lord and to keep His commandments and His testimonies and His statutes, with all his heart and all his soul, to perform the words of this covenant that were written in this book. And all the people took a stand for the covenant.

In addition to the book being found in Solomon's Temple—a building constructed in the tenth century BC specifically to worship the God revealed in the Torah—the return to the religion of the 'covenant ... written in this book' indicates that the Mosaic 'Book of the Law' had attained a position of reverence well before the seventh century BC, even if it was not always followed.[19]

Although a book might have been composed in an earlier era, generations could pass before it achieved its final written form. One example of this is found in Proverbs 25:1, where it states that 'These also are proverbs of Solomon which the men of Hezekiah king of Judah copied', indicating that, although the sayings originated in the mid-900s BC during Solomon's reign, they were not collected into a more structured format until some two centuries later. Following Jerusalem's destruction by Nebuchadnezzar II in the sixth century BC, many of the Biblical texts were preserved in their final form. With the Temple burned and the bulk of the people taken to Babylon, the exiled survivors had to come to terms with their apparent loss of national identity and divine favour.[20] Reflecting upon their history and the prophecies of Jeremiah, they observed that:

According to the books of both Deuteronomy and Jeremiah, the promises of God were conditional. Their fulfillment was dependent on Israel's obedience to the Torah ... It was not the case that God had abandoned Israel. On the contrary, Israel had abandoned God by failing to observe the law God had given. The defeat suffered at the hands of the Babylonians was a divine punishment. But it was not the last word. God may punish but would also restore, bringing Israel back to the land and rebuilding its temple.[21]

Recommitting themselves to God, the Jewish leaders compiled Israel's religious history into a written format that could be passed down more easily to future generations, with the books of Joshua, Judges, 1-2 Samuel and 1-2 Kings likely assuming a more organised form during this era.[22] Editors did not invent a glorious non-existent past, but sought to preserve and present records of Israel's history and its relationship with God. Portions of books might have been written centuries after the events they described, but they also included many passages that were already ancient. The Song of Deborah in Judges 5 is believed to date from the twelfth century BC during the actual time of the Judges, whilst other passages such as the Blessings of Jacob and Moses in Genesis 49 and Deuteronomy 33, and the Oracles of Balaam in Numbers 23-24, also evidence earlier forms of Hebrew.[23] Although debate would continue for some time about which books were considered canonical, the Tanakh was complete by the fourth century BC.[24]

2. THE SEPTUAGINT TRANSLATION

During the reign of Ptolemy II Philadelphus in the third century BC, the Hebrew scriptures were translated into Greek in Alexandria.[25] Beginning with the Torah and continuing with the Nevi'im and Ketuvim, the work was largely complete by 132 BC and was the first time a religious translation of that size had ever been attempted.[26] Known as the Septuagint after the supposed seventy Jewish scholars who assisted with the translation, it was an invaluable resource for Jews who no longer understood Hebrew, and within a matter of decades it had become the 'de facto text of countless synagogues'.[27] In addition to making the Scriptures more accessible to foreigners and the Jewish diaspora, the Septuagint also left a lasting impression on our vocabulary—few have probably heard of the Book of Bereshith, for instance, although most will likely be familiar with its Greek name, Genesis.[28] By the first century AD, there was widespread acceptance of the books that comprised the Tanakh and the textual arrangements within each book. In *Against Apion*, a defence of Judaism's antiquity in contrast to the inventions of Greek mythology, the Jewish historian Josephus wrote:

we have not an innumerable multitude of books among us, disagreeing from and contradicting one another, [as the Greeks have,] but only twenty-two books, which contain the records of all the past times, which are justly believed to be divine. And of them, five belong to Moses, which contain his laws and the traditions of the origin of mankind till his death. This interval of time was little short of three thousand years; but as to the time from the death of Moses till the reign of Artaxerxes, king of Persia, who reigned after Xerxes; the prophets, who were after Moses, wrote down what was done in their times in thirteen books. The remaining four books contain hymns to God, and precepts for the conduct of human life. ... and how firmly we have given credit to these books of our own nation, is evident by what we do: for during so many ages as have already passed, no one hath been so bold as either to add any thing to them, to take any thing from them, or to make any change in them; but it is become natural to all Jews, immediately and from their very birth, to esteem those books to contain divine doctrines, and to persist in them, and, if occasion be, willingly to die for them.[29]

Although it is unclear which two books of the customary twenty-four Josephus did not mention or whether he simply chose to group them with others, his account—along with what we know of the Septuagint—gives a reasonable picture of the scriptural landscape at the start of the Christian era.

3. The Christian Writings

In the first century AD, a group of Jews who would become the first Christians declared that Jesus of Nazareth was the Messiah whose arrival had been prophesied in the Tanakh. Rather than being a political saviour who would restore the Jews' national independence, Christianity taught that He had come instead to atone for the sins of the world through His death and resurrection. By the middle of the century, written references to Jesus and His teachings were appearing. Paul, a Jewish Pharisee who 'persecuted the church of God beyond measure' prior to his conversion to Christianity, wrote several of the books that would form the New Testament, with his first letter to the Thessalonians considered by some to be the earliest New Testament book and the first writing to mention Jesus.[30] Dating from around AD 50—a mere twenty years after Jesus' crucifixion—it notes how the Thessalonians 'became imitators of the churches of God which are in Judea in Christ Jesus. For you also suffered the same things from your own countrymen, just as they did from the Judeans, who killed both the Lord Jesus and their own prophets, and have persecuted us'.[31] Although Paul was not one of the original Apostles, his unique status as 'Apostle to the Gentiles' gave his writings particular prominence.[32]

While the chronological sequence of Paul's letters is still debated, they are generally believed to predate the four Gospels and the Book of Acts.[33] Although the churches Paul wrote to may not have possessed written accounts of Christ's life, his letters nevertheless reveal their familiarity with key Christian teachings, such as the observance of the Lord's Supper in 1 Corinthians 10:16, a letter written in the mid-50s: 'The cup of blessing which we bless, is it not the communion of the blood of Christ? The bread which we break, is it not the communion of the body of Christ?'[34] Paul's letters also show that the churches had concern for one another, with many of them taking up collections for the church in Jerusalem, which was then experiencing persecution and hardship.[35]

In addition to Paul's letters, the early churches soon came to possess narrative accounts of Jesus' life and ministry. Known to us as gospels from the Old English 'godspel'—a translation of the Greek word εὐαγγελίου, or 'good news'—four accounts quickly gained prominence: the Gospels according to Matthew, Mark, Luke, and John.[36] Attributed to Matthew (a former tax collector and Apostle), Mark (an assistant to the Apostle Peter), Luke (a companion of the Apostle Paul), and John (another Apostle), the first three books are known as the Synoptic Gospels after the similar perspective in which they recorded details from Jesus' life.[37] The fourth Gospel, according to John, offers a different, but not conflicting, perspective of Jesus' life, death, and resurrection.[38] Mark is believed to have been written first and John written last, with suggested composition dates potentially as early as the 40s and 50s.[39]

Beyond the Gospels and Pauline letters, a number of other writings relating to Jesus and his teachings circulated amongst the churches by the end of the first century. The Book of Acts gives an account of the development of Christianity in its first few decades. Written by the author of the Gospel of Luke as a follow-up to that work, it was likely published by the mid-70s and focuses on many of Paul's missionary experiences.[40] The anonymously-written Letter to the Hebrews recounts many events from Israel's history and tells how God provided salvation to his people through Christ, while the shorter books of James, 1-2 Peter, 1-3 John, and Jude contain, among other things, warnings against sin and exhortations for holy living.[41] The Book of Revelation, written by AD 96, contains messages to seven churches in the Roman province of Asia (now western Turkey), followed by a series of apocalyptic prophecies and visions relating to the second coming of Christ.[42]

Although these books are recognisable to anyone who has ever looked through a Bible, they were by no means the only ones produced about Jesus. As with the Tanakh, a process of canonisation occurred in which some texts—such as the Gospels of Matthew and Mark—were determined to be divinely-inspired, whilst others—such as the Gospels of Peter and Thomas—were dismissed as spurious or heretical. In contrast to the Tanakh's canonisation which, owing to the time involved in its writing, unfolded over a period of centuries, the canonisation of the New Testament occurred relatively rapidly. By the end of the first century AD, many of the New Testament books were known to the early churches and cited in correspondence. Around AD 95, Clement of Rome wrote a letter to the Corinthians alluding to the books of 1 Corinthians, Acts, Romans, Galatians, Ephesians, Philippians, 1 Timothy, Titus, Hebrews, 1 Peter, the three Synoptic Gospels—and potentially the Gospel of John—while also making extensive use of the Septuagint.[43] About fifteen years later, Ignatius of Antioch, traveling under guard to Rome to be executed by wild beasts, wrote a series of letters to the neighbouring churches which also referenced most of Paul's writings in addition to setting out a firm doctrinal position on 'Jesus Christ our God'.[44] In his *Epistle to the Trallians*, he advised the local church to:

> Stop your ears, therefore, as often as anyone shall speak contrary to Jesus Christ, who was of the race of David, of the Virgin Mary; who was truly born, and did eat and drink; was truly persecuted under Pontius Pilate; was truly crucified and dead; both those in heaven and on earth, and under the earth, being spectators of it. Who was also truly raised from the dead by his Father, after the manner as He will also raise up us who believe in him, by Christ Jesus, without whom we have no true life.[45]

Contemporaneous with Ignatius was Polycarp, Bishop of Smyrna and a fellow student of the Apostle John. In a letter to the Philippian church written around AD 110, he referred to 1-2 Corinthians, Romans, Galatians, Ephesians, Philippians, 1-2 Thessalonians, and the pastoral letters of 1-2 Timothy, in addition to noting that a collection of Paul's letters could be found at Philippi, since 'when he was absent, [Paul] wrote you letters. By the careful perusal of his letters you will be able to strengthen yourselves in the faith given to you'.[46] As the writings of these early leaders show, by the beginning of the second century a majority of the New Testament books were already regarded as authoritative by the early churches. Amidst the ongoing persecutions from Rome, this era also saw the first 'apologies', or formal written defences in support of Christianity, addressed to the imperial government. One such apology, written by Aristides of Athens to the

Emperor Hadrian in the mid-120s, illustrates how the 'gospel writing' was already considered to be 'holy' by the early church:

> Christians trace their origin to the Lord Jesus Christ. He that came down from heaven in the Holy Spirit for the salvation of men is confessed to be the Son of the Most High God. He was born of a holy Virgin without seed of man, and took flesh without defilement; and He appeared among men so that He might recall them from the error of polytheism. When He had accomplished His wonderful design, by His own free will and for a mighty purpose He tasted of death on the cross. After three days, however, He came to life again and went up into the heavens. It is possible for you, O king, to learn to know the report of His coming in the holy gospel writing, as it is called by us—should you chance to come upon a copy.[47]

As the second century unfolded, the books that would form the New Testament continued to spread across the Roman world, including to one city that would offer a glimpse into Christianity's early growth. In 1897, two Oxford scholars named Bernard Grenfell and Arthur Hunt excavated the ruins of the ancient Egyptian city of Oxyrhynchus.[48] Whilst their initial impressions were unfavourable, they did discover a large quantity of papyri buried in the sands outside the city.[49] Although 'Some hundreds of thousands of fragments [were initially] dismissed as practically useless', further examination began to reveal their value—seven of the lost books of Livi's *History of Rome* were recovered in summary form, along with portions of Menander's comedies and the oldest and most complete diagrams of Euclid's *Elements*.[50]

Over six seasons, more than 500,000 scraps of papyri were recovered, making it 'the best-documented provincial city anywhere in the Mediterranean world'.[51] Two of the recovered fragments, known as Papyrus 90 and Papyrus 104, contain portions of the Gospels of John and Matthew. Both date from the middle of the second century, with the latter believed to be the earliest surviving text of Matthew.[52] A third fragment known as Papyrus 52 was also uncovered in Egypt, containing verses from the Gospel of John. Dating from the first quarter of the second century—a mere twenty years or so after the original was written—it is believed to be the oldest surviving fragment from a New Testament book.[53]

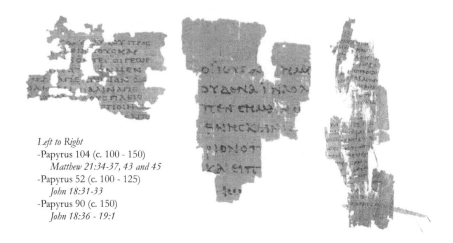

Left to Right
-Papyrus 104 (c. 100 - 150)
  Matthew 21:34-37, 43 and 45
-Papyrus 52 (c. 100 - 125)
  John 18:31-33
-Papyrus 90 (c. 150)
  John 18:36 - 19:1

While the discovery of the Egyptian papyri establishes that at least two of the Gospels were circulating in a small desert town 160 kilometres southwest of Cairo within a few decades after they were written, these were by no means the only New Testament books known to the African churches. In a trial held in Carthage on July 17, 180, seven men and five women were convicted and subsequently executed for having 'confessed that they live[d] after the Christian fashion'.[54] As recorded in the *Acts of the Scillitan Martyrs*:

> The proconsul Saturninus said, 'Do you persevere in being a Christian?'
> Speratus said, 'I am a Christian,' and they all agreed with him. ... The
> proconsul Saturninus said, 'What things do you have in your box?'
> Speratus said, 'The books, and the epistles of Paul, a just man.'[55]

Although it is unclear which 'books' Speratus was referring to, the mention of 'the epistles of Paul' indicates that by the year 180, a collection of Paul's writings had spread as far as modern-day Tunisia and were regarded highly enough to have accompanied the martyrs to their trial. Many passages from their testimony also establish their familiarity with the New Testament books, such as an exchange with Saturninus in which Speratus said 'I serve that God whom no man sees or can see with these eyes', a reference to 1 Timothy 6:16, and the remark of one of the female martyrs about 'Honour to Caesar as Caesar, but fear to God', in an apparent reference to 1 Peter 2:17.[56]

By the middle of the second century, the use of apostolic writings had become an established part of Christian life. In addition to what we see from the Scillitan trial, the Christian author Justin Martyr's *First Apology* to the Emperor Antoninus Pius, written around 155, records how 'On the day which is dedicated to the sun [Sunday], all those [Christians] who live in the cities or who dwell in the countryside gather in a common meeting, and for as long as there is time the Memoirs of the Apostles or the writings of the prophets are read'.[57] Even the pagan author Lucian of Samosata took notice of this, writing in the *Death of Peregrinus* that, when the philosopher Peregrinus was in prison, the Christians came to visit him 'and they read their sacred books together'.[58]

4. HERESY AGAINST ORTHODOXY

Toward the latter half of the second century, the question of which books were to be considered as canonical took on a greater urgency in response to heretical teachings—most notably Marcionism—that challenged the orthodox view of Jesus' life and purpose. Around the year 138, a wealthy ship-owner named Marcion came to Rome with the argument that the Hebrew scriptures were inferior to the Christian writings, and consequently had 'no part of authoritative revelation'.[59] Believing the world to have been created by a 'cruel god of battles and bloody sacrifices' known as the Demiurge, Marcion sought to rid Christianity of 'every trace of Judaism', insisting that the New Testament revealed a different 'God of love' superior to the Old Testament deity.[60] By the year 140, he had produced a list of the books he claimed were the sole authoritative basis of genuinely Christian teaching, consisting of selectively edited versions of the Gospel of Luke and ten of Paul's letters.[61]

While this 'canon', along with his unorthodox views, led to Marcion's expulsion from the Roman church in 144, it prompted an important discussion about which writings were to be regarded as authoritative scripture.[62] Although the four Gospels of Matthew, Mark, Luke, and John had been in use for much of the second century—with the early churches showing 'little interest' in other gospels—they received their most vocal defence in Irenaeus of Lyon's *Against Heresies*, written around 180:

> It is not possible that the Gospels can be either more or fewer in number than they are. For, since there are four zones of the world in which we live, and four principal winds, while the church is scattered throughout all the world, and the 'pillar and ground' of the church is the gospel and the spirit of life; it is fitting that she should have four pillars, breathing out immortality on every side, and vivifying men afresh.[63]

Irenaeus' belief in the authority of the four gospels was hardly unique. Around the same time as *Against Heresies* was published, the Muratorian Canon was produced, listing the books that were considered canonical by the Latin churches. Named after the Italian historian Lodovico Antonio Muratori, who discovered it in Milan in the 1700s, its first few lines have been lost, but note that 'The third book of the Gospel is that according to Luke ... The fourth of the Gospels is that of John', before going on to list Acts, thirteen of Paul's letters, Jude, two of John's letters, and Revelation as canonical, along with the works of several other authors.[64]

Even though some Christian writings, such as 1 Clement or the Shepherd of Hermas, were not considered canonical by most of the early churches, they were nevertheless regarded as having some intrinsic value.[65] This was not the case, however, with works that were determined to be fraudulent. The Muratorian Canon specifically rejected two letters attributed to Paul—the epistles to the Laodiceans and Alexandrians—as forgeries created by the Marcionites, and when a priest in Asia produced the 'Acts of Paul' around 170 out of respect for the apostle, he was rebuked before a church council and dismissed from his position.[66] Just because a book was alleged to have been written by an apostle, it did not follow that it was accepted without question. The Gospel of Peter, for instance, would have been a valuable perspective on Jesus' ministry if it had actually been written by Peter, but even the most cursory glance reveals why it was rejected as a forgery. Unlike the traditional accounts of the resurrection, the Gospel of Peter describes a completely different scene, replete with a crowd of Jewish elders who had come to watch the event, angels carrying Jesus out of the tomb, and a floating cross that could speak.[67] Apart from disagreeing with more than a century of church teaching, the presence of the Jewish elders alone would have been highly unlikely, given their claims that Jesus had not been resurrected.[68]

5. THE EMERGENCE OF THE NEW TESTAMENT

By the third century, the New Testament had assumed a recognisable form. In his *Prescription Against Heretics*, written around the year 200, the African theologian Tertullian first used the phrase 'New Testament' to describe the Christian scriptures.[69] Toward the middle of the century, a clearer picture of the New Testament appeared in the writings of Origen, one of the early church's most distinguished scholars.[70] In Homily 7 of his *Homilies on Joshua*, he wrote:

> Matthew first sounded the priestly trumpet in his Gospel; Mark also; Luke and John each played their own priestly trumpets. Even Peter cries out with trumpets in two of his epistles; also James and Jude. In addition, John also sounds the trumpet through his epistles, and Luke, as he describes the Acts of the Apostles. And now that last one [Paul] comes, the one who said, 'I think God displays us apostles last,' and in fourteen of his epistles, thundering with trumpets, he casts down the walls of Jericho and all the devices of idolatry and dogmas of philosophers, all the way to the foundations.[71]

Another of Origen's writings indicates that, by the year 230, these books had long been regarded as divinely inspired in the same way as the Old Testament. In Book 4 of *On First Principles*, he wrote, 'Nor was it only with regard to those Scriptures which were composed down to the advent of Christ that the Holy Spirit thus dealt; but as being one and the same Spirit, and proceeding from one God, He dealt in the same way with the evangelists and apostles'.[72] In contrast to the arguments of some that the New Testament was merely the creation of fourth-century Roman councils, Origen's writings show that around 90% of what would eventually comprise the New Testament was already regarded as canonical by the middle of the third century, more than sixty years before Christianity received legal recognition under the Edict of Milan.[73] Rather than facilitating the New Testament's development, the Roman Empire became increasingly hostile toward Christianity in the decades leading up to the grant of toleration. Although Christians had faced persecutions since the days of Nero in the first century, the third century saw a rise in this activity—beginning with the Decian persecution in 250 in which citizens were required to produce certificates showing they had sacrificed to the gods, or else were liable to be arrested and executed.[74] Fifty years later, the Emperor Diocletian ordered copies of the New Testament to be burned as part of an effort to stamp out Christianity.[75] In what would become known as the 'Great Persecution':

> an imperial edict was announced everywhere ordering that the churches be demolished and the Scriptures destroyed by fire. Any [Christians] who held high places would lose them, while those in households would be imprisoned if they continued to profess Christianity. ... Soon, however, other edicts appeared ordering that the presidents of the churches everywhere be thrown into prison and then forced by every sort of device to offer sacrifice.[76]

Within a few months, these edicts reached Oxyrhynchus. In a letter written by a Christian named Copres to his wife Sarapias—preserved as Papyrus P.Oxy. XXXI 2601—he noted that, while traveling on business to resolve a court case, 'it was made known to us that those who appear in court are compelled to sacrifice and I made a power of attorney to my brother and ... we have instructed an advocate ... so that the matter about the *arourai* might be brought into court'.[77] Rather than appear in person, which would have required him to make an idolatrous sacrifice, Copres empowered non-Christians to argue on his behalf.

While it is unclear whether this tactic succeeded, others had no choice but to report to the Roman authorities. Christians were purged from the army, stripped of their privileges, sent to work in the mines, and executed by the thousands.[78]

Even children were not immune from suffering, with a twelve-year-old girl named Eulalia purportedly martyred in Spain in 304.[79] Amidst a scene of levelled churches, burned books, broken bodies, and ruined lives, the notion that the New Testament was the production of a Roman diktat or bureaucratic vote, à la *The Da Vinci Code*, exposes itself as a hollow fiction.[80]

6. THE COMPLETION OF THE BIBLE

With the end of the Great Persecution in 311 and the grant of religious toleration in 313, Christianity entered a new historical phase.[81] To record what had gone on in the centuries before, Eusebius, the Bishop of Caesarea, produced a ten-volume *Ecclesiastical History* in 324. In Book 3, Chapter 25, he divided the main Christian writings that were then in circulation into four categories based upon their reception by the churches across the Empire:[82]

Acknowledged as Genuine	Disputed but Well-Known	Spurious	Heretical, Absurd and Impious
Matthew	James	Acts of Paul	Gospel of Peter
Mark	Jude	Apocalypse of Peter	Gospel of Thomas
Luke	2 Peter	Epistle of Barnabas	Gospel of Matthias
John	2 John	Didache	Acts of Andrew
Acts	3 John	Shepherd of Hermas	Acts of John
Romans		Gospel of the Hebrews	
1 Corinthians		Revelation*	
2 Corinthians			
Galatians			
Ephesians			
Philippians			
Colossians			
1 Thessalonians			
2 Thessalonians			
1 Timothy			
2 Timothy			
Titus			
Philemon			
Hebrews			
1 Peter			
1 John			
Revelation*			

Although the five 'disputed' books were not recognised as genuine by all, they were nevertheless 'well known and approved by many' and were still regarded as part of the New Testament.[83] Apart from questions about the Book of Revelation—which Eusebius listed as both 'Genuine' and 'Spurious' since the eastern churches rejected it and the western churches accepted it—his New Testament is identical to the modern text.[84] Moreover, the concerns of the eastern churches had less to do with the book's content and more with the fact that some heretical groups also referred to it.[85]

Notably, Eusebius' list predates by forty years the Council of Laodicea that met in 364—the first church council to consider which books formed the Bible—providing further evidence of the scriptures' organic development.[86] In 367, Athanasius, the Bishop of Alexandria, issued a letter that, for the first time, contained the complete New Testament canon. In *Festal Letter 39*, he wrote:

> it is not tedious to speak of the [books] of the New Testament. These are, the four Gospels, according to Matthew, Mark, Luke, and John. Afterwards, the Acts of the Apostles and Epistles (called Catholic), seven, viz. of James, one; of Peter, two; of John, three; after these, one of Jude. In addition, there are fourteen Epistles of Paul, written in this order: The first, to the Romans; then two to the Corinthians; after these, to the Galatians; next, to the Ephesians, then to the Philippians; then to the Colossians; after these, two to the Thessalonians, and that to the Hebrews; and again, two to Timothy; one to Titus; and lastly, that to Philemon. And besides, the Revelation of John. These are fountains of salvation, that they who thirst may be satisfied with the living words they contain. In these alone is proclaimed the doctrine of godliness. Let no man add to these, neither let him take ought from these.[87]

While the Council of Laodicea had discussed the Biblical canon a few years earlier, it had left out Revelation.[88] Athanasius' letter is therefore the earliest reference to the twenty-seven-book New Testament that we have today. Within a matter of years, this list was endorsed by the Council of Hippo in 393 and the Council of Carthage in 397.[89] The New Testament canon—and along with it, the Christian Bible—was finally complete.

5

The Transmission of the Bible

Having seen how the Bible came to be, we will now consider how it has come down through the ages. With something as significant as the very word of God itself, it is important to have confidence that the text available today conveys the same information as the original readers had centuries ago. Given that some have argued—principally from secular or Islamic perspectives—that the scriptures have been corrupted over time, it is necessary to dispel these assertions before considering its teachings in detail.[1] To do so, we must study the history of the Bible's preservation and its transmission to the present day.

If our intention was to re-create an exact word-for-word copy of the books of the Bible as they were originally written, we would quickly become frustrated by the challenge of the undertaking. Looking at the New Testament alone, about 20,000 ancient manuscripts—totalling over 2.5 million pages—have been discovered in various languages to date, containing an estimated 300,000 to 400,000 textual variations between them.[2] While the vast majority of these are mere differences in spelling, and less than one percent could be considered to have a meaningful impact on interpretation, this would still present a challenge for anyone attempting to arrive at the precise original wording for all of the books.[3] Fortunately, our inquiry does not demand an unattainable standard of textual reconstruction. Instead of attempting to establish whether the Gospel of Mark originally contained the longer ending in 16:9-20, or if the mark of the beast in the Book of Revelation is 666 or 616, as the earliest surviving version has it, it is of far greater significance to establish whether the central teachings of the Bible have remained unchanged.[4] Did the Bible of the early church contain the same accounts of Jesus' life, death, and resurrection as the ones available today? Did the first Christians have the same sense of His ministry and purpose as we do? Can we be confident that doctrinal corruptions have not crept in over time? Before we can consider what the Bible says, we must first be sure that it has not undergone a material change through time and translation.

1. Early Translations

The books of the Old Testament were originally written in two Semitic languages, Hebrew and Aramaic—with the latter appearing only minimally throughout the Old Testament.[5] As for Hebrew, the Old Testament reflects multiple stages of linguistic development—from passages of Archaic Hebrew (used until around 1000 BC), Standard Iron Age Hebrew (1000 - 586 BC) and Post-Exilic Hebrew (450 - 200 BC).[6] Although these books received linguistic updates as necessary, the ancient editors took care when revising one version of Hebrew into another.[7] The majority of the Torah, for instance, is now written in a style that developed centuries after Moses, but many of its songs have retained their archaic dialect, given that their language 'did not lend itself to updating without destroying their literary quality', thus providing a measure of linguistic authenticity.[8] Such updates were occasionally necessary to aid the reader, just as ancient works are sometimes treated today—the Anglo-Saxon epic *Beowulf* would be unintelligible to anyone who could not read ninth-century Old English, for instance, but can readily be understood by those with a modern translation.[9]

Following Alexander the Great's conquests in the fourth century BC, Koine or 'common' Greek became the dominant language of the Mediterranean world.[10] This was the language the Alexandrian Jews used to produce the Septuagint translation, and it was also the language the New Testament was first written in.[11] While the Septuagint was undoubtedly influential, however, it was simply one of many Greek Old Testament translations circulating across the Roman Empire. To help make sense of them all, the Christian scholar Origen produced a side-by-side comparison of the leading texts around the year 240.[12] Estimated to have spread across fifty volumes, his *Hexapla* featured six columns from left to right containing the text in Hebrew characters, the Hebrew text transliterated into Greek, along with the Greek translations of Aquila, Symmachus, the Septuagint, and Theodotion.[13] For some books, Origen also affixed to the right of Theodotion's text a fifth, sixth, and even seventh translation, leading to as many as nine versions of Biblical text on a single page.[14] Scholars could readily determine whether there were any discrepancies among the translations of a particular passage simply by comparing all of the versions that appeared.[15] In his *Commentary on Matthew*, Origen wrote that 'We have been able, with God helping us, to repair the difference between the copies of the Old Testament, by using the remaining versions as a criterion'.[16] Because of its size, it is likely that the *Hexapla* only ever existed as a single work in the Christian library at Caesarea, where it is believed to have remained until the library's destruction in the Muslim invasion of 638.[17]

While collections of Biblical writings formed relatively early, it is unlikely that most Christians prior to the fourth century would have ever seen anything resembling what we now think of as the Bible.[18] A church might have possessed some of Paul's writings or a gospel or two, as we see from the Oxyrhynchus papyri, but full versions of the Bible would have been rare.[19] The earliest surviving Bible—the *Codex Vaticanus*—dates from around 325-340 and would have taken a tremendous amount of time and money to produce.[20] Although several sections have been lost, it is still a massive work, with its 759 remaining leaves carefully preserved in the Vatican Library.[21] Similar in age is the *Codex Sinaiticus*, another Greek Bible containing the complete New Testament.[22]

Important though Greek was, it soon became necessary to translate the Bible into other languages. By 360, Ulfilas had produced a Gothic translation, while Frumentius had translated part of the Bible into the Ethiopian dialect of Ge'ez.[23] A Syriac translation known as the Peshitta was produced, and translations were made into the Coptic dialects of Sahidic and Bohairic.[24] By 434, an Armenian translation was published by Mesrob Mashtots which drew upon the *Hexapla*.[25] As difficult as the process of translation could be, however, it was often compounded by native illiteracy; before Ulfilas and Mesrob could translate the Bible into their respective languages, for instance, they first had to invent alphabets for them.[26]

2. THE VULGATE & MEDIEVAL ERA

While Latin translations of parts of the Bible had existed for many years, collectively known as the *Vetus Latina*, no systematic translation had been undertaken by the mid-fourth century.[27] Around 380, Pope Damasus I tasked his assistant Jerome with revising the Church's Latin texts to produce a more accurate version.[28] Classically trained in rhetoric and philosophy before converting to Christianity, Jerome had initially found the Bible's writing style to be 'most irritating' in comparison with the works of pagan literature, but soon discovered that it could be both beautiful and poetic.[29] By 384, he had translated the Gospels and Psalms, but was driven out of Rome following Damasus' death.[30] Settling in Bethlehem, he received financial support from Paula, a Christian convert from one of Rome's richest senatorial families, and soon gained access to the library in Caesarea where his efforts were enhanced by the use of the *Hexapla*.[31] By 390, he was translating directly from the Hebrew Tanakh, believing that it represented 'a more ancient and less corrupt authority' than many of the Greek translations then available.[32]

Fifteen years later, the Latin translation that would become known as the Vulgate was complete.[33] With his mastery of Hebrew, Greek, and Latin, the superior merits of his translation soon became evident.[34] While the *Vetus Latina* continued to circulate for some time, Jerome's translation was destined to become the primary medium through which the gospel arrived in Western Europe, particularly since knowledge of Greek was becoming less prevalent in the Latin-speaking world.[35] By the end of the fourth century, Greek instruction in the West had steeply declined, with many areas struggling to find suitable teachers.[36] The Vulgate therefore gave the Latin Church a version of the Bible it could read with confidence.

As the fifth century unfolded, geopolitical developments led to significant changes in the Christian world. With the Roman Empire stretching from northern England to the banks of the Euphrates, the challenges of administering more than five million square kilometres of territory eventually proved too much for a single government.[37] Following crises in the third and fourth centuries, along with the establishment of Constantinople as the 'New Rome', the Empire's cohesion became permanently strained and in 395 it was formally divided into East and West.[38] Life for most people continued as it had before, but in August 410 Rome was sacked by the Visigoths—the first time in 800 years that it had been attacked by foreign invaders.[39] Three days of 'looting, torture, rape, murder and captivity' ensued, with many of the city's inhabitants suffering terribly.[40] Although the Western Roman Empire would nominally survive until 476 when its last emperor was deposed, the sack of Rome underlined the contrast in fortunes between the two divisions.[41] The East was strong, rich, and culturally Greek whilst the West was fractured, poorer, and culturally besieged.[42] In the midst of such different environments, the Church began to develop along Greek and Latin lines of influence. In the East, with its strong imperial court and functioning civil service, it was increasingly subordinated to the state—even to the point of allowing the emperor to issue edicts on doctrinal matters.[43] In contrast, it frequently fell to the Western Church to perform the most basic functions of government.[44] Following the sack of Rome, Pope Innocent I was forced to oversee the city's reconstruction after the emperor fled to Ravenna, and when Attila the Hun invaded Italy in 452, he was turned back by a delegation led by Pope Leo I rather than any of the once-fearsome Roman legions.[45]

As the Western Roman Empire disintegrated, its inhabitants found themselves increasingly cut off from Greek learning and culture.[46] In the absence of Greek—let alone Hebrew—texts to study from, Jerome's Latin translation became the only complete version of the Bible they possessed. As Christianity spread into areas that were less familiar with Latin, however, it became necessary to translate the Vulgate into local dialects. In seventh-century England, the poet Caedmon is believed to have sung stories from it in Anglo-Saxon, and the Venerable Bede, a Northumbrian monk and historian, is said to have produced an Anglo-Saxon translation of the Gospel of John around 735.[47] In 789, the Frankish king Charlemagne enjoined the clergy in his *General Admonition* to teach children to read, since 'often it happens that people have the admirable desire to pray to God, but they address him in an inappropriate way, because their books are uncorrected. … if it is necessary to write a Gospel book, psalter or missal, have mature men write those with all diligence'.[48] As Charlemagne understood, 'if there is less care in writing, there is also much less wisdom for understanding the Holy Scriptures than there ought to be'.[49]

While translations were produced in several languages across Europe—such as Otfrid von Weissenburg's *Evangelienbuch*, a rendition of the Gospels in Old High German from around 870—the Anglo-Saxons were particularly diligent translators.[50] The earliest surviving Anglo-Saxon translation of the Bible is the Vespasian Psalter, an interlinear gloss of the Book of Psalms dating from around 850.[51] Pictured below, an excerpt from Psalm 26 is written in Latin with the Mercian dialect appearing above each line in a smaller brown script.[52]

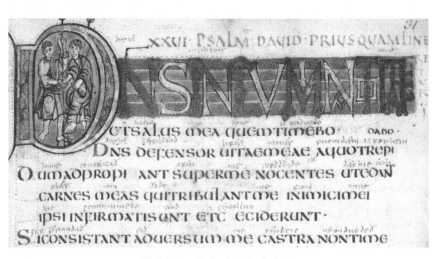

The Vespasian Psalter (c. 850) - Psalm 26

Toward the end of the ninth century, the quest for an Anglo-Saxon translation of the Bible received royal support. Much like Charlemagne a century before, Alfred the Great recognised the need for a Bible people could understand. Following the deaths of his older brothers, Alfred had become king of the West Saxons at the age of twenty-two.[53] Scholarly and religious, he was the only English king prior to Henry VIII to write a book, and the last ten years of his reign were spent promoting the revival of literacy and learning.[54] With respect to the Bible, he wrote in the preface to his translation of Pope Gregory I's *Pastoral Care*:

> I wondered very greatly at the good and wise men who were once in England … why they did not wish to translate [books] into their own language. But then I immediately answered myself and said, 'They did not think that men would ever become so careless and learning so fallen away; they neglected this out of a desire that there would be more wisdom here in the country the more languages we knew.' Then I remembered how the law was first found in the Hebrew language, and then, when the Greeks learned it, they translated it all into their own language … and then Latin speakers in the same way … translated it all, through wise interpreters, into their own language. And also all other Christian peoples translated some part of it into their own language.[55]

Putting his beliefs into practice, Alfred translated the Ten Commandments and much of the Mosaic Law, and within a hundred years the four Gospels had been translated into the West Saxon dialect.[56] Pictured below is an excerpt from the West Saxon Gospel of Matthew containing the Lord's Prayer.[57]

The Lord's Prayer in West Saxon

Fæder ure þu þe eart on heofonum, si þin nama gehalgod. To becume þin rice, gewurþe ðin willa, on eorðan swa swa on heofonum. Urne gedæghwamlican hlaf syle us todæg, and forgyf us ure gyltas, swa swa we forgyfað urum gyltendum. And ne gelæd þu us on costnunge, ac alys us of yfele. Soþlice.[58]

Following the Norman Conquest of England in 1066, English ceased to be the language of government.[59] Although versions of the Anglo-Saxon Biblical texts continued to be read by some after the Conquest, the introduction of Norman French by the new ruling class brought about such radical changes in spoken English that 'before long the Old English versions of the tenth century must have been unintelligible to the great mass of the English people'.[60] As French was the language of the court and Latin the language of the Church, translations of the Bible into English 'virtually ceased'.[61]

Elsewhere across Europe, local translations were beginning to lose favour for other reasons. By the time of the Third Lateran Council in 1179, the Church had become increasingly wary of unauthorised translations of the Bible—partly due to quality concerns, but also on account of certain heresies that were beginning to spread via unqualified preachers.[62] In 1199, the Bishop of Metz wrote to Pope Innocent III seeking advice about how to handle a group that had scorned the local priests and argued that their personal translation of the Bible was superior to the Vulgate. Although the Pope advised the Bishop that 'the desire to understand sacred Scripture and the zeal to adhort according to them was not to be rebuked, but rather commended', he also instructed him to:

> Inquire and find out the truth: who was the translator of that translation, what was the intention of the translator, what do its users believe, why do they teach, and do they uphold the apostolic see and the catholic faith? We will better be able to understand what must be done to track down the truth about these and others after we are instructed by your letters.[63]

As Innocent III recognised, the use of a vernacular translation did not, by itself, make someone a heretic. In the absence of any proof that a translation was inaccurate or heretical, it was best to proceed cautiously before condemning it.[64] There was a great difference, after all, between a translation that had been clumsily done and one that had been deliberately produced to undermine the doctrines of the Church. Although the Vulgate was not without its flaws, it had served the Church reliably for eight centuries and was not to be lightly swept aside. Around 1204, it also received an important upgrade when a lecturer at the University of Paris named Stephen Langton introduced chapter divisions into the text.[65] While it would be another 350 years before verses were added, this greatly increased the speed and accuracy with which one could search through the Bible.[66] Langton's choices about where to divide chapters were 'occasionally artificial and not without mistakes', but his apparent motivation was to create passages of fairly equal size, and his approach soon became the standard system of Biblical reference.[67]

In 1208, the debate over vernacular translations took on greater significance when the Church was forced to confront the Cathar heresy in France. Similar in certain respects to the second-century Marcionites and their belief in both a loving God and a cruel demiurge, the Cathars believed that there were 'two gods or lords without beginning and without end, one good, the other wholly evil'.[68] To the Cathars, the material world was the creation of the 'power of evil', with the souls of humans imprisoned in material bodies and subject to reincarnation until they could finally escape through a ceremony known as the *consolamentum*.[69] Sex, marriage, and procreation were regarded as inventions of the Devil, and passages from the New Testament were 'radically reinterpret[ed]' so that Jesus' crucifixion and resurrection were seen as having occurred only metaphorically.[70]

Eccentric and heretical as Cathar theology was, one particularly troublesome manifestation of their belief system was the idea that, since the material world was irrevocably tainted by evil, Cathars were not subject to the control of any civil authority.[71] Finding a friend in Raymond VI, Count of Toulouse, the Cathars took advantage of the region's weak political environment to establish their own church hierarchy and power base.[72] Although monks were sent to debate the Cathar leaders and challenge their theological errors, the heresy continued to spread.[73] In January 1208, a meeting to discuss the situation ended in acrimony when the Pope's ambassador, Pierre de Castelnau, was threatened by Raymond VI.[74] Within days, Castelnau was assassinated and the Count—already suspected of heresy—was accused of arranging his murder.[75]

Upon receiving news of Castelnau's death, Innocent III reacted swiftly. Summoning an army to 'wipe out the treachery of heresy and its followers', the Pope denounced the 'perverters of our souls [who] have become also the destroyers of our flesh', and authorised the confiscation of Raymond VI and other heretics' lands.[76] The Albigensian Crusade—named after the city of Albi, a Cathar stronghold—had begun.[77] Twenty-one years later, an exhausted Raymond VII, son of the by-then-deceased Raymond VI, signed the Treaty of Paris with the French King Louis IX, officially ending the Crusade.[78] With the Cathars defeated, the Church then turned to the question of how to prevent such conflicts from occurring in the future. Although the Crusade had taken on a political context as members of the nobility fought to acquire territory, its root cause had been the Cathar heresy, which had arisen from a flawed interpretation of the Bible.[79] The Church had recognised the potential threats unapproved translations could present for some time, and the Albigensian Crusade had shown these dangers to be all too real. Thousands had died over the course of the conflict, and the Church was determined to ensure that such heresies could never happen again in order to avoid further bloodshed.[80]

To this end, a Church council was convened in France at Toulouse to adopt protocols for the prevention of heresy. Recognising the danger that could come from unqualified people giving flawed interpretations of the Bible, it decided to take the Bible out of their hands completely, decreeing in Canon 14:

> We prohibit also that the laity should be permitted to have the books of the Old or the New Testament; unless anyone from motives of devotion should wish to have the Psalter or the Breviary for divine offices or the hours of the blessed Virgin; but we most strictly forbid their having any translation of these books.[81]

Four years later in 1233, a similar decree was issued at the Council of Tarragona in Spain.[82] Possession of the Bible in the 'vernacular dialect' was prohibited, and if anyone had such a Bible and neglected to bring it within eight days to be burnt, 'he should be regarded, whether clergyman or layman, as suspected of heresy until he had purged himself'.[83] In time, the prohibition on vernacular translations extended to include sermons and commentaries, with the Holy Roman Emperor Charles IV instructing his agents in 1369 to 'diligently investigate the possession of sermons, treatises, and other writings in the vernacular', in what is now Belgium and the Netherlands, as the laity were not allowed to possess 'any vernacular books dealing with sacred scripture'.[84]

Although the dangers of heresy were undoubtedly real, as the fourteenth century progressed some began to feel that the Church had gone too far. Rather than protecting people from false teaching, the lack of access to the Bible instead meant that they had no way of knowing whether a teaching was Biblically correct. The Church might have made itself the Bible's guardian and interpreter, but many of its clergy disregarded its commandments. Religious corruption was becoming increasingly prevalent, with wealthy families often able to purchase church offices for their children.[85] Disapproving of this, an English clergyman named John Wycliffe argued that the prohibition on translations went against the will of God and the practice of the early church:

> The friars with their followers say that it is heresy thus to write God's law in English ... It seems first that the knowledge of God's law should be taught in that language which is best known, because this knowledge is God's Word. ... Also, the Holy Spirit gave to the apostles at Pentecost knowledge to know all manner of languages to teach the people God's law thereby; and so God willed that the people be taught his laws in diverse tongues. But what man on God's behalf should reverse God's ordinance and his will? For this reason Saint Jerome labored and translated the Bible from diverse tongues into Latin that

it might after be translated into other tongues. Thus Christ and his apostles taught the people in that tongue that was best known to them. Why should men not do so now?[86]

Believing that everyone should have access to the Bible in a language they could understand—and that such knowledge would help curtail the growing abuses inside the Church—Wycliffe and his supporters began preparing an English translation of the Vulgate.[87] By 1382 it was complete, and a group of 'poor parishioners' known as Lollards began traveling throughout England 'reading the Scriptures in their mother tongue to all who would hear God's word'.[88] Unfortunately for Wycliffe and his fellow reformers, their beliefs soon became linked in the minds of the authorities with the Peasants' Revolt, with the Wycliffe Bible regarded as subversive.[89] In 1401, the political establishment reacted harshly to what it saw as the Lollard heresy and its deviations from the teachings of the Church. In a statute known as *De Heretico Comburendo*, or 'On the Burning of a Heretic', the English Parliament condemned the:

> false and perverse people of a certain new sect [who] under the colour of dissembled holiness, preach and teach ... divers new doctrines and wicked, heretical and erroneous opinions, contrary to the same faith and blessed determinations of the holy church. And of such sect and wicked doctrine and opinions they ... make and write books [and] do wickedly instruct and inform people...[90]

It then went on to command that 'this wicked sect [and its] doctrines and opinions should from henceforth cease and be utterly destroyed', with anyone 'having such books or any writings of such wicked doctrines or opinions' required to deliver them up to the authorities.[91] If an individual failed to comply, he was liable to be fined, or, if sufficiently unrepentant, taken before the people 'to be burnt, that such punishment might strike in fear to the minds of other[s]'.[92] Eight years later, the Constitutions of Oxford declared it heretical as a matter of law to possess or produce an unlicensed English translation.[93] Although a licence could theoretically be obtained, in practice they were strictly forbidden, with the ownership of an English Bible regarded as proof of capital heresy.[94]

3. THE RENAISSANCE

To underscore the severity of these purportedly-heretical activities, in 1428 the Bishop of Lincoln ordered Wycliffe's remains—long since deceased—to be exhumed, burned, and scattered into the River Swift.[95] Few actions could have been more symbolic of the establishment's attitude toward challenges to the status quo, even if the challenger—in Wycliffe's case—had been dead for over forty years by that point. What the bishop could not have foreseen as Wycliffe's ashes floated downstream, however, was that events were about to unfold that would transform Europe's knowledge of the Bible.

The first pivotal event occurred in the 1440s, when a German goldsmith named Johannes Gutenberg invented the movable-type printing press, making it possible to mass-produce written information.[96] After borrowing extensively to purchase the necessary materials, Gutenberg embarked on the ambitious project of printing the entire Bible.[97] By 1455, he had produced a printed version of the Vulgate, the first book in Europe to be mechanically printed.[98] Although it took some three years to complete, its impact was immediate—in the time it would have taken a monastic scribe to produce a single Bible by hand, Gutenberg had produced 180 copies.[99] While the project ultimately forced him into bankruptcy, the technology he had unleashed in a small workshop inspired a communications revolution.[100] Within a few decades, book production costs fell by 85-90%, leading to an unparalleled expansion of knowledge.[101]

At the same time as Gutenberg's Bibles were being printed, a second pivotal event occurred 2,500 kilometres away in the city of Constantinople. While the Eastern Roman Empire had been in decline for centuries, by the 1450s its condition had become terminal.[102] Having lost nearly all of its wealth, power, and territory around the Mediterranean and Middle East, the once-great civilisation had been reduced to a narrow strip along the Bosporus.[103] On May 29, 1453, Ottoman forces overran the imperial city's defences after a fifty-three day siege.[104] Constantine XI, the last Roman emperor, died fighting on the city walls, and—in an echo of the sack of Rome centuries before—the invading army subjected the conquered city to three days of plundering.[105] Men, women, and children were slain in the streets, nuns killed themselves to avoid being raped and enslaved, and upon entering the city, the Ottoman Sultan Mehmed II ordered the *adhan* to be said in the ancient church of Hagia Sophia to convert it into a mosque.[106] 977 years after the collapse of its western half—and 1,480 years since its establishment under the first emperor, Augustus—the Roman Empire was finally at an end.

While the fall of Constantinople marked the end of an era, it also brought about a transformation of Western Biblical knowledge. As Ottoman influence had grown around the eastern Mediterranean in the decades leading up to 1453, Greek scholars had begun immigrating to the West. In 1423, a school had opened in Italy that taught Greek as an important part of the curriculum, and that same year an Italian historian named Giovanni Aurispa had returned from Greece with a collection of 238 manuscripts.[107] As more texts became available to study, Western scholars began to rediscover an entire body of long-forgotten knowledge. In the

1430s, a monk named Ambrogio Traversari translated many of the Greek Christian Fathers' works into Latin, and when news of Constantinople's fall reached Rome, Pope Nicholas V quickly dispatched agents to rescue as many manuscripts as possible.[108] Following his death, other collectors continued to acquire knowledge from the East, including Cardinal Basilios Bessarion—a former imperial advisor who amassed over 470 manuscripts containing 'the essential texts, Classical and Christian' from the ancient world.[109] By the 1480s, the Vatican Library contained thousands of manuscripts, including what would eventually be recognised as the world's oldest Bible, the *Codex Vaticanus*.[110]

As the revival of interest in classical literature led to an emphasis on textual criticism, attention soon turned to the Bible.[111] Now over 1,000 years old, the Vulgate was no longer the fresh translation Jerome had published in 405. Having been copied hundreds of times across Europe by scribes of varying quality, many of the versions in circulation left much to be desired.[112] While this was hardly a new development—Charlemagne had tasked Alcuin of York with producing a corrected edition in the eighth century—by the 1450s it had reached the point that the Pope's own secretary, Lorenzo Valla, was able to write a book listing many of the Vulgate's flaws.[113]

As the sixteenth century began, two separate efforts emerged to produce a more accurate Biblical text. In 1502, scholars in the Spanish city of Alcalá began working on a translation that would become known as the Complutensian Polyglot.[114] Led by Diego López de Zúñiga and financed by the powerful Cardinal Francisco Ximénez de Cisneros, the project took fifteen years to complete and resulted in a six-volume edition of the Bible in Hebrew, Greek, Aramaic, and Latin.[115] Separately from this team, the Dutch scholar Desiderius Erasmus published a Greek version in 1516 as part of his *Novum Instrumentum Omne*, a revised Latin translation of the New Testament.[116] Although the Complutensian New Testament was actually the first to be printed in 1514, a delay in editing the Old Testament meant that it could not be published until 1520, when Erasmus' publishing privilege expired.[117]

Although Erasmus' Greek New Testament was a tremendous leap forward for Biblical scholarship, his first edition was marred by imperfections. None of the seven manuscripts available to him in Basel were complete copies of the New Testament, nor were they particularly ancient—the earliest dated from the twelfth century.[118] Having completed his translation in less than a year, the finished product also contained numerous errors.[119] Three months after its publication, Erasmus resolved to produce a second edition, which duly appeared in 1519.[120] This *Novum Testamentum*, as it was now called, corrected many of the first edition's mistakes and came to over 3,000 pages.[121] Within a few years, it had sold over

2,000 copies—one of which made its way to a German theologian named Martin Luther.[122] In 1522, Luther used it to publish a German translation of the New Testament, which Jacob van Liesvelt used in turn to produce a Dutch translation in 1526.[123] After 1,100 years, vernacular translations from the Greek were once again possible.

At the same time as Erasmus' translation was changing Europe's understanding of the New Testament, scholars also gained a Hebrew version of the Old Testament. In 1525, the *Miqra'ot Gedolot* was published in Venice by the Italian printer Daniel Bomberg.[124] Containing the Hebrew Tanakh and commentaries from some of Judaism's most prominent rabbis, this edition soon became the definitive Rabbinic Bible.[125] Drawing upon a vast number of manuscripts collected by the Masoretic scholar Jacob ben Hayyim ibn Adonijah, Bomberg's publication represented the culmination of centuries of effort to develop a standardised Hebrew text.[126]

Although accuracy had always been important for the Tanakh—with possession of an imperfect copy deemed to transgress the admonition in Job 11:14 to 'Let not iniquity reside in thy tents'—debates over the language and spelling of words had emerged in the first and second centuries.[127] Prior to the fall of Jerusalem in AD 70, scribes had revised all Biblical scrolls against a master copy held at the Temple, but following its destruction, textual control had shifted out of necessity to the rabbis.[128] One second-century rabbi, Akiva ben Joseph, 'attached importance to every particle and grammatical peculiarity' of the scriptures, since the 'traditional spelling of the Scribes [was] a fence to the law'.[129] As the Tanakh originally lacked vowels or accent marks, a system of vocalisation had to be created to preserve its traditional reading.[130] This 'Masoretic Text' had stabilised by the twelfth century under the Ben Asher school, and won approval from the renowned Jewish scholar Maimonides.[131] Following its publication by Bomberg, the *Miqra'ot Gedolot* became a quick success across Europe, establishing itself as a useful tool for both Biblical scholars and Hebrew linguists.[132]

4. The English Bibles

By the end of the 1520s, the Biblical landscape in the West had changed significantly. While the Latin Vulgate still retained supremacy in the Catholic Church, translations were taking hold across Protestant Europe. In addition to Luther's German and Liesvelt's Dutch translations, a French translation appeared in 1530, followed by a Swiss-German translation a year later.[133] Notably absent, however, was a translation in English. Copies of Wycliffe's banned fourteenth-century Bible undoubtedly circulated in secret, but few would have had access to one or been able to read it.[134] In 1523, a scholar named William Tyndale sought permission from the Bishop of London to translate the Greek New Testament into English.[135] When permission was denied, he left England to find a more suitable place to carry out what would become his life's calling.[136] As a child, he was apparently influenced by John Trevisa's translation of the *Polychronicon*, a fourteenth-century history arguing that 'Englisshe preching ys verey Englisshe translacioun. And sich Englisshe prechying is gode and nedeful; thane Englisshe translacioun is gode and nedeful'.[137]

Under this logic, an oral translation already occurred when preaching was conducted in English, so by extension a written translation would be equally 'good and needful'. In 1526, Tyndale published his translation of the New Testament.[138] Within months, several thousand copies were smuggled into England, where the authorities 'tried to stem the flood by hunting down and burning the contraband, warning booksellers, threatening readers, and imprisoning the smugglers'.[139] That October, he was denounced and a campaign of persecution ensued.[140] In 1530, a man named Thomas Hitton was burned after being found with a copy of Tyndale's translation.[141] The following year, Richard Bayfield was executed for smuggling his books into England, and in 1532, a London lawyer named James Bainham was burned after appearing in church with two such books.[142] In 1535, Tyndale himself was arrested for heresy.[143] On October 6, 1536, he was strangled and burned, his last words reportedly, 'Lord, open the King of England's eyes'.[144] But although Tyndale was now dead, his efforts did not die with him. Having translated the entire New Testament and over half of the Old Testament prior to his arrest, he left his supporters a powerful intellectual legacy.[145] Within months of his death, one of his associates, John Rogers, published *The Translation of Thomas Matthew*, an English Bible containing all of Tyndale's work along with translations of the portions he had not had time to complete.[146] This 'Matthew Bible' concealed Tyndale's involvement to avoid controversy and was dedicated to King Henry VIII—the very man who, for so long, had opposed an English Bible.[147]

When the Matthew Bible reached England, its reception was very different from that which had befallen its principal translator. In a letter dated August 4, 1537, Thomas Cranmer—the Archbishop of Canterbury—wrote to the king's chief minister, Thomas Cromwell:

> My especial good Lord, after most hearty commendations unto your Lordship … you shall receive by the bringer thereof a Bible, both of a new translation, and of a new print, dedicated unto the King's Majesty … which in mine opinion, is very well done; and therefore I pray your Lordship to read the same. And, as for the translation, so far as I have read thereof, I like it better than any other translation

heretofore made ... I pray you, my Lord, that you will exhibit the book unto the King's Highness, and obtain of his Grace, if you can, a license that the same may be sold and read of every person, without danger of any act, proclamation, or ordinance heretofore granted to the contrary, until such time that we, the Bishops, shall set forth a better translation, which I think will not be till a day before doomsday![148]

Within a week, Cranmer's request was granted and the Matthew Bible received a royal licence. In a letter dated August 13, Cranmer wrote to Cromwell that 'You have showed me more pleasure herein than if you had given me a thousand pounds, and I doubt not but that hereby such fruit of good knowledge shall ensue, that it shall well appear hereafter, what high and acceptable service you have done unto God and the King'.[149] With the prohibition on English Bibles now over, efforts turned to spreading them across the kingdom. In October 1538, Cromwell issued an injunction requiring 'one book of the whole Bible of the largest volume in English' to be placed in every parish church so that the people might be able to read it.[150]

In 1539, an authorised version known as the 'Great Bible' was published under the editorship of Miles Coverdale.[151] As he had worked with Tyndale and portions of his translations had been used in the Matthew Bible, he was well-placed to undertake such a task.[152] 2,500 copies were initially printed in Paris, but after most of them were 'condemned to the flames' by the Inquisition, Coverdale returned to London where printing could be undertaken with greater safety.[153] Although the Protestant Reformation had finally come to England, a Catholic Counter-Reformation was unfolding across France and much of Europe. In 1546, the Council of Trent declared that 'the old Latin Vulgate Edition ... in use for so many hundred years', was the 'authentic' Bible of the Catholic Church, and warned that no one should 'dare or presume under any pretext whatsoever to reject it'.[154] In 1555, this became the official position in England when Henry VIII's Catholic daughter Mary became Queen. The Great Bible ceased to be printed, and Coverdale, along with many others, was sent into exile.[155] Having escaped persecution in Switzerland, one group of exiles decided to produce a new translation, which appeared in 1560.[156] This 'Geneva Bible' was the first English edition to incorporate verses, using the system developed by Robert Estienne in 1551.[157] Over 350 years after Stephen Langton's introduction of chapters, readers could finally cite passages from the Bible with precision.[158]

With the death of Mary in 1558 and accession of her Protestant sister, Elizabeth I, the political climate changed once again in favour of English translations of the Bible. In 1561, the Queen granted an exclusive patent to John Bodley to print the Geneva Bible for seven years, which was extended for a further twelve years at the urging of Matthew Parker, the Archbishop of Canterbury.[159] Although the Geneva Bible was never appointed for use in the English churches on account of certain passages reflecting 'a more radical Reformed viewpoint than that favoured in the Elizabethan religious settlement', Parker nevertheless wrote in 1565 that nothing should hinder its use, since it would 'rather do much good to have diversity of translations and readings'.[160]

In 1568, a successor to the Great Bible was published under Parker's direction.[161] While this 'Bishops' Bible' quickly overtook the Great Bible as the official church text, the Geneva Bible became the household Bible of English-speaking Protestants.[162] This was the Bible of Shakespeare, and in Scotland a law was passed in 1579 requiring every household with sufficient means to own a copy.[163] In addition to the Biblical text, the Scottish edition also contained some 300,000 words of commentary, including annotations that were against church hierarchies and 'notoriously opposed to the "divine right" theories of the Stuart monarchy'.[164] While meant to guide readers in understanding 'the hard places' of the Bible, the commentary posed a challenge to the Scottish king James VI's absolutist views on royal authority—something he would not forget.[165]

In 1582, an English translation of the New Testament was produced at the Catholic seminary in Douay, France for Catholics who could not read Latin.[166] Underscoring the transformation that had occurred since the ban on vernacular translations 350 years earlier, the preface described it as:

> The New Testament of Jesus Christ, translated faithfully into English, out of the authentical Latin, according to the best corrected copies of the same, diligently conferred with the Greek and other editions in divers languages ... for the discovery of the corruptions of divers late translations, and for clearing the controversies in religion of these days...[167]

By 1610, the Old Testament had also been translated, and the Douay-Rheims Bible, as it would become known, was complete.[168] Although it was treason to attempt to convert anyone to the 'Romish religion', and English Catholics faced heavy penalties for refusing to attend Protestant services, the Douay-Rheims New Testament ironically managed to escape censure after an Anglican clergyman published it in 1589 in a book arguing for the superiority of the Bishops' Bible.[169] As the text was contained in a work that had received official approval, English Catholics were able to lawfully possess it.

In 1603, an event that would have significance for the development of the English Bible occurred when Elizabeth I died and her Scottish relative James VI became king.[170] While travelling from Scotland to claim the English throne, he was presented with a 'Humble Petition of the Ministers of the Church of England, desiring Reformation of certain Ceremonies and Abuses of the Church', signed by over 800 members of the clergy.[171] Listing the matters they felt warranted reformation, the petition indicated the dissatisfaction many felt toward the Elizabethan religious settlement.[172] Although the Act of Supremacy in 1558 had 'clearly extinguished' all 'foreign power and authority, spiritual and temporal' over the English church as a matter of law, a growing faction known as 'Puritans' felt that the Reformation had not gone far enough in practice.[173]

Faced with the worrying possibility of religious instability, the king—now known as James I—convened a conference of 'learned men' at Hampton Court Palace in January 1604.[174] Attended by many of the country's leading bishops, including representatives of 'the puritan element', the conference set about to debate the problems of the church.[175] Although many of the petitioners' grievances were politely ignored, the most significant development occurred when one of the Puritan leaders, John Reynolds, 'moved his Majesty, that there might be a new Translation of the Bible, because those which were allowed in the Reign of King Henry the Eight, and Edward the sixt, were corrupt, and not answerable to the truth of the original'.[176] After Reynolds cited three verses in the Bishops' Bible which he felt had been improperly translated, the Bishop of London dismissively remarked that 'if every man[']s humour should be followed, there would be no end of translating'.[177] With all eyes on the king, James I then expressed his wish:

> that some special paines should be taken in that behalf for one uniform translation (professing that he could never, yet, see a Bible well translated in English, but the worst of all his Majesty thought the Geneva to be) and this to be done by the best learned in both the universities, after them to be reviewed by the Bishops, and the chief learned of the Church; from them to be presented to the Privy Councel; and lastly, to be ratified by his Royal Authority. And so this whole Church to be bound unto it, and none other.[178]

The king then stressed that no marginal notes should be added, since in the Geneva Bible he had found 'some Notes very partial, untrue, seditious, and savouring too much of dangerous, and traiterous conceits'.[179] The new edition was also to retain 'the old ecclesiastical words' and phrasing which supported the established religious hierarchy, such as using 'church' instead of 'congregation' and 'bishop' instead of 'overseer'.[180]

In July 1604, the king announced the appointment of fifty-four translators to six committees—two meeting at Oxford, two at Cambridge, and two at Westminster.[181] Although they were to base their work on the Bishops' Bible, with the text to be 'as little altered as the truth of the original will permit', they were allowed to consult other versions where they felt they agreed better with the Hebrew and Greek texts.[182] The Masoretic Text in the *Miqra'ot Gedolot* was to be the primary source for the Old Testament, with many of the country's experts in Hebrew and the traditions of Judaism appointed to the committees.[183] For the New Testament, they were to work from the Greek text, using primarily Theodore Beza's 1598 edition which built upon the work of Erasmus and Robert Estienne.[184] While Erasmus had only had access to seven manuscripts for his Greek New Testament in 1516, Estienne had used at least fifteen to produce his editions in the 1550s, to which Beza had joined a further two, the *Codices Bezae* and *Claromontanus*, in the 1580s.[185] Beza's edition also reflected comparisons with Immanuel Tremellius' 1569 translation of the Syriac New Testament, and included references to a number of textual variations that occurred across the manuscripts available to him.[186]

Seven years later in 1611, the translators' work was finished and the first copies of *The Holy Bible, conteyning the Old Testament and the New, newly translated out of the Originall Tongues, and with the former Translations diligently compared and revised by his Majesties special Comandement* were printed in London by Robert Barker.[187] What had emerged from the committee rooms of Oxford, Cambridge, and Westminster bore little stylistic resemblance to the Bishops' Bible they had been instructed to revise.[188] Conscious of this, the translators included a lengthy preface to the new Bible justifying the scope of their work:

> Truly (good Christian Reader) wee never thought from the beginning, that we should need to make a new translation, nor yet to make of a bad one a good one ... but to make a good one better, or out of many good ones one principall good one ... having and using as great helpes as were needful, and fearing no reproch for slownesse, nor coveting praise for expedition, we have at the length, through the good hand of the Lord upon us, brought the worke to that passe that you see.[189]

Although it quickly overtook the Bishops' Bible as the official English Bible—helped in part by the other no longer being printed—its impact was initially limited.[190] In a sample of fifty sermons preached between 1611 and 1630, for instance, the new Bible was used only seven times, compared to twenty-seven times for the Geneva Bible and five for the Bishops' Bible.[191] Lancelot Andrewes, one of the Westminster translators, almost never used it, but continued to preach almost exclusively from the Geneva Bible.[192] When the Pilgrims boarded the Mayflower for the New World in 1620, they took the Geneva Bible with them, and in Scotland it was not even published until 1633—eight years after James' death.[193] As late as 1663, when John Eliot translated the Bible into Algonquin for the Massachusetts Indians, he based his *Mamusse Wunneetupanatamwe Up-Biblum God* upon the Geneva Bible, rather than the new translation.[194] By the end of the 1660s, however, it had come into its own as 'the Bible of King James's translation', and by 1723, a historian noted that it was 'commonly called King James's Bible'.[195]

In 1769, it received an update when Benjamin Blayney published a revision of the text.[196] As the Universities of Oxford and Cambridge had both claimed the right to print copies of the Bible in the mid-1600s, differences had arisen over time between their editions.[197] Blayney re-checked the original source texts, corrected mistakes, revised punctuation and spelling, and added over 30,000 marginal references.[198] After nearly four years of editing, his edition was released to wide acclaim, becoming the standard text from which subsequent printings of the King James Bible would be based.[199] One such printing occurred in 1782 when Robert Aitken produced the first English Bible to be printed in America.[200] Responding to a shortage of Bibles caused by the American Revolution, Aitken produced 10,000 copies in Philadelphia.[201] After the Congress of the Confederation was notified of his efforts, they requested a report from the Congressional chaplains on the work's quality, who advised that 'Having selected and examined a variety of passages throughout the work, we are of opinion, that it is executed with great accuracy as to the sense, and with as few grammatical and typographical errors as could be expected in an undertaking of such magnitude'.[202] In response to the chaplains' findings, it was resolved on September 12, 1782 that:

> the United States in Congress assembled, highly approve the pious and laudable undertaking of Mr. Aitken, as subservient to the interest of religion as well as an instance of the progress of arts in this country, and being satisfied from the above report, of his care and accuracy in the execution of the work, they recommend this edition of the bible to the inhabitants of the United States, and hereby authorize him to publish this recommendation in the manner he shall think proper.[203]

5. THE CRITICAL EDITIONS

By the middle of the eighteenth century, the debate over vernacular translations had entered a new phase. Rather than being condemned as dangerous and heretical, attention had shifted to what sources they should be based upon. While the Vulgate still had its defenders, few were prepared to create a new translation that drew exclusively from a now-1,300-year-old Latin translation. In 1782, the Scottish priest Alexander Geddes summed up the feelings of many when he wrote that he was 'determined to translate from the Originals; as I find it impossible to make a tolerable one of the Vulgat[e]'.[204]

A key problem for Geddes and like-minded scholars, however, was that the 'Originals' no longer existed. Moreover, among the ancient copies that had survived, there were often slight variations that made it difficult to establish exactly what the original text had been. Erasmus had encountered this problem in 1516, but others such as Robert Estienne and Theodore Beza had struggled with the same issue.[205] To produce a Bible that most closely approximated the original text, it would be necessary to consult a much greater number of manuscripts.[206] In 1627, one such manuscript had arrived in England after the Patriarch of Constantinople had given Charles I a Greek Bible, the *Codex Alexandrinus*.[207] Although missing part of the Gospel of Matthew, the codex, which would later be dated to the first half of the fifth century, was essentially complete.[208] Thirty years after its arrival, Brian Walton used it to produce his Polyglot Bible.[209] Drawing upon over forty Greek manuscripts, he produced an edition of the New Testament in Greek, Latin, Syriac, Arabic, Ethiopic, and Persian.[210] In 1675, John Fell improved upon Walton's efforts by producing a Greek New Testament that drew upon more than 100 manuscripts, in addition to using the Coptic and Gothic New Testaments as comparators.[211]

While the increase in manuscripts might have produced a more broad-based text, it did not automatically follow that each was equally important. In 1734, a German theologian named Johann Albrecht Bengel published a Greek New Testament that attempted to address this concern.[212] Believing that manuscripts 'must be weighed and not merely counted', he introduced a system that ranked variations based upon how close to the original he believed them to be, with readings from older manuscripts favoured over later ones.[213] Bengel also employed the interpretive approach of *proclivi scriptioni praestat ardua*, ('the difficult is to be preferred to the easy reading'), when evaluating variations, since scribes were more likely to have made a difficult passage easier to understand, rather than made an easier passage more difficult.[214] In 1775, Johann Jakob Griesbach built upon this for his critical edition, which, in addition to ranking variations by their likely probability, also divided the underlying manuscripts into three families—the Alexandrian, Western, and Byzantine—based upon shared similarities.[215] Alexandrian-type manuscripts tended to be characterised by a 'terseness and unrefined Greek style and grammar', as opposed to the 'more expansive and paraphrastic' Western-type manuscripts, while the text of Byzantine-type manuscripts was 'generally slightly longer and more polished'.[216]

In 1831, a German scholar named Karl Lachmann published a Greek New Testament that attempted to replicate the Biblical text as it had existed in the fourth century.[217] Rather than basing his efforts on the editions of Erasmus, Estienne, and Beza, collectively known as the 'Textus Receptus', Lachmann sought to rely upon 'the usage of the most ancient eastern churches'.[218] In place of Byzantine-type manuscripts from the medieval era, he searched for the oldest manuscripts he could find—chiefly the *Codex Vaticanus*—which he then compared with citations from the writings of Origen and Irenaeus.[219] While the age of a manuscript was important, Lachmann also gave consideration to where it had been found:

> Above all we shall take account of the most ancient [witnesses], and among these of such ones as derive from the most widely separated places. ... Where manuscripts from distant regions agree with one another, this is likely to have been propagated from very ancient sources into the various places.[220]

In 1859, one distant region yielded an incalculable find when Constantin Tischendorf discovered the *Codex Sinaiticus*.[221] After receiving his doctorate at twenty-three, he had devoted himself to searching for early Biblical manuscripts, desiring to 'reconstruct, if possible, the exact text, as it came from the pen of the sacred writers'.[222] On one such excursion through the Egyptian desert in 1844, he visited the Monastery of Saint Catherine at Mount Sinai.[223] Located some 250 kilometres north of Sharm el-Sheikh, the monastery had been built by the Emperor Justinian in the sixth century and housed some 3,300 ancient codices and manuscripts.[224] While his initial visit only resulted in the discovery of a partial version of the Septuagint, Tischendorf returned in 1859 with the backing of the Russian tsar, Alexander II, to seek out additional manuscripts.[225]

Shortly before he was to depart, Tischendorf was shown a fourth-century manuscript in near-perfect condition containing the entire New Testament and about half of the Old Testament.[226] As the tsars had become the protectors of the Greek Orthodox Church following the fall of Constantinople, Tischendorf eventually obtained the manuscript with Alexander II's assistance, and in 1862 he published a four-volume facsimile of the *Codex Sinaiticus*, with special ink 'made to resemble that of the original in colour, and the type being greatly varied, so as to imitate the [manuscript's] various shapes and sizes of letters'.[227] Seven years later, he published a critical edition that drew upon the three oldest Greek manuscripts known—the *Codices Alexandrinus, Vaticanus, and Sinaiticus*.[228] Reflecting upon the current state of Biblical scholarship, he noted that:

> Since the sixteenth century, Greek manuscripts have become known far older than those of Erasmus and [Estienne], and besides the Greek, also Syriac, Egyptian, Latin, and Gothic, into which languages the original text was translated in the second, third, and fourth centuries; moreover, in the works of the Christian Fathers who wrote in the second and following centuries, many citations from texts of the New Testament have been found and compared.[229]

As this edition showed, scholars now possessed a wealth of information about the early Bible that would have been unimaginable to previous generations. From an ignorance of Greek in the medieval era to a handful of manuscripts in the Renaissance, researchers now possessed hundreds of ancient New Testament texts—with one scholar, J.M.A. Scholz, single-handedly collecting 616 new manuscripts prior to his death in 1852.[230] With many of them also much older and more complete than had previously been known, a comprehensive picture of the early New Testament was starting to emerge. In 1881, two theologians, B.F. Westcott and F.J.A Hort, published *The New Testament in the Original Greek*, drawing upon twenty-eight years of research.[231] Although favouring the *Vaticanus* over the *Sinaiticus* and other ancient manuscripts, the two noted the significant degree of harmony between Biblical manuscripts as a whole—writing that 'the words in our opinion still subject to doubt only make up about one sixtieth of the whole New Testament ... [and] the amount of what can in any sense be called substantial variation ... can hardly form more than a thousandth part of the entire text'.[232] Moreover, 'there are no signs of deliberate falsification of the text for dogmatic purposes', with the two scholars observing that:

> Accusations of wilful tampering with the text are not unfrequent in Christian antiquity: but, with a single exception, wherever they can be verified they prove groundless, ... The one known exception is in the case of Marcion's dogmatic mutilation of the books accepted by him [which did not have] any influence outside [his] sect. ... The books of the New Testament as preserved in extant documents assuredly speak to us in every important respect in language identical with that in which they spoke to those for whom they were originally written.[233]

As the nineteenth century came to a close, two further developments occurred that would shape the course of Biblical scholarship. In 1897, Bernard Grenfell and Arthur Hunt excavated the ruins of Oxyrhynchus, mentioned earlier in Chapter 4.[234] Uncovering a host of Biblical manuscripts that had been buried, including portions of Matthew and John from the mid-second century, their work yielded an important glimpse of the New Testament from long before the legalisation of Christianity.[235] Having survived the ravages of time, the papyri helped affirm the antiquity of the Alexandrian family of manuscripts and the overall stability of the New Testament texts.[236]

A year after the expedition to Oxyrhynchus, a second important development occurred when Eberhard Nestle produced a critical edition that refined the work of Tischendorf, Westcott, and Hort.[237] Although unable to take advantage of the newly-discovered papyri, Nestle's *Novum Testamentum Graece* moderated

Tischendorf's partiality to the *Sinaiticus* and Westcott and Hort's reliance on the *Vaticanus* to produce a composite text for scholars and translators.[238] While this was an important development for researchers, Nestle's work took on even greater prominence in 1904 when his fourth edition was chosen by the British and Foreign Bible Society to replace the Erasmus-Estienne-Beza 'Textus Receptus' as their source for the New Testament, on account of its 'recognised eminence'.[239] Combining scholastic quality with continuous research, Nestle ensured that updated editions were released as new manuscripts and evidence became available. Upon his death in 1913, his son Erwin took his place and continued to gradually refine the text.[240] By the middle of the twentieth century, the Nestle text had become the world's preeminent New Testament critical edition.[241]

6. THE MODERN ERA

In contrast to the councils that had once restricted access to the Bible, the nineteenth and early twentieth centuries witnessed a proliferation of groups dedicated to spreading it around the world.[242] In 1939, representatives from six national Bible societies met in the Netherlands to discuss ways they could cooperate in distributing Bibles and ensuring high-quality translations.[243] Although the meeting ended positively, their plans to form a Council of Bible Societies suffered a severe setback when Germany invaded Poland five days later.[244] Following the end of World War II, they reconvened in England with seven additional societies to form the United Bible Societies.[245] Responding to the shortage of Bibles in war-torn Europe, the American Bible Society produced 250,000 German Bibles and 900,000 New Testaments, in addition to sending 550 tons of pulp to Germany so local mills could produce the paper for an additional one million Bibles.[246] Arrangements were also made to produce Bibles in Russian and Greek.[247] Before a translation could be published, it was carefully reviewed to ensure that it made sense, represented the customary usage of the language, and—above all—conformed to the meaning of the original text.[248]

As Europe and Asia continued to rebuild, events unfolded in the Middle East that would transform the world's knowledge of the Old Testament. In 1947, shepherds exploring a cave near the Dead Sea discovered seven scrolls that had been sealed in jars.[249] Taking their findings to Bethlehem, they attempted to sell the scrolls to a local antiquities dealer, who—fearing they had been stolen—refused to purchase them.[250] After passing through a series of intermediaries, several of the scrolls were eventually purchased by a local monastery.[251] In 1948, an official at the monastery contacted the American School of Oriental Research in Jerusalem to arrange for an examination of the scrolls to establish their authenticity.[252] On the appointed day, one of the monastery's monks wrapped them in newspaper and carried them across the city in a leather briefcase, where they were presented to the school's interim director, John C. Trevor.[253] Believing the scrolls to be quite old, Trevor photographed them and sent the images to the United States for analysis.[254] Three weeks later, William F. Albright—one of the world's preeminent archaeologists—wrote to him with his 'heartiest congratulations on the greatest [manuscript] discovery of modern times!', noting that he believed the scrolls to date from around 100 BC, making them the oldest Biblical manuscripts ever found.[255]

Before the discovery of what would become known as the Dead Sea Scrolls, the oldest complete Hebrew-language Biblical manuscript was the eleventh-century *Codex Leningradensis*.[256] When news broke that texts that were over 1,000 years older had been discovered, an international search began to locate the cave where they had been stored.[257] In 1949, it was located near the ruins of Khirbet Qumran, and over the next seven years it and ten others yielded hundreds of ancient documents.[258] One cave in particular—Cave 4—produced 137 Biblical manuscripts, including the remains of every book of the Old Testament, save for Esther and Nehemiah.[259] Although it was unclear who had placed the scrolls in the caves or why they had done so, manuscripts found alongside the Biblical texts indicated that an isolated religious community had existed at Qumran for nearly 200 years.[260] While some textual variations were observed, they confirmed the overall stability of the Masoretic Text while also revealing clues about its relationship with the Greek Septuagint.[261] Many had presumed that the Masoretic Text reflected the 'original' Old Testament, but the Qumran discoveries showed that the Septuagint translation often referenced an even earlier version.[262] Much like Origen's lost third-century *Hexapla*, they offered an invaluable insight into the Biblical landscape of Roman Judea.[263] With the advent of carbon dating, Albright's estimate of their age was also vindicated, with the Biblical manuscripts found to date from c. 275 BC to 135 AD.[264]

Contemporaneous with the search for the Dead Sea Scrolls, the quest for the original New Testament text continued. In 1952, a German theologian named Kurt Aland joined Erwin Nestle to co-edit the twenty-first edition of the *Novum Testamentum Graece*, which incorporated a number of previously-unknown manuscripts.[265] Influential as the 'Nestle-Aland' critical edition had become, however, the weight it assigned to textual variations still rested upon the judgment of two scholars. Recognising the limits of this approach, a member of the United Bible Societies proposed in 1954 that an international committee be created to prepare an edition of the Greek New Testament that would be useful to translators and students.[266] The following year, five scholars met to begin work, using Westcott and Hort's edition as a base, along with the editions of Tischendorf, Nestle-Aland, and several others for comparison.[267] Data on several thousand sets of variants were studied—including some 600 variations in punctuation—to produce what the committee felt was the closest reading to the original text.[268] Following ten years of effort, the new edition was published in 1966.[269] Two years later, a second edition appeared, followed by a third in 1975 that incorporated the latest papyri discoveries.[270] So influential was this edition that, in 1979, the Nestle-Aland editors requested and received permission to replace their text with it, thus harmonising the world's two leading editions.[271]

With the advent of computers, the resources available to Biblical scholars increased dramatically. At the University of Münster, the Institute for New Testament Textual Research developed the aim of researching 'the textual history of the New Testament and [reconstructing] its Greek initial text on the basis of the entire manuscript tradition'.[272] In an undertaking that would have staggered the imaginations of earlier researchers, it spent years developing a database containing information on all ancient New Testament manuscripts ever discovered.[273] Whilst Erasmus could only draw from seven manuscripts to prepare his edition, the database now contains more than 700 manuscripts for the Gospel of Matthew alone—thirteen of which predate the legalisation of Christianity.[274] Even 3 John, the shortest book in the New Testament by word count, has over 130 manuscripts presently catalogued.[275] The Institute is currently using this database to prepare the *Editio Critica Maior*, a critical edition that will document the history of the Greek text through the first millennium, with work expected to be completed by 2030.[276] Recent efforts have also focused on the Old Testament, with a number of editions presently underway that seek to establish the earliest attainable text for translators and interpreters.[277]

The quantity of ancient Biblical manuscripts is all the more striking when we consider the relative scarcity of other ancient manuscripts. Only *ten* manuscripts of Julius Caesar's *Gallic Wars* still survive, with the oldest dating from nearly 900 years after the original text was composed.[278] Only *eight* ancient copies of Thucydides' *Peloponnesian War* remain, with the oldest copy dating more than 1,300 years after it was originally written.[279] Then there is Euclid's *Elements*— the most successful mathematical textbook of all time—whose earliest surviving manuscript dates from about 1,200 years after its original composition.[280] Such manuscripts—copied roughly 1,000 years after their originals were made—are seen by experts to be faithful representations of their subject matter. So how much more must we objectively regard the Biblical manuscripts—counted in the thousands, and with dates sometimes only *decades* from when the originals were written—to be accurate reflections of the events their first manuscripts described? In terms of documentary richness, they are without comparison.

Having thus seen how the Bible has come down to the present day, we must return to the question of potential corruption raised at the beginning of the chapter. With respect to whether we can be confident that the modern Biblical text is the same in doctrine and spirit as that which the early Christians had, the answer must be an unequivocal yes. Researchers might still quibble about the placement of an occasional word or comma—and reasonable minds can disagree about the interpretation of certain passages—but the fact remains that no major doctrine is affected by any of the variations presently known.[281] This is particularly evident when one considers Ignatius of Antioch's *Epistle to the Trallians* from AD 108, in which—centuries before the adoption of any official church creed—he expressed Christianity's core beliefs in a single paragraph:

> Jesus Christ, who was of the race of David, of the Virgin Mary; who was truly born, and did eat and drink; was truly persecuted under Pontius Pilate; was truly crucified and dead; both those in heaven and on earth, and under the earth, being spectators of it. Who was also truly raised from the dead by his Father, after the manner as He will also raise up us who believe in him, by Christ Jesus, without whom we have no true life.[282]

Doctrinally harmonious as this might be, however, we must still consider the second—and more important—part of the credibility question, namely whether the original Biblical accounts were truthful in what they asserted. For this, let us now turn our attention to Chapter 6.

6

The Authenticity of the Bible

Whilst the previous two chapters have respectively considered the Bible's creation and transmission, we must now turn to that most critical of questions, whether what it proclaims is true. If it is indeed the record of God's revelations to mankind—the very 'word of God, which also effectively works in you who believe', as 1 Thessalonians 2:13 declares it to be—it would be the height of foolishness to ignore it. But how can we be sure that it reflects the truth? Chapter 5 disposed of the argument that the Biblical text has been corrupted through time and translation, but how can we establish that its authors were correct in their assertions?

In considering the Bible's authenticity, or truthfulness, a multi-disciplinary approach is useful since different forms of proof can be put forward. This chapter will examine five types of such evidence—the historical and archaeological record, the fulfilment of Old Testament prophecy, the style of the Biblical text, the conversion of the Apostle Paul, and the spread of Christianity in its first few centuries despite great persecution. Each approach has certain strengths, and together they reveal a whole greater than the sum of its parts—collectively affirming the truth of what has been written. A broad spectrum of Biblical history will be considered, showing that across all ages its authors have written with an authority that we may trust—even if, in the case of the Old Testament prophets, they did not always appreciate the full significance of what had been revealed to them. With the Bible's authenticity established, we will then be able to consider its doctrines for what they are—the authoritative revelation of the universe's creator to His creation.

1. THE HISTORICAL RECORD

The first form of proof for the Bible's authenticity comes from historical and archaeological records. Although we must be careful to avoid placing more reliance on these accounts and artefacts than they can legitimately support, they often corroborate Biblical accounts of certain events. Much remains unknown about the ancient world, but a considerable body of evidence has developed over the centuries to aid our understanding. New discoveries are also continuously emerging. In 1881, for instance, the *Encyclopædia Britannica's* entry for the Hittites noted with scepticism that 'the lists [in the Bible] of these pre-Israelitish populations cannot be taken as strictly historical documents', and 'It is not surprising that at least two eminent Egyptologists ... should absolutely deny the identity of the [Hittites]'.[1] Twenty-five years later, archaeologists discovered the Hittite capital of Hattusa, including hundreds of tablets containing contracts and official documents, instruction in cult practice, folklore, and historical texts.[2] Today, one can even learn to read Hittite through the University of London—something that would have been unthinkable to nineteenth-century sceptics.[3]

Although the Old Testament—and specifically the Book of Genesis—was primarily written from a Hebrew-centric perspective, it speaks of many events of wider significance. The first of these to consider here is the flood, the great deluge recorded in Genesis 7. The scriptures do not depict this as a mere overflowing of a stream or bursting of a local riverbank, but a terrible flood of judgment so destructive that only eight people and a large number of animals survived in a purpose-built ark.[4] In the face of claims by some that this is merely a fiction—and an unoriginal one at that—adapted from an earlier Mesopotamian flood myth in the *Epic of Gilgamesh*, we must consider whether corroborative evidence can be found.[5] Did such a flood actually happen?

To address a common objection, it is not surprising that the Genesis account would share similarities with another flood story. If anything, this is one of the strongest arguments in its favour. It would be far *more* unusual for the Bible to be the *only* source to mention the flood, given that an event of such cataclysmic magnitude would have left a permanent impression on those who survived it—a collective trauma that would be passed down over generations. Rather than being surprised at the existence of non-Biblical flood stories, we should, if anything, expect to find them in abundance in the legends of ancient cultures around the world. Although they might have small differences in their respective retellings, we should expect enough similarities to link them to the same event. Turning to the aforementioned *Epic of Gilgamesh*, this Babylonian tale from around 1700 BC contains a collection of earlier Sumerian stories.[6] Of immediate interest is an account in Tablet XI of when 'the great gods decided to send down the Deluge'.[7] After agreeing to destroy humanity, one of the gods warned the story's hero, Uta-napishti, to demolish his house and 'build a boat! Abandon wealth, and seek survival! Spurn property, save life! Take on board the boat all living things' seed!'[8] The boat was to be built with equal dimensions and covered with a roof. Uta-napishti then divided it into six decks before sealing the hull with pitch.[9] Eventually the promised flood came:

> The stillness of the Storm God passed over the sky, and all that was bright then turned into darkness. [He] charged the land like a bull [on a rampage,] he smashed [it] in pieces [like a vessel of clay.] For a day the gale [winds flattened the country,] quickly they blew, and [then came] the [Deluge.] Like a battle [the cataclysm] passed over the people. One man could not discern another, nor could people be recognized amid the destruction. Even the gods took fright at the Deluge, they left and went up into the heaven of Anu, lying like dogs curled up in the open.[10]

Despite sharing basic similarities with the Genesis account—a warning is given to build a ship to guard against a coming flood, few are saved, the vessel comes to rest on a mountain, and a sacrifice is then made to the gods—there are also clear differences.[11] Apart from Uta-napishti's ark being built essentially as a square with six decks instead of three and only taking a few days to build, the reason for the flood is never stated, the gods are surprised that anyone survives, and Uta-napishti and his wife are given immortality at the end of the story as compensation for their trouble.[12] It is both similar, and yet dissimilar, to the Biblical account. But before concluding as some have that the version in Genesis is merely a Hebrew copy of a Sumerian legend—despite key details either differing or being left out entirely—we must ask whether there are other accounts of the flood beyond the *Epic of Gilgamesh*. If so, their existence would corroborate the alternative view that Genesis instead preserves a record of humanity's most devastating disaster—an event so awful that it left a mark on the cultures that emerged from the survivors.

Continuing our inquiry in Mesopotamia, in addition to the story preserved in the *Epic of Gilgamesh* we find an account recorded by the Babylonian historian Berossus around 300 BC of how the god Kronos:

> appeared to Xisouthros in a dream and revealed that on the fifteenth of the month Daisios humankind would be destroyed by a great flood... He was to build a boat and board it with his family and best friends. He was to provision it with food and also to take on board wild animals and birds and all four-footed animals. ... He did not stop working until the ship was built. ... After the waters of the Great Flood had come and

quickly left, Xisouthros freed several birds. They found neither food nor a place to rest, and they returned to the ship. After a few days he set free some other birds, and they too came back to the ship, but they returned with claws covered with mud. Then later for a third time he set free some other birds, but they did not return to the ship.[13]

Turning next to Greece, the writer Pseudo-Apollodorus similarly recorded that:

when Zeus would destroy the men of the Bronze Age, Deucalion … constructed a chest, and having stored it with provisions he embarked in it with [his wife] Pyrrah. But Zeus by pouring heavy rain from heaven flooded the greater part of Greece, so that all men were destroyed, except a few who fled to the high mountains in the neighbourhood. It was then that the mountains in Thessaly parted, and that all the world outside the Isthmus and Peloponnesus was overwhelmed. But Deucalion, floating in the chest over the sea … drifted to [Mount] Parnassus, and there, when the rain ceased, he landed and sacrificed to Zeus…[14]

Journeying to India, we find in the ancient Hindu *Satapatha-Brahmana*, written around 700 BC, a warning from a fish to a man named Manu of a flood that would 'sweep away' all creatures:

in … such a year, then the flood will come; thou shalt, therefore, construct a ship, and … embark in the ship when the flood rises … When the flood rose, Manu embarked in the ship. The fish swam towards him. He fastened the cable of the ship to the fish's horn. By this means he passed over this northern mountain. … The fish said, 'I have delivered thee; fasten the ship to a tree. But lest the water should cut thee off whilst thou art on the mountain, as much as the water subsides, so much shalt thou descend after it.' … Now the flood had swept away all these creatures; so Manu alone was left here.[15]

In Mexico, the native historian Ixtlilxóchitl—descended from the rulers of Texcoco—wrote how:

It is found in the histories of the Toltecs that this age and first world as they call it, lasted 1716 years; that men were destroyed by tremendous rains and lightning from the sky, and even all the land without the exception of anything, and the highest mountains, were covered up and submerged in water 'caxtolmoletli,' or fifteen cubits, and here they add other fables of how men came to multiply from the few who escaped from this destruction in a 'toptlipetlacali,' … this word nearly signifies a close chest…[16]

Other cultures have similar accounts.[17] In Wales, the *Trioedd Ynys Prydein* speaks of one of the 'three awful events' of history being 'the rupture of the Lake of Floods, and the going of an inundation over the face of all the lands, so that all the people were drowned, except Dwyvan and Dwyvach, who escaped in a [mastless] ship, and from them the Isle of Britain was re-peopled'.[18] Their ship was no ordinary vessel, but 'carried in it the male and female of all living, when the Lake of Floods was broken'.[19] In northern Canada, the Cree tribe spoke of Wissaketchak, who 'built a great raft and gathered upon it pairs of all animals and all birds, and in that way saved his own life and the lives of the other creatures' from a flood that 'covered not only the earth but the highest mountains'.[20] Another tribe, the Hareskin, spoke of Kunyan, who told his wife that he was building a great raft to save them from a coming flood:

> He told his plan to other men on the earth, but they laughed at him ... Nevertheless [Kunyan] made a great raft, joining the logs together by ropes made of roots. All of a sudden there came a flood such that the like of it had never been seen before. The water seemed to gush forth on every side. Men climbed up in the trees, but the water rose after them, and all were drowned. But [Kunyan] floated safely on his strong and well-corded raft. As he floated he ... gathered by twos all the herbivorous animals, and all the birds, and even all the beasts of prey he met with on his passage. 'Come up on my raft', he said to them, 'for soon there will be no more earth.' Indeed, the earth disappeared under the water, and for a long time nobody thought of going to look for it.[21]

Despite their cultural nuances, all of these stories share the common elements of (i) a chosen figure, (ii) supernatural warnings, (iii) destruction by an unnaturally-devastating flood, and (iv) survival of the chosen via an unusual vessel. Whether the ship is described as the Biblical ark, a floating square, mastless ship, chest, or great raft, it was constructed not as a normal boat on a normal scale but as a large purpose-built vessel of salvation. That such disparate peoples from the Toltecs, Sumerians, and Welsh to the Hindus, Greeks, and Cree all share *the same basic story* proves that the Genesis account could not have been a mere literary invention. The number of differences between it and the *Epic of Gilgamesh*, however—to say nothing of the comparatively minor role Tablet XI plays in the larger story—also diminishes the argument that it was simply copied from a Babylonian text.

Questions still remain about when—and how—the flood occurred, although a variety of theories have been advanced.[22] Common to all flood accounts, however, is the view that the deluge was unnatural—both for the volume of water involved and the speed with which it arrived. We hear of no gradual rises in the water level or slow submersion, but a violent 'smash[ing] in pieces' of the land, a 'breaking' of the Lake of Floods, and water seeming to 'gush forth on every side'. Genesis 7 is no different in this respect, but contains a further detail in verse 11 not mentioned by any other account: 'on that day all the fountains of the great deep were broken up'.

In contrast to the accounts that just mention rain as the source of the flood water, the Bible refers to a second hydrological source—the earth itself. Although further interpretation of this passage ventures into the realm of speculation, the concept of a great volume of water bursting forth from deep within the earth is not inconceivable. As NASA's Cassini spacecraft demonstrated in its flybys of Saturn's moon Enceladus, such a phenomenon can be observed right now in our solar system. Pictured below are some of the moon's 101 known geysers blasting water vapour up to 50-100 kilometres above its southern pole.[23]

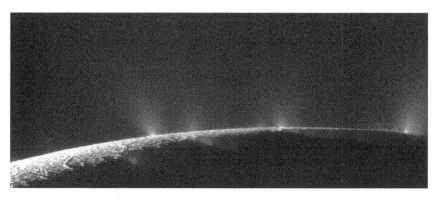

Geysers erupting near the south pole of Enceladus, NASA/JPL (2010)[24]

Could similar eruptions have accounted for Genesis 7:11? Enceladus is different in many ways, but the earth has no shortage of subterranean water. Based upon studies of the earth's mantle, it is estimated that up to three times the entire volume of the world's oceans are stored within its transition zone.[25] Even if this were ignored solely in favour of water in the top two kilometres of the earth's crust, however, there is still enough groundwater to cover the global land surface to a depth of 180 metres—more than sufficient to contribute to a flood.[26]

Other Biblical events are also mentioned in ancient records. With respect to the Tower of Babel in Genesis 11, the Greek historian Alexander Polyhistor recorded how 'giants'—men of great prowess—once 'erected the tower of which history gives account; but that it was overthrown by the mighty power from God, and consequently the giants were scattered abroad over the whole earth'.[27] Abydenus—another Greek historian—wrote of the Assyrians that:

There are some who say that the first men sprang out of the earth; that they boasted of their strength and size; that they contemptuously maintained themselves to be superior to the gods; that they erected a lofty tower where now is Babylon; then, when it had been carried on almost up to heaven, the very winds came to assist the gods, and overthrew the vast structure upon its builders. ... The men, who before had possessed one tongue, were brought by the gods to a many-sounding voice...[28]

Also mentioned are Sodom and Gomorrah—the cities destroyed by heavenly fire in Genesis 19. The Roman historian Tacitus wrote that, near the Dead Sea, there was 'a plain, once fertile, they say, and the site of great cities ... consumed by fire from heaven'.[29] The Greek geographer Strabo recorded 'the common tradition of the natives, that thirteen cities once existed there, the capital of which was Sodom, but that a circuit of about sixty stadia around it', or eleven kilometres, was destroyed by earthquakes and 'eruptions of flames and of hot springs, containing asphaltus and sulphur' and that 'some of the cities were swallowed up, others were abandoned by such of the inhabitants as were able to make their escape'.[30]

Moving further into the Old Testament, we come to the era of physical artefacts. The first item for consideration involves the Biblical account in Numbers 22, where the Moabite king Balak sends for 'Balaam the son of Beor' to curse the Israelites.[31] In verses 5-6, the king pleads for Balaam's help:

Look, a people has come from Egypt. See, they cover the face of the earth, and are settling next to me! Therefore please come at once, curse this people for me, for they are too mighty for me. Perhaps I shall be able to defeat them and drive them out of the land, for I know that he whom you bless is blessed, and he whom you curse is cursed.

Could a mysterious person like Balaam have actually existed? In 1967, archaeologists uncovered the Deir 'Alla Inscription in what is now Jordan.[32] Written on lime plaster on the wall of what was once possibly a shrine, fragments dating from around 800 BC revealed details that not only corroborated Balaam's existence, but also his reputation for spiritual abilities.[33] The first group of fragments—known as Combination I—begins with:

These are the visions of Balaam the son of Beor the man who was a seer of the gods. As to him the gods came to him in the night ... *and Shgr spoke to* Balaam the son of Beor thus: a blazing fire *never dying out* I want to kindle, a fire which will not...[34]

A second group of fragments—known as Combination II—then revealed how unknown individuals 'said to Balaam: you did take in foolishness and silliness an iniquitous word on your tongue … it will be impossible for you to curse anymore'.[35] In their book *Aramaic Texts from Deir 'Alla*, the scholars who discovered the inscription compared the Biblical accounts of Balaam against the fragments and archaeology of the Deir 'Alla site, writing that:

> Much of this [Old Testament] tradition is confirmed by the find of our texts. The text speaking of him is found east of the Jordan. The *stele* on which it was possibly written once stood in a building which to all probability was a sanctuary or at least some kind of sacred place. There is no sign whatever that this sanctuary was dedicated in one way or other to [the God of the Bible], or that He was worshipped there … We meet Balaam here in a setting which lacks any typically Israelite trait. That we find here texts speaking of him and recording his words … proves that he was an important figure in the local religious tradition (even up to the seventh century BC). … Returning to our text, it is not amazing, from what we have seen above, that a prophecy, which stood in the name of Balaam, was still considered an important document in the seventh or eighth century BC.[36]

Even if many of the details about Balaam's life have been lost—likely damaged by earthquakes over the centuries—the surviving texts from Deir 'Alla corroborate the account in the Book of Numbers that he existed, was 'the son of Beor' and that he was believed to have the power of cursing others.

Fragments of the Deir 'Alla Inscription (c. 800 BC)
referring to Balaam in the second line

The second artefact to consider is the Merneptah Stele. Discovered in 1896 in the ruins of an Egyptian mortuary temple, it records with pharaonic bombast Merneptah's victories over his regional adversaries.[37] Much of its propaganda is directed against Libya, but toward the end it states:

The kings are overthrown, saying: 'Salâm!' Not one holds up his head among the Nine Bows. Wasted is Tehenu, Kheta is pacified, plundered is Pekanan with every evil, carried off is Askalon, seized upon is Gezer, Yenoam is made as a thing not existing. Israel is desolated, his seed is not...[38]

The Merneptah Stele
(c. 1208 BC)
with hieroglyphs for 'Israel' inset
The Wellcome Library

Dating from 1208 BC, this is the earliest extra-Biblical reference to Israel in the historical record, with the Egyptians' choice of hieroglyphs corroborating details about the Israelites found in the Book of Judges.[39] Unlike the hieroglyphs employed for Askalon, Gezer, and Yenoam which refer to city-states, the hieroglyphs for Israel—a throw stick plus a man and woman over three vertical lines—were used to denote a rural people without a fixed urban home.[40] Combined with the reference to 'seed' or crops, it reveals that by the thirteenth century BC, Israel had been settled in Canaan long enough to have become an agrarian socioethnic entity powerful enough to be mentioned alongside major city-states, but not so far organised that it could be regarded as a separate country.[41] This is very much the picture of the Israelites recorded in the Book of Judges. Rather than being united under a single king ruling from an urban capital, the scriptures record that they were spread out across the land.

We also see in Judges 2:14 that, when Israel would sin, God would give them 'into the hands of their enemies all around', with a reference to an oppression by the Egyptians in Judges 10:11. Whether this refers to Merneptah is unclear, but his stele confirms Israel's presence in Canaan at the time covered by the Book of Judges, whilst also corroborating details about its pre-monarchical condition.

Eventually the Israelites did organise into a political state. Three kings—Saul, David, and David's son, Solomon—ruled in succession over a united Israel, but in the tenth century BC the country split into the Kingdom of Israel in the north and the Kingdom of Judah in the south.[42] Two artefacts from the ninth century BC reflect this national division, the Tel Dan and Mesha steles. Although neither stele is complete—with the latter purposefully broken by Bedouin tribesmen in the 1800s—they provide important details about the political environment in the ancient Middle East.[43] The Mesha Stele records how 'Omri was king of Israel. He humbled Moab many days because Kemosh was angry with his land. His son succeeded him and he also said "I will humble Moab!" In my days he spoke thus. But I gloated over him and his house. And Israel has certainly fled forever!'[44]

This aligns with the account in 2 Kings 3, which refers to Mesha's revolt against Israel. Furthermore, although the fragments make a precise identification impossible, there is a potential reference to the 'House of David' around line 31, which would be the earliest reference to the Davidic dynasty in Judah.[45] A clear reference to the 'House of David' does appear in the Tel Dan stele, however. Created for the Aramean king Hazael, it records how:

> the king of Israel entered previously in my father's land. ... I slew seventy kings, who harnessed thousands of chariots and thousands of horsemen. I killed Jehoram son of Ahab king of Israel, and I killed Ahaziahu son of Jehoram king of the house of David. And I set their towns into ruins and turned their land into desolation.[46]

This aligns with 2 Kings 8:28, which records how Ahaziah, the King of Judah, 'went with Joram the son of Ahab to war against Hazael king of Syria at Ramoth Gilead; and the Syrians wounded Joram'.

The Mesha Stele (c. 840 BC)
The British Museum

In addition to these Egyptian, Moabite, and Aramean discoveries, artefacts from Assyria also confirm many Biblical details. The first of these, the Shalmaneser III Monolith, commemorates his victory over an alliance of twelve armies at the Battle of Qarqar in 853 BC, mentioning 2,000 chariots and 10,000 soldiers fielded by 'Ahab the Israelite'.[47] Although the Assyrian propagandists might have overstated the number of troops who took part in the battle, the inscription nevertheless reveals that Israel was a significant military power—able to marshal far more than the '200 soldiers of the Usanateans', '500 soldiers of the Gueans', or '1,000 soldiers of the Musreans', who were also considered important enough to warrant inclusion on the inscription.[48] Twelve years after Qarqar, Shalmaneser III caused further hardship for Israel when Jehu—who became king after killing Ahab's family in 2 Kings 9-10—had to pay tribute to him to avoid further conflict. Depicted on the Black Obelisk of Shalmaneser III, Jehu is shown prostrate before the Assyrians, with the inscription above it reading 'The tribute of Jehu, the [son of Omri]. Silver, gold, a golden bowl, a golden vase, golden goblets, golden pitchers, tin, a *hutartu* for the hand of the king, and *puašhatu*, I received from him'.[49]

Left:
*The Shalmaneser III Monolith
(c. 852 BC)*

Right:

*The Black Obelisk of
Shalmaneser III (c. 824 BC)
with image of Jehu inset*

The British Museum

Two generations later, another Assyrian king—Adad-nirari III—continued his grandfather's policies against Israel. Declaring himself on the Tel al-Rimah stele to be the 'king of the universe', he 'received the tribute of Ia'asu [Jehoash] the Samaritan', the king of Israel mentioned in 2 Kings 13:10.[50] Although Jehoash was allowed to remain in power, time was running out for his kingdom. Seventy years later, his successor unsuccessfully tried to escape Assyrian vassalage by forming an alliance with Egypt.[51] But as 2 Kings 17:6-24 records:

> the king of Assyria took Samaria and carried Israel away to Assyria ... Then the king of Assyria brought people from Babylon, Cuthah, Ava, Hamath, and from Sepharvaim, and placed them in the cities of Samaria instead of the children of Israel; and they took possession of Samaria and dwelt in its cities.

This is confirmed by the annals of the Assyrian king Sargon II, who conquered the Kingdom of Israel in 720:

> I besieged and conquered Samaria. I deported 27,290 inhabitants. I removed from thence fifty war chariots. People out of all lands, prisoners of mine, I settled there. I placed my officials over them as governors. I laid tribute upon them in the Assyrian fashion.[52]

Although the Kingdom of Israel had been destroyed, the Kingdom of Judah to its south still remained. Tablet K.3751, an inscription recovered in 1873 from the ruins of the city of Nimrud, mentions tribute being paid by 'Jehoahaz of Judah', the king described in 2 Kings 16.[53] His son, Hezekiah, would feature prominently in Biblical and Assyrian records—undertaking several public works to strengthen Jerusalem's defences. In addition to

Nimrud Tablet K.3751 (c. 733 BC)
The British Museum

Hezekiah's construction of the Broad Wall, noted in 2 Chronicles 32:5, he also 'made a pool and a tunnel and brought water into the city' via an underground passage.[54] An inscription discovered in this tunnel dating from Hezekiah's reign records how the stone-cutters, working from opposite sides, 'flowed water from the source to the pool for 1,200 cubits', a feat of engineering that could only have been undertaken by a reasonably advanced state.[55]

In 701 BC, the Assyrians invaded Judah. Lachish—the kingdom's second-most important city—quickly fell after a brief siege.[56] This is recorded in 2 Chronicles 32:9 and also in a series of stone reliefs that once adorned the walls in the Assyrian South-West Palace in Nineveh. Pictured below is one such relief, showing the moment King Sennacherib gave the order for Lachish's destruction.

Inset from the Lachish Reliefs (c. 700 BC). The cuneiform text reads 'Sennacherib, the mighty king, king of the country of Assyria, sitting on the throne of judgment before the city of Lachish. I give permission for its slaughter'.[57]
The British Museum

Turning to Jerusalem, however, the Assyrians experienced disappointment. Despite laying siege and attempting psychological warfare—with a variety of their religious insults preserved in 2 Chronicles 32:10-19—the city did not fall, with verse 22 noting that God 'saved Hezekiah and the inhabitants of Jerusalem from the hand of Sennacherib the king of Assyria'. Moreover, in contrast to the opulent commemoration of his conquest of Lachish, Sennacherib's annals contain a far more modest account of his campaign against Jerusalem:

> As for Hezekiah, the Jew, who did not submit to my yoke, 46 of his strong cities, as well as the small cities in their neighbourhood, which were without number ... I besieged and took. ... Himself, like a caged bird I shut up in Jerusalem, his royal city.[58]

After returning to Assyria, Sennacherib was assassinated. 2 Kings 19:37 records that 'as he was worshiping in the temple of Nisroch ... his sons Adrammelech and Sharezer struck him down with the sword; and they escaped into the land of Ararat. Then Esarhaddon his son reigned in his place'. This is confirmed in the Esarhaddon Prism, in which Sennacherib's son and heir recorded how his brothers, disappointed by their father's succession plans:

Esarhaddon Prism (c.673 BC) The British Museum

> went mad and whatever was wicked against the gods and men they did, and plotted evil: they drew the sword in the midst of Nineveh godlessly ... Like a lion I roared and my spirit was stirred. To carry on the royal rule of my father's house I clapped my hands ... those scoundrels who were making rebellion and revolt, they heard of the march of my expedition and ... fled to an unknown land.[59]

After reigning for twelve years, Esarhaddon was succeeded by his son, Ashurbanipal—a highly-literate king who assembled a vast library in Nineveh.[60] On a tablet recounting his intellectual pursuits, he wrote how 'I read the beautiful clay tablets from Sumer and the obscure Akkadian writing which is hard to master. I had my joy in the reading of inscriptions on stone from the time before the flood'—the great deluge noted earlier.[61] Following his death in 627 BC, however, Assyria started to collapse.[62] In 605 BC, the remnant of its army was defeated by the Babylonians at

Carchemish, bringing an end to one of the world's most ancient empires.[63] The leader of the Babylonian army was the crown prince, Nebuchadnezzar—later to reign as Nebuchadnezzar II.[64] Following his victory over the Assyrians, he eventually moved south to conquer Jerusalem. Jeremiah 39:3 records the Babylonians' arrival, even listing prominent officials like 'Nebo-Sarsekim, a chief officer'.[65] This is significant since it reveals the importance of accuracy to the Biblical authors and the contemporaneous nature of the writing—only someone familiar with the event could have recorded it in such detail. As the clay tablet below illustrates, Nebo-Sarsekim was indeed an important official. Documenting the transfer of gold to a temple, it reads:

> 1.5 minas (0.75 kg) of gold, the property of Nabu-sharrussu-ukin, the chief eunuch, which he sent via Arad-Banitu the eunuch to [the temple] Esangila: Arad-Banitu has delivered [it] to Esangila. In the presence of Bel-usat, son of Aplaya, the royal bodyguard, [and of] Nadin, son of Marduk-zer-ibni. Month XI, day 18, year 10 [of] Nebuchadnezzar, king of Babylon.[66]

As the British Museum's curator noted, Nabu-sharrussu-ukin and Nebo-Sarsekim 'are clearly one and the same person', with the difference in spelling 'due to the fact that the Hebrew text was originally written without all the vowels … The name represents an attempt to record a strange Babylonian name, where the details of the words were unfamiliar'.[67] Another artefact of interest is the Jehoiachin Ration Tablet, listing the allowance of provisions for 'Jehoiachin, King of the land of Judah'.[68] This corroborates the account in Jeremiah 52 in which Jehoiachin—who reigned for less than four months before the conquest of Jerusalem—was treated kindly in exile and 'as for his provisions, there was a regular ration given him by the king of Babylon, a portion for each day until the day of his death, all the days of his life'.[69]

The Nebo-Sarsekim Tablet (c. 595 BC)
The British Museum

Jehoiachin's Ration Tablet (c. 595-570 BC)
The Pergamon Museum

Taken together, the accounts and artefacts discussed herein—along with others which, if included, would have swelled the chapter to an unreasonable length—reveal an Old Testament thoroughly grounded in the historical record. Although there is much that history and archaeology may never be able to confirm, what it does confirm gives us confidence that the Biblical authors wrote with reliability. From Egyptian hieroglyphs on stone to Babylonian cuneiform in clay, we see a broad congruence between the Biblical accounts and those produced by disinterested—if not hostile—contemporary sources.

2. THE FULFILMENT OF PROPHECY

A second form of proof for the Bible's authenticity comes from the prophecies found in the Old Testament. These prophecies are not mere predictions about what *might* happen in the future, but rather divine declarations about what *will* happen—specific enough to be recognised after their completion, but not so detailed that they could be fulfilled by conscious design. Many of them speak of the fate of individuals, whilst others foretell the destiny of cities and empires. It is to one of these latter types that we now turn.

There are many such prophecies that could be cited in support of the Bible's divine character, but which would require too much of a detour into the historical record to be of use in this chapter. Those interested in exploring them in detail would be well-served by Thomas Newton's *Dissertations on the Prophecies*, which offers a comprehensive treatment of more than two dozen of them.[70] The prophecies against Babylon are notable, however, both for the circumstances of their fulfilment and their continuing impact. Although some might be tempted to argue that Biblical prophecies are only histories written after the events had happened in a prophetic style and manner—an accusation that has never been successfully vindicated—Babylon's fate shows this to be impossible.[71] One must either, to quote the aforementioned Newton, 'renounce your senses, and deny what you may read in your Bibles, together with what you may see and observe in the world; or else must acknowledge the truth of prophecy, and, in consequence of that, the truth of Divine Revelation'.[72]

The city of Babylon was founded along the banks of the Euphrates as early as the twenty-third century BC.[73] From its initial settlement, it grew into one of the richest, most populous, and powerful city-states on earth. Wealth from the east and west flowed to it, with the Greek historian Herodotus noting that:

> in magnificence there is no other city that approaches it. ... In the circuit of the wall are a hundred gates, all of brass, with brazen lintels and side posts. ... The houses are mostly three and four stories high; the streets all run in straight lines ... [and] there was a tower of solid masonry, a furlong in length and breadth, upon which was raised a

second tower, and on that a third, and so up to eight. The ascent to the top is on the outside, by a path which winds round all the towers. When one is about half way up, one finds a resting-place and seats, where persons are wont to sit some time on their way to the summit.[74]

Such was the might and majesty of Babylon. In a time when many throughout the Middle and Near East lived in primitive tents or rudimentary settlements, Babylon was a city of straight roads, multi-level housing, opulent public works, and even an early skyscraper. Centuries before Herodotus' commentary, however, a different description was given by the two Biblical prophets Isaiah and Jeremiah. Warning of the dangers that would come from the Kingdom of Judah's idolatry, they prophesied that its people would be carried off into captivity by the Babylonians.[75] Babylon would be instrumental in God's chastisement of the Jews, but the prophets also recorded that it would eventually become overly oppressive and would itself face divine punishment for its behaviour. So severe would its idolatrous pride and confidence in its own strength ultimately be, its fate would be nothing short of utter desolation. Recorded in Isaiah 13:19-22:

> And Babylon, the glory of kingdoms, the beauty of the Chaldeans' pride, will be as when God overthrew Sodom and Gomorrah. It will never be inhabited, nor will it be settled from generation to generation; nor will the Arabian pitch tents there, nor will the shepherds make their sheepfolds there. But wild beasts of the desert will lie there, and their houses will be full of owls; ostriches will dwell there, and wild goats will caper there. The hyenas will howl in their citadels, and jackals in their pleasant palaces. Her time is near to come, and her days will not be prolonged.

To its initial audience, such a prophetic denouncement must have seemed impossible to imagine—akin to one foretelling the destruction of London or New York today. By the time of Isaiah's prophecy, Babylon had existed for over 1,500 years, boasting strong walls, a large army, and a reputation for unrivalled opulence.[76] Even if the city were attacked, as it frequently had been over its history, the notion that a day would come when it would 'never be inhabited, nor will it be settled from generation to generation', would have struck many as absurd. The Assyrian king Sennacherib might have flattened parts of the city in 689 BC, for instance, but within a few years of his death his son Esarhaddon had repaired the damage.[77] Babylon might not have been invincible, but it had a strong record of survival.

Separately from Isaiah, the prophecies of Jeremiah recorded that the defeat of Babylon, which would deliver God's people from captivity, would be accompanied by a series of unusual events. First, it would fall without a battle, with

Jeremiah 51:30 recording that 'The mighty men of Babylon have ceased fighting, they have remained in their strongholds; their might has failed'. Secondly, the king of Babylon would not witness this himself, but—per verse 51:31—would be informed of it after the city had fallen:

> One runner will run to meet another, and one messenger to meet another, to show the king of Babylon that his city is taken on all sides;

Thirdly, verse 51:36 records the prophecy that the city's 'sea' and 'springs' would be made dry, whilst verse 57 states that God would:

> make drunk Her princes and wise men, her governors, her deputies, and her mighty men. And they shall sleep a perpetual sleep and not awake, says the King, whose name is the Lord of hosts.

Judgment was coming for Babylon, but for many years nothing seemed to happen. Following the Jewish people's unrepentant idolatry, Jerusalem was conquered by the Babylonian king Nebuchadnezzar II in 597 BC, and then destroyed by him ten years later after a brief uprising.[78] The city's inhabitants were forcibly removed to Babylon under the prophesied Jewish captivity, losing both their homeland and independence. As for Babylon itself, under Nebuchadnezzar its influence and opulence reached new heights—ruling an empire from the Mediterranean Sea to the Persian Gulf.[79]

Babylon appeared to be rising from strength to strength. In 539 BC, however—two centuries after the time of Isaiah and a century and a half after Jeremiah—its fortunes changed when the armies of the Persian king, Cyrus the Great, approached the city. Although he had conquered other nations, Cyrus recognised that the conquest of Babylon would prove more difficult. Chief amongst his problems were the city's walls and the Euphrates River. As recorded by the historian Xenophon, the Persians realised after surveying the walls that they could not be taken by a direct assault—they were simply too strong and too high.[80] As for the river that flowed through the city, it was—if anything—an even better defender, being not only wide but deep so that two men standing on top of one another could not have reached its surface.[81] Compounding their difficulties, the Babylonians also refused to come out and fight.[82] Plans were made for a siege to starve the city into submission, but a defector informed them that it had enough provisions to hold out for more than twenty years.[83] Well-guarded and well-fed, Babylon by all appearances was unconquerable.

Nevertheless, Cyrus ordered the construction of a series of deep trenches along the city perimeter, using the excavated soil to erect guard towers. To the Babylonian defenders on the city walls, these muddy fortifications were laughable.[84] Secure in their stronghold, they even engaged in revelry. The Book of Daniel records how the city's ruler, Belshazzar, 'made a great feast for a thousand of his lords, and drank wine in the presence of the thousand'.[85] To appropriately celebrate the occasion, he ordered the gold and silver cups that had been taken from the Jerusalem temple to be brought out for his guests to drink from.[86] But as they were drinking and praising their national deities, 'the fingers of a man's hand appeared and wrote opposite the lampstand on the plaster of the wall of the king's palace'.[87] Frightened, Belshazzar ordered his astrologers and wise men to inspect the writing, stating that 'Whoever reads this writing, and tells me its interpretation, shall be clothed with purple and have a chain of gold around his neck; and he shall be the third ruler in the kingdom'.[88]

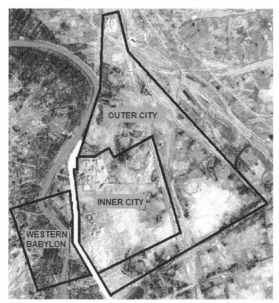

An aerial image of the ruins of Babylon taken in 1965 before the construction efforts of Saddam Hussein altered the site, showing the outline of the city's old walls (in black) and the original riverbed of the Euphrates River (in white) running through the middle of the city.

The Euphrates' course was changed by Cyrus' conquest of the city in 539 BC, and then altered further by Alexander the Great's engineers two centuries later in the 320s BC. In the intervening centuries, it has drifted to cover much of Western Babylon in sediment and water.

Image provided courtesy of the U.S. State Department

Try as they might, the Babylonian officials could not make sense of it. Observing Belshazzar's growing fear, the queen then recalled how, in the days of Nebuchadnezzar, a prophet named Daniel had been able to interpret dreams and explain enigmas. Summoning him to the banquet, Belshazzar repeated his offer of riches and the position of third ruler in the kingdom if he could reveal the writing's significance.[89] After rebuking him for his pride, Daniel gave the interpretation: 'MENE: God has numbered your kingdom, and finished it; TEKEL: You have been weighed in the balances, and found wanting; PERES: Your kingdom has been divided, and given to the Medes and Persians'.[90] Sobering as this undoubtedly was, what Belshazzar did not know was that—at that very moment—hundreds of cubic feet of water were pouring every second from the Euphrates into the Persian trenches. The primitive mud fortifications the Babylonians had laughed at earlier had been a ruse—Cyrus' army had not been digging barrier ditches, but a canal.[91] Having learned that the city's elite would be engaged in an all-night festival, the Persians had waited until dark to breach their upstream trench to drain the river away from the city.

With the river bed now dry, they had a direct, unguarded route into the heart of Babylon.[92] Entering the city with many of its inhabitants asleep or intoxicated, they quickly made their way to the palace where, to quote Xenophon:

> As a great clamour and noise ensued, those who were within [the palace] heard the tumult, and as the king ordered them to see what was the matter, some of them threw open the gates and rushed out. Those who were with [the Persian commander], as soon as they saw the gates unclosed, burst in, and pursuing those who fled, and dealing blows amongst them, came up to the king, and found him in a standing posture with his sword drawn. The [Persians] being numerous, mastered him; those who were with him were killed, one holding up something before him, another fleeing, and another defending himself in whatever way he could.[93]

The Nabonidus Cylinder (c. 540 BC)
The British Museum

Just as Jeremiah had prophesied a century and a half before, Babylon had fallen without a battle, with its 'springs' dried up and 'Her princes and wise men, Her governors, her deputies, and her mighty men' killed in the very hall where they had gotten drunk hours earlier.[94] Moreover, Belshazzar himself had been slain the night of the feast, as Daniel 5:30 recorded. But what of the prophecy about the king of Babylon only learning of the city's fall after the event? Did Belshazzar's death preclude its fulfilment? One could be forgiven for thinking so, particularly since Xenophon referred to the 'king' fighting for his life. But as the evidence shows, it was indeed fulfilled in an unexpected way. Although Belshazzar ruled the city *as* a king, the actual king was his father, Nabonidus. As the Nabonidus Chronicle, a small clay tablet now in the British Museum, shows, the king preferred for many years to live in the Arabian oasis of Tayma.[95] In the ninth year of his reign, for instance, the Chronicle records that 'Nabonidus, the king, stayed in Tayma. The prince, the officers, and the army were in Akkad', with similar entries for other years.[96] Although the prince is unnamed in the Chronicle, we can be sure that it refers to Belshazzar thanks to the Nabonidus Cylinder, which contains a prayer of Nabonidus to the moon-god for his son:

> And as for me, Nabonidus, the king of Babylon, protect thou me from
> sinning against thine exalted godhead, and grant thou me graciously
> a long life; and in the heart of Belshazzar, my first-born son, the off-
> spring of my loins, set the fear of thine exalted godhead, so that he may
> commit no sin and that he may be satisfied with the fulness of life![97]

These artefacts establish that Belshazzar was the crown prince, and that he and
the government remained at home running the country whilst Nabonidus lived
in Tayma. They also explain why he could only offer the position of 'third ruler'
in the kingdom, since his father was the first ruler and he was the second.[98] But
if Belshazzar was the 'king' killed by Cyrus' army, where was Nabonidus? Here, a
second account of the Persian conquest proves useful. As recorded by the historian Berossus, Nabonidus had confronted Cyrus after his army had crossed into
Babylonia, but after being defeated had 'fled with certain others and shut himself
up in Borsippa', some eighteen kilometres southwest of Babylon.[99] Following the
attack on Babylon, Cyrus marched to Borsippa to organize another siege, but
'Nabonidus did not await the end of the siege, and surrendered'.[100] The entry for
his seventeenth year in the Nabonidus Chronicle records that:

> In the month of Tešrit, Cyrus having joined battle with the army
> of Akkad at Upû on the [bank] of the Tigris, the people of Akkad
> fell back. … The fourteenth, Sippar was taken without a struggle.
> Nabonidus fled. The sixteenth, Governor Ugbaru of Gutium and the
> army of Cyrus made their entrance into Babylon without fighting.
> Later, having returned, Nabonidus was taken in Babylon.[101]

Having fled to Borsippa after the fall of Sippar, a defeated Nabonidus returned
several days later to his conquered capital, which had fallen 'without fighting' in
confirmation of Jeremiah's prophecies. But what of the prophecies of Isaiah that
foretold its destruction? Babylon might have been taken, but its people, wealth,
and walls still remained. In fact, following two centuries of importance in the
Persian Empire, it was even chosen by the Macedonian king Alexander the Great
to be his capital—placing it at the heart of an empire from Greece to India.[102] To
the Babylonians living four hundred years after Isaiah, his prophecy of desolation,
to the extent they even knew about it, must have seemed like little more than
wishful thinking. Following Alexander's death in 323 BC, however, Babylon went
into terminal decline.[103] Within fifty years, the majority of its inhabitants had been
transported to the neighbouring city of Seleucia.[104] The few who remained were
unable to keep the city's neglected irrigation system from silting up, causing nature
to start reclaiming the abandoned ruins.[105]

By the first century BC, the Greek writer Strabo recorded that it 'is in great part deserted, so that no one would hesitate [to say] "The great city is a great desert"'.[106] By the fourth century, a Persian monk reported that its ruins had been reduced to a hunting ground for wild beasts.[107] Eventually even the animals and hunters left, with the Jewish traveller Benjamin of Tudela writing in the twelfth century that Babylon was not only uninhabited, but uninhabitable. Nebuchadnezzar's palace—once the opulent seat of power where kings ruled over nations and Alexander the Great lived and died—had become so dangerous that 'Men fear to enter there by reason of the serpents and scorpions, which are in the midst of it'.[108] In 1574, a German physician named Leonhard Rauwolf echoed this after his visit to the ruins, noting that:

> This country is so dry and barren, that it cannot be tilled, and so bare that I could never have believed that this powerful city, once the most stately and renowned in all the world ... could ever have stood there ... the ruins of its fortifications are still visible, though demolished and uninhabited. Behind it, and pretty near to it, did stand the tower of Babylon. It is still to be seen, and is half a league in diameter; but so ruinous, so low, and so full of venomous creatures, which lodge in holes made by them in the rubbish, that no one durst approach nearer to it than within half a league, except during two months in the winter, when these animals never stir out of their holes.[109]

Just as Isaiah had prophesied 2,300 years before, Babylon's desolation was total—having become home to only 'wild beasts of the desert' and creatures that dwelled in the ruins of its 'pleasant palaces'. Significantly, none of this could have been predicted by human effort when the prophecy was given. By the time Alexander embarked on his transformation of the city, even deploying workers to try to redirect the Euphrates back to its old channel, the Book of Isaiah had been in its final form for over a century.[110] It was simply not possible for it to have been edited to include details about Babylon's ultimate fate. Long before its inhabitants left and its buildings crumbled, its destruction had been foretold.

Furthermore, Babylon's desolation was not to be a temporary misfortune, but an ongoing judgment—a *continuing* prophecy that the city would 'never be inhabited, nor will it be settled from generation to generation'.[111] Even the megalomaniacal ambitions of Iraq's twentieth-century dictator Saddam Hussein—combined with the country's tremendous oil wealth—could not overcome it. In an article appearing in the British newspaper *The Guardian* on 4 January 1999, a journalist who had been granted an official tour of the site wrote:

It was supposed to have stood for all time as an emblem of Saddam Hussein's greatness, but the reconstruction of the ancient city of Babylon has hit a sticky patch ... When he first conceived his plan to rebuild [Babylon ...] Iraq was reaping an oil harvest and money was no object. But the years of sanctions have left their mark and Babylon has suffered from neglect. When we arrived for our official tour the site seemed deserted ... At the height of the Iran-Iraq war he channelled millions of dollars to the project, commissioning millions of new bricks to build 60ft-high walls ... [But ...] the walls of the new Babylon ... are already deeply cracked less than 10 years after they were built. ... The first stage, completed in the late 1980s, was supposed to have given way to even grander designs, including the reconstruction of the Hanging Gardens - one of the Seven Wonders of the ancient world - and the Tower of Babel. Now the site has all the atmosphere of a stranded housing project in a state where its only cash-cow has been slaughtered. Deep down among the foundations, where Nebuchadnezzar's ice-house may once have stood, the air is fetid and dank. Oddly, the new Babylon seems to have built-in impermanence.[112]

Given that the prophecies of Isaiah were indisputably recorded long before the city fell into disarray, their fulfilment must be accounted for in one of two ways. Either Isaiah was astonishingly good at guessing—able to imagine what would befall a city he had never seen, in a country he had never visited, in an era far beyond his own—or he was divinely inspired. Consider too the prophecies of Jeremiah—could mere guesswork have foretold that the strongest city in the world's preeminent military power would fall without a battle, or that its conqueror would dry up the river that ran through it, when the Babylonians themselves never considered such a possibility? Could anyone other than a prophet have written that the country's elite would die *en masse* after becoming drunk, or that its king would only be informed of his city's fall after it had already been taken? Histories and archaeological records, written in distant lands for separate purposes long after the prophecies were recorded, corroborate in detail the city's fall to the Persians and ultimate ruin. Only one with divine foreknowledge could have spoken of these events so confidently hundreds of years before they occurred.

3. THE STYLE OF THE TEXT

A third form of proof for the Bible's authenticity comes from an examination of the text itself. Although written by a variety of authors with different personalities over more than 1,000 years, it contains a series of hallmarks that fraudulent writers would have been unlikely to include. The first of these involves the criterion of embarrassment, or the unlikelihood that embarrassing details would have been included if the accounts containing them were not true. Although a sceptic might counter that an embarrassing detail is precisely the sort of thing a cunning writer might include to give their fraud greater credibility, the Bible records too many items of a scandalous nature to support such an argument. When we consider the Jews' zeal for the Law of Moses—particularly after their return from Babylon—it is difficult to imagine them inventing a mythical history full of violators of the very law they so diligently sought to preserve. What pious Jew would have fabricated Abraham—their national patriarch—marrying his half-sister in violation of Leviticus 18:9, or Jacob, the father of their twelve tribes, marrying two sisters in violation of Leviticus 18:18? Would they have been likely to invent a tale about Judah—the very namesake of the southern kingdom—impregnating his daughter-in-law in violation of Leviticus 18:15, or David—King of Israel in its golden age—ordering the death of Bathsheba's husband to cover up his adultery?

These are not minor embarrassments that add colour to a story, but abominations that would have disgraced the violators.[113] Moreover, many Biblical figures are presented with negative personality traits. Moses might have been the Jews' chief lawgiver, but he was afraid of public speaking. Jonah might have preached repentance to the Ninevites, but he was fearful and peevish. In the New Testament, if Jesus' disciples were not squabbling about who was the greatest or abandoning their master in His hour of betrayal, they were slow to understand His parables and initially missed the purpose of His ministry. All of this the Bible records without any effort at concealment. But apart from *what* the Bible reveals, there is also the matter of *how* it reveals it. The majority of the Bible is written in a style that is plain, direct, and without any attempt at countering the anticipated objections of its readers. Rather than presenting an overly sunny account of Jesus' ministry, for instance, the New Testament writers preserved details that acknowledged the difficulties many had with His teachings. Would writers who dealt in suppression and fraud have recorded in John 6:66 that 'From that time many of His disciples went back and walked with Him no more' or in Matthew 13:58 that 'He did not do many mighty works there because of their unbelief'? Would anyone wishing to present him in an attractive light have included teachings which appear at first glance to be unduly harsh? In Luke 9:59-60, Jesus tells a prospective disciple who recently lost his father to 'Let the dead bury their own dead', and in John 6:53-55 He scandalises many by saying 'unless you eat the flesh of the Son of Man and drink His blood, you have no life in you. Whoever eats My flesh and drinks My blood has eternal life, and I will raise him up at the last day'. Verse 60 records the crowd's reaction: 'many of His disciples, when they heard this, said, "This is a hard saying; who can understand it?"'

Then there is the inclusion of details that fabricators would have been unlikely to invent due to the risk of getting them wrong. In Genesis 37:28, the price paid by the slave traders for Joseph is noted as twenty shekels of silver, a detail that could have been safely left out—and indeed *was* left out in the Quran—without detriment.[114] The price accurately reflects, however, the value of slaves in that era. In the Babylonian Code of Hammurabi, the value of a slave is listed as 'one-third mina of silver', with a mina equal to sixty shekels.[115] By the time of Moses centuries later, the price had risen to thirty shekels, and by the eighth century BC it had risen to sixty shekels, showing fluctuation over time.[116] Although one might anticipate that a fabricator would try to add historical detail to build credibility, they are unlikely to have been experts in Bronze-Age slave trading, particularly given the difficulties of acquiring such information.

Other details are sufficiently unusual that it is unclear why they would have been included if they were not true.[117] One instance appears in Mark 14:51-52, which records how, following Jesus' arrest in the Garden of Gethsemane, 'a certain young man followed Him, having a linen cloth thrown around his naked body. And the young men [sent to arrest Jesus] laid hold of him, and he left the linen cloth and fled from them naked'. Why would a fraudulent scribe have inserted this into the narrative about Jesus' arrest? It does nothing to advance the story, nor does it reveal who the naked man was or why he was there. It is the sort of bizarre detail which would not have arisen by chance or design, but which only a real witness to the event would have recalled. Furthermore, the reference to certain Biblical figures by name suggests that they were still alive, and could be called upon as witnesses, when the scriptures were written. Simon of Cyrene, who assisted in carrying Jesus' cross, is identified in Mark 15:21 as 'the father of Alexander and Rufus'—a detail that would have been irrelevant if they had not been sufficiently well-known to a first-century audience. In 1 Corinthians 15:5-8, the Apostle Paul mentions an entire list of such witnesses who saw and interacted with the risen Jesus—the majority of whom were still alive and able to attest to it at the time of his writing:

> He was seen by Cephas, then by the twelve. After that He was seen by over five hundred brethren at once, of whom the greater part remain to the present, but some have fallen asleep. After that He was seen by James, then by all the apostles. Then last of all He was seen by me also...

More unusual still, however, is that the Biblical writers placed women as key witnesses to pivotal events when men would have been seen at the time as more credible. Although women could, and occasionally did, give evidence in Roman society, they were not viewed as optimal witnesses.[118] Discussing this cultural bias in the context of female guardianship, the Roman jurist Gaius acknowledged in his *Institutes* the 'argument commonly accepted' in his era that women, 'on account of their weakness of intellect, are often deceived'.[119] Nevertheless, all four gospels present women, rather than men, as the first witnesses to Jesus' resurrection.[120] John 4:4-26 further upends societal expectations by recording Jesus revealing Himself as the Messiah to a Samaritan woman. To an audience that regarded Samaritans in general as lower than dogs, Samaritan women as ritually unclean, and this particular woman—coming to a well alone at midday, and having had five previous husbands—as an immoral outcast, such an account would have been shocking to the point of scandal.[121] And yet, even as the text records how 'Jews have no dealings with Samaritans', it was to a *Samaritan woman* that Jesus revealed the purpose of His ministry.

As these examples illustrate, much can be learned from the Bible's writing style which supports the truth of its accounts. From the inclusion of embarrassing histories, obscure facts and unusual details, to seemingly-awkward teachings and unexpected witnesses, it is written in a way that fraudulent writers would have been unlikely to produce. That the Bible contains these hallmarks offers valuable evidence for the truth of its assertions—particularly when compared to actual fraudulent texts from antiquity. We must also consider the duration of the writing process. The centuries involved in the Bible's creation make coordination amongst fabricators impossible—a scribe in one century could hardly collude with another centuries later to produce a cohesive narrative, nor could a fraud predict with certainty what would befall a foreign city long after their time. Simply put, if fabricators had attempted to invent the Bible, it would almost certainly have been less colourful, more polished, and with tighter doctrinal presentation than the one we have, even as it omitted details that could not have been known with certainty—in short, far more like the Quran.

4. THE CONVERSION OF PAUL

A fourth type of evidence arises from the conversion of the Apostle Paul. Just as much can be learned from a study of the Bible's writing style, even more can perhaps be gleaned from a study of its most prolific writer, who went from being one of Christianity's worst adversaries to one of its greatest advocates.[122] Given his authorship of much of the New Testament, his motivation for writing is worthy of examination—why did he write what he did?

We first meet Paul under unfavourable circumstances. Stephen—very soon to become the first Christian martyr—has just given a bold defence of his faith before the Jewish Sanhedrin, the same council that demanded Jesus' execution. Furious at what they perceive to be blasphemy, they have dragged him outside to be stoned to death—placing their cloaks in the care of 'a young man named Saul', as Paul was then known, who 'was consenting to his death'.[123] Following Stephen's execution, he enthusiastically took part in the ongoing persecution against Christians, making 'havoc of the church, entering every house, and dragging off men and women, committing them to prison'.[124] Brief as these verses are, they reveal an abundance of detail. It was no accident that he was present at the Sanhedrin's execution of Stephen. Young though he might have been, he was one of them in spirit if not in rank—a rising star educated since childhood by Judaism's greatest teachers, familiar to the rich and powerful.[125] He was a man capable of breaking into homes to carry his enemies off to prison, and—not the type to shrink from violence—could watch approvingly as Stephen was pelted to death with baseball-sized rocks over a ten to twenty-minute period.[126] So committed was he to the cause of persecution that he even received permission for a special assignment to round up Christians in Damascus.[127] Armed with guards and letters from the high priest authorising his mission, he entered Syria full of confidence in the righteousness of his cause.

And then, his life changed forever. As he would later tell King Agrippa and Porcius Festus, the Roman governor presiding over his trial, at midday on his journey he suddenly 'saw a light from heaven, brighter than the sun' shining around him and his companions.[128] After falling to the ground, he then heard a voice saying 'Saul, Saul, why are you persecuting me?,' which identified itself as 'Jesus, whom you are persecuting'.[129] After being instructed to proceed to Damascus, Paul—the very man who had previously rounded up Christians with enthusiasm, 'punished them often in every synagogue', and cast votes for their executions— became a Christian himself.[130] How are we to explain this unusual transformation? One moment he was pursuing a mission of vengeance against the Christians, and less than a week later he had become one. Furthermore, he did not simply become a quiet follower in obscurity, but gained prominence as a long-suffering and widely-travelled apostle—founding, visiting, and writing to churches all across the Mediterranean world, before ultimately losing his life as a martyr in Rome. Only three possible explanations could account for this behaviour, which will now be considered in detail. First, there is the possibility that he was an imposter—someone who knew that Christianity was untrue but who faked a conversion and went along with it for his own benefit. Secondly, that he was a religious enthusiast, or someone who genuinely thought he had experienced something real, but because of a weak mind or excitable imagination actually had not. Under these possibilities, Paul either knowingly set out to deceive, or deceived himself. Finally, we are left with the conclusion that what he experienced was real—so real that his life could never be the same.

Looking first at the possibility that Paul was an imposter, he would have had no rational motive for pretending to be an apostle, nor could he have carried out such a trick successfully. Consider the circumstances in which he converted to Christianity. Jesus had recently been put to death as an imposter and blasphemer. His crucifixion between two criminals had been lengthy and excruciating. His disciples had abandoned Him, only to regroup days later to spread the word that He had risen from the dead. The chief priests had escalated their persecutions—throwing some of His followers in prison and even putting some to death. Paul had approved of all this and had been instrumental in attacking the church. He was, by his own description, a 'Hebrew of the Hebrews', a loyal Pharisee zealous for the Jewish law, and someone inimically hostile to Christianity.[131]

At this moment and under these circumstances, Saul the Pharisee became Paul the Christian. If we consider that he did so knowing that it was all a lie, what motive could have driven him? Was it for wealth? By converting, he not only lost all that he had, but the hope of ever acquiring more. Those he left behind were the wealthy and powerful—those he joined were the impoverished and oppressed. As he would tell the Corinthians in his first letter, 'To the present hour we both hunger and thirst, and we are poorly clothed, and beaten, and homeless. And we labour, working with our own hands'.[132] Later in the Book of Acts when saying goodbye to the elders at Ephesus, he reminds them that 'I have coveted no one's silver or gold or apparel. Yes, you yourselves know that these hands have provided for my necessities, and for those who were with me'.[133] From the poverty of the church when he joined it and his behaviour inside it, Paul could have had no plausible thought of increasing his wealth.

But what about for reputation? Many will sacrifice a lucrative career for a prestigious one, but here again we come up short. Those Paul left behind were the leaders of society; those he joined were then viewed with the greatest contempt. The leaders of the newly-formed church were of the lowest birth, education, and rank. They did not have a single advantage of skill, learning or achievement to recommend them. Their doctrines went against those taught by the people considered to be the wisest in society. Their miracles were imputed to either magic or fraud. The very author of their faith had been crucified as a criminal. Could Paul really hope to flatter himself by joining a group like this? And what about outside Judea? As he would write in 1 Corinthians 1:23, 'we preach Christ crucified, to the Jews a stumbling block and to the Greeks foolishness', before recording how 'We have been made as the filth of the world, the offscouring of all things until now'.[134] For an ambitious man, this would have been an unlikely way of seeking a glorious reputation.

But if not for reputational gain, then what about power? But power over whom—sheep driven to the slaughter, whose very shepherd had been murdered only a little while before? All Paul could have hoped to gain from this power would have been a greater dose of wrath. Could he expect more mercy from the chief priests than they had shown to Jesus? Would they not have been even angrier with the betrayer of their cause than against someone who had never been a part of their circle? Was power over such a poor and contemptible group really worth the risk and danger? Although some are so fond of power that they will seek to attain it no matter what, and be pleased to wield it no matter over whom, Paul does not fit this profile. In 1 Corinthians 15:9, he states 'I am the least of the apostles, who am not worthy to be called an apostle, because I persecuted the church of God'. Even in the churches he established, he never pretended to any superiority over the other apostles. In 1 Corinthians 1:12-15 and 3:5, he wrote:

> each of you says, 'I am of Paul,' or 'I am of Apollos,' or 'I am of Cephas,' or 'I am of Christ.' Is Christ divided? Was Paul crucified for you? Or were you baptized in the name of Paul? I thank God that I baptized none of you except Crispus and Gaius, lest anyone should say that I had baptized in my own name. ... Who then is Paul, and who is Apollos, but ministers through whom you believed, as the Lord gave to each one?

Paul might have been instrumental in guiding the church, but he never sought to rule it nor did he use his position to satisfy a worldly pleasure. We do not find him granting himself special privileges like Muhammed—allowed eleven wives instead of the four permitted to other Muslim men—nor did he make himself the head of a political community like the Mormon founder Joseph Smith.[135] The authority he exercised was purely of a spiritual nature, without any mixture of worldly dominion, wealth, or personal gratification so frequently sought after by religious imposters.

If we accept that Paul had nothing to gain by being an imposter, what did he stand to lose? To start with, all of the wealth he could have hoped to obtain was lost. He became a traitor to his friends and gave up a reputation acquired by the work of his whole life. As he wrote in Galatians 1:14, 'I advanced in Judaism beyond many of my contemporaries in my own nation, being more exceedingly zealous for the traditions of my fathers'. Paul was not simply a Jew but a Pharisee—the strictest sect in their culture—and one who had been held in esteem by his peers and elders. Would he really have given up all this—his wealth, friendships, prestige, and culture—for something he knew to be untrue? Moreover, these losses came with tremendous suffering. Recounting his experiences in 2 Corinthians 11:24-29:

> From the Jews five times I received forty stripes minus one. Three times I was beaten with rods; once I was stoned; three times I was shipwrecked; a night and a day I have been in the deep; in journeys often, in perils of waters, in perils of robbers, in perils of my own countrymen, in perils of the Gentiles, in perils in the city, in perils in the wilderness, in perils in the sea, in perils among false brethren; in weariness and toil, in sleeplessness often, in hunger and thirst, in fastings often, in cold and nakedness—besides the other things, what comes upon me daily: my deep concern for all the churches.

Are these experiences really those of an imposter? Some will suffer—and perhaps even die—for what they believe to be true, but Paul was a living witness to Christianity's foundation, making it unreasonable for him to have endured all this in the knowledge that it was false, *and for no apparent gain*. It would also have been impossible for him to have been an imposter on his own. The faith he became a leader in was not of his own invention, meaning he lacked the power to create its doctrines. He had never met with Jesus before His death nor with the apostles, except perhaps as their persecutor. If he was to pretend to be one, however, he would have needed a precise knowledge of what would eventually be recorded in the gospels. The New Testament had not been written yet, so he could not simply open a Bible to read about Christianity. And yet, if he was to succeed as an imposter it was imperative that he got everything right since he would have exposed himself as a fraud to those with more knowledge than he had. He might have picked up a few ideas about Christianity from those he persecuted, but not enough to qualify him to be an apostle through guesswork.

He would also have needed an apparent power of working miracles, since the apostles appealed to this as proof of their divine mission. Without this, how could he gain admission to their inner circle? Would a group that stood firm in the face of persecution and death really confess themselves as fraudulent magicians to their tormentor, in the hope that he would become their accomplice? Consider too that, when he arrived in Damascus with a tale of a light from heaven which struck him blind, it would have been easy to ask his travelling companions if this had really happened. What could motivate them to betray their orders and lie for someone they might not even have known prior to the journey?

Assuming Paul managed to convince the believers in Damascus, his position as an apostle could never be secure until he had been accepted by the other apostles—particularly since he had recently been their mortal enemy. The quicker he was recognised as their equal, the safer his position would be. And yet, we read in Galatians 2:14 how Paul confronted the Apostle Peter in Antioch in front of the other disciples, writing that 'If you, being a Jew, live in the manner of Gentiles and not as the Jews, why do you compel Gentiles to live as Jews?' If Paul was an imposter, how could he afford to offend the one person it was in his greatest interest to please? Such freedom of speech belongs to truth alone.

Having shown that Paul would have had no motive or opportunity to become an imposter, and that he would have required considerable help to pull it off with any chance of success, we must now consider whether he was a religious enthusiast who deceived himself into believing something untrue. We know that there are some who are convinced, perhaps due to mental illness or an overactive imagination, that they have experienced something highly implausible. Moreover, a 2012 article in the *Journal of Neuropsychiatry and Clinical Neurosciences* observed that 'as many as 60% of those with schizophrenia have religious grandiose delusions consisting of believing they are a saint, God, the devil, a prophet, Jesus, or some other important person'.[136] Was Paul such a case?

It would undoubtedly strike some as implausible that he could have seen the risen Jesus, and yet the evidence does not support a charge of him being an enthusiast. If we look at the historical profile of religious enthusiasts, several common themes emerge. Often there can be an underlying diagnosis of bipolar disorder, with those who report hallucinations typically less educated and suffering from higher anxiety than the general population.[137] Religious delusions also generally take one of three forms: 'persecutory (often including the Devil), grandiose (involving messianic beliefs) and belittlement (including beliefs about having committed unforgiveable sins)'.[138] In psychotic states, the onset of these beliefs often marks a change in the person's life, with a 'deterioration of social skills and personal hygiene'.[139] To these psychological elements we might add the characteristics of enthusiasm condemned by eighteenth and nineteenth-century writers when it was on the rise: ignorance, gullibility, and vanity.[140]

Taking these in turn, did Paul possess a mental disorder? His writings show that he had a passion for his endeavours, zealous in his persecution of the church and later in his work to spread the Gospel. But having a passionate streak does not necessarily make someone a religious enthusiast. Paul's zeal was strong, but also tempered with prudence and civility. We read in 1 Corinthians 9:20-22 how he did not allow it to compromise his efforts in a blind or inconsiderate manner, but—on issues which were not doctrinally critical—he became all things to all people so that by all possible means he might save some: 'to the Jews I became as a Jew, that I might win Jews; to those who are under the law, as under the law ... to the weak I became as weak, that I might win the weak'. His personality gave him a passion for preaching, but he did so with sensitivity to his audience.

But what about a depressive or melancholy state? We know that Paul was capable of feeling negative emotions, but nothing in his writings shows that he was more inclined to them than anyone else or experienced them to an unhealthy degree. He certainly felt great remorse for his persecutions of the early church, but we do not read of any gloomy sacrifices or extravagant, self-inflicted wounds such as we see with some who fall into the enthusiast category.[141] He bore the sufferings he met with, but brought none on himself if they could be avoided. On the contrary, after being taken into the Roman barracks in Jerusalem for questioning after a disturbance at the Temple, he pleaded the privilege of being a Roman citizen to avoid being whipped.[142]

As for ignorance, Paul appears to have been a master not only of the Jewish learning, but also of the Greek. In Acts 22:3, he recounts how he was brought up in Jerusalem 'at the feet of Gamaliel, taught according to the strictness of our fathers' law'. Gamaliel was not only one of the most senior members of the Sanhedrin but also one of Judaism's most prominent teachers—revered for his wisdom long after his death.[143] We must also note that, in an age in which less than 3% of the population in Judea were estimated to be able to read and write, Paul composed letter after letter—many of which are included in the New Testament.[144] He was also a keen observer of his surroundings and familiar with Greek philosophy and culture. In Acts 17:28 when preaching before the Athenian philosophers, he speaks of God by saying 'for in Him we live and move and have our being, *as also some of your own poets have said,* "For we are also His offspring"'.[145] Paul was clearly not an ignorant man.

As for gullibility, the history of his life shows that he was hardly the type to believe in something on the basis of insufficient evidence. Instead, he seems to have been completely unmoved before his conversion by the stories of Jesus' miracles, which he would have undoubtedly heard about living in Jerusalem as a Pharisee—one of the groups Jesus often preached against. When Peter and John healed a crippled man at the Temple, their account of the miracle to the High Priest and scribes did not sway him, nor did he believe when news of the apostles' miraculous escape from prison became known.[146] Far from being the type who believed in something too easily, he appears to have been so prejudiced against Christianity that nothing less than the irresistible evidence of his own senses, clear from all possibility of doubt, could have overcome his unbelief.

Finally, we come to vanity. This can lead people of a warm temper and religious mindset to think they are worthy of special favours from God. In extreme cases, it can lead to claims that they have been given a new revelation, such as Joseph Smith's publication of the Book of Mormon in 1830, supposedly copied from golden tablets left by ancient prophets in New York. With Paul, however, no such charge can be made. In Ephesians 3:8, he describes himself as 'less than the least of all saints'. In Philippians 2:3, he instructs Christians to 'Let nothing be done through selfish ambition or conceit, but in lowliness of mind let each esteem others better than himself'. And, in 1 Timothy 1:15, he states 'Christ Jesus came into the world to save sinners, of whom I am chief'. These are not the words of vanity, nor does their context suggest false modesty.

From the evidence presented, Paul lacked the characteristics of an enthusiast. Far from being manic, vain, or ignorant, he was instead humble, intelligent, and discerning. But allowing for the sake of argument that his passion was enough to make him an enthusiast, it is still unlikely that he could have deceived himself into believing he was an apostle called by Jesus. The delusions of an enthusiast are undoubtedly strong, but they typically act in conformity to the mind's pre-existing opinions. When he set out for Damascus with authority to bring Christians by force to Jerusalem, his mind was firmly against Jesus and His followers. With such a mental state, it would have been less surprising if he had claimed to have seen a vision from heaven declaring the anger of God against the Christians and commanding him to persecute them without mercy. But at that very instant, when he was on a mission of vengeance, he was called to be an apostle of the same Jesus who but a minute before he had deemed an imposter and blasphemer. Could this really be the effect of enthusiasm? His passion was carrying him violently in one direction when his senses and reason suddenly and irreversibly took him in the opposite direction. The conduct of the remainder of his life proves that he was no enthusiast.[147] Then there are his multiple demonstrations of miraculous power, from surviving a shipwreck in Malta and venomous snakebite on the beach to healing the father of one of the island's leading citizens—an act which led to the conversion of the nation.

Having seen that Paul could not have been an imposter or enthusiast, the sole remaining explanation for his conduct is that what he experienced and wrote about was true. Drawing upon his knowledge of Jewish and Greek learning, he preached the sacrificial death and resurrection of Jesus across the Mediterranean world—repeatedly proving his divine mandate with miraculous power. His life was one of hardship and discomfort, dominated by the preaching of a message to those who were often unwilling to hear it. Like many early Christians, he also sealed his testimony through the blood of martyrdom in Rome.[148]

5. The Spread of Christianity

The martyrdom of Paul, along with many of the other first Christians, leads to the final type of evidence this chapter will consider—the spread of Christianity. When we examine the difficulties faced by the early Christians in their interactions with the pagan world, their adherence to their faith—even to the point of death—offers strong evidence in favour of the Bible's teachings. Although the remnants of paganism today consist of little more than historical artefacts—myths and marble statues—in the first century it was a vibrant world of colours, smells, and sounds. Serious men studied the flight of birds for omens of war, and government priestesses in Rome carefully tended sacred fires.[149] Cities across the empire felt pride at their glittering array of temples, which often contributed significantly to their local economies.[150] Paganism was the religion of the state, the time-honoured faith, and a confident force at its apex.

Against this religious kaleidoscope stood a motley collection of Christian fishermen and other converts from Judaism—a religion despised across much of the empire for its beliefs. To the Romans, Christianity seemed almost designed to cause offence. Its founder, hailing from a provincial backwater, had been shamefully executed between two criminals. Its teachers—apart from a few notable exceptions—were minimally educated, if not illiterate. Its adherents were generally poor, with the upper and educated classes having largely rejected it.[151] Its doctrines were not only austere but exclusivist—denying the truth of every article of their mythology and every object of their worship. It accepted no compromise with paganism, but pronounced its gods false and their worship in vain.[152] Assimilation into the pantheon of religious belief was impossible.

Faced with these unfavourable circumstances, how did such a religion ever attract anyone—much less transform the world? In contrast to Islam, it did not spread through conquest, nor did it offer prospective followers sensual delights and worldly gratification. Instead, it denounced mankind's sinfulness whilst proclaiming the need for repentance, self-denial, and spiritual renewal.[153] Though lacking all worldly advantages that could have aided it, however, what it did possess was sheer miraculous power. Men who might never have seen the inside of a school could suddenly preach in foreign languages with native fluency.[154] Burly fishermen who had never studied medicine could heal the sick or lame with a touch.[155] Disciples who had once timidly forsaken their master now boldly proclaimed His resurrection before the very men who had arranged His execution.[156] Such unnaturalness undoubtedly drew the attention of those who witnessed it, particularly those in the lower ranks who were not part of the pagan politico-economic system. The result was an unparalleled number of Christian conversions across the Roman world. In a letter to the Emperor Trajan, one Roman governor reported with alarm how Christianity had quickly spread throughout his province:

> I have never been present at the resolutions taken concerning the Christians ... Are those, who repent, to be pardoned? Or is it to no purpose to renounce Christianity, after having once professed it? ... the sum total of their fault, or of their error, consisted in assembling upon

a certain stated day before it was light, to sing alternatively among themselves hymns to Christ, as to a God; binding themselves by oath, not to be guilty of any wickedness … To me an affair of this sort seems worthy of your consideration, principally from the multitude involved in the danger. For many persons of all ages, of all degrees, and of both sexes, are already, and will be constantly brought into danger by these accusations. Nor is this superstitious contagion confined only to the cities, it spreads itself through the villages and country.[157]

The speed and extent of Christianity's spread across the Roman world was unprecedented. By comparison, Stoicism—despite sharing many of Christianity's views on self-denial and moral reformation—never became a mass movement and even after 350 years remained largely confined to the cultural elite.[158] Something extraordinary had to convince so many to reject the inclusive comforts of paganism—at great risk to themselves—for a strict new religion that utterly opposed it, and the only explanation that can satisfactorily account for this is the miraculous power that accompanied its propagation.

Much can be cited in support of this from the Bible, but accounts from sources highly antagonistic to Christianity also testify to such power. The Jewish Talmud denounced Jesus as a powerful sorcerer who enticed Israel into idolatry.[159] The satirist Lucian of Samosata recorded Him as a 'famous' magician who 'was crucified … for having introduced these novel mysteries into the world'.[160] Celsus, a philosopher, claimed that Jesus' miracles were merely the products of dark arts learned in Egypt, and that it was 'a most intolerable Thing, that from the same Actions He by all Means, must be denominated a God, and Others be branded with the Infamous Title of Magicians' for performing them.[161] Even the Emperor Julian—Rome's last pagan emperor and one of Christianity's greatest adversaries—candidly admitted in his treatise *Against the Galileans* that miracles were performed, although he curiously dismissed them as 'no deed which deserves to be mentioned, unless any one fancies that to cure the blind and the lame, and to exorcise those possessed by demons in the villages of Bethsaida and Bethania rank among the greatest undertakings'.[162]

All of these sources were united by a severe dislike of Christianity and would not have credited it with supernatural powers unless they could not be ignored. Even if one were to disregard the Biblical accounts of Christianity's spread, the clear impression from pagan accounts is that *something* supernatural accompanied it. Stronger testimony still, however, comes from the deaths of the first-century martyrs. Not only did they have the best opportunity to evaluate the Bible's credibility first-hand, but its truth was of the highest concern to their fate and happiness. As the English writer Samuel Johnson once remarked, 'when a man knows he is to be hanged … it concentrates his mind wonderfully', and their refusal to denounce Christianity in their final hours—knowing the horrors that awaited them if they refused, and the release they could expect if they relented—testifies to their certainty that what they had witnessed was true.[163] They died because the facts had so completely convinced them of Christianity's truth that nothing else—including death—mattered.[164] All religions may have some willing to die for what they *believe* to be true, but none would willingly embrace a brutal execution for what they *know* to be false.

Imagine the difficulties of their final moments. Suppose that you were accused of belonging to a religion regarded as traitorous by the state. As your children watch, you are dragged away to join one of your co-religionists who has been fixed by the chin to a stake and covered in pitch to burn as a human candle. As the flames draw near to your tortured friend, you are told that the same will very shortly happen to you. In these circumstances, how convinced would you have to be that your religion was true? Would anything short of *utter certainty* be enough for you to forsake the love of family and life to—quoting the first-century writer Juvenal—'stand burning in [your] own flame and smoke' for a religion you had recently converted to?[165] This, for the avoidance of doubt, actually occurred in AD 64 when the Emperor Nero attempted to shift blame for the Great Fire of Rome onto the Christians. As recorded by Tacitus:

> Nero fastened the guilt and inflicted the most exquisite tortures on a class hated for their abominations, called Christians by the populace. Christus, from whom the name had its origin, suffered the extreme penalty during the reign of Tiberius at the hands of one of our procurators, Pontius Pilatus, and a most mischievous superstition, thus checked for the moment, again broke out not only in Judaea, the first source of the evil, but even in Rome, where all things hideous and shameful from every part of the world find their centre and become popular. Accordingly, an arrest was first made of all who pleaded guilty; then, upon their information, an immense multitude was convicted, not so much of the crime of firing the city, as of hatred against mankind. Mockery of every sort was added to their deaths. Covered with the skins of beasts, they were torn by dogs and perished, or were nailed to crosses, or were doomed to the flames and burnt, to serve as a nightly illumination, when daylight had expired. Nero offered his gardens for the spectacle, and was exhibiting a show in the circus, while he mingled with the people in the dress of a charioteer or stood aloft on a car. Hence, even for criminals who deserved extreme and exemplary punishment, there arose a feeling of compassion; for it was not, as it

seemed, for the public good, but to glut one man's cruelty, that they were being destroyed.[166]

Tacitus' account reveals several items of importance. It corroborates the Gospel accounts of Jesus' execution with its mention of 'Christus', His crucifixion ('the extreme penalty'), the era in which He died ('the reign of Tiberius'), the official who presided over it ('Pontius Pilatus') and the place where it occurred ('Judaea'), whilst also revealing that, by AD 64, Christianity was sufficiently established in Rome—a city of over 1,000,000 people—that its adherents constituted a distinct class that could readily be identified as scapegoats.[167] Within a mere thirty years of Jesus' crucifixion, the city had gone from having no Christians to 'an immense multitude' prepared to suffer terribly rather than renounce their faith in Him. That many of them actually did suffer unimaginable consequences is all too apparent, with their executions eventually giving rise to 'a feeling of compassion', even amongst those who initially felt they deserved such 'extreme and exemplary punishment'.[168]

The impact on those who interacted with the early Christians could also be long-lasting and life-altering. As a youth, Polycarp, the Bishop of Smyrna, had studied under the Apostle John and others who had seen and known Jesus. Years later as an old man, he calmly refused to denounce his faith despite repeated attempts by the Roman proconsul—ultimately meeting his death in an arena surrounded by a baying mob.[169] His contemporary and fellow bishop, Ignatius of Antioch, wrote to the Christians in Rome whilst awaiting his own execution that 'I know what is expedient for me. ... Come fire and cross and conflicts with wild beasts, wrenching of bones, mangling of limbs, crushing of the whole body; come grievous torments of the devil upon me—only may they aid me in attaining unto Jesus Christ'.[170] These men, and many others like them, died after a lifetime of mature reflection on the credibility of those who first proclaimed Christianity. Their writings do not show them to be rash, intemperate sorts who latched onto any cause for self-glorification, but sober-minded, even-tempered scholars who were convinced by the truth of their assertions. They did not regard the Bible as a mere collection of stories, but a revelation of truth as real as the blades at their throats and flames at their feet. For them, there could be no doubt as to the veracity of its teachings—they had experienced them first-hand.

Taken together, it is difficult to imagine more effective proofs for the Bible's authenticity. History and archaeology corroborate important facts, a study of the text reveals its unscripted nature, and the fulfilment of prophecy shows an unmistakeable power behind its claim to inspiration. Early Christians willingly went to their often-brutal deaths convinced of these truths. They did not rely upon second-hand knowledge as we must, but witnessed the supernatural acts that accompanied Christianity's propagation—power well-attested by writers critical of their beliefs. Within a generation of Jesus' crucifixion, the number believing He had risen from the dead had exploded in spite of the prejudice and violence they received from the governing authorities. When the New Testament books were written by Paul and others, their accounts agreed with what their early readers had seen and heard to be true. Their confidence in the Bible's veracity then further justifies our confidence in it today. From a consideration of the evidence, we may truly regard the Bible as the inspired word of God.

7

The Great War

To summarise the preceding three chapters, we have seen how the Bible was created and preserved over millennia without material change, giving us confidence that the text we have today is effectively identical to the original manuscripts. We have also seen how a variety of evidence points to the truthfulness of its accounts, from archaeology and prophecy to its textual composition and reception. This is all the more significant when we appreciate that no other religious text offers anything remotely comparable in terms of establishing its divine authority. It is indeed the one worthy foundation for the one true religion. But having recognised it for what it is, we must now consider a more important question—why was it given?

The Bible's principal purpose is to reveal God's will to us. Beyond setting out commandments and revealing elements of the divine character, however, it offers an answer to that most important of questions—why things are the way they are. Central to this is an understanding of humanity's fall into sin—how it happened, why it was permitted, and what has been done about it. In revealing this, it teaches that we are not alone in the vast expanse of the universe, but in fact occupy the key battleground in the greatest and most terrible war ever fought—the angelic rebellion against God. By understanding this ongoing conflict and our place within it, we will be able to view the scriptures as a unified history of God's unfailing love for His creation. From the first promise of a deliverer and the prophecies of the Messiah, to Jesus' death and resurrection, the Bible reveals the course of the war and the final day of judgment when it will be brought to an end.

1. THE REBELLION

To understand the nature of this war and the subsequent need for a divine revelation, we must begin not with the Book of Genesis, but in Ezekiel. In chapter 28 verse 12, a lamentation is given for, ostensibly, the King of Tyre—the ruler of a rich Mediterranean coastal city. As its verses establish, however, the passage has a secondary meaning that cannot apply to any mortal ruler:

> You were the seal of perfection, full of wisdom and perfect in beauty. You were in Eden, the garden of God; … You were anointed as a guardian cherub, for so I ordained you. You were on the holy mount of God; you walked among the fiery stones. You were blameless in your ways from the day you were created till wickedness was found in you. … Your heart became proud on account of your beauty, and you corrupted your wisdom because of your splendour.

Isaiah 14:12-15 then details this being's offence:

> How you are fallen from heaven, O Lucifer, son of the morning! How you are cut down to the ground, you who weakened the nations! For you have said in your heart: 'I will ascend into heaven, I will exalt my throne above the stars of God; I will also sit on the mount of the congregation on the farthest sides of the north; I will ascend above the heights of the clouds, I will be like the Most High.' Yet you shall be brought down to Sheol, to the lowest depths of the Pit.

These verses collectively reveal the initial rebellion of the angel Lucifer, a being 'full of wisdom and perfect in beauty' who, corrupted by pride, wickedly sought to ascend the throne of God. How this was attempted the scriptures do not reveal, but other passages record that he acted as the leader of a faction. Jude 1:6 condemns 'the angels who did not keep their proper domain,' noting their confinement in 'everlasting chains under darkness for the judgment of the great day'. Revelation 12:10 denounces 'that serpent of old, called the Devil and Satan' whose 'angels were cast out with him'.

However Lucifer and his angels fought against God, the result was a swift and unequivocal defeat, with Ezekiel 28:16 recording how God 'cast [him] as a profane thing out of the mountain of God'. What happened immediately thereafter is unknown, although he soon launched another offensive. Genesis 3 records his temptation of Adam and Eve in the garden of Eden. Armed with superior wisdom and the cunning of 'a roaring lion, seeking whom he may devour', he used the allure of forbidden fruit and its accompanying knowledge to facilitate our first parents' disobedience.[1] Although the scriptures do not fully reveal his motive, John Milton's poem *Paradise Lost* perhaps captures it with the belief that—in sight of their disobedience—the all-holy God:

> May prove their foe, and with repenting hand
> Abolish his own works. This would surpass
> Common revenge, and interrupt his joy
> … when his darling sons,
> Hurl'd headlong to partake with us, shall curse
> Their frail original, and faded bliss,
> Faded so soon.[2]

Such demonic hatred—'so deep a malice … to spite the Great Creator', as Milton put it—rested upon a cold logic borne from experience.[3] With the punishment for *their* disobedience being divine separation, corrupted natures, and the ultimate doom of 'everlasting fire', it was only natural to expect that, once marred by sin, mankind would be equally condemned.[4] Their enemy might reign supreme in heaven, but they could attempt revenge and bring hell to His 'very good' creation, even causing the consignment of humanity—made in the very image of God—to eternal damnation.[5] Forcing such an exercise of divine justice would do nothing to alleviate their pain, but would aggravate His.

2. THE FALL

With the disobedience of Adam and Eve, the ruin of mankind seemed assured. Their sin—so devastating that creation itself 'was subjected to futility' and delivered into 'the bondage of corruption'—resulted in God's declaration that they would experience pain, hardship, and death.[6] This was nothing less than justice, since God had previously declared the fatal consequence of disobedience.[7] But in addition to judgment, an unexpected grace was promised to our fallen ancestors. Directing His attention to their tempter, God declared that from the seed of the woman would come one who 'shall bruise your head' even as he would 'bruise His heel'.[8]

This is the first prophecy of a deliverer who would destroy Lucifer's power.[9] Although the former would be wounded in the process, the damage inflicted upon the latter would be far greater, with the original Hebrew signifying a degree of violence akin to Lucifer being crushed, ground to powder, and pulverized.[10] Man would have to live with the consequences of sin, but all hope was not lost. The Old Testament points to this singular promise and records God's reiteration of it to Abraham, the separation of his descendants as a nation dedicated to His worship, the institution of a sacrificial system foreshadowing the atoning work of the redeemer, and prophecies that would teach them how to recognise His arrival. The New Testament then records Jesus' life, death, and victory on our behalf as that redeemer, which will be considered in detail in Chapter 8. Both parts were written for our instruction, that we might have hope.[11]

Hopeful though we might be, however, this is the point where serious questions often emerge. Why would an all-powerful God permit evil to exist? Why did there have to be a Fall? Why did Lucifer's rebellion have to escalate into an all-consuming war on earth? The history of humanity makes for grim contemplation—billions dead, creation spoiled, and untold misery suffered by those seemingly most unable to bear it. In light of this, it is unsurprising that many would turn to the trilemma purportedly advanced by the Greek philosopher Epicurus about the power and goodness of God:

> Is God willing to prevent evil, but not able? Then he is not omnipotent. Is he able but not willing? Then he is malevolent. Is he both able and willing? Whence then is evil?[12]

We have already dealt with the evidence for God's existence—arguments that atheism cannot, if it is being honest with itself, refute—but now we must speak to God's fairness. Some, perhaps, have rejected God after a dispassionate contemplation of the universe, but many more have done so out of anger and despair. How could a God described as 'merciful and gracious, longsuffering, and abounding in goodness and truth' permit pandemics, tsunamis, and Alzheimer's?[13] How could a God who 'loves righteousness and justice' allow murder and war, if they were preventable?[14]

These are important questions, and few who ask them will have been untouched by tragedy. Even for those not directly affected by loss, the world offers abundant reminders of life's fragility—every day a new crisis emerges, forever altering the lives of those involved. In the midst of this, it is natural to seek answers. Why did *my* baby die? What did we do to deserve *that* diagnosis? Why would a good God allow *this* to happen? Significantly, underlying all of these questions is the presumption of an answer. The Australian poet Les Murray captured this in *The Knockdown Question*:

> Why does God not spare the innocent?
> The answer to that is not in
> the same world as the question
> so you would shriek from me
> in terror if I could answer it.[15]

Recognising that the ability to answer such a question would involve powers that would overwhelm anyone who encountered them, Murray nevertheless identified a key truth—there *is* an answer, even if it is partly unknowable here. We may lack understanding of particular cases—why *this* child suffered or *that* man died—but all will one day be revealed. As Isaiah 55:8 declares, "'My thoughts are not your thoughts, nor are your ways My ways," says the Lord'.

One example of this comes from Genesis 37, in which Joseph—one of the twelve sons of Israel—was sold into slavery by his brothers. It is difficult to imagine a more painful betrayal than to be sold into a life of misery by one's family. How often, in the burning heat of day or the frigid cold of night, must he have wondered why God would have allowed such a fate to befall him? Years passed with little change, until one day when everything changed. Elevated from prison to second-in-command of Egypt, he was able to save countless lives when a regional drought brought years of famine. As he later recognised in Genesis 45:7 when speaking to his brothers, 'God sent me before you to preserve a posterity for you in the earth, and to save your lives by a great deliverance. So now it was not you who sent me here, but God'.

Not all suffering admits to such a clear purpose, to be sure, and there is much that to us may appear gratuitous or unfair. The private tragedies of life include many sorrows known only to the sufferer and God, to say nothing of the public calamities that affect communities and nations. Nevertheless, we are told that the day is coming when 'God will wipe away every tear from their eyes; there shall be no more death, nor sorrow, nor crying. There shall be no more pain, for the former things have passed away'.[16] Wonderful as this promised future will be, however, we are still left with the question of why evil is permitted to exist *now*, when God—being all-powerful—presumably could have avoided its existence entirely.

Turning back to Epicurus' trilemma, the flaw in its reasoning does not relate to God's omnipotence, but rather that, by being 'able but not willing' to prevent evil, God is malevolent. At first glance, the notion that God would permit evil seems not only malevolent but monstrous—a slander upon the scriptural proclamation that 'God is love' and an insult to His divine character.[17] What sort of 'love' would allow the evils we see on a daily basis to arise, let alone continue? The very idea strikes us with repugnance. But this is to rely upon human reasoning. God's thoughts are higher than our thoughts, Isaiah 55:9 declares, and there are valid reasons why He would not rescue us from every malady or frustrate the plans of all who would cause harm. To appreciate this, we must remove the false images of God as a sort of a divine Father Christmas working tirelessly to deliver happiness or a master utilitarian seeking to maximise the world's pleasures. The scriptures record His desire to bless us, but His ultimate desire is for a relationship with His creation—for us to be holy, as He is holy.[18] Having been created in the image of God, mankind once possessed this holy relationship before losing it in the Fall. But why was it lost? Returning to Genesis 3, we see that it was due to acts of choice. Lucifer might have tempted our first parents to disobedience, but they were the ones who *chose* to disobey.

These acts of choice—of free will—illustrate the fundamental reason why God has not, in His providence, removed our capacity for evil. Rather than creating our first parents to be biological robots, He endowed them with reason, giving humanity moral agency. Man could, like Lucifer and his fallen angels, choose to do evil, but could also choose to do good. The doll that says 'I love you' when touched does not think for itself or care about its owner, but merely repeats what it has been programmed to say—to borrow from Martin Luther, it can do no other.[19] Far from being malevolent in allowing free will, God bestowed a supreme gift—even if it came with the possibility of abuse.

It is sometimes forgotten that the tree of the knowledge of good and evil, from which Adam and Eve ate their fateful fruit, was not planted in Eden by Lucifer, but by God. It was, as part of His creation, good.[20] What its purpose was or would have been if they had continued in obedience is unclear, but by placing it there and giving the admonition that 'of [that tree] you shall not eat, for in the day that you eat of it you shall surely die', God gave them the *choice* to obey Him.[21] This singular act bestowed an incomparable dignity upon our first parents that no robot or animal could ever possess. Even after the Fall, when tainted by sin they lived under judgment, they still retained this capacity. Genesis 4:6-7 records God's message to Cain that 'If you do well, will you not be accepted? And if you do not do well, sin lies at the door. And its desire is for you, but you should rule over it', a warning that would have been meaningless if he had not possessed at least some degree of agency. Then there is Deuteronomy 30:19, which records God's declaration to the Israelites that He had 'set before [them] life and death, blessing and cursing', with the hope that they would 'choose life, that both [they] and [their] descendants might live'.

Scripture and common experience affirm our capacity for choice, but why could God not, in His omnipotence, have created us to *always* make the right choice—thereby avoiding evil? This argument was made by the Australian philosopher J.L. Mackie, who wrote:

> if God has made men such that in their free choices they sometimes prefer what is good and sometimes what is evil, why could he not have made men such that they always freely choose the good? ... Clearly, his failure to avail himself of this possibility is inconsistent with his being both omnipotent and wholly good.[22]

Seductive as this argument might initially appear, it ultimately demands the impossible. Although Revelation 19:6 declares God to be the Lord omnipotent, with other passages affirming His ability to 'do everything' and nothing being 'too hard' for Him, it does not follow from these verses that He is therefore capable of doing *any* thing.[23] Apart from not being able to perform the logically impossible—such as causing Himself to not exist—the Bible itself records certain qualifications on God's power, in that He cannot do anything contrary to His character. Titus 1:2 declares that He cannot lie. James 1:13 declares that He cannot be tempted by evil, nor does He Himself tempt anyone. 2 Timothy 2:13 declares that He cannot deny Himself, but remains faithful. Viewed accordingly, verses about God's omnipotence necessarily contain a silent caveat, that He is capable of doing *all things that can be done.*

In response to Mackie's argument, the American philosopher Alvin Plantinga argued that, whilst it was possible for God to create a world with persons possessing free will but without evil—the very world described in Genesis 1-2—it was a logical impossibility for God to create a world containing persons with 'free will' whose actions were controlled so they always made the 'choice' for moral good:

> God could have created a world containing no moral evil only by creating one without significantly free persons. ... the creation of a world containing moral good is a co-operative venture; it requires the uncoerced concurrence of significantly free creatures. ... Of course it is up to God whether to create free creatures at all; but if he aims to produce moral good, then he must create significantly free creatures upon whose co-operation he must depend. Thus is the power of an omnipotent God limited by the freedom he confers upon his creatures.[24]

It was certainly within God's power to create a world without the possibility of evil, but such a world would have lacked *us*—persons possessing free will.[25] Mackie and those sympathetic to his argument appeared ready to condemn God for allowing choice, rather than creating morally-perfect robots—a complaint similar to the thirteenth-century king Alfonso X's arrogant remark that, 'if I had been of God's counsel at the Creation, many things would have been ordered better'.[26] As C.S. Lewis put it in *Mere Christianity*, however:

> Some people think they can imagine a creature which was free but had no possibility of going wrong; I cannot. If a thing is free to be good it is also free to be bad. And free will is what has made evil possible. Why, then, did God give them free will? Because free will though it makes evil possible, is also the only thing that makes possible any love or goodness or joy worth having. A world of *automata*—of creatures

that worked like machines—would hardly be worth creating. The happiness which God designs for His higher creatures is the happiness of being freely, voluntarily united to Him and to each other in an ecstasy of love and delight compared with which the most rapturous love between a man and a woman on this earth is mere milk and water. And for that they must be free.[27]

Some have tried to argue that this freedom is illusory and that God bears responsibility for our actions. This, in turn, would make His punishment of our sins unjust. Taking issue with God's omniscience, the American philosopher David Griffin argued that, when assigning blame for sin, we must ask whether someone could have done otherwise.[28] For Griffin, free will:

> is not compatible with an omniscient being who knows the details of what is still the future for us. If this being knows infallibly that next year I will do A, instead of B or C, then it is necessary that I will do A. It may seem to me then as if I make a real choice among genuine alternatives, but this will be illusory. I really could not do otherwise.[29]

Rather than joining those in John Wolcot's poem *Ode to the Devil* who, when caught in sin, cried 'The Devil made me do it', this argument appears to rest on the opposing supposition that, due to His foreknowledge, 'God made me do it'.[30] As Augustine of Hippo argued in the fifth century, however, 'a man does not therefore sin because God foreknew that he would sin. Nay, it cannot be doubted that it is the man himself who sins when he does sin'.[31] God's foreknowledge is infallible and all-encompassing, but the person who 'wills not, sins not'.[32]

To illustrate why Augustine is right, let us suppose that it were possible to travel back in time. As you sit in the audience at Ford's Theatre on April 14, 1865 watching the performance of *Our American Cousin*, you are, in Griffin's argument, the 'being who knows the details of what is still the future'. Thanks to this knowledge, you know that John Wilkes Booth will soon assassinate Abraham Lincoln—doing 'A', in Griffin's words, instead of options 'B or C' of returning home or continuing to watch the play. But on what ground does it follow that it is *necessary* that Booth shoot Lincoln? How does your knowledge render Booth's choices 'illusory', to the point that he 'really could not do otherwise'? Did your foreknowledge cause him go up the stairs? Did it make him pull the trigger? You know Booth's future, but his actions are what will cause it to unfold.

At this point, one might assert that, if Booth were to do otherwise than shoot Lincoln, your 'immutable, infallible knowledge', as the stand-in for God, 'would be in error and this is impossible'.[33] Moreover:

if there is a being who eternally knows all things, then every single 'choice' in [Booth's] life prior to wicked deed A and the desire to do it is as devoid of real alternatives as the wicked deed A itself. Hence [Booth is] not responsible for [his] character any more than [he] will be for that particular decision.[34]

What this argument fails to address is the element of causation, or how foreknowledge would *cause* Booth, and by extension all of humanity, to not have a real choice in their actions. In our example, all you have done is sit knowingly in the theatre as an observer—in no sense can it be said that your foreknowledge has *caused* Booth to carry out his evil deeds. In the same way, God's foreknowledge does not implicate Him in our exercise of free will. Returning to Augustine, 'it does not follow that, though there is for God a certain order of all causes, there must therefore be nothing depending on the free exercise of our own wills, for our wills themselves are included in that order of causes which is certain to God, and is embraced by His foreknowledge'.[35]

As Isaiah 46:9-10 shows, time is a different concept for God: 'I am God, and there is none like Me, declaring the end from the beginning, and from ancient times things that are not yet done'. What is time to Him, then, but a book or recording whose ending is known? In this sense, God infallibly knows the choices we will make not because he compels them, but because *He has already seen us make them*. Griffin's subjects really can 'do otherwise' by choosing B or C instead of A, but simply choose not to. That these choices happen to occur in the future does not change the fact that they are still *their* choices.

If Epicurus had taken his trilemma to its natural conclusion, he would have realised that a God who stopped *all* evil from occurring would have rendered freedom impossible—a totalitarian in the truest sense of the word. Short of turning humanity into docile robots, such a God would have effectively had to imprison us in our own bodies—still possessing the capacity for evil, but with the certainty that any attempt at expressing it would be thwarted by immediate and irresistible divine force. Like a toddler strapped in a chair or someone with an itch that could never be scratched, our frustration and resentment at these restraints would have eventually overthrown even the most placid of minds, to say nothing about removing opportunity for moral good. Life, if one could have called it that, would have been little more than an utopian straightjacket. That God spared us from such a fate is hardly malevolence, but mercy.

But what of natural evil, or those afflictions that do not result from human agency? We can understand why the existence of moral evil would be necessary for free will, but what can justify the pain we see around us? The ground brings forth thorns and thistles. Our bodies return to dust. Corruption and decay eventually consume all. Even for those who survive disasters and diseases to reach advanced age, infirmities of the mind can wipe away the memories of a lifetime. But before asking why God would permit such suffering, we must understand its origin. As with moral evil, the scriptures reveal natural evil to be a consequence of our first parents' sin. The Fall subjected us to death, but Romans 8:20-22 records how it also subjected the world to 'futility', with the result that 'the whole creation groans and labours'. Our present world—with its cancers, cyclones, droughts, and diseases—is fallen, cursed in Genesis 3:17.

Understanding this is essential, since it allows us to properly make sense of our experiences. Sin did not simply alter *us*, it also altered *nature*. The world was not meant to suffer from disaster and decay, just as we were not meant to suffer from disease and death. Natural evil is in fact deeply *un*natural—an aberration from God's design. The day is coming, however, when 'creation itself also will be delivered from the bondage of corruption'.[36] Until then, we must pass through a damaged world, experiencing it not as it was intended, nor as it will ultimately remain. We may not know why individual afflictions strike us, but their collective cause is Biblically clear.

We must also recognise that suffering, even if we may not understand how, can be made to bring about a higher purpose. When Jesus' disciples asked in John 9 about whose sins caused a man to be born blind, He answered that 'Neither this man nor his parents', but that out of his blindness 'the works of God should be revealed in him'.[37] Romans 8:28 declares that 'all things work together for good to those who love God, to those who are the called according to His purpose'. Even if the things themselves are not good, good can still emerge in the fulfilment of God's plan. As Joseph told his brothers in Genesis 50:20 referencing his sale into slavery, 'you meant evil against me; but God meant it for good'. Trials can also help shape us for God's purpose, and—as 2 Corinthians 1:4 reveals—equip us to serve others in need, 'that we may be able to comfort those who are in any trouble, with the comfort with which we ourselves are comforted by God'.

Furthermore, although we must suffer amidst a fallen world, the scriptures reveal that we do not suffer alone and we are told specifically to turn to God in such times. Matthew 11:28 says 'come to Me, all you who labour and are heavy laden, and I will give you rest'. Hebrews 13:5 states that God will never leave or forsake us. The warrior King David recognised this when he wrote Psalm 23:4 'Though I walk through the valley of the shadow of death, I will fear no evil; For You are with me; Your rod and Your staff, they comfort me'. Lamentations 3:22 explains that 'Through the Lord's mercies we are not consumed, because His compassions fail not'. To those who love God, such trials will be but temporary sufferings along the pathway to eternal glory.

3. The Promise

Although we might recognise that the allowance of evil is necessary for the existence of freedom and moral good, it likely comes as cold comfort to the one experiencing it. Worse still, these evils, whether moral or natural, all operate as secondary tragedies. The primary tragedy is our separation from God as a result of our sin. Fallen from our original nature, we live subject to decay and under the sentence of death. All have sinned and fallen short of the glory of God, Romans 3:23 declares, placing us firmly—if unwittingly—onto the side of Lucifer in his war of rebellion. This can be shocking when first understood. What quarrel do we have with God? We may not be perfect, of course, but surely we are not *that* bad? Many of us, in fact, strive to live decently—raising families, giving to charities, volunteering for worthy causes, and undertaking a variety of good works. We can understand the justice of God punishing the tyrants who have ruled with murderous abandon, but people like *us*? Do we truly stand condemned alongside them and the very prince of hell himself?

'Every way of a man is right in his own eyes, but the Lord weighs the hearts', as Proverbs 21:2 reveals. Whatever the earthly merits of our actions, they count for nothing beneath the crushing weight of our sin. Every lie, impure thought, and unholy deed have all offended our sovereign creator whose eyes are too pure to behold iniquity.[38] Isaiah 53:6 describes us as sheep who have gone astray, whilst Romans 3:10 declares that, in the sight of God, 'there is none righteous, *no, not one*'. We are by nature 'children of wrath' whose good works without God are little more than 'filthy rags'.[39] Romans 5 reveals that in our sinful condition, we have rejected God and stand as His enemies—awaiting the terrible judgment promised in Isaiah 66:14-16:

> The hand of the Lord shall be known to His servants,
> And His indignation to His enemies.
> For behold, the Lord will come with fire
> And with His chariots, like a whirlwind,
> To render His anger with fury,
> And His rebuke with flames of fire.
> For by fire and by His sword
> The Lord will judge all flesh;
> And the slain of the Lord shall be many.

Lest we be tempted to complain about our first parents' original sin and the injustice of being punished for it, scripture reveals how we have aggressively compounded it with our own. Isaiah 66:3-4 reminds the reader that 'they have chosen their own ways, and their soul delights in their abominations', whilst Isaiah 59:18

states that 'According to their deeds … [God] will repay, fury to His adversaries, recompense to His enemies'. The details of this fury and recompense are unclear, but they will undoubtedly be terrible. Isaiah 33:14 speaks not only of the fearfulness that will seize 'the hypocrites', but the eternal nature of the punishment: 'Who among us shall dwell with the devouring fire? Who among us shall dwell with everlasting burnings?' The eighteenth-century minister Jonathan Edwards warned of this in a sermon to a New England congregation:

> It would be dreadful to suffer this fierceness and wrath of Almighty God one moment, but you must suffer it to all eternity; there will be no end to this exquisite horrible misery. When you look forward, you shall see a long forever, a boundless duration before you, which will swallow up your thoughts, and amaze your soul; and you will absolutely despair of ever having any deliverance, any end, any mitigation, any rest at all; you will know certainly that you must wear out long ages, millions and millions of ages, in wrestling and conflicting with this almighty merciless vengeance; and then when you have so done, when so many ages have actually been spent by you in this manner, you will know that all is but a point to what remains. So that your punishment will indeed be infinite.[40]

As enemies of God, it matters not how great or small our part in the war of rebellion might have been. The wages of sin is death, Romans 6:23 records, with the consequence of our actions being a final condemnation to 'the everlasting fire prepared for the devil and his angels'.[41] Lucifer's war might not have been of our own making, but we have contributed to it with varying degrees of enthusiasm—failing to see our position on the losing side. Some battles still remain to be fought, but the outcome is assured. Against omnipotent power there can be no victory—only the most ignominious of defeats. But though our guilt places us deservedly alongside Lucifer and his fallen angels, we must remember the promise made in Genesis 3:15 of the one who would crush his power. Scripture records that there will be no relief for the angelic rebels, but for us there is still hope.[42] Though we have sinned against God and deserve nothing but divine justice, the Bible also records that He who created our first parents in His image chose to extend an offer of mercy as an expression of His divine love. We do not have to remain children of wrath. We do not have to stay on the losing side. We do not have to face the everlasting flames. What remains to be considered in the next chapter is how to recognise this all-important mercy.

8

The Messiah

Sinners though we are before an almighty God, we are also unimaginably loved by Him. As the previous chapter noted, God in His mercy promised our first parents a redeemer who would crush Lucifer's power, even as they—and we, their descendants—had to face the consequences of sin. In time, He communicated further prophecies about this redeemer to the Jewish people, who duly recorded them in what we know as the Old Testament. Intermingled in their histories, songs, and other writings, it is to these prophecies that we now turn. Who is this redeemer, how may we recognise Him, and by what means does our redemption come?

Central to an understanding of this is the Hebrew concept of *ha-mashiah*, or 'the Messiah'.[1] In its narrowest sense, the term refers to someone 'anointed', although its broader meaning refers to one anointed or chosen by God for a special purpose.[2] Kings or other Old Testament figures might have been technical 'messiahs' by virtue of being chosen for particular tasks, but this chapter is concerned with one Messiah—*the* Messiah foretold in scripture.[3] Christianity holds this figure to be Jesus, a position rejected by Judaism. This disagreement and its resolution is of critical importance to both religions—as writers ancient and modern have recognised, the truth of one necessarily invalidates the other.[4] Nevertheless, this chapter proceeds from a common framework: Christianity and modern Judaism are both heirs of first-century Judaism, having emerged from the same theological environment.[5] The Messianic prophecies are our common heritage, with the disagreement arising over their interpretation. The most obvious of these prophecies have been grouped here by type and are examined in detail—relating to the place and time of the Messiah's coming, the characteristics He would possess, and the nature of His mission. Jewish sources are cited where appropriate to provide further clarity and to demonstrate Christianity's continuity with ancient Jewish thought.

1. THE PROPHECIES OF PLACE

The first prophetic category we will consider relates to place, or those prophecies that connect the Messiah to a particular heritage, lineage, and location. The first of these is found in Genesis 12:3, in which God promised to Abraham that 'in you all the families of the earth shall be blessed'. This is also evident in Genesis 18:18, which repeated that 'all the nations of the earth shall be blessed' through Abraham's line. This blessing was to be of great importance. The apostles Peter and Paul both applied it to the coming of the Messiah, and even within Judaism we find an ancient recognition that it was to be more than a general blessing.[6] In the seventeenth-century, Rabbi Isaiah Horowitz wrote in his influential *Shnei Luhot ha-Berit* how, when God spoke about Abraham becoming 'great' in Genesis 18:18:

> we have the implied promise that in the future, as a result of someone like Abraham, that configuration described as 'there were' will eventually be changed to the configuration 'will be' … the original design for the world will materialise: that *the fall from grace due to having eaten from the tree will be reversed.*[7]

In Genesis 26:4, this promise of a line through whom 'all the nations of the earth shall be blessed' narrowed to descendants of Abraham's son Isaac, and then in Genesis 28:14 to descendants of Isaac's son Jacob. Centuries later, King David—one of Jacob's descendants—was given another prophecy in 2 Samuel 7:16 that, after his death, God would raise up one of his descendants whose 'throne shall be established forever'. Isaiah 11:1 echoed this, with the prophecy that 'There shall come forth a Rod from the stem of Jesse, and a Branch shall grow out of his roots'. Christianity and Judaism both apply this to the Messiah, with *Berakhot 17b* of the Jerusalem Talmud, written around the year 400, noting that 'the King Messiah' would be of royal stock, with the verse in Isaiah referring to 'the birth of a Messiah of the line of David'.[8] A further prophecy in Micah 5:2 then revealed that this Messiah would be born in Bethlehem:

> But you, Bethlehem Ephrathah, though you are little among the thousands of Judah, yet out of you shall come forth to Me the One to be Ruler in Israel, whose goings forth are from of old, from everlasting.

These prophecies foretold that the Messiah would come from the lines of Abraham, Isaac, and Jacob, be a descendant of the Davidic monarchy, and be born in the Judean city of Bethlehem—collectively ruling out the vast majority of mankind as potential Messianic candidates. Applying them to Jesus, we see that He was not only born in Bethlehem, but was repeatedly hailed as the 'Son of David' by people across the region during His ministry—to say nothing of the details of His genealogical descent from Abraham, Isaac, Jacob, and David recorded in Matthew and Luke.[9] As for the site of His birth, by the third century—long before Christianity received official toleration—it had become sufficiently famous that Origen noted in *Against Celsus* that:

> As for our Saviour's being born at Bethlehem, if any person be dissatisfied with the prophecy of Micah, and the account which is given by the Evangelists, let him only consider, that the cave, in which he was born, and the manger, in which he lay, are to be seen at the fore-mentioned place to this very day. And this is a truth so well known, and so credibly attested, that even they, who are strangers to the Christian Religion, are frequently heard to say, 'Here is the cave, in which that Jesus, who is worshipped by the Christians, was born.'[10]

From an examination of the Biblical text and historical record, Jesus satisfied the Messianic prophecies of place.

2. The Prophecies of Time

We next come to the prophecies of time that foretold when the Messiah would appear. Two such prophecies, the first in Genesis 49, and the second in Daniel 9, address this with a degree of specificity that cannot be ignored, although modern Judaism has attempted to read inferences into them that go beyond the plain meaning of the text. In Genesis 49:10, we find Jacob—the father of the twelve tribes that would form the nation of Israel—giving his last words to his children. With respect to his fourth son, Judah, not only would his siblings 'bow down' to him, but 'The sceptre shall not depart from Judah, nor a lawgiver from between his feet, until Shiloh comes'. This last phrase is significant. As *Sanhedrin 98b* in the Babylonian Talmud records, 'Shiloh' was regarded within ancient Judaism as one of the names of the Messiah.[11] To remove any doubt about this interpretation, *Sanhedrin 5a* also clarifies the verse's Messianic nature:

> The verse states: 'The sceptre shall not depart from Judah nor the ruler's staff from between his feet until Shiloh comes' (Genesis 49:10). The term 'Shiloh' is understood as a reference to the Messiah, and therefore the verse is interpreted as delineating the authority of Jewish rulers during the exile, before the Messiah comes.[12]

Notwithstanding the Talmud's interpretation of the prophecy being limited to 'Jewish rulers during the exile' rather than to Jewish rulers *in general* as conveyed by a plain reading of the text, *Sanhedrin 5a* further explains that the 'sceptre' refers to 'a ruler with actual power of governance', in contrast to 'a legislator with limited power'.[13] Read plainly, Genesis 49 therefore foretold that the Messiah would come whilst a Jewish ruler possessed actual sovereign power. Narrowing the Messiah's timing further, a second prophecy in Daniel 9:24-26 declared that the Messiah would come before the destruction of Jerusalem and the Temple:

> Seventy weeks are determined for your people and for your holy city, to finish the transgression, to make an end of sins, to make reconciliation for iniquity, to bring in everlasting righteousness, to seal up vision and prophecy, and to anoint the Most Holy.
>
> Know therefore and understand, that from the going forth of the command to restore and build Jerusalem until Messiah the Prince, there shall be seven weeks and sixty-two weeks; the street shall be built again, and the wall, even in troublesome times.
>
> And after the sixty-two weeks Messiah shall be cut off, but not for Himself; and the people of the prince who is to come shall destroy the city and the sanctuary.

Various theories have been advanced about when the number of 'weeks' or seven-year periods would begin and end, but the prophecy's central element is that the Messiah would be 'cut off'—or killed—before 'the prince who is to come shall destroy the city and the sanctuary'.

Before considering whether Jesus fulfilled these prophecies, we must address two erroneous interpretations that commonly arise from the passage in Daniel. The first interpretation—apparently unknown before the third-century writings of the pagan philosopher Porphyry—is that it was written after-the-fact to refer to Antiochus Epiphanes, the Seleucid king and purported 'prince who is to come' who persecuted Judea in the second century BC.[14] This argument raises two problems, however. First, Antiochus neither destroyed the Temple nor Jerusalem, but in fact caused a rebellion that led to the reestablishment of the Jewish monarchy *in* Jerusalem.[15] Secondly, given that the Septuagint translation of the Tanakh was completed around 132 BC—a mere thirty years after Antiochus' death—it is unclear how a back-dated Daniel 9 that cryptically referred to him could have been written, gained canonical acceptance, and then been translated into Greek with such extraordinary rapidity. The oldest Daniel manuscript found at Qumran amongst the Dead Sea Scrolls dates to 125 BC, for instance, proving the high regard the book had already obtained by that era.[16]

The second erroneous interpretation—which puzzlingly continues to enjoy support within Judaism—comes from the work of a twelfth-century French rabbi named Shlomo Yitzchaki.[17] Known as 'Rashi' from an abbreviation of his title and name, he was the foremost commentator on the Babylonian Talmud and wrote what soon became the standard commentary on the Torah—an authoritative scholar whose influence continues to this day.[18] With respect to Daniel 9:26, his interpretation was that the one who 'will be cut off' referred to 'Agrippa, the king of Judea, who was ruling at the time of the destruction, [and who] will be slain', with the 'prince who is to come' referring to the Roman leader 'Titus and his armies', who destroyed Jerusalem and the Temple in AD 70.[19]

Although Rashi was right about Titus, he was wrong about Agrippa. Not only was Agrippa, the last Judean king, *not* slain during the war, he actually *served on the Roman side*—commanding 5,000 troops at the siege of Jerusalem and even hosting the victorious conquerors afterward in his capital, Caesarea Philippi, for celebratory games.[20] Agrippa in fact lived for a further thirty years after the fall of Jerusalem and destruction of the Temple—dying, apparently of natural causes, in his seventies around the year 100.[21] Rashi correctly identified the Roman general Titus—son of the emperor Vespasian and later emperor himself—as the 'prince who is to come' to 'destroy the city and the sanctuary'. Yet his attribution of Agrippa as the Messiah that 'shall be cut off' is historically incorrect.

Instead, applying these two prophecies to the Messiah as they were intended yields a clear deadline by which He would have had to appear. The prophecy in Genesis 49:10 that the 'sceptre shall not depart from Judah, nor a lawgiver from between his feet, until Shiloh comes' foretold that the Messiah would come whilst a Jewish ruler possessed the *actual* power to govern. Although the prophecy in Daniel imposed an ultimate end date of AD 70 with the destruction of 'the city and the sanctuary', the Genesis prophecy takes this back even further to AD 6, when the Romans deposed the Jewish ruler Herod Archelaus and exiled him to Vienna.[22] Thereafter, Judea was subject to Roman political control, with imperial officers like Pontius Pilate exercising actual power even if a nominal king like Herod Agrippa ceremonially reigned alongside them.[23] To satisfy both prophecies, the Messiah would have had to come prior to the 'sceptre' departing in AD 6.

We see from several accounts that Jesus satisfied these prophecies. Matthew 2:1 refers to him being born during the reign of Herod the Great, who ruled until around 4 BC.[24] Luke 3:23 speaks of Him being 'about thirty years of age' when He began His public ministry in the fifteenth year of Tiberias (AD 29).[25] Having satisfied Genesis 49:10, Jesus then applied Daniel 9 directly to Himself, warning His disciples in Matthew 24, Mark 13, and Luke 21 of Jerusalem and the Temple's coming destruction, in which 'not one stone shall be left upon another that shall not be torn down'.[26] From a plain reading of the Biblical text and historical record, Jesus satisfied the Messianic prophecies of time.

3. THE PROPHECIES OF CHARACTER

Having seen how the Messiah would come from the Jewish people, be of royal descent through the line of David, and be born in Bethlehem before the sceptre departed and Jerusalem was destroyed, the number of individuals in all of history who could potentially claim to be the Messiah narrows to perhaps a few hundred at most. To remove all possibility of doubt about the Messiah's identity, however, the scriptures also contain an abundance of prophecies about His character and the attributes He would display.

The first of these is found in Genesis 3:15, in which God revealed to our first parents how the 'seed' of 'the woman' would one day bruise their tempter's head, even as the latter would bruise their descendant's heel. As Chapter 7 noted, the English translation of this verse fails to fully convey the violence reflected in the 'bruising' of Lucifer's head—instead of a mere injury, it denotes a crushing, pulverizing blow tantamount to being ground into powder.[27] Although the seed of the woman would also be injured through the figurative bruising of the heel, He would fully *crush* Lucifer—an extraordinary power for any human given that our first parents failed to resist even moderate temptation.

Christianity has long interpreted this as applying to the Messiah, and Judaism once did as well. Notwithstanding Rashi's silence on the 'seed' in his commentary—ignoring it in favour of his claim that the serpent wanted to marry Eve and tempted her first 'only because women are easily enticed'—a more ancient Jewish source recognised it as referring to the Messiah.[28] In the *Genesis Rabbah*, dating from around 400-450, the commentary on the birth of Seth in Genesis 4:25 noted how Eve 'beheld that other seed which was to come forth from another place, and who is that? *It is the King Messiah*'.[29] Seth would not be Eve's saviour, but this indicates the thought within fifth-century Judaism that the promised 'seed' of Genesis 3:15 was indeed Messianic. It is also arguable that Genesis 3:15 contains a clue about how the Messiah's birth would be unusual. As the fourth-century Egyptian bishop Serapion observed about the reference to 'her seed':

> a woman does not have seed, only man does. How then was it said of
> The Woman? Is it clear that it was said of Christ whom the undefiled
> Virgin brought forth without seed? Certainly, He is a singular seed,
> not seeds in the plural.[30]

This was echoed by another fourth-century bishop, Epiphanius of Salamis, and by the fifth-century bishop Isidore of Pelusium:

> That Seed of The-Woman, whom God commands to be inimical and hostile to the Serpent is Our Lord Jesus Christ. For He is the Seed of The-Woman, alone born from her in such a manner, namely, that neither the life-germ of man intervened, nor was chastity diminished at all.[31]

In the entirety of the Old Testament, there are only five instances in which the word *zerah* or 'seed' is used with a feminine possessive, and two of them do not refer to individuals.[32] Of the three that do, the references to Hagar and Rebekah's descendants in Genesis 16:10 and 24:60 both use the noun in the collective sense, with only Genesis 3:15 using it in the singular.[33] Then there is the matter of context—by comparison, *zerah* in the masculine or neutral sense appears over forty times in Genesis alone, and the references to Hagar and Rebekah occur whilst the men they would have children with were absent, making them the focus of conversations about descendants.[34] Genesis 3:15's use of 'her seed', particularly when Adam was present, is scripturally unique.

Suggestive as this might be, the circumstances of the Messiah's birth were dealt with explicitly in Isaiah 7:14. Given 700 years before the birth of Jesus, this prophecy came at a time of national crisis in which Judah was threatened with invasion from the allied forces of Syria and Israel.[35] When King Ahaz was told to request a sign from God as proof that it would not happen, he stubbornly refused—causing Isaiah to then give a sign to the 'house of David': 'Behold, the virgin shall conceive and bear a Son, and shall call His name Immanuel', or God-with-us.[36] Central to this prophecy is the word *almah*, which modern Judaism translates as 'young woman' instead of 'virgin'.[37] If Isaiah had intended to refer to a virgin, some within Judaism argue, he would have used the word *bethulah*.[38] Rashi even claimed that the *almah* was, in fact, a reference to Isaiah's wife.[39]

Arguments from Jewish apologetics that *almah* has been mistranslated by Christians overlook the fact that *ancient Judaism itself* translated the word as 'virgin' not once, but twice.[40] Over 150 years before the birth of Jesus, Jewish scribes translating Isaiah 7:14 into Greek as part of the Septuagint used the word *parthénos*—or virgin—for *almah*.[41] Similarly, when translating the Tanakh into Syriac in the first and second centuries AD, other Jewish scribes used the cognate word *bĕtûlâ* to signify 'virgin' in Isaiah 7:14.[42] Even if one were to allege that this translation was somehow susceptible to an unproven Christian influence—despite its 'halakic and haggadic interpretations and the indications that it was used in the synagogues for the weekly lessons'—no such argument can be made for the Septuagint.[43] Furthermore, the Gospel of Matthew, written specifically for a Jewish audience, took care in verses 1:18-23 to show how Jesus' birth fulfilled Isaiah 7:14—an unusual and unnecessary act if the concept of a virgin giving birth to 'God-with-us' was not already established in Jewish thought. It was also not until the Jewish convert Aquila's revision of the Septuagint in the mid-second century AD, well after the start of the Christian era, that 'virgin' was replaced with 'young woman' after centuries of use—a variation whose timing and content cannot help but raise questions of theological bias.[44]

Then there is the context in which *almah* is used. Of the six instances other than Isaiah 7:14 in which it appears, none involve circumstances in which the woman in question was *not* a virgin.[45] As for Rashi's claim that the *almah* was a reference by Isaiah to his wife, this fails on two grounds. First, by virtue of being married she would not have been an *almah* but an *ishah*.[46] We also know that Isaiah did not refer to her as an *almah* since only a few verses later in Isaiah 8:3, he called her 'the prophetess', or *neviah*. Secondly, the child she subsequently bore was not called 'God-with-us', but 'quick-to-plunder-swift-to-the-spoil'—hardly a sign of comfort for the House of David.[47] Had Isaiah intended to link the prophecy in 7:14 to his wife, he could have easily used either *ishah* or *neviah* in place of *almah*, and given his son a different name. He would scarcely have referred—as Rashi would have it—to his wife as a young unmarried woman, given that they already had a child together. As for the argument that *bethulah* would have been a more specific term, this is not dispositive—the prophet Jeremiah used *bethulah* several times when referring to Israel as a wife who had gone astray, and Joel 1:8 told the people to 'lament like a *bethulah* girded with sackcloth for the husband of her youth', which complicates the use of the term as Judaism's preferred meaning.[48] From a plain interpretation of the text, recognised by Jewish translators of the Septuagint in the pre-Christian era and of the Syriac centuries later, Isaiah 7:14 foretold of a virgin conceiving a son who would be 'God-with-us', a reference that can only apply to Jesus.

Isaiah also prophetically revealed other characteristics the Messiah would possess. In Isaiah 35:3-6, it was foretold that He would perform certain recognisable miracles as Jesus did:

> Strengthen the weak hands, and make firm the feeble knees. Say to those who are fearful-hearted, 'Be strong, do not fear! Behold, your God will come with vengeance, with the recompense of God; He will come and save you.' Then the eyes of the blind shall be opened, and the ears of the deaf shall be unstopped. Then the lame shall leap like a deer, and the tongue of the dumb sing.

It was also noted of the Messiah in Isaiah 61:1—which Jesus applied to Himself in the synagogue sermon in Luke 4:17-21—that:

> The Spirit of the Lord God is upon Me, because the Lord has anointed Me to preach good tidings to the poor; He has sent Me to heal the brokenhearted, to proclaim liberty to the captives, and the opening of the prison to those who are bound…

Modern Judaism has generally ignored these passages. The weekly *haftarah* reading cycle omits them entirely, for instance, with *Ki Tavo*, or Week 50, covering all of Isaiah 60 and then skipping to Isaiah 61:10 the following week.[49] Rashi portrayed them as allegorical, with the 'ears of the deaf' diminished figuratively to those 'who did not hearken to the voice of the prophets'.[50] But it was not always so within Judaism. Among the Dead Sea Scrolls discovered at Qumran was a manuscript (4Q521) from the first century BC that had been copied from an earlier second century work.[51] Known today as the *Messianic Apocalypse*, it reveals the belief of the Qumran Jews—long before Jesus was born—that these verses were Messianic and spoke of how the Messiah would rule heaven and earth, heal the blind and lame, and raise the dead:

> heaven and earth will obey his messiah, [and all th]at is in them will not turn away from the commandments of holy ones. You who seek the Lord, strengthen yourselves in his service. … For he will glorify the pious on the throne of an eternal kingdom, releasing captives, giving sight to the blind and raising up those who are bo[wed down]. Forever I will cleave to [those who] hope, and in his kindness … The fru[it of a] good [wor]k will not be delayed for anyone and the glorious things that have not taken place the Lord will do as he s[aid] for he will heal the wounded, give life to the dead and preach good news to the poor…[52]

The parallels between this passage and Matthew 11:4-5 are striking. When messengers from John the Baptist enquired of Jesus as to whether He was the Messiah, He 'said to them, "Go and tell John the things which you hear and see: the blind see and the lame walk; the lepers are cleansed and the deaf hear; the dead are raised up and the poor have the gospel preached to them"'. Even more striking, however, is the realisation that 4Q521 is the only manuscript of its kind ever discovered, was originally composed 200 years before the Christian era, and was likely hidden in a cave prior to the Gospel of Matthew being written.[53] It therefore could have exerted no influence on the gospel's composition, but affirms with *exact precision*—even down to the sequence of healing, resurrection, and preaching of good news to the poor—that the signs of the Messiah the Qumran Jews looked for, based upon Isaiah 35 and 61, were the very same which John's disciples could report had been manifested by Jesus.

A final prophetic attribute this section will consider comes from Zechariah 9:9. Written some 500 years before Jesus' birth, it foretold that the Messiah would enter Jerusalem riding upon a donkey:

> Rejoice greatly, O daughter of Zion! Shout, O daughter of Jerusalem!
> Behold, your King is coming to you; He is just and having salvation,
> lowly and riding on a donkey, a colt, the foal of a donkey.[54]

Christianity and Judaism agree on the Messianic nature of this passage, with Rashi commenting that 'It is impossible to interpret this except as referring to the King Messiah'.[55] The ancient writers of the Babylonian Talmud concurred, with Rabbi Alexandri noting in *Sanhedrin 98a*:

> Rabbi Yehoshua ben Levi raises a contradiction between two depictions of the coming of the Messiah. It is written: 'There came with the clouds of heaven, one like unto a son of man...and there was given him dominion and glory and a kingdom...his dominion is an everlasting dominion' (Daniel 7:13-14). And it is written: 'Behold, your king will come to you; he is just and victorious; lowly and riding upon a donkey' (Zechariah 9:9). Rabbi Alexandri explains: If the Jewish people merit redemption, the Messiah will come in a miraculous manner with the clouds of heaven. If they do not merit redemption, the Messiah will come lowly and riding upon a donkey.[56]

Notwithstanding Rabbi Alexandri's notion that the manner of the Messiah's coming would depend upon how worthy the Jewish people were to receive Him, Matthew 21:1-10, Mark 11:1-10, Luke 19:28-44, and John 12:12-15 all affirm that Jesus entered Jerusalem to popular acclaim upon a young donkey, thereby satisfying Zechariah 9:9. In doing so, He paralleled Solomon's entry into Jerusalem on a donkey 1,000 years earlier to claim the throne of David in 1 Kings 1:33-48. When combined with His birth in Bethlehem to a virgin, numerous miracles of healing, resurrection of the dead, and proclamation of 'good news' to the poor—all before the destruction of Jerusalem—it becomes readily apparent that Jesus is the sole figure in history who satisfied the Messianic prophecies of place, time, and character.

4. THE PROPHECIES OF SUFFERING

Having narrowed the application of these prophecies to one person, we may have confidence that Jesus is the promised Messiah. But the scriptures do not stop there. In addition to the prophecies of place, time, and character, there are many others that speak of the suffering and rejection the Messiah would experience. When we consider that all of them were given centuries before Jesus' crucifixion, their parallels with that event illustrate all too clearly the divine nature of their inspiration and fulfilment—providing further evidence that the Messianic prophecies can only refer to Him. Chief amongst these is Isaiah 53, which foretold that the Messiah would be despised, rejected, and executed:

> Who has believed our report? And to whom has the arm of the Lord been revealed? For He shall grow up before Him as a tender plant, and as a root out of dry ground. He has no form or comeliness; and when we see Him, there is no beauty that we should desire Him. He is despised and rejected by men, a Man of sorrows and acquainted with grief. And we hid, as it were, our faces from Him; He was despised, and we did not esteem Him.

> Surely He has borne our griefs and carried our sorrows; yet we esteemed Him stricken, smitten by God, and afflicted. But He was wounded for our transgressions, He was bruised for our iniquities; the chastisement for our peace was upon Him, and by His stripes we are healed. All we like sheep have gone astray; we have turned, every one, to his own way; and the Lord has laid on Him the iniquity of us all.

> He was oppressed and He was afflicted, yet He opened not His mouth; He was led as a lamb to the slaughter, and as a sheep before its shearers is silent, so He opened not His mouth. He was taken from prison and from judgment, and who will declare His generation? For He was cut off from the land of the living; for the transgressions of My people He was stricken. And they made His grave with the wicked—but with the rich at His death, because He had done no violence, nor was any deceit in His mouth.

> Yet it pleased the Lord to bruise Him; He has put Him to grief. When You make His soul an offering for sin, He shall see His seed, He shall prolong His days, and the pleasure of the Lord shall prosper in His hand. He shall see the labour of His soul, and be satisfied. By His knowledge My righteous Servant shall justify many, for He shall bear their iniquities. Therefore I will divide Him a portion with the great, and He shall divide the spoil with the strong, because He poured out

His soul unto death, and He was numbered with the transgressors, and
He bore the sin of many, and made intercession for the transgressors.

This prophecy—perhaps more than any other—illustrates the divergence
between Christianity and Judaism; the former applies it to the Messiah, the latter
to Israel as a whole.[57] Rashi wrote of verse 2 that 'he came up like a sapling' or
plant referred to 'This people, before this greatness came to it', and in verse 3 that
'despised and rejected by men' was Isaiah's way of 'mention[ing] all Israel as one
man'.[58] Jewish apologetics also frequently refer to the Christian scholar Origen's
third-century work *Against Celsus* as containing an ancient mention of this interpretation, in which he referred to Jews who applied the prophecy 'to the whole
body of their own nation' in a debate against Christianity.[59] Ancient though this
interpretation might be, however, it was by no means universally held by the
Jews in either Origen's day or Rashi's. Turning first to the Babylonian Talmud,
Sanhedrin 98b contains a collection of references to the Messiah's name:

> Apropos the Messiah, the Gemara asks: What is his name? The school
> of Rabbi Sheila says: Shiloh is his name … The school of Rabbi Yannai
> says: Yinnon in his name … And the Rabbis say: The leper of the
> house of Rabbi Yehuda HaNasi is his name, as it is stated: 'Indeed our
> illnesses he did bear and our pains he endured; yet we did esteem him
> injured, stricken by God, and afflicted' (Isaiah 53:4).[60]

Here we have a third-century rabbi, Yehuda HaNasi, who specifically linked
Isaiah 53 to the Messiah rather than to Israel. Moreover, he was no ordinary rabbi,
but the *nasi*—or leader—of the Sanhedrin for fifty years until his death around
AD 220.[61] As the rabbi *par excellence* who collected the Jews' oral law into the
Mishnah, he was well-placed to expound upon the scriptures.[62] That he declared
this prophecy to be in reference to the Messiah is as close to a definitive statement
of orthodoxy as one can obtain from the second and third centuries—carrying far
greater weight than the unnamed scholars noted by Origen.

We then have the *Ruth Rabba*, compiled around AD 600.[63] In a discussion
about the meanings that could arise from Boaz telling Ruth to 'Come hither, and
eat of the bread, and dip your morsel in the vinegar', Rabbi Yonatan referred to
the various interpretations each phrase could carry. Like Yehuda HaNasi, he too
applied Isaiah 53 to the Messiah:

> The fifth explanation for 'come here' is the King Messiah. 'Come
> here': that is draw near to kingship. 'And eat from the bread': that
> is the bread of kingship. 'And dip your morsel in the vinegar': that is

his chastisements, as it is said: 'But he was wounded because of our transgressions (Isaiah 53:5)'.[64]

In the tenth century, the Jewish scholar Yefet ben Elī ha-Levi al-Baṣrī produced an extensive commentary on the Tanakh in Arabic.[65] With respect to Isaiah 52-53, he wrote:

> The commentators differ concerning this section. The *Fayyumi* lost his senses applying it to the prophets generally ... His explanation is not indeed of a kind towards which any one would feel attracted ... I am inclined, with Benjamin of Nehawend, to regard it as alluding to the Messiah, and as opening with a description of his condition in exile, from the time of his birth to his accession to the throne ... from the words 'he was wounded for our transgressions,' we learn two things: 1. that Israel had committed many sins and transgressions, for which they deserved the indignation of God; 2. that by the Messiah bearing them they would be delivered from the wrath which rested upon them...[66]

We then come to the *Zohar*, a Jewish Kabbalah text composed in Spain in the late thirteenth century.[67] In section 2:212, a passage referring to the 'souls which are in the garden of Eden' speaks of how they:

> contemplate all those that are possessed of pains and sicknesses and ... then return and announce it to the Messiah. And as they tell him of the misery of Israel in their captivity, and of those wicked ones among them who are not attentive to know their Lord, he lifts up his voice and weeps for their wickedness: and so it is written, 'He was wounded for our transgressions', ... There is in the garden of Eden a palace called the Palace of the sons of sickness: this palace the Messiah then enters, and summons every sickness, every pain, and every chastisement of Israel; they all come and rest upon him. And were it not that he had thus lightened them off Israel and taken them upon himself, there had been no man able to bear Israel's chastisements for transgressions of the law: and this is that which is written, 'Surely our sicknesses he hath carried.'[68]

What these texts illustrate is that, up until the late Middle Ages, several of Judaism's most distinguished scholars regarded Isaiah 53 as applying to the Messiah. Although there were, as Origen and Yefet ben Elī's writings show, differing views on this passage, it is significant that, even after the emergence of Christianity, prominent rabbis affirmed its Messianic nature for centuries—including the very leader of the Sanhedrin.[69] Modern Judaism's application of it to the nation of Israel is therefore at variance with its traditional interpretation. It is also logically flawed, as the wording 'for the transgressions of My people He was stricken' in verse 8 reveals. Isaiah 52:4-6 repeatedly establishes that 'My people' is a reference to Israel, so how can the 'He' placed beside 'My people' also refer to Israel? Furthermore, Isaiah 52:14 distinguishes between 'My people' and the 'Servant' who forms the subject of Isaiah 53 ('Just as many were astonished at *you* [My people] so *His* visage…'). The very syntax requires the 'He' to be a single figure, and not Israel as a whole.[70]

Christianity correctly applies the prophecy to Jesus, with the gospels recording in detail His satisfaction of its characteristics. The Messiah would appear without splendour (53:2), and He was born in a stable and worked as a carpenter.[71] The Messiah would be a man of sorrows (53:3), and He suffered many trials.[72] The Messiah would bear the people's sicknesses and pains (53:4), and He healed many.[73] The Messiah would be wounded for the transgressions and iniquities of others (53:5), and He gave His life as a ransom.[74] The Messiah would be led as a lamb to the slaughter but remain silent (53:7), and He refused to speak when questioned by Herod Antipas before His execution.[75] The Messiah's grave would be made 'with the wicked, but with the rich at His death' (53:9), and He was crucified between criminals before being buried in the tomb of a wealthy man.[76] Most importantly, the Messiah would be made 'an offering for sin' yet would 'see the labour of His soul, and be satisfied' (53:10-11), and Jesus died for the sins of the world before rising from the dead.[77]

In addition to Isaiah 53 with its broad overview of the Messiah's purpose, rejection, and suffering, other prophecies refer to specific events leading up to His death. Zechariah 11:12-13 foretold the price that would be paid for His betrayal, and what would ultimately happen to the money:

> So they weighed out for my wages thirty pieces of silver. And the Lord said to me, 'Throw it to the potter'—that princely price they set on me. So I took the thirty pieces of silver and threw them into the house of the Lord for the potter.

Rashi struggled to assign a meaning to this beyond what plainly appears, writing that 'I do not know how to explain the expression here of thirty pieces of silver exactly', and the Babylonian Talmud's only reference in *Chullin 92a* curiously connects it with righteous men and barley—commenting that 'there are forty-five righteous men in every generation' and, applied to the pieces of silver, thirty of them must have been in Israel.[78] This is at odds with the passage's context, however. Rather than speaking highly of the thirty pieces of silver as one would expect if they referred to righteous men, the verse's subject regarded them as contemptible—referring to the sum sarcastically as 'that princely price they set on me'. As Exodus 21:32 records, thirty pieces of silver were the damages payable if an ox gored a slave—hardly a monumental amount.[79]

Christianity in contrast regards the passage as clearly referring to the payment of actual silver, with the prophecy fulfilled in two stages—first, when Judas agreed to betray Jesus in Matthew 26:15 in exchange for thirty pieces of silver, and secondly in Matthew 27:3-9 when, full of remorse, he returned them. When the priests and elders refused to take them back on account of the coins being blood money, verse 5 records how he 'threw down the pieces of silver in the temple and departed, and went and hanged himself'. After consulting on what to do with the money, the priests 'bought with them the potter's field, to bury strangers in', which, as Acts 1:18-19 records, was where Judas had killed himself.[80] Just as Zechariah 11:12-13 had foretold 500 years earlier, the thirty pieces of silver weighed out for Jesus' betrayal were ultimately thrown back into the house of the Lord before being paid to the potter.[81] Isaiah also foretold in verses 50:5-6 that the Messiah would not offer resistance as He was insulted, struck, and spat upon:

> The Lord God has opened My ear; and I was not rebellious, nor did I turn away. I gave My back to those who struck Me, and My cheeks to those who plucked out the beard; I did not hide My face from shame and spitting.

This was fulfilled in multiple stages prior to Jesus' crucifixion. Mark 14:65 records how members of the Sanhedrin 'began to spit on Him, and to blindfold Him, and to beat Him, and to say to Him, "Prophesy!" And the officers struck Him with the palms of their hands'. Once transferred into Roman custody, Matthew 27:27-30 records how:

> the soldiers of the governor took Jesus into the Praetorium and gathered the whole garrison around Him. And they stripped Him and put a scarlet robe on Him. When they had twisted a crown of thorns, they put it on His head, and a reed in His right hand. And they bowed the knee before Him and mocked Him, saying, 'Hail, King of the Jews!' Then they spat on Him, and took the reed and struck Him on the head.

Other prophecies revealed how the Messiah's humiliation would continue to the point of death. Psalm 69:21 foretold that He would be given 'gall for my food, and for my thirst they gave me vinegar to drink', which was fulfilled when the Roman soldiers gave Jesus 'sour wine mingled with gall' on the cross in Matthew 27:34. Psalm 22:18 foretold that the Messiah's garments would be divided 'among them, and for my clothing they cast lots', which was fulfilled when the same soldiers 'crucified Him, and divided His garments, casting lots'.[82] Psalm 22:6-8 spoke of the Messiah as:

> a worm, and no man; a reproach of men, and despised by the people. All those who see Me ridicule Me; they shoot out the lip, they shake the head, saying 'He trusted in the Lord, let Him rescue Him; Let Him deliver Him, since He delights in Him!'

This was fulfilled by the priests in Matthew 27:41-43, who called out as Jesus was dying 'He saved others; Himself He cannot save' and 'He trusted in God; let Him deliver Him now if He will Have Him, for He said, "I am the Son of God."'

5. Salvator Mundi

The remarkable fulfilment by Jesus of these prophecies, along with others which would have swelled the chapter to an unreasonable length if included, shows with unmistakable clarity that He is the Messiah foretold by scripture. Although Judaism rejects Jesus as the Messiah, two issues emerge that complicate its theological position. First, Judaism has never challenged the basic facts about Jesus presented by the Gospels, apart from His divine nature and resurrection. *Sanhedrin 43a* of the Babylonian Talmud records how 'Jesus the Nazarene' was killed on Passover Eve 'because he practiced sorcery, incited people to idol worship, and led the Jewish people astray', even though 'the gentile authorities were interested in his acquittal'.[83] Elaborating on the reasons for Jesus' death in his *Epistle to Yemen*, the influential Jewish scholar Maimonides wrote in 1172 that He:

> impelled people to believe that he was a prophet sent by God to clarify perplexities in the Torah, and that he was the Messiah that was predicted by each and every seer. He interpreted the Torah and its precepts in such a fashion as to lead to their total annulment, to the abolition of all its commandments and to the violation of its prohibitions. The sages, of blessed memory, having become aware of his plans before his reputation spread among our people, meted out fitting punishment to him. Daniel had already alluded to him when he presaged the downfall of a wicked one and a heretic among the Jews who would endeavour to destroy the Law, claim prophecy for himself, make pretences to miracles, and allege that he is the Messiah, as it is written, 'Also the children of the impudent among thy people shall make bold to claim prophecy, but they shall fall.' (Dan. 11:14).[84]

These passages confirm the gospel accounts of Jesus (i) growing up in Nazareth, (ii) having a reputation for performing miracles, (iii) teaching an interpretation of the law, and (iv) being executed on the eve of Passover. Although Maimonides' characterisation of Jesus' teachings is somewhat biased, his application of Daniel 11:14 to Him is simply wrong. Apart from the verse's mention of plural figures instead of a single person ('the *children* of the impudent among thy people'), it is also part of a longer prophecy about the wars between the Seleucids and Ptolemies *200 years before Jesus*, with the people in question being Jews who assisted Antiochus III in his campaign against Egypt—an effort which did indeed 'fall' when the Egyptian general Scopas re-captured Judea.[85] *Bava Metzia 105a* in the Talmud linked the verse to robbers and shedders of blood, and even Rashi—no friend of Christianity—did not believe it alluded to Jesus, but interpreted it as applying to 'the renegades of Israel and their company'.[86]

Maimonides also curiously disregarded the Messianic nature of Isaiah 35:3-6 and 61:1. In what would have surprised the Jewish community at Qumran who carefully preserved the belief—expressed in manuscript 4Q521—that the Messiah would perform miracles of healing and raise the dead, he wrote in his *Mishneh Torah* that 'It should not occur to you that the King Messiah must bring wondrous signs or perform marvels or invent new things or revive the dead or anything like what the fools say. It is not so'.[87] This illustrates the second issue complicating Judaism's claims about Jesus not being the Messiah—the numerous instances, evident from its own sources, of historical revision and prophetic reinterpretation necessary to render Messianic passages inapplicable to Him. Why was 'virgin' in Isaiah 7:14 only re-translated as 'young woman' a century into the Christian era? Why did Rashi claim that the Messiah in Daniel 9:26 who would be cut off before Jerusalem's destruction was 'Agrippa, the king of Judea', when Agrippa died of old age in luxury for helping Rome destroy Jerusalem? Why were the Qumran Jews— far closer to the time of Isaiah's prophecies than Maimonides—'fools' for believing that the Messiah would perform miracles and raise the dead? What did later Jews find in Isaiah 53 to link it to Israel which the ancient Rabbis Yehuda HaNasi, Yonatan, Yefet ben Elī ha-Levi al-Baṣrī, and the author of the *Zohar* missed in applying it to the Messiah? Why did thirty pieces of silver need to refer to something more than just actual pieces of silver?

These questions, and others of a similar nature that could be asked, collectively illustrate the pains modern Judaism has taken to distance itself from the prophetic interpretations of Christianity and many of its own ancient sages. Whilst agreement exists that certain passages are Messianic, others have been neutralised through practical omission—like Isaiah 61:1—or interpretive redefinition. This is all to its loss, as a careful examination of the scriptures reveals Judaism's importance in preserving the knowledge of the true religion against the errors of the ancient world. From the very first prophecy in Genesis 3:15, mankind received the promise of a deliverer who would one day crush Lucifer's power. When ignorance and superstition threatened to overrun the world, Genesis 12:3 recorded God's separation of Abraham as a chosen figure through whom 'all the families of the earth shall be blessed'. Rabbi Isaiah Horowitz saw the truth of this when he wrote in the *Shnei Luhot ha-Berit* that this blessing signified nothing less than that 'the original design for the world will materialise [and] the fall from grace due to having eaten from the tree will be reversed'.[88]

Centuries later, Israel received the Mosaic law to separate them from the surrounding nations, with the institution of a sacrificial system to focus their minds on the guilt humanity bore before an all-powerful God. In time, the blessing of Genesis 3:15 and 12:3 was revealed to be a descendant of the Davidic monarchy, but one whose 'throne shall be established forever'.[89] This Messiah would be human, but with an unmistakeably divine nature—able to not only crush Lucifer's power, but rule forever.[90] In the age of the prophets, further details about this Messiah were given, from the timing and place of His appearing to the signs the people should look for to recognise Him. Specific miracles of healing were foretold, as the Qumran Jews recognised, along with the sign given to the House of David that He would be born of a virgin.[91] He would arrive in Jerusalem to rejoicing, but 'lowly and riding upon a donkey'.[92]

The Messiah would also experience unparalleled suffering—being made 'an offering for sin', as Isaiah 53 records, who would be bruised by God Himself. This was a radical revelation—in place of lambs and other burnt offerings established under the Mosaic law, the *Messiah* would be God's 'righteous Servant [who] shall justify many, for He shall bear their iniquities'.[93] In doing so, the Messiah would be killed—cut off and stricken 'for the transgressions of My people'—but in the unusual circumstances of His grave being made with the wicked, but with the rich at His death.[94] Other prophecies foretold specific forms of suffering and degradation He would undergo, from being beaten and spat upon to watching as lots were cast for His clothing.[95] Thirty pieces of silver would be paid for His betrayal, but the money would ultimately be thrown back into the temple for the potter.[96]

All of these prophecies, carefully preserved by the Jews for centuries, were fulfilled by Jesus. Born of a virgin in Bethlehem prior to the destruction of Jerusalem, He was hailed as the Son of David who healed multitudes of their sicknesses and injuries. He died as an offering for sin at the very hour the Passover lambs were being sacrificed at the Temple, crucified between 'the wicked' and buried in the tomb of the rich.[97] Furthermore, just as Psalm 16:10 foretold that God would not allow his 'Holy One' to see decay, Jesus rose bodily from the dead on the Sunday following His crucifixion. Having 'poured out His soul unto death' to bear the sins of others, His resurrection fulfilled the prophecy in Isaiah 53:11 that, despite experiencing death two verses earlier, He would 'see the labour of His soul, and be satisfied'. It also demonstrated in the clearest terms the fulfilment of Genesis 3:15. Jesus, the seed of the woman, had been 'bruised' via the crucifixion, but in doing so He had thoroughly *crushed* Lucifer's power. No longer would mankind have to suffer under the weight of sin—the 'Lamb of God who takes away the sin of the world' had finally come.[98]

Clear as the fulfilment of these prophecies are, a core objection of Judaism is that Jesus did not fulfil *all* the Messianic qualifications noted in the Old Testament.[99] This objection possesses a technical degree of truth, but lacks the persuasive force many in Judaism assign to it. Judaism and Christianity agree that the Messiah must fulfil all the Messianic qualifications recorded in scripture, but disagree over the timing of their fulfilment; the former looks for their occurrence in a single Messianic age, whilst the latter divides them between Jesus' first and second coming.[100]

The second coming of the Messiah is not, as some within Judaism would claim, a theological dodge to avoid admitting that Jesus 'failed to fulfil these essential Messianic passages', but a plain scriptural truth.[101] This is evident throughout the Old Testament when the Messiah is presented in purportedly contradictory terms—the one who 'shall have dominion from sea to sea' and whose 'enemies will lick the dust' in Psalm 72:8-9, and yet would be 'despised and rejected by men, a man of sorrows and acquainted with grief' in Isaiah 53:3.[102] Both are equally Messianic, but clearly relate to separate periods. Ancient Judaism itself acknowledged this duality—even if it failed to understand it—with *Sanhedrin 98a* in the Talmud noting:

> a contradiction between two depictions of the coming of the Messiah. It is written: 'There came with the clouds of heaven, one like unto a son of man...and there was given him dominion and glory and a kingdom...his dominion is an everlasting dominion' (Daniel 7:13-14). And it is written: 'Behold, your king will come to you; he is just and victorious; lowly and riding upon a donkey' (Zechariah 9:9).[103]

Rather than interpret this as evidence that the Messiah would come twice, first in a 'lowly' form and secondly with the full glory of heaven, the Talmud noted Rabbi Alexandri's explanation instead that 'If the Jewish people merit redemption, the Messiah will come in a miraculous manner with the clouds of heaven. If they do not merit redemption, the Messiah will come lowly and riding upon a donkey'.[104] The problem with this interpretation is that the prophecy was never conditional. It also runs afoul of Psalm 119:160: 'The *entirety* of Your word is truth'.[105] To claim that Daniel 7:13-14—in which the Messiah comes with the clouds of heaven and is 'given dominion and glory'—might not be true if the Jews failed to merit redemption, is to elevate man's actions over God's. But as Isaiah 14:24-27 reveals about God's will, 'Surely, as I have thought, so it shall come to pass, and as I have purposed, so it shall stand … For the Lord of hosts has purposed, and who will annul it?' Human unworthiness could no more cancel Daniel 7 in favour of Zechariah 9 than it could extinguish the sun or reverse time. These passages show there must *necessarily* be two Messianic comings.

The nature of these comings is also revealed in scripture. Just as Zechariah 9:9 foretold, the first coming saw the Messiah appear with salvation, 'lowly and riding on a donkey'—a symbol of peace.[106] Jesus the Messiah came to live among us, provide instruction, and serve as an offering for sin, with the Lord laying upon Him 'the iniquity of us all'.[107] In doing so, He proved Himself *salvator mundi* or saviour of the world, with John 3:16-17 revealing the extent of God's mercy toward His fallen creation:

> For God so loved the world that He gave His only begotten Son, that whoever believes in Him should not perish but have everlasting life. For God did not send His Son into the world to condemn the world, but that the world through Him might be saved.

In the second coming, however, the Messiah will appear with the full power of heaven—no longer the baby of Christmas or suffering servant of Isaiah 53, but the sovereign judge of all. Daniel 7:14 spoke of the Messiah being given 'everlasting dominion' that 'all peoples, nations, and languages should serve Him'. At *this* coming, every knee shall bow and every tongue confess that Jesus the Messiah is Lord.[108] Jesus Himself spoke of this in Matthew 25:31-41, in which He would come again in glory with the angels of heaven:

> All the nations will be gathered before Him, and He will separate them one from another, as a shepherd divides his sheep from the goats. And He will set the sheep on His right hand, but the goats on the left. Then the King will say to those on His right hand, 'Come, you blessed of My Father, inherit the kingdom prepared for you from the foundation of the world … Then He will also say to those on the left hand, 'Depart from Me, you cursed, into the everlasting fire prepared for the devil and his angels'.

Central to this judgment are the words of Jesus in John 3:18-19 about His Messianic role. As these verses reveal:

> He who believes in Him is not condemned; but he who does not
> believe is condemned already, because he has not believed in the name
> of the only begotten Son of God. And this is the condemnation, that
> the light has come into the world, and men loved darkness rather than
> light, because their deeds were evil.

As Chapter 7 noted, we stand by default as rebels against God—all having sinned and fallen short of His standard.[109] Offensive as this truth might be to our pride, it is perilous to our eternal welfare if we ignore it, for 'the wages of sin is death' and on our own merit we could only hope to tremble before an all-righteous judge.[110] But we must remember the divine mercy promised in Genesis 3 and Isaiah 53. As the Apostle Paul wrote in Romans 5:8-9, 'God demonstrates His own love toward us, in that while we were still sinners, Christ died for us. Much more then, having now been justified by His blood, *we shall be saved from wrath through Him*', to which we may recall the very words of Jesus Himself in John 3:18, that '*He who believes in Him is not condemned*'.[111]

These verses establish the terms for our salvation. But what does it mean to 'believe' in Jesus? As James 2:19 notes, 'Even the demons believe—and tremble!' John 3:18 clarifies that it is more than mere intellectual assent to His existence, with the 'condemned' not believing '*in the name* of the only begotten Son of God'.[112] The nature of the belief therefore relates to His Messianic identity. To believe in Jesus is to accept that He is who the scriptures proclaim Him to be, acknowledging Him as our Saviour. Isaiah 61:1 declares Him to be the preacher of good tidings, the healer of the broken-hearted, and the proclaimer of liberty to the captives. Isaiah 53 declares Him to be the man of sorrows who 'poured out His soul unto death' and 'bore the sin of many, and made intercession for the transgressors'. Zechariah 9:9 declares Him to be our king. John 1:14 declares Him to be God incarnate, who 'became flesh and dwelt among us'. Acts 4:12 declares Him to be the only 'name under heaven given among men by which we must be saved', and in John 14:6 He declares of Himself that 'I am the way, the truth, and the life. No one comes to the Father except through me'.[113]

To believe in Jesus is to accept Him as Lord, the sovereign judge of heaven who—in the utmost expression of mercy—came as an infant, lived as a man, and died for our sins as the sinless Lamb of God. In doing so, He fulfilled the prophecies that spoke to His first coming, and He will come again in glory to fulfil the remainder at His second. It is also to recognise our position as sinners who have offended Him in thought, word, and deed. By right we stand on the losing side as rebels with all the forces of darkness and evil—enemies of God awaiting the terrible day of judgment. But in the midst of our ruin and despair, God Himself became man—God-with-us, *Immanuel*—to bear the punishment we deserved.

All have sinned and fallen short of God's law, Romans 3:23 declares, but 1 John 1:9 records the divine declaration that 'If we confess our sins, He is faithful and just to forgive us our sins and to cleanse us from all unrighteousness'. No longer rebellious but righteous in His sight, we look to the assurance of John 1:12 that 'as many as received Him, to them He gave the right to become children of God, to those who believe in His name'.

This is no fairy-tale promise or deluded hope. As the previous chapters illustrate, an examination into the origins of the universe and the emergence of life from non-living matter proves the existence of an uncaused first cause who manifested incalculable power to bring about the natural world. This being, whom we call God, then created a host of lesser beings endowed with free will, some of whom left their angelic stations to rebel against His authority. In time, their war came to the earth and our first parents who, through a tragic exercise of their own free will, also chose disobedience. All would have been lost without a supreme act of mercy—the promise of a redeemer. Generations later, God in His providence called Abraham to be the progenitor of the nation that would produce this redeemer. He subsequently revealed Himself to Abraham's descendants and shaped them into a political and theological state. Prophecies were given concerning the coming Messiah, and the sacrificial system was instituted as a foreshadowing of the atonement for sin. To safeguard the knowledge of our future redemption, these revelations were committed to writing in what we know as the Old Testament. Included among them were stories of Israel's history, showing God's providential role in the Jewish people's preservation. Small though they might have been, He allowed events to position their religion for global influence—first the conquest of the east by Alexander the Great, and secondly the rise in the west of the Roman Empire. With a perfect confluence of timing and geography, the Messiah then appeared in the centre of the then-known world at the very moment a common language and political system prevailed across much of it. This allowed the news of His coming to spread with greater ease than would have otherwise been possible—evidenced by the growth of Christianity in its first few centuries. By the fourth century it had become the official religion of the Roman Empire, the heavenly stone and kingdom identified in Daniel 2:34-45 that would stand forever, even as Rome and its empire fell. As Rashi wrote, but failed to appreciate, in his commentary on Daniel 2:44:

> when the kingdom of Rome is still in existence ... the God of heaven
> will set up a kingdom: *The kingdom of the Holy One, blessed be He,*
> *which will never be destroyed, is the kingdom of the Messiah.*[114]

Although Rashi might have still hoped in his day for another Messiah, since the 'kingdom of Rome' nominally survived via the Byzantine Empire, the Ottoman conquest of it in 1453 brought it to a final end—ending with it any future possibility of a Messiah other than Jesus. By his own interpretation of Daniel 2:44, the time for the 'kingdom of the Messiah' to appear ended in the fifteenth century. Judaism's hope for a different Messiah is therefore—on its own terms—prophetically time-barred. Rashi was correct, however, in acknowledging that 'the kingdom of the Holy One ... the kingdom of the Messiah' would be set up whilst the kingdom of Rome was 'still in existence'; he simply refused to see that it pointed to Christianity.

Just as the scriptures foretold, Jesus the Messiah has come as our saviour. When He appears a second time in glory it will be as our sovereign. The terms of our salvation are simple—belief and trust in His name, acceptance of His mercy, and repentance from our sins. We must be made righteous in God's sight through Jesus' perfect sacrifice on our behalf. No other currency will be accepted by God at the day of judgment. Salvation cannot be bought, earned, or achieved through merit, but simply received with gratitude as the gift Ephesians 2:8-9 declares it to be: 'For by grace you have been saved through faith, and that not of yourselves; it is the gift of God, not of works, lest anyone should boast'.

The Messiah has come.
Jesus is Lord.
Christianity is true.

9

The Rational Faith

To return to the Introduction, the purpose of this book has been to advance two interconnected themes—that Christianity is rational and, above all else, true. This was the West's understanding for much of the last 2,000 years, but events over the last few centuries have caused some to question these once-unshakeable premises. Even in William Wilberforce's day two centuries ago, unbelief was rapidly spreading amongst the cultural elite. Only a few years before he published his book, revolutionary France had sought to abolish Christianity in favour of 'the new faith of liberty and reason'—instituting a reign of terror intended, with no trace of irony, to return 'fanaticism' to 'the hell from which it was devised'.[1] With the subsequent rise of scientism, communism, world wars, and the sexual revolution, popular religious belief was undermined even further to form the increasingly-irreligious world we see today. A consideration of the evidence, however, proves Christianity to be the *true* faith of liberty and reason. Now more than ever before, atheism is vulnerable as its logical and scientific assumptions are shown to be false. We now understand with greater insight that the universe had a beginning, which could only have been accomplished by an incomparably-powerful force outside of time and space—God, the uncaused first cause. We know that the simplest life forms are too complex to have randomly arisen in the time the universe has existed—even assuming a hitherto-unknown process of generation. These are not speculative hypotheses but logical deductions that, as the eleventh century monk Anselm of Canterbury would have appreciated, can be recognised 'by the force of reason alone'.[2] Amidst our existence in a finely-tuned universe, belief in a creator is *inherently* rational.

But reason, powerful though it might be, can only take us so far. We can use it to discern which of the world's religions hold false—and therefore uninspired—views about the existence of the universe, but a divine revelation is required for us to know more. This was duly given to the Jewish people, who preserved records of God's interaction with them in the Tanakh, or Old Testament. Central to this was the promise of a Messiah who would redeem humanity, along with prophecies about how to recognise His appearance. In the fullness of time Jesus was revealed to be this Messiah, with the books of the New Testament recording details of His life, ministry, and commandments. These two testaments—collectively known as the Bible—have been faithfully transmitted to the present day with the same doctrinal clarity their original audiences received generations ago. Though some details might cause perplexity with the passage of time and lack of familiarity with ancient customs, the core message remains unchanged and easily grasped—in our sinful rebellion we are deserving of wrath, but God in His mercy became man, died for our sins, and rose from the dead to assure the promise of salvation to those who believe in Him.

All of this the previous chapters have demonstrated, using the latest scientific evidence, histories ancient and modern, and the best commentaries the author could procure—some 1,100 citations in total. To the inquiring mind diligently searching for truth, we submit this book in the hope that it will be examined with the full seriousness it deserves. We also pray that the seeker's path would be illumined with that spiritual grace promised in James 1:5-6, that 'If any of you lacks wisdom, let him ask of God, who gives to all liberally and without reproach, and it will be given to him. But let him ask in faith, with no doubting, for he who doubts is like a wave of the sea driven and tossed by the wind'.

There is a certain mind, however, upon which this book will regrettably have no effect. As the psychologist William James once noted, 'If your heart does not *want* a world of moral reality, your head will assuredly never make you believe in one'.[3] The atheist Thomas Nagel touched upon this with an unusual degree of openness in his book *The Last Word*:

> In speaking of the fear of religion … I am talking about something much deeper—namely, the fear of religion itself. I speak from experience, being strongly subject to this fear myself: I want atheism to be true and am made uneasy by the fact that some of the most intelligent and well-informed people I know are religious believers. It isn't just that I don't believe in God and, naturally, hope that I'm right in my belief. It's that I hope there is no God! *I don't want there to be a God; I don't want the universe to be like that.*[4]

Three centuries before Nagel, the French mathematician and Christian apologist Blaise Pascal considered the importance of this *want*, or motivation. Expressing nothing but 'hearty compassion' for 'those who labour with all their force to obtain instruction', he reserved harsher judgment for 'those who live without giving themselves any trouble, or so much as any thought in this affair':

> We know very well how men, under this indifferency of spirit, behave themselves in the case. They suppose themselves to have made the mightiest effort towards the instruction of their minds, when they have spent some hours in reading the scriptures, and have asked some questions of a clergyman concerning the articles of faith. When this is done, they declare to all the world, that they have consulted books and men without success. I shall be excused if I refrain not from telling such men (what I have often told them) that this neglect of theirs is insupportable. It is not a foreign or a petty interest which is here in debate: we are ourselves the parties, and all our hopes and fortunes are the depending stake.[5]

What Pascal recognised was a fundamental distinction between two types of unbelievers—those who lacked knowledge but were earnestly seeking it, and those who were indifferent or hostile and happy to remain so. For some of the latter, no amount of evidence would ever be sufficient since they did not *wish* for it to be sufficient. Some might have conducted a superficial inquiry into religion, but without the diligence appropriate to the subject—fixating on a question or perceived contradiction as if no one in the history of the church had ever considered and answered it. Instead of examining the scriptures in context or seeing what others over the centuries might have thought, it was easier to declare the matter an impossible barrier to belief and ridicule Christianity for its apparent absurdities—notwithstanding that some of history's greatest minds had examined the same points and resolved them satisfactorily.

It is understandable, however, why some might avoid inquiring too closely into such matters. Acknowledging God's existence involves acknowledging *other* things. At a stroke, the universe ceases to be a purposeless accident in which our actions bear no consequences beyond their immediate effects, but a realm governed by an almighty sovereign in which they carry *eternal* consequences. In such a universe, mercy and love sit alongside justice and purity. To the soul that wants, as Aldous Huxley put it, 'to prove that there is no valid reason why he personally should not do as he wants to do', this is not only repugnant, but terrifying.[6] It is far easier to deny God's existence than to accept that, under His justice, they are among the damned. As Jesus declared in John 3:19-20, 'this is the condemnation, that the light has come into the world, and men loved darkness rather than light, because their deeds were evil. For everyone practicing evil hates the light and does not come to the light, lest his deeds should be exposed'.

However industriously some might have avoided these considerations, whether through denial or distraction, judgment still approaches. Romans 1:18 declares 'the wrath of God is revealed from heaven against all ungodliness and unrighteousness of men, who suppress the truth'. Through creation, His 'invisible attributes' and 'eternal power' are evident to all, so that, as verse 20 states, *they are without excuse.* It will be no defence to say 'I never thought of God' when the very heavens declare His glory.[7] The problem faced by this sort of individual therefore has less to do with reason and more to do with perceptions of liberty. Instead of acknowledging the sovereignty of their creator, they would deny His existence to escape His judgment. Living as they wish, they erect the most formidable of mental barriers upon the flimsiest of pretexts to safeguard their apparent autonomy. *Creatio ex nihilo* is denounced as impossible, but infinite universes and strings with ten dimensions—which no one can actually find—are regarded as 'too good to be false'.[8] The creation of life by an omnipotent God is dismissed as childish, but spontaneous generation—notwithstanding its inherent impossibility—is touted as the foundation of biology.[9] How much greater must the atheist's faith be in comparison to that of a Christian!

Yet these matters must be pondered seriously, especially since our time is short. As James 4:14 reminds us, 'you do not know what will happen tomorrow. For what is your life? It is even a vapour that appears for a little time and then vanishes away'. No matter how vibrant or full of 'positive energy' one might be today, death—that king of terrors spoken of in Job 18:14—is always victorious. The French minister Charles Drelincourt made the point well in 1651:

> The great Alexander, and the triumphant Caesars, who have made all the world to tremble … could never find anything that might protect them from Death's power. When magnificent statues and stately trophies were raised to their honour, Death laughed at their vanity, and made sport with their persons. The rich marbles, where so many proud titles are engraved, cover nothing but a little rotted flesh, and a few bones, which Death hath broken and reduced to ashes.[10]

To be careless of—or worse, disinterested—in this is to do an eternal disservice to one's soul. So long as one lives, there is still hope for the salvation promised in the scriptures and detailed in the preceding chapter. Jesus, the prophesied Messiah, entered this world—tainted though it was with evil—and died *for you*. But He did not stay dead. Rather, as the scriptures foretold, He rose from the dead victorious, proving that even though 'all die, even so in Christ all shall be made alive'.[11] This is not a speculative wish or—as Stephen Hawking once claimed—a mere crutch for those 'who are afraid of the dark'.[12] It is an objective truth.

For those who desire the truth but have not yet found it, the years it has taken to write this book have been for you. Every effort has been made to assist your quest for the truth, but, as the nineteenth-century theologian Thomas Chalmers once wrote, it is up to you to follow where 'the light of argument may conduct'.[13] Some might claim, like the old Cult of Reason, that Christianity cannot 'endure the brilliancy of the light' in modern times, but the evidence reveals that *only* Christianity can endure it.[14] However critically you examine it, Christianity will not fall. The same cannot be said for other belief systems.

Whether one has grown up without a religion, in a different religion, or considers themselves to be 'spiritual but not religious', it must be recognised that truth exists. We live in a universe governed by rules. No matter the country or culture, two plus two will always equal four. It would be illogical in the extreme to imagine that the God who created the universe with such finely-tuned parameters would be indifferent to how He was worshipped. As Matthew 7:21 makes clear, 'Not everyone who says to Me, 'Lord, Lord,' shall enter the kingdom of heaven, but he who does the will of My Father in heaven'. Jesus' words in John 14:6 are even more explicit: 'I am the way, the truth, and the life. No one comes to the Father except through Me'. God does not sit atop a mountain that can be climbed via different paths, but, as Acts 4:12 declares, 'there is no other name under heaven given among men by which we must be saved' beyond Jesus. Any belief system that would proclaim otherwise is, by definition, false.

Such exclusivity is jarring to the modern mind, just as it was to the pagan pantheism of first-century Rome. And yet, a consideration of the evidence proves it to be right. The cosmological shortcomings of Hinduism, Buddhism, Mormonism, and other such religions are evident. If they cannot account for a fundamental question like how the universe began, how can they speak to our eternal happiness? Even for the belief systems that survive this hurdle, the problem of evil presents an additional challenge. Others, such as Islam or the Jehovah's Witnesses, prove themselves false through their contrasts with the very scriptures they purport to affirm. God is not schizophrenic, nor do His prophecies fail. As Chapter 3 demonstrated, the contradictions between the Quran and the Torah prove that they cannot have come from the same source. God is not a man, that He should lie.[15] Deuteronomy 18:22 also declares that if a prophet speaks in the name of God and the event does not occur, 'the prophet has spoken it presumptuously; you shall not be afraid of him'. Notwithstanding the dozens of predictions about the date of the end of the world made by the Jehovah's Witnesses as part of their key teachings, not one has come true.[16] Colossians 2:8 warns us to beware, lest anyone cheat us 'through philosophy and empty deceit, according to the tradition of men ... and not according to Christ'.

Whatever their background, we must speak with compassion to those who were once affiliated with religion but left in anger or despair—particularly those who escaped a cult-like group or suffered deception or betrayal. Looking at some religious groups today, there is indeed much to be angry about—chief among them false teachings, spiritual manipulation, and the abuse of the vulnerable entrusted to their care. Matthew 7:15 condemns those 'false prophets, who come to you in sheep's clothing, but inwardly they are ravenous wolves'. Even the church can be vulnerable to leaders who do not appropriately handle themselves or the word of God, desiring—as 1 Timothy 1:7 puts it—'to be teachers of the law, understanding neither what they say nor the things which they affirm'. Others might abuse their position for personal gain, failing to 'shepherd the flock of God' as Jesus—our true 'good shepherd' who gave His life for the sheep—intended.[17] But just as counterfeit money does not negate, but rather affirms, the existence of genuine currency, so the wickedness of some does not take away from Christianity's inherent truth. Jesus taught in Matthew 13:24 that the kingdom of heaven is like a man who sowed good seed in his field, which was spoiled when his 'enemy' came and sowed tares—a weed resembling wheat that would cause headaches and sickness when eaten.[18] Rather than immediately pluck the tares out, which would have uprooted the wheat as well, the harvesters were instructed to gather them together at the end when the tares would be burned. Our experience with such people might have been grievously bitter, but they do not undermine the existence of the true wheat.

However you might have been hurt, the salvation of your soul is far too precious to be put off from true Christianity by the sinful actions of human tares. In the church you will undoubtedly find hypocrites, since it is the best place for their spiritual growth. When the religious leaders asked why Jesus associated with the 'sinners and tax collectors'—those considered to be the worst in society—He answered in Mark 2:17 that 'Those who are well have no need of a physician, but those who are sick. I did not come to call the righteous, but sinners, to repentance'. Even the hardest of hearts can be changed and renewed by an awakening of the Holy Spirit. Few who saw the fast-living, slave-trading, God-hating 'infidel and libertine' John Newton in his younger years could have imagined that he would be transformed by faith into a repentant clergyman and staunch abolitionist who would denounce the sins of his youth and pen the words to 'Amazing Grace' in 1772:

> Amazing grace! (how sweet the sound,) that sav'd a wretch like me! I
> once was lost, but now am found, was blind but now I see. 'Twas grace
> that taught my heart to fear, and grace my fears reliev'd; how precious
> did that grace appear the hour I first believ'd![19]

To the sceptics, we would return to Baron Albrecht von Haller's statement in the Introduction: *truth loses nothing by being closely examined*.[20] This was written by one of the eighteenth century's sharpest minds—a physician, botanist, and poet who encouraged his daughter and others to discover the truth of Christianity. This book offers you the same encouragement. Read the Bible diligently. Pray for wisdom. Ask the hard questions. Search for the answers. Be patient and *do not give up*. The first disciples often lacked understanding. Paul originally persecuted Christianity before ending his days proclaiming it. Augustine of Hippo initially 'despaired of finding [truth]' in the fourth-century church, but later became one of its most influential theologians.[21] His contemporary Jerome found the Bible's writing style to be 'most irritating' at first, before producing the edition that proclaimed the gospel to Europe for a thousand years.[22] The history of the church is full of examples like these who initially struggled—sometimes mightily—before coming to a resolute faith in Christianity. Modern times are also not lacking when it comes to such examples, from the writers C.S. Lewis and Evelyn Waugh to the geneticist Francis Collins, rocket scientist Werhner von Braun, and many others. As Matthew 7:7 promises, 'seek, and you will find'.

The road to faith is not always smooth. The Bible reveals what we *need* to know concerning salvation, but it does not address all questions we might possibly have. In this life we see through a glass darkly, as 1 Corinthians 13:12 declares, but the day is coming when we shall know as we are known. It is perfectly legitimate to have questions, and your author will confess to still having many, but this is the case for everyone and we must accept that some will remain unanswered on this side of eternity. Nevertheless, what the Bible does reveal is sufficient to establish its authenticity. Some elements might be 'hard to understand' as the apostle recognised in 2 Peter 3:16, but a careful reading will illuminate its truth, goodness, and beauty. Persevere in your study, with the recognition of Proverbs 9:10 that 'The fear of the Lord is the beginning of wisdom, and the knowledge of the Holy One is understanding'.

To the Christian reader, we must now address a different message. As Chapter 1 noted, the world faces a renewed 'cult of reason' more influential than its eighteenth-century forerunner. The decline of Christianity across the West is undoubtedly real, with as few as one-in-ten under the age of thirty confessing it in some countries.[23] But although this suggests a dismal future, it does not have to turn out that way. As Jesus reminded His disciples in Matthew 19:26, with God all things are possible. It is true that we face 'a liberality which is intolerant against all who hold definite truth as from God', as one nineteenth-century scholar called it, but every age has produced witnesses who rose up in defence of that truth.[24] Now is the time for us to make a similar stand. Not only do we have the advantage of divine revelation itself—accompanied by history, logic, and science—we also have the opportunity of timing. The sexual revolution has aged badly; rather than offering an abundance of liberation and happiness, it has brought forth unparalleled ruin—immiseration, broken marriages, incurable diseases, and deaths of the unborn in the hundreds of millions. Even in the 1990s, economists studying the breakdown of social norms could quantify its negative impact.[25] A generation later, we struggle with a 25% spike in suicides and historic increases in other 'deaths of despair'.[26] All is clearly not well.

The promises of the sexual revolution have failed because they were based upon a lie—that man could live in opposition to God's commandments and still flourish. This was Lucifer's original temptation, that our first parents could order their lives better than God without consequence. From the beginning of history down to the present hour, man has been similarly seduced. All around us we see its impact. Consider, for instance, that between 1960 and 2016, the percentage of American children living without fathers nearly tripled to 23%, with such children at an increased risk of negative behavioural and emotional outcomes.[27] If online pornography were a country, its GDP would be higher than Kenya's.[28] Over 200,000 hospital admissions occur in England annually because of self-harm.[29] In recent years, the US has seen a 'disproportionate national increase' in such incidents amongst *middle-aged* adults—outpacing the rate of increase among young people.[30] 28% of US and 29.5% of UK households now consist of only one person—significant increases from historic figures.[31] This social breakdown has had far-reaching impacts, with the US Surgeon General soberly noting that 'loneliness and weak social connections are associated with a reduction in lifespan similar to that caused by smoking 15 cigarettes a day and even greater than that associated with obesity'.[32] Notwithstanding our advances in technology, the West is far sicker in many ways than it once was. As too many have discovered at great cost, the barriers God established were not fences to keep us from pleasure, but guardrails to shield us from pain.

Whatever misery might have been avoided if this had been understood is likely to be eclipsed by what will unfold if we do not boldly proclaim Christianity to a sick and dying world. We are commanded in Matthew 28:19 to make disciples of all nations, and each of us has a role in that commission. William Wilberforce's words to the Christians of 1797 are just as timely now:

> Let [Christians] on their part seriously weigh the important stations
> which they fill, and the various duties which it now peculiarly enforces
> on them. ... the progress of irreligion, and the decay of morals ... are
> such as to alarm every considerate mind, and to forebode the worst
> of consequences, unless some remedy can be applied to the growing
> evil. ... Let true Christians then, with becoming earnestness, strive
> in all things to recommend their profession, and to put to silence
> the vain scoffs of ignorant objectors. Let them boldly assert the cause
> of Christ in an age when so many who bear the name of Christians
> are ashamed of Him: and let them consider as devolved on them the
> important duty of serving, it may be of saving, their country, not by
> busy interference in politics, (in which it cannot but be confessed
> there is much uncertainty,) but rather by that sure and radical benefit
> of restoring the influence of religion, and raising the standards of
> morality. ... Let them pray continually for their country in this season
> of national difficulty.[33]

Whatever our station in life, each of us has the power through the Holy Spirit
to influence others for Christ, even if this influence may not be widely seen. As
George Elliot wrote in *Middlemarch*, 'the growing good of the world is partly
dependent on unhistoric acts; and that things are not so ill with you and me as
they might have been, is half owing to the number who lived faithfully a hidden
life, and rest in unvisited tombs'.[34] No effort in the service of Christ is insignifi-
cant—as Jesus declared in Matthew 10:42, 'whoever gives one of these little ones
only a cup of cold water in the name of a disciple, assuredly, I say to you, he shall
by no means lose his reward', and in Matthew 25:40, 'inasmuch as you did it to
one of the least of these My brethren, you did it to Me'. Through our daily choices,
conversations, and general conduct, we all have the capacity to promote the res-
toration of Christianity.

Such actions may, from time to time, call for an element of courage. The
parable of the sower in Matthew 13 illustrates all too well that some will simply
reject what we have to say—perhaps denouncing our motivations as hatred against
a particular group or cultural orthodoxy. We must recognise, however, that such
attacks for sharing Christian teachings are often based upon:

> the hope ... that the believer will eventually relent and accuse himself
> of failing to love that offended person, who is made to feel 'unsafe'
> when contradicted. The attempt here is not to convince by reason, but
> to intimidate into submission by making 'love of neighbour' into an
> ideological cudgel. ... In the order of knowledge, the most charitable
> thing one can do is share the truth with others. In the case of those who

reject that truth, charity demands that we not affirm that rejection out of a misguided notion that contradicting them is hurtful and offensive, hence un-Christian.[35]

Matthew 5:16 tells us to let our light shine before the world. Faith is not meant to be hidden privately, but lived publicly. Even the atheist writer and magician Penn Jillette appreciated this, stating that 'Proselytizing is annoying, but not proselytizing is immoral ... If you believe in everlasting life and don't annoy me about it, if you're polite and let me believe what I want, even though I'm going to spend eternity in real ... hell, what kind of scumbag are you?'[36] If we truly love our neighbours as ourselves, as Matthew 22:39 requires, we must be honest about what the scriptures reveal.

We must also be careful to avoid pride, however, and recognise that we are merely instruments in this task. To quote John 3:30, 'He must increase, but I must decrease'. As Paul wrote in 1 Corinthians 3:5-7 to a church that was beginning to elevate the personalities of the workers over the work itself:

> Who then is Paul, and who is Apollos, but ministers through whom
> you believed, as the Lord gave to each one? I planted, Apollos watered,
> but God gave the increase. So then neither he who plants is anything,
> nor he who waters, but God who gives the increase.

Whether one plants or waters, the increase ultimately comes from God. We must always be ready, as 1 Peter 3:15 states, to 'give a defence to everyone who asks' why we believe, but we should not imagine that our defence—however eloquent or ineloquent it might be—plays the decisive role. The Bible declares in Romans 8:7 that the worldly mind is hostile to God, and in 1 Corinthians 1:21 that wisdom has its limits—it is the '*message preached* to save those who believe' which possesses true power. Logic and science are all very well, but 'faith comes by hearing, and hearing by the word of God'.[37] Paul did not charge the young minister Timothy to preach human reasoning, but to '*Preach the word*'.[38]

This is not to say, however, that reason is without value. Rather, as Martin Luther understood, it is properly the 'handmaiden' or servant, of faith.[39] In every age, Christianity has benefitted from arguments advanced by its defenders, even as the arguments have changed to respond to the prevailing cultural challenges. In the second century, Quadratus—the first known apologist—wrote a defence or 'apology' to the Roman emperor Hadrian describing how, as a young man, he had encountered many who had been the beneficiaries of Jesus' miracles and could testify to the truth of Christianity:

The works of our Lord have never ceased to be visible, because they were true. We could convince ourselves of the reality of the miracle long after He healed the sick or awakened the dead to life, for they remained with us as living proofs even after our Savior's death, the lives of some amongst them being prolonged to our own day.[40]

Later that century, another testament came from Tertullian's *Apologeticus*, in which he noted how the noon-time darkness of Jesus' crucifixion was sufficiently unnatural that the Romans themselves had preserved a record of it:

In the same hour, too, the light of day was withdrawn, when the sun at the very time was in his meridian blaze. Those who were not aware that this had been predicted about Christ, no doubt thought it an eclipse. *You yourselves have the account of the world-portent still in your archives.*[41]

In addition to these evidentiary appeals, early apologists also defended Christianity philosophically. Justin Martyr's *First Apology* to the emperor Antoninus Pius sought justice for Christianity against the false accusations of hostile magistrates—firmly grounding it in reason and truth:

Reason directs those who are truly pious and all true philosophers to honour and love only what is true, to decline to follow traditional opinions if these be worthless. Not only does sound reason direct us to refuse the guidance of those who taught anything wrong; but it is incumbent upon the lover of truth, by all means and even if death be threatened … to choose to say and to do what is right.[42]

Two centuries later in the aftermath of Rome's invasion by the Visigoths, Augustine of Hippo defended Christianity against claims that the suppression of pagan worship had led to the city's fall. Not only was Christianity responsible for much of the city's preservation, but the pagan deities were 'useless, and their worship superfluous':

they cannot complain against the Christian religion, as if it were that which gave offence to the gods and caused them to abandon Rome, since the Roman immorality had long ago driven from the altars of the city a cloud of little gods, like as many flies. And yet where was this host of divinities, when, long before the corruption of the primitive morality, Rome was taken and burnt by the Gauls? Perhaps they were present, but asleep?[43]

Augustine also wrote against the follies of superstition, demonstrating that fate, or 'the position of the stars at the time of each one's conception or birth, is an unmeaning word, for astrology itself is a delusion'.[44] In contrast to Mediterranean mythology, Christianity was a revealed and rational religion. In the sixth century, John Philoponus argued against Aristotle's eternal universe to show that the Biblical view of creation was compatible with logic.[45] 500 years later, Anselm of Canterbury developed the ontological argument for the existence of God. In the 1200s, Thomas Aquinas wrote of the unmoved mover and first cause. In the 1600s, Isaac Newton declared that the 'most beautiful' solar system 'could only proceed from the counsel and dominion' of God.[46] Three centuries later, the priest and physicist Georges Lemaître wrote how Christianity and science were compatible, notwithstanding atheism's claims to the contrary.[47] Innumerable figures have defended Christianity over millennia using a variety of apologetic arguments. Their tools are available to you, even if they will only ever be supporting arguments for the Gospel's proclamation.

The present hour may seem daunting, but we must recall the words of Solomon in Ecclesiastes 1:9 that 'there is nothing new under the sun'. At its core, humanity's rebellion against God remains unchanged. We can draw encouragement, however, from the fact that the West has recovered from spiritual disillusionment before and could do so again. In 1736, the Anglican clergyman Joseph Butler began his *Analogy of Religion* with this dispiriting preface:

> It is come, I know not how, to be taken for granted by many persons, that Christianity is not so much as a subject of inquiry; but that it is, now at length, discovered to be fictitious. And accordingly they treat it as if, in the present age, this were an agreed point among all people of discernment; and nothing remained but to set it up as a principle subject of mirth and ridicule … for its having so long interrupted the pleasures of the world.[48]

Two years after this was written, John and Charles Wesley discovered the transformative power of real Christian faith. Out of this came the Methodist movement, with small groups of believers meeting together for Bible study, discussion, and prayer. As the historian Herbert Schlossberg wrote:

> Along with the spread of these groups in myriad mining, fishing, and textile towns, scattered Anglican parishes came to life …. by the end of the century there were influential concentrations of evangelicals all over England. Societies to extend mission and to do good works sprang up all over the nation, and publications at all levels (from tracts intended for near-illiterates to collections of sermons to journals full

of historical, political, and theological reasoning) began appearing, supplemented by newspapers and pamphlets.[49]

Within a century of Butler's pessimistic remarks, evangelicals like William Wilberforce and John Newton had led the charge to abolish the slave trade, enacted laws mitigating the harshness of the industrial revolution, and established charities for the protection of the vulnerable and marginalised.[50] Schools were transformed into training grounds for Christian leaders.[51] Society as a whole was so altered as to be almost unrecognisable. Even those who disliked Christianity—such as Francis Place, a clothing merchant, political activist, and ardent Malthusian— could nevertheless reflect that, in comparison with their childhood, society was very much improved:

> The circumstances ... I have mentioned relative to the ignorance, the immorality, the grossness, the obscenity, the drunkenness, the dirtiness and depravity of the middling and even of a large portion of the better sort of tradesmen, the artisans, and the journeymen tradesmen of London in the days of my youth, may excite a suspicion that the picture I have drawn is a caricature, the parts of which are out of keeping and have no symmetry as a whole.[52]

Place's description was *not* a caricature, however—the England of his childhood really *had been* that different. Alongside the revival's political reforms, a profound cultural change had occurred:

> The ignorant became readers, writers, and leaders; the indigent began working and learning to excel at their work; housewives raised their children to be good family people, citizens, and neighbours; paupers and drunks began to earn a living, to save and invest and send their children to the universities and their grandchildren to the House of Commons. An often brutal society in which a woman walking alone on the street could expect to be at least verbally molested, in which the highways were unsafe for the unarmed, in which political corruption was common, in which sexual promiscuity was the norm, had by the early years of the new century become kinder, more loving, and (dare we say it?) more Christian.[53]

How might such a transformation occur today? With the collapse of many denominations and institutional forms of religion, Christianity in some ways is now reverting to its earlier pre-Edict-of-Thessalonica form—a time before the year 380 when it became the Roman Empire's state religion and could depend upon public support. Although the early church might have lacked access to the halls of power or wealth of cathedrals, it nevertheless brought about an utter transformation of the Mediterranean world. This was done one relationship at a time—frequently in homes where people gathered to learn and worship.[54] As the professor of historical theology, Ephraim Radner, noted, such a model might well be suited for today:

> Times of instability are frequently times of insight and even creativity. … But steadiness is also needed—the kind of intellectual stability of discipline, expectations, and time that relative isolation, prayer, and monastic virtues once permitted … What will this look like? There will no doubt be a spectrum of formats in play … something for smaller groups of committed theological spirits, bound to the holiness of life and humility of mind, given over to the 'indwelling Word of Christ' (Col. 3:16), and gathering in churches or homes, using forms of long-term learning that are already well-tested. They would study Scripture, theology, and the church's history at a slow and regular pace and in a rhythm of gathering that is adapted to the toil of our daily existence.[55]

The challenges we face are similar to those encountered by earlier reformers. Although their eras had not been shaped by scientism, world wars, communism or the sexual revolution, they were all too familiar with spiritual poverty, indifference, and hostility. Our time has witnessed a resurgence of these characteristics, frequently aided by the tools of prosperity. But even as we must fight once more the spiritual battles won by previous generations, we do so as followers of the rational faith—armed with divine revelation, scientific and historical knowledge, and centuries of collective wisdom. If God is for us, who can be against us?[56] Whatever our circumstances, let us work with all diligence for the good of the kingdom, standing firm and proclaiming the truths of God in sincere tenderness to those whom He loves and died for. Let us not be ashamed of the gospel of Christ, for it is the power of God to salvation for everyone who believes.[57] Jesus declared that the harvest is plentiful but the labourers few, so let us pray that the Lord of the harvest would send us out, wherever we might be, for the glory of His name—and that we might prove ourselves worthy of the calling.

Notes to the Introduction

1   Kevin Belmonte, *William Wilberforce: A Hero for Humanity* (Zondervan 2007) 17 and 62; William Wilberforce, *A Practical View of the Prevailing Religious System of Professed Christians, in the Higher and Middle Classes in this Country, Contrasted with Real Christianity* (4th edn, Glasgow 1833).

2   Wilberforce (n 1) 366.

3   Richard Dawkins, *The God Delusion* (First Mariner Books 2008) 74.

4   See respectively Barry Ritholtz, 'Are the Poor Better Off Than King Louis XIV?', *Bloomberg* 16 January 2015, <www.bloomberg.com/view/articles/2015-01-16/are-the-poor-better-off-than-king-louis-xiv> accessed 1 October 2020, noting that 'Let me remind you of the Dark Ages, the centuries of intellectual and economic regression that came after the collapse of the Roman Empire. It was the Church that wouldn't allow knowledge to be disseminated, fought scientific inquiry and limited literacy'; Transcript for March 11 Show, 'Scarborough Country', 11 March 2004, <www.nbcnews.com/id/4515474/#.V-souPkrLIV> accessed 1 October 2020; and Ian Sample, 'Stephen Hawking: "There is no heaven; it's a fairy story"', *The Guardian*, 15 May 2011, <www.theguardian.com/science/2011/may/15/stephen-hawking-interview-there-is-no-heaven> accessed 1 October 2020.

5   See Baron Albrecht von Haller, *Letters from Baron Haller to His Daughter, on the Truths of the Christian Religion* (London 1803) 145-46 and 5, respectively.

6   Thomas Chalmers, *The Evidence and Authority of the Christian Revelation* (4th edn, Edinburgh 1817) 216.

Notes to Chapter 1 - The Cult of Reason

1   H.D. Traill (ed), *The Works of Thomas Carlyle*, vol 4 (Cambridge Univ. Press 2010) 228.

2   ibid 227-28.

3   M.A. Thiers, *The History of the French Revolution* (London 1845) 374.

4   ibid.

5   See R. Phillips (ed), *Biographical Anecdotes of the Founders of the French Republic, and of Other Eminent Characters, who have Distinguished Themselves in the Progress of the Revolution* (London 1797) 97 and Charly Coleman, *The Virtues of Abandon: An Anti-Individualist History of the French Enlightenment* (Stanford Univ. Press 2014) 268.

6   Cloots was executed on March 24, 1794, with Chaumette following on April 13, 1794, see Gregory Fremont-Barnes (ed), *Encyclopedia of the Age of Political Revolutions and New Ideologies, 1760-1815*, vol 1 (Greenwood Press 2007) 119 and 329.

7   J.F. Maclear (ed), *Church and State in the Modern Age: A Documentary History* (Oxford Univ. Press 1995) 88.

8   See Gregory A. Smith, 'A growing share of Americans say it's not necessary to believe in God to be moral', 16 October 2017, <www.pewresearch.org/fact-tank/2017/10/16/a-growing-share-of-americans-say-its-not-necessary-to-believe-in-god-to-be-moral/> accessed 1 October 2020; '"Nones" on the Rise', 9 October 2012, <www.pewforum.org/2012/10/09/nones-on-the-rise/> accessed 1 October 2020; and Aileen M. Kelly, *Views from the Other Shore: Essays on Herzen, Chekhov, & Bakhtin* (Yale Univ. Press 1999) 217.

9   Emma Green, 'The False Equation of Atheism and Intellectual Sophistication', 14 March 2014, <www.theatlantic.com/international/archive/2014/03/the-false-equation-of-atheism-and-intellectual-sophistication/284406/> accessed 1 October 2020.

10   See Nandhini Narayanan, 'Why the world no longer needs religion', 13 November 2015, <www.dukechronicle.com/article/2015/11/why-the-world-no-longer-needs-religion>

accessed 1 October 2020.

11   David R. Law, 'Franz Overbeck: Kierkegaard and the Decay of Christianity', in Jon Stewart (ed), *Kierkegaard's Influence on Theology: Tome I: German Protestant Theology* (Ashgate 2012) 238.

12   Terence Irwin, *Aristotle's First Principles* (Oxford Univ. Press 1990) 3.

13   See specifically the Old Roman Symbol, the Apostles' Creed, and the Nicene Creed.

14   Angus Stevenson and Maurice Waite (eds), *Concise Oxford English Dictionary* (12th edn, Oxford Univ. Press 2011) 1193 and 610, respectively.

15   Thomas C. Brickhouse and Nicholas D. Smith, *Socrates on Trial* (Clarendon Press 2002) 13-15 and Plato, *Symposium and the Death of Socrates* (Tom Griffith tr, Wordsworth Editions 1997) 210.

16   ibid.

17   ibid.

18   Brickhouse and Smith (n 15) 20-24 and Robin Waterfield, *Why Socrates Died: Dispelling the Myths* (Emblem 2010) 5-7.

19   Luis E. Navia, *Socrates: A Life Examined* (Prometheus Books 2007) 76. See also Lisa Wilkinson, *Socratic Charis: Philosophy without the Agon* (Lexington Books 2013) 124.

20   Neil Ormerod, *A Public God: Natural Theology Reconsidered* (Fortress Press 2015) 132.

21   Walter Woodburn Hyde, *Paganism to Christianity in the Roman Empire* (Univ. Pennsylvania Press, 1946), 4.

22   John Rickards Mozley, *The Divine Aspect of History*, vol 2 (Cambridge Univ. Press 2011) 216.

23   David Rollason, *Early Medieval Europe 300-1050: The Birth of Western Society* (Routledge 2014) 254.

24   Eric Lund (ed), *Documents from the History of Lutheranism, 1517-1750* (Fortress Press 2002) 32.

25   Mark Galli and Ted Olsen (eds), *131 Christians Everyone Should Know* (Christianity Today 2000) 344.

26   ibid.

27   Carter Lindberg, *The European Reformations* (2nd edn, Wiley-Blackwell 2010) 181.

28   R. Ward Holder, *Crisis and Renewal: The Era of the Reformations* (Westminster John Knox Press, 2009) 216.

29   Allyson F. Creasman, *Censorship and Civic Order in Reformation Germany, 1517-1648: "Printed Poison and Evil Talk"* (Ashgate 2012) 109.

30   ibid.

31   Jeffrey M. Shaw and Timothy J. Demy (eds), *War and Religion: An Encyclopedia of Faith and Conflict*, vol. 1 (ABC-CLIO 2017) 847.

32   Phil Orchard, *A Right to Flee: Refugees, States, and the Construction of International Cooperation* (Cambridge Univ. Press 2014) 52.

33   Robert A. Kann, *A History of the Habsburg Empire 1526-1918* (Univ. California Press 1980) 45.

34   Bardo Fassbender and Anne Peters (eds), *The Oxford Handbook of the History of International Law* (Oxford Univ. Press, 2012) 106.

35   ibid 105-06.

36   See James B. Bell, *Empire, Religion and Revolution in Early Virginia, 1607-1786* (Palgrave Macmillan, 2013) 6, and 'The Charter of Massachusetts Bay', 1629 <http://avalon.law.yale.edu/17th_century/mass03.asp> accessed 1 October 2020.

37   'An Act Concerning Religion', 21 September 1649 <http://avalon.law.yale.edu/18th_century/maryland_toleration.asp> accessed 1 October 2020.

38   William Penn, 'Frame of Government of Pennsylvania, Article XXXV', 5 May 1682 <http://avalon.law.yale.edu/17th_century/pa04.asp> accessed 1 October 2020.

39   Andrew W. Robertson (ed), *Encyclopedia of U.S. Political History*, vol 1 (CQ Press 2010) 123-24.

40   Máire Cross and David Williams 'New Dawns in the Making of Modern France: the Consequences of Revolutionary Change' in Máire F. Cross and David Williams (eds), *The French Experience from Republic to Monarchy, 1792-1824: New Dawns in Politics, Knowledge and Culture* (Palgrave 2000) 3 and Michael L. Kennedy, *The Jacobin Clubs in the French Revolution, 1793-1795* (Berghahn Books 2005) 151.

41   Kennedy (n 40) 151-54.

42   ibid 155.

43   Christopher Hibbert, *The Days of the French Revolution* (Perennial 2002) 30.

44   Kennedy (n 40) 155.

45   Nigel Aston, *Religion and Revolution in France, 1780-1804* (Cath. Univ. of America Press 2000) 188.

46   Lynn Hunt and Jack R. Censer, *The French Revolution and Napoleon: Crucible of the Modern World* (Bloomsbury Academic 2017) 107.

47   Jonathan Israel, *Revolutionary Ideas: An Intellectual History of the French Revolution from the Rights of Man to Robespierre* (Princeton Univ. Press 2014) 489.

48   Hunt and Censer (n 46).

49   Aston (n 45) 193.

50   ibid.

51   ibid 188.

52   Kennedy (n 40) 158.

53   Colin Jones, *The Longman Companion to the French Revolution* (Routledge 2013) 119-20.

54   James Hitchcock, *What is Secular Humanism? Why Humanism Became Secular and How it is Changing our World* (Servant Books, 1982) 43.

55   Lloyd S. Kramer, 'The French Revolution and the Creation of American Political Culture', in Joseph Klaits and Michael H. Haltzel (eds), *The Global Ramifications of the French Revolution* (Cambridge Univ. Press, 2002) 47.

56   ibid.

57   ibid 48.

58   Stewart J. Brown and Peter B. Nockles (eds), *The Oxford Movement: Europe and the Wider World 1830-1930* (Cambridge Univ. Press, 2012) 3-4.

59   Eric Richards, 'Margins of the Industrial Revolution', in Patrick O'Brien and Roland Quinault (eds), *The Industrial Revolution and British Society* (Cambridge Univ. Press 1998) 212-13.

60   John Hinshaw and Peter N. Stearns, *Industrialization in the Modern World: From the Industrial Revolution to the Internet*, vol 1 (ABC-CLIO 2014) 392.

61   Chet Bowers, *A Critical Examination of STEM: Issues and Challenges* (Routledge 2016) 102.

62   Lawrence M. Principe, 'Scientism and the Religion of Science', in Richard N. Williams and Daniel N. Robinson (eds), *Scientism: The New Orthodoxy* (Bloomsbury Academic 2015) 44.

63   ibid.

64   ibid 43.

65   David Amigoni and Jeff Wallace (eds), *Charles Darwin's The Origin of Species: New Interdisciplinary Essays* (Manchester Univ. Press, 1995) 9.

66   Delos B. McKown, *The Classical Marxist Critiques of Religion: Marx, Engels, Lenin, Kautsky* (Martinus Nijhoff, 1975) 17.

67   ibid 17-18.

68   ibid 18. See also (n 2) of the Introduction.

69   Karl Marx, 'The Decay of Religious Authority', in Eleanor Marx Aveling and Edward Aveling (eds), *The Eastern Question: A Reprint of Letters written 1853-1856 dealing with the events of the Crimean War* (London 1897) 482.

70   ibid 483.

71   ibid 483-84.

72   Henry Bayman, 'Nietzsche, God, and Doomsday: The Consequences of Atheism', in Weaver Santaniello (ed), *Nietzsche and the Gods* (State Univ. of New York, 2001) 184.

73   ibid 183.

74   Louise Mabille, *Nietzsche and the Anglo-Saxon Tradition* (Continuum 2009) 133.

75   M.M. Mangasarian, *The Truth About Jesus: Is He a Myth?* (Indep. Religious Soc. 1909) 29-30.

76   Michael Burleigh, *Sacred Causes: The Clash of Religion and Politics, from the Great War to the War on Terror* (HarperCollins 2006) 1.

77   Allan K. Davidson, 'Christianity and National Identity: The Role of the Churches in "the Construction of Nationhood"', in John Stenhouse and others (eds), *The Future of Christianity: Historical, Sociological, Political and Theological Perspectives from New Zealand* (ATF Press 2004) 25.

78   Sue Bradford Edwards, *Trench Warfare* (Abdo Publishing 2016) 38.

79   Peter Hitchens, *The Abolition of Britain: The British Cultural Revolution from Lady Chatterley to Tony Blair* (Quartet Books 1999) 109.

80   István D. Rácz, *Philip Larkin's Poetics: Theory and Practice of an English Post-war Poet* (Brill 2016) 124.

81   Russell Freedman, *The War to End All Wars: World War I* (Clarion Books 2010).

82   See respectively Articles 13 and 65(d) of the 1918 Constitution of the Russian Soviet Federated Socialist Republic.

83   'Comr Latsis is completely right when he says that Communism and Religion are mutually exclusive and is also deeply right that no other apparatus is capable of destroying religion apart from the apparatus of the VChK'. Felix Corley, *Religion in the Soviet Union: An Archival Reader* (Macmillan 1996) 23.

84   Peter Hitchens, *The Rage Against God: How Atheism Led Me to Faith* (Zondervan 2010) 197.

85   Sidney and Beatrice Webb, 'Is Soviet Communism a New Civilisation?' *The Left Review*, November 1936, 20.

86   Stéphane Courtois and others, *The Black Book of Communism: Crimes, Terror, Repression* (Jonathan Murphy and Mark Kramer trs, Harvard Univ. Press, 1999) 126.

87   ibid.

88   Thomas Hardy, *The Poetical Works of Thomas Hardy*, vol 1 (Macmillan 1919) 307-08.

89   D.D. Paige, *The Selected Letters of Ezra Pound, 1907-1941* (New Directions 1971) 97-98.

90   Pericles Lewis, *Religious Experience and the Modernist Novel* (Cambridge Univ. Press 2010) 142.

91   Klaus-Jürgen Müller, *The Army, Politics and Society in Germany, 1933-45: Studies in the Army's Relation to Nazism* (Manchester Univ. Press 1987) 13.

92   Jack Rogers, *Presbyterian Creeds: A Guide to the Book of Confessions* (Westminster John Knox Press 1991) 176.

93   Arthur C. Cochrane, *The Church's Confession Under Hitler* (2nd edn, Pickwick Publications 2009) 241.

94   David G. Schultenover (ed), *50 Years On: Probing the Riches of Vatican II* (Lit. Press 2015) xlvi.

95   'Encyclical of Pope Pius XI on the Church and the German Reich to the Venerable Brethren the Archbishops and Bishops of Germany and other Ordinaries in Peace and Communion with the Apostolic See', *Mit Brennender Sorge* <http://w2.vatican.va/content/pius-xi/en/encyclicals/documents/hf_p-xi_enc_14031937_mit-brennender-sorge.html> accessed 1 October 2020.

96   Archer Jones, *The Art of War in the Western World* (Univ. Illinois Press 2001) 508.

97   Martin Middlebrook, *The First Day on the Somme* (rev. edn, Pen & Sword 2016) 263-64 and Erik Koppe, *The Use of Nuclear Weapons and the Protection of the Environment during International Armed Conflict* (Hart Publishing 2008) 35.

98   Jessica M. Chapman, 'The Vietnam War', in Robert J. McMahon and Thomas W. Zeiler (eds), *U.S. Foreign Policy: A Diplomatic History*, vol 1 (SAGE 2012) 337.

99   Daniel Peris, *Storming the Heavens: The Soviet League of the Militant Godless* (Cornell Univ. Press 1998) 2.

100   Dianne Kirby, 'Harry Truman's Religious Legacy: The Holy Alliance, Containment and the Cold War', in Dianne Kirby (ed), *Religion and the Cold War* (Palgrave Macmillan, 2003) 86.

101   Jonathan P. Herzog, *The Spiritual-Industrial Complex: America's Religious Battle against Communism in the Early Cold War* (Oxford Univ. Press 2011) 88.

102   ibid 91.

103   Toward the end of Pius' decree, it was expressed that 'If Christians declare openly the materialist and antichristian doctrine of the communists, and, mainly, if they defend it or promulgate it', they would face automatic excommunication, Pius XII, 'Decree against communism', (1949) MONTFORT Associação Cultural <http://www.montfort.org.br/eng/documentos/decretos/anticomunismo/> accessed 1 October 2020. See also Merrilyn Thomas, *Communing with the Enemy: Covert Operations, Christianity and Cold War Politics in Britain and the GDR* (Peter Lang 2005) 76.

104   Kirby (n 100).

105   ibid 93.

106   ibid 97.

107   ibid 99.

108   T. Jeremy Gunn, *Spiritual Weapons: The Cold War and the Forging of an American National Religion* (Praeger 2009) 65-66.

109   Nathanial Davis, *A Long Walk to Church: A Contemporary History of Russian Orthodoxy* (Westview Press 2003) 33 and Dimitry V. Pospielovsky, *A History of Soviet Atheism in Theory and Practice, and the Believer: Soviet Studies on the Church and the Believer's Response to Atheism*, vol 3 (Macmillan 1988) 209 and 124.

110   Testimony of Rev. Richard Wurmbrand before the United States Senate Committee on the Judiciary - Subcommittee to Investigate the Administration of the Internal Security Act and Other Internal Security Laws of the Committee on the Judiciary, May 6, 1966, <https://babel.hathitrust.org/cgi/pt?id=uc1.$b643027;view=1up;seq=15> accessed 1 October 2020.

111   ibid.

112   Gerhard Simon, *Church, State and Opposition in the U.S.S.R.* (Kathleen Matchett tr, Univ. California Press 1974) 170-71.

113   ibid 171.

114   ibid.

115   ibid.

116   ibid.

117   Hitchens (n 79) 270.

118   Hera Cook, *The Long Sexual Revolution: English Women, Sex, and Contraception 1800-1975* (Oxford Univ. Press 2005) 279 and Hitchens (n 79).

119   Cook (n 118) 283.

120   Aldous Huxley, *Ends and Means: An Inquiry into the Nature of Ideals* (Transaction Publishers 2012) 315

121   James Hull, *Aldous Huxley, Representative Man* (Lit Verlag Münster 2004) 321.

122   Huxley (n 120) 318-19.

123   Callum G. Brown, 'The secularization decade: the 1960s', in Hugh McLeod and Werner Ustorf (eds), *The Decline of Christendom in Western Europe, 1750-2000* (Cambridge Univ. Press 2003) 31-34.

124   Theodore Caplow and others, *Recent Social Trends in the United States 1960-1990* (McGill-Queen's Univ. Press 1994) 279.

125   Andrew Singleton, *Religion, Culture and Society: A Global Approach* (SAGE 2014) 97.

126   ibid 96.

127   'Nightmare in the Catskills', 18 August 1969, *The New York Times* <http://woodstockpreservation.org/Gallery/NYT-PDF/17_NightmareInTheCatskills.pdf> accessed 1 October 2020.

128   See s 1 of the Abortion Act 1967 and ss. 58-59, Offences Against the Person Act 1861.

129   Leslie Friedman Goldstein, *The Constitutional Rights of Women: Cases in Law and Social Change* (Univ. Wisconsin Press 1989) 358.

130   Anne Sa'adah, *Contemporary France: A Democratic Education* (Rowman & Littlefield 2003) 119.

131   Joseph Chinyong Liow, *Dictionary of the Modern Politics of Southeast Asia* (4th edn, Routledge 2015) 54.

132   Raymond A. Schroth, *The American Jesuits: A History* (New York Univ. Press 2007) 230.

133   Robert E. Emery, *Marriage, Divorce, and Children's Adjustment* (2nd edn, SAGE 1999) 11-12 and Marvin B. Sussman and others (eds), *Handbook of Marriage and the Family*, vol 1 (2nd edn, Springer 1999) 530.

134   See Kathleen Kiernan and others, *Lone Motherhood in Twentieth-Century Britain: From Footnote to Front Page* (Oxford Univ. Press 2004) 34; 'Table 1, Characteristics of women who obtained legal abortions – United States, 1973-2005', <www.cdc.gov/mmwr/preview/mmwrhtml/ss5713a1.htm> accessed 1 October 2020; Jay Cassel, 'Public Health in Canada', in Dorothy Porter (ed), *The History of Public Health and the Modern State* (Wellcome Trust 2006) 298; and Kelly Boyer Sagert, *The 1970s* (Greenwood Press 2007) 66.

135   David Farber and Beth Bailey, *The Columbia Guide to America in the 1960s* (Columbia Univ. Press 2001) 240.

136   G.I.T. Machin, *Churches and Social Issues in Twentieth-Century Britain* (Clarendon Press 1998) 213 and Robert D. Putnam (ed), *Democracies in Flux: The Evolution of Social Capital in Contemporary Society* (Oxford Univ. Press 2004) 408.

137   See (n 122) and George D. Chryssides, 'Defining the New Age', in Daren Kemp and James R. Lewis (eds), *Handbook of New Age* (Brill 2007) 5-8.

138   Peter B. Levy, *Encyclopedia of the Reagan-Bush Years* (Greenwood Press 1996) 25.

139   ibid.

140   William C. Martel, *Grand Strategy in Theory and Practice: The Need for an Effective American Foreign Policy* (Cambridge Univ. Press 2015) 244.

141   William C. Wohlforth, 'The Stability of a Unipolar World', in Michael E. Brown and others (eds), *Primacy and Its Discontents: American Power and International Stability* (MIT Press 2008) 11 and Ariel Cohen, *Russian Imperialism: Development and Crisis* (Praeger Publishers 1998) 23.

142   Martel (n 140).

143   Kenneth A. Oye, 'Explaining the End of the Cold War: Morphological and Behavioral Adaptations to the Nuclear Peace?', in Richard Ned Lebow and Thomas Risse-Kappen (eds), *International Relations Theory and the End of the Cold War* (Columbia Univ. Press 1995) 74.

144   Andrew Cherry and others (eds), *Substance Abuse: A Global View* (Greenwood Press 2002) 174.

145   Ann Cooper, 'Women Fault Soviet System for Abortion', 28 February 1989, *The New York Times*, <http://www.nytimes.com/1989/02/28/world/women-fault-soviet-system-for-abortion.html> accessed 1 October 2020.

146   Clyde Hertzman and others (eds), *East-West Life Expectancy Gap in Europe: Environmental and Non-Environmental Determinants* (Kluwer Academic 1996) 30. Mortality calculations based upon the 1985 infant mortality rates in the USSR (26/1,000), the USA (10.4/1,000), and the UK (9.4/1,000); see Michael Ryan, 'Infant Mortality in the Soviet Union', 19 March 1988, 296 British Medical Journal 850, 'Infant Mortality by Birthweight and Other Characteristics: United States, 1985 Birth Cohort', July 1994, US Dept of Health and Human Services 3, and 'Trends in births and deaths over the last century', 15 July 2015 <https://visual.ons.gov.uk/birthsanddeaths/> accessed 1 October 2020.

147   Rett R. Ludwikowski, *Constitution-Making in the Region of Former Soviet Dominance* (Duke Univ. Press 1996) 191.

148   Kira V. Tsekhanskaia, 'Russia: Trends in Orthodox Religiosity in the Twentieth Century', in Marjorie Mandelstam Balzar (ed), *Religion and Politics in Russia: A Reader* (Routledge 2015) 11.

149   Catherine Wanner, *Communities of the Converted: Ukrainians and Global Evangelism* (Cornell Univ. Press 2007) 130.

150   Tsekhanskaia (n 148).

151   David Held, *Models of Democracy* (3rd edn, Stanford Univ. Press 2006) 218.

152   Jeffrey A. Engel (ed), *The Fall of the Berlin Wall: The Revolutionary Legacy of 1989* (Oxford Univ. Press 2009) 17.

153   Dinissa Duvanova, *Building Business in Post-Communist Russia, Eastern Europe, and Eurasia: Collective Goods, Selective Incentives, and Predatory States* (Cambridge Univ. Press 2013) 142.

154   Angela E. Stent, *The Limits of Partnership: U.S.-Russian Relations in the Twenty-First Century* (Princeton Univ. Press 2014) 1.

155   ibid.

156   'End of the Soviet Union; Text of Bush's Address to Nation on Gorbachev's Resignation', 26 December 1991, *The New York Times* <https://www.nytimes.com/1991/12/26/world/end-soviet-union-text-bush-s-address-nation-gorbachev-s-resignation.html> accessed 1 October 2020.

157   Francis Fukuyama, 'The End of History?' Summer 1989, *The National Interest* 3-5.

158   Christian Parenti, 'Planet America: The Revolution in Military Affairs as Fantasy and Fetish', in Ashley Dawson and Malini Johar Schueller (eds), *Exceptional State: Contemporary U.S. Culture and the New Imperialism* (Duke Univ. Press 2007) 90.

159   Koichi Iwabuchi, *Resilient Borders and Cultural Diversity: Internationalism, Brand Nationalism, and Multiculturalism in Japan* (Lexington Books 2015) 14.

160   Alamin M. Mazrui, *English in Africa: After the Cold War* (Multilingual Matters 2004) 14-15.

161   Iwabuchi (n 159).

162   Neal M. Rosendorf, 'Hollywood, Dictatorship and Propaganda: Samuel Bronston's Special Relationship with the Franco Regime, 1957-1973', in Kenneth A. Osgood and Brian C. Etheridge (eds), *The United States and Public Diplomacy: New Directions in Cultural and International History* (Martinus Nijhoff 2010) 103.

163   Joseph D. Straubhaar, *World Television: From Global to Local* (SAGE, 2007) 119-24 and Janna Quitney Anderson, *Imagining the Internet: Personalities, Predictions, Perspectives* (Rowman & Littlefield 2005) 4.

164   *Voice of America Programming Handbook: 50 years of Broadcasting to the World* (3rd edn, Voice of America 1991) 96.

165   'Hits of the World', *Billboard* (14 November 1992) 46.

166   'Mortal Marketing', *GamePro* (February 1994) 187 and S. Kline and others, *Digital Play: The Interaction of Technology, Culture, and Marketing* (McGill-Queen's Univ. Press 2005) 133.

167   Kevin D. Impellizeri, 'Use Your Joystick, 007: Video Games and the Interactive Bond Experience', in Robert G. Weiner and others (eds), *James Bond in World and Popular Culture: The Films are Not Enough* (2nd edn, Cambridge Scholars Publishing 2011) 12-13.

168   Jeffrey Ian Ross (ed), *Encyclopedia of Street Crime in America* (SAGE 2013) 182.

169   'Most Offensive: Grand Theft Auto 3', GameSpy Best of 2001, *GameSpy*, <https://web.archive.org/web/20060110195949/http://archive.gamespy.com/goty2001/special/24.shtml> accessed 1 October 2020 (emphasis added).

170   See 'NPD Reports Annual 2001 U.S. Interactive Entertainment Sales Shatter Industry Record', *NPD Techworld* (February 7, 2002) <https://web.archive.org/web/20040814133238/http://www.npd.com/dynamic/releases/press_020207.htm> accessed 1 October 2020, 'Game of the Year - Second Annual Game Developers Choice Awards', *Game Developers Conference* <www.gamechoiceawards.com/archive/gdca_2nd.html> accessed 1 October 2020, and ' Take-Two Interactive Software, Inc. Recommendation of the Board of Directors to Reject Electronic Arts Inc.'s Tender Offer March 2008', <https://web.archive.org/web/20080408234728/http://taketwovalue.com/documents/TTWO_Value.pdf#page=12> accessed 1 October 2020.

171   Dick Thornburgh and Herbert S. Lin (eds), *Youth, Pornography, and the Internet* (National Academies Press 2002) 72-73.

172   George A. Akerlof and others, 'An Analysis of Out-of-Wedlock Childbearing in the United States', May 1996, The Quarterly Journal of Economics, 277, 278-97 (emphasis added).

173   Pope Paul VI, *Humanae Vitae*, 25 July, 1968, <http://w2.vatican.va/content/paul-vi/en/encyclicals/documents/hf_p-vi_enc_25071968_humanae-vitae.html> accessed 1 October 2020.

174   Rebecca O'Neill, 'Experiments in Living: The Fatherless Family', September 2002, *Civitas* <www.civitas.org.uk/research/family/family-archive-of-factsheets-from-2002/> accessed 1 October 2020.

175   *Publications of the American Statistical Association*, vol 11 (Amer. Statistical Assn, 1910) 495.

176   U.S. Census Bureau, Table 1292 'Marriage and Divorce Rates by Country: 1980 to 2006', *Statistical Abstract of the United States: 2009* (128th edn, Washington, DC 2008) 818. To produce a comparable sample to the data in n 166, the figures in this table were multiplied by 100 to show 'per 100,000 population' totals, rather than 'per 1,000 population' totals.

177   'Table 1 – Illegitimate Births per 1000 Births (excluding still-born)' *Encyclopædia Britannica*, vol 14 (11th edn New York 1910) 301.

178   U.S. Census Bureau (n 176), Table 1291 'Births to Unmarried Women by Country: 1980 to 2006'.

179   U.S. Census Bureau, 'Illegitimate Births', *Birth Statistics for the Birth Registration Area of the United States 1919, Fifth Annual Report* (Washington, DC 1921) 21.

180   See US Census Bureau, 'Table 73: Self-Described Religions Identification of Adult Population: 1990 and 2001' in *Statistical Abstract of the United States: 2007* (126th edn, Wash-

ington, DC 2006) 59, and Russell Sandberg, *Religion, Law, and Society* (Cambridge Univ. Press 2014) 54. See also *The Gallup Poll: Public Opinion 2013* (Rowman & Littlefield 2015) 13.

181 Gary Wolf, 'The Church of the Non-Believers', 1 November 2006, *Wired*, <www. wired.com/2006/11/atheism/> accessed 1 October 2020.

182 ibid.

183 Alona Wartofsky, 'The Last Word', 19 February 2001, *The Washington Post* <www.washingtonpost.com/archive/lifestyle/2001/02/19/the-last-word/4bad376f -4ab7-441c-9c50-afc7e63dd192/?utm_term=.3b780be000f0> accessed 1 October 2020.

184 Richard Dawkins, *The God Delusion* (First Mariner Books, 2008) 358 and Simon (n 112).

185 See Sam Harris, 'Science Must Destroy Religion', <https://samharris.org/science-must-destroy-religion/> accessed 1 October 2020 and John S.C. Abbott, *The French Revolution of 1789 as Viewed in the Light of Republican Institutions*, vol 2 (New York 1859) 360.

186 See Christopher Hitchens, *God is Not Great: How Religion Poisons Everything* (McClelland & Stewart 2008) 25 and Sam Harris, 'Science Must Destroy Religion', 2 January 2006, *The Huffington Post*, <www.huffingtonpost.com/sam-harris/science-must-destroy-reli_b_13153. html> accessed 1 October 2020, and see (n 46).

187 Wolf (n 181).

188 Stephen Bullivant, 'Europe's Young Adults and Religion: Findings from the European Social Survey (2014-16) to inform the 2018 Synod of Bishops', 21 March 2018, Benedict XVI Centre for Religion and Society, <www.stmarys.ac.uk/research/centres/benedict-xvi/ docs/2018-mar-europe-young-people-report-eng.pdf> accessed 1 October 2020.

189 Harriet Sherwood, '"Christianity as default is gone": the rise of a non-Christian Europe', 20 March 2018, *The Guardian*, <www.theguardian.com/world/2018/mar/21/ christianity-non-christian-europe-young-people-survey-religion> accessed 1 October 2020.

190 ibid.

191 ibid.

192 Peter Hitchens, 'A Church That Was', May 2016, *First Things*, <www.firstthings.com/ article/2016/05/a-church-that-was> accessed 1 October 2020.

193 Thiers (n 3).

194 Abrahám Kovács, 'The Challenge of the Post-Christendom Era: The Relation of Christian Theology to World Religions', in Stephen R. Goodwin (ed), *World Christianity in Local Context: Essays in Memory of David A. Kerr*, vol 1 (Continuum 2009) 11.

195 See W.R. Sorley, *Moral Values and the Idea of God* (2nd edn, New York 1921) 456. See e.g. Samuel Chandler, *Reflections on the Conduct of the Modern Deists, in their late Writings against Christianity* (London 1727); Charles Leslie, *Deism Refuted: Or, the Truth of Christianity Demonstrated* (London 1755); and Monsieur Bergier, *Deism Self-Refuted; or an Examination of the Principles of Infidelity Scattered Throughout the Different Works of Mons. Rousseau*, vol 1 (4th edn, Paris 1775).

196 Timothy Kusky (ed), *Encyclopedia of Earth and Space Science* (Facts on File 2010) 413.

197 Chad Denton, *Decadence, Radicalism, and the Early Modern French Nobility: The Enlightened and Depraved* (Lexington Books 2017) 70.

198 ibid 70-73.

199 ibid 74 and 80.

200 Alison Conway, *The Protestant Whore: Courtesan Narrative & Religious Controversy in England, 1680-1750* (Univ. Toronto Press 2010) 3-4 (emphasis added).

201 Matthew Jenkinson, *Culture and Politics at the Court of Charles II, 1660-1685* (Boydell Press 2010) 6.

202 ibid 88.

203 ibid 88-89.

204 See (n 122).

205 See (n 72).

206 'Sermon Preached before the Court at Christ Church Chapel in Oxford', in Robert South, *Sermons Preached Upon Several Occasions*, vol 1 (New York 1866) 4, 11.

207 ibid 3-7.

208 See (n 119).

209 For statistics in England and Wales, see 'Table 1: Legal abortions: Number and rates; resident status and purchaser, 1968 to 2019', in *Abortion Statistics, England and Wales: 2019* <https://assets.publishing.service.gov.uk/government/uploads/system/uploads/attachment_data/file/915150/abortion-statistics-2019-data-tables.ods> accessed 1 October 2020 showing a collective 8,844,910 abortions. For statistics in the United States, see Table 1 in 'Abortion Surveillance – United States 2005' for historical data from 1973 to 2005, <www.cdc.gov/mmwr/preview/mmwrhtml/ss5713a1.htm> accessed 1 October 2020 showing a collective 37,311,516 abortions, and then annual abortion surveillance documents thereafter up to 2016, the last year of reported data, showing a further 8,062,460. The population of Kenya as of July 2020 was estimated at 53,527,936, per the CIA World Factbook.

210 For statistics in the UK from 1960-2002, see 'A Summary of Recorded Crime Data from 1898 to 2001/02', showing 118,150 recorded rapes, <www.gov.uk/government/statistics/historical-crime-data>, and for data reported from England and Wales from 2003-2017 showing 289,009 recorded rapes, see 'Crime in England and Wales: Bulletin Tables' for year ending June 2017 <www.ons.gov.uk/peoplepopulationandcommunity/crimeandjustice/datasets/crimeinenglandandwalesbulletintables>. For statistics in the US from 1960-2014, a search of the Uniform Crime Reporting Tool showed 4,232,419 rapes, <www.ucrdatatool.gov/Search/Crime/State/RunCrimeStatebyState.cfm> whilst the 'Crime in the United States: 2019' report showed an additional 677,794 recorded rapes for 2015-19, <https://ucr.fbi.gov/crime-in-the-u.s/2019/crime-in-the-u.s.-2019/topic-pages/tables/table-7>. All data accessed 1 October 2020.

211 For data in England and Wales, see 'Appendix table 2.05a: Offences currently recorded as homicide for all victims by relationship of victim to principal suspect and sex of victim, numbers, year ending March 2006 to year ending March 2016', recording 1,232 homicides, <www.ons.gov.uk/peoplepopulationandcommunity/crimeandjustice/datasets/appendixtablesfocusonviolentcrimeandsexualoffences>. For data from the US for the same time period, see 'Expanded Homicide Data Table 10' for the years 2008-2016 (2006-2007 appear under Table 9), <https://ucr.fbi.gov/crime-in-the-u.s> showing 12,912 comparable homicides. All data accessed 1 October 2020.

212 See <www.cdc.gov/nchhstp/newsroom/docs/factsheets/std-trends-508.pdf> for the US figure of approximately $16 billion, and <https://www.fpa.org.uk/sites/default/files/unprotected-nation-sexual-health-full-report.pdf> for the UK figure of £620 million, accessed 1 October 2020.

213 For data from England, see 'Table 1 (a): Number of new STI diagnoses in England by gender, 2007 – 2016', <https://www.gov.uk/government/uploads/system/uploads/attachment_data/file/626359/2016_Table_1_STI_diagnoses___rates_in_England_by_gender.pdf> and for US data see <https://www.nichd.nih.gov/health/topics/stds/conditioninfo/risk>. All data accessed 1 April 2018.

214 For data for England and Wales, see 'Divorces in England and Wales: 2016', <www.ons.gov.uk/peoplepopulationandcommunity/birthsdeathsandmarriages/divorce/bulletins/divorcesinenglandandwales/2016> showing 1,285,118 divorces from 2006-2016; for US data, see 'Provisional number of divorces and annulments and rate: United States, 2000-2016', <www.cdc.gov/nchs/data/dvs/national_marriage_divorce_rates_00-16.pdf>. Dividing the averaged total yielded 2 divorces every minute. Data accessed 1 October 2020.

215 Mark A. Noll, *The Scandal of the Evangelical Mind* (Wm. B. Eerdmans 1995) 3-4.
216 ibid 5.
217 ibid 21.

Notes to Chapter 2 - This We Call God

1   Anselm of Canterbury, *Monologion - Chapter 1*, <https://sourcebooks.fordham.edu/basis/anselm-monologium.asp#CHAPTER%20I> accessed 1 October 2020; Brian Davies and Brian Leftow (eds), *The Cambridge Companion to Anselm* (Cambridge Univ. Press 2004) 11.
2   ibid.
3   Brian Davies and G.R. Evans, *Anselm of Canterbury: The Major Works* (Oxford Univ. Press, 1998) xii.
4   Lawrence M. Principe, 'Scientism and the Religion of Science', in Richard N. Williams and Daniel N. Robinson (eds), *Scientism: The New Orthodoxy* (Bloomsbury Academic 2015) 44.
5   ibid 43.
6   Art Harris, 'Second View: Sagan on Encounters', in Tom Head (ed), *Conversations with Carl Sagan* (Univ. Press of Mississippi, 2006) 47.
7   Charles Alfred Coulson, *Science and Christian Belief* (Oxford Univ. Press 1955) 20.
8   Alan Richardson and John Bowden (eds), *The Westminster Dictionary of Christian Theology* (Westminster Press 1983) 242.
9   See 'Hubble Reveals Observable Universe Contains 10 Times More Galaxies Than Previously Thought', 13 October 2016, National Aeronautics and Space Administration, <www.nasa.gov/feature/goddard/2016/hubble-reveals-observable-universe-contains-10-times-more-galaxies-than-previously-thought> accessed 1 October 2020, and Jean-René Roy, *Unveiling Galaxies: The Role of Images in Astronomical Discovery* (Cambridge Univ. Press 2018) ix.
10   David Sadava and others (eds), *Life: The Science of Biology* (8th edn, Macmillan 2006) 21.
11   See James F. Petersen and others, *Fundamentals of Physical Geography* (Brooks/Cole, Cengage Learning, 2011) 18; Lloyd Motz and Jefferson Hane Weaver, *The Concepts of Science: From Newton to Einstein* (Springer 2013) 75; and Joseph C. Amato and Enrique J. Galvez, *Physics from Planet Earth: An Introduction to Mechanics* (CRC Press 2015) 418 for the respective calculations.
12   See Santhosh Mathew, *Essays on the Frontiers of Modern Astrophysics and Cosmology* (Springer, 2014) 15 and George M. Williams, *Handbook of Hindu Mythology* (Oxford Univ. Press 2008) 90.
13   Bruce G. Trigger, *Understanding Early Civilizations: A Comparative Study* (Cambridge Univ. Press 2003) 463.
14   See Jacques Brunschwig and others (eds), *Greek Thought: A Guide to Classical Knowledge* (Catherine Porter tr, Harvard Univ. Press 2000) 578 and Constantine J. Vamvacas, *The Founders of Western Thought – The Presocratics: A Diachronic Parallelism Between Presocratic Thought and Philosophy and the Natural Sciences* (Robert Crist tr, Springer 2009) 220.
15   S. Marc Cohen and others (eds), *Readings in Ancient Greek Philosophy: From Thales to Aristotle* (5th edn, Hackett Publishing 2016) 449.
16   See George Karamanolis, 'Plethon and Scholarios on Aristotle' in Katerina Ierodiakonou (ed) *Byzantine Philosophy and its Ancient Sources* (Clarendon Press, 2004) 274 and Rupert W. Anderson, *The Cosmic Compendium: The Ultimate Fate of the Universe* (Lulu 2015) 6.
17   David Deming, *Science and Technology in World History - Volume 1: The Ancient World and Classical Civilization* (McFarland & Co. 2010) 131.
18   ibid.

19   Maurice A. Finocchiaro, *Defending Copernicus and Galileo: Critical Reasoning in the Two Affairs* (Springer, 2010) 3-4 and Ernest Zebrowski, Jr., *A History of the Circle: Mathematical Reasoning and the Physical Universe* (Rutgers Univ. Press 2000) 90.

20   Linda K. Glover and others (eds), *National Geographic Encyclopedia of Space* (National Geographic 2004) 32.

21   John Marenbon (ed), *The Oxford Handbook of Medieval Philosophy* (Oxford Univ. Press 2012) 49.

22   David C. Lindberg (ed), *Science in the Middle Ages* (Univ. Chicago Press 1978) 11.

23   Marenbon (n 21) 688.

24   Garth Fowden, *Before and After Muhammad: The First Millennium Refocused* (Princeton Univ. Press 2014) 135.

25   See Helge S. Kragh, *Entropic Creation: Religious Contexts of Thermodynamics and Cosmology* (Ashgate, 2008) 12 and Linda Zagzebski and Timothy D. Miller (eds), *Readings in Philosophy of Religion: Ancient to Contemporary* (Wiley-Blackwell 2009) 66.

26   Zagzebski and Miller (n 25) 67.

27   Robin Gill, *A Textbook of Christian Ethics* (3rd edn, T&T Clark 2006) 285 and Edward Craig (ed), *The Shorter Routledge Encyclopedia of Philosophy* (Routledge 2005) 44-45.

28   Brian Davies, *Thomas Aquinas's* Summa Contra Gentiles*: A Guide and Commentary* (Oxford Univ. Press 2016) 8.

29   Craig (n 27).

30   Book 2, Chapter 38, Sections 4-15. Thomas Aquinas, Summa Contra Gentiles, <http://dhspriory.org/thomas/ContraGentiles.htm> accessed 28 November 2017.

31   ibid, Book 1, Chapter 13, Section 3.

32   ibid, Book 1, Chapter 13, Section 33.

33   ibid, Book 2, Chapter 20, Section 5.

34   ibid, Book 2, Chapter 16, Section 2.

35   Marcus Plested, *Orthodox Readings of Aquinas* (Oxford Univ. Press 2012) 113.

36   ibid.

37   Thomas Hibbs, *Aquinas, Ethics, and Philosophy of Religion: Metaphysics and Practice* (Indiana Univ. Press, 2007) 165 and Marcus Plested, '"Light from the West": Byzantine Readings of Aquinas', in George E. Demacopoulos and Aristotle Papanikolaou (eds), *Orthodox Constructions of the West* (Fordham Univ. Press 2013) 67.

38   'On 4 March 1391, Pope Boniface IX issued a bull authorizing the establishment of a university in Ferrara. In grandiloquent language, it explained that a university would produce men of mature advice, crowned and decorated in virtue, and learned in the principles of different subjects. Further, the community would have a flowing fountain to quench the thirst of all who desired lessons in letters and science. Other bulls for other universities echoed such sentiments, sometimes in the same words.' Paul F. Grendler, *Renaissance Education Between Religion and Politics* (Ashgate 2006) 2.

39   John Freely, *Celestial Revolutionary: Copernicus, the Man and His Universe* (I.B. Tauris 2014) 9.

40   ibid 9-10. See also Michael J. Crowe, *Theories of the World from Antiquity to the Copernican Revolution* (2nd edn rev., Dover Publications 2001) 83.

41   ibid 83-84.

42   Jerzy Dobrzycki, 'Nicholas Copernicus – His Life and Work', in Barbara Bieńkowska (ed), *The Scientific World of Copernicus: On the Occasion of the 500th Anniversary of his Birth 1473-1973* (Christina Cenkalska tr, D. Reidel Publishing Co. 1973) 36.

43   N.M. Swerdlow and O. Neugebauer, *Mathematical Astronomy in Copernicus's De Revolutionibus, Part 1-2* (Springer 1984) 8.

44 Wolfgang Neuber and others (eds), *The Making of Copernicus: Early Modern Transformations of the Scientist and his Science* (Brill 2015) 55.

45 ibid.

46 'Letter of Nicholas Schönberg to Nicholas Copernicus', in Jerzy Dobrzycki (ed), *Nicholas Copernicus on the Revolutions* (Edward Rosen tr, Macmillan Press 1978) xvii.

47 ibid.

48 Nicholaus Copernicus, *On the Revolutions of Heavenly Spheres* (Charles Glenn Wallis tr., Prometheus Books 1995) 12.

49 ibid 14-17, emphasis added.

50 Clifford A. Pickover, *Archimedes to Hawking: Laws of Science and the Great Minds Behind Them* (Oxford Univ. Press 2008) 52.

51 Rhonda Martens, *Kepler's Philosophy and the New Astronomy* (Princeton Univ. Press 2000) 79, 81.

52 S.M. Chitre, 'Overview of Solar Physics', in H.M. Antia and others (eds), *Lectures on Solar Physics* (Springer 2003) 1.

53 William J. Hinze and others, *Gravity and Magnetic Exploration: Principles, Practices, and Applications* (Cambridge Univ. Press 2013) 28 and Debora M. Katz, *Physics for Scientists and Engineers: Foundations and Connections*, vol. 1 (Cengage Learning 2016) 191.

54 Katz (n 53).

55 Isaac Newton, *The Mathematical Principles of Natural Philosophy*, Book III (Andrew Motte, tr., New York 1848) 504-05.

56 Steve Adams, *Relativity: An Introduction to Space-Time Physics* (Taylor & Francis 1997) 228.

57 Thomas Wright, *An Original Theory or New Hypothesis of the Universe* (London 1750) 83-84.

58 ibid 50.

59 Kamill Klem-Musatov and others (eds), *Classical and Modern Diffraction Theory* (Society of Exploration Geophysicists 2016) 101.

60 Thomas Young, *A Course of Lectures on Natural Philosophy and the Mechanical Arts*, vol 1 (London 1845) 365.

61 Alex Byrne and David R. Hilbert (eds), *Readings on Color*, vol. 2 (MIT Press 1997) 3-4.

62 Alec Eden, *The Search for Christian Doppler* (Springer-Verlag Wien 1992) 31.

63 ibid.

64 John M. Henshaw, *An Equation for Every Occasion: Fifty-Two Formulas and Why They Matter* (John Hopkins Univ. Press 2016) 19.

65 Boris V. Alexeev, *Nonlocal Astrophysics: Dark Matter, Dark Energy and Physical Vacuum* (Elsevier 2017) 177.

66 V.M. Slipher, 'The Radial Velocity of the Andromeda Nebula' (1912) Lowell Observatory Bulletin No. 58, vol 2 56.

67 ibid 57.

68 V.M. Slipher, 'Spectographic Observations of Nebulae' (1915) Popular Astronomy, vol 23, 23.

69 The Andromeda Galaxy, for instance, is believed to contain approximately one trillion stars. David Blatner, *Spectrums: Out Mind-boggling Universe from Infinitesimal to Infinity* (Bloomsbury 2012) 42.

70 Adams (n 56).

71 S. Cotsakis and E. Papantonopoulos (eds), *Cosmological Crossroads: An Advanced Course in Mathematical, Physical and String Cosmology* (Springer 2002) 17.

72 Rodney D. Holder and Simon Mitton (eds), *Georges Lemaître: Life, Science and Legacy* (Springer 2012) 1-2.

73　A. Zee, *Einstein's Universe: Gravity at Work and Play* (Oxford Univ. Press 2001) 69.

74　Joseph Cambray, *Synchronicity: Nature & Psyche in an Interconnected Universe* (Texas A&M Univ. Press 2009) 18.

75　Immo Appenzeller, *High-Redshift Galaxies: Light from the Early Universe* (Springer 2009) 8.

76　Cambray (n 74).

77　ibid.

78　G. Lemaître, 'The Beginning of the World from the Point of View of Quantum Theory', (1931) 127 Nature 706.

79　Helge Kragh, *Cosmology and Controversy: The Historical Development of Two Theories of the Universe* (Princeton Univ. Press 1999) 52.

80　See Adam Curtis, 'A Mile or Two Off Yarmouth', *BBC* 24 February 2015, <www.bbc.co.uk/blogs/adamcurtis/entries/512cde83-3afb-3048-9ece-dba774b10f89> accessed 1 October 2020.

81　ibid.

82　Kragh (n 79) 59.

83　ibid 60.

84　Helge Kragh, *Matter and Spirit in the Universe: Scientific and Religious Preludes to Modern Cosmology* (Imperial College Press 2004) 143.

85　Joseph A. Angelo, Jr., *Encyclopedia of Space and Astronomy* (Facts on File 2006) 83-84.

86　Rhodri Evans, *The Cosmic Microwave Background: How It Changed Our Understanding of the Universe* (Springer 2015) 69.

87　ibid.

88　Amadeo Balbi, *The Music of the Big Bang: The Cosmic Microwave Background and the New Cosmology* (Springer 2007) 44-45.

89　ibid.

90　ibid 46.

91　ibid.

92　Angelo, Jr. (n 85) 85.

93　Jed Buchwald and Robert Fox (eds), *The Oxford Handbook of the History of Physics* (Oxford Univ. Press 2013) 909.

94　Norriss S. Hetherington (ed), *Encyclopedia of Cosmology: Historical, Philosophical, and Scientific Foundations of Modern Cosmology* (Garland Publishing 1993) 307.

95　John L. Heilbron (ed), *The Oxford Guide to the History of Physics and Astronomy* (Oxford Univ. Press 2005) 78.

96　Angelo, Jr. (n 85) 85.

97　ibid.

98　Hetherington (n 94), noting that 'One can show by a straightforward calculation that [one trying to achieve thermal equilibrium] would have to communicate at more than ninety times the speed of light to achieve their goal of creating a uniform temperature across the visible universe within 100,000 years after the big bang.' See also page 282, where it states that 'if the universe expanded according to the standard model, calculations show that the sources were as much as ninety horizon distances apart at the time the radiation was emitted, in which case there is no physical process by which the sources could have reached equilibrium.'

99　Tai L. Chow, *Gravity, Black Holes, and the Very Early Universe: An Introduction to General Relativity and Cosmology* (Springer 2008) 123.

100　Stephen Hawking and Leonard Mlodinow, *A Briefer History of Time* (Bantam Dell 2008) 68.

101　William D. Heacox, *The Expanding Universe: A Primer on Relativistic Cosmology* (Cambridge

Univ. Press 2015) 184.

102   Hawking and Mlodinow (n 100) 69.

103   Carl Sagan, *The Demon-Haunted World: Science as a Candle in the Dark* (Ballantine Books 1997) 278.

104   Edward Wakin, 'God and Carl Sagan: Is the Cosmos Big Enough for Both of Them?' in Tom Head (ed), *Conversations with Carl Sagan* (Univ. Press of Mississippi 2006) 70.

105   Email from Stephen Barr to author (6 September 2020).

106   Eric G. Swedin, *Science in the Contemporary World: An Encyclopedia* (ABC CLIO 2005) 40.

107   See Nola Taylor Redd, 'How Big is the Universe?', 6 June 2017 <www.space.com/24073-how-big-is-the-universe.html> accessed 1 October 2020.

108   Tony Roark, *Aristotle on Time: A Study of the Physics* (Cambridge Univ. Press 2011) 36.

109   See Maurizio Gasperini, *The Universe Before the Big Bang: Cosmology and String Theory* (Springer 2008) 186 and Katrin Becker and others, *String Theory and M-Theory: A Modern Introduction* (Cambridge Univ. Press 2006) 587.

110   Shing-Tung Yau and Steve Nadis, *The Shape of Inner Space: String Theory and the Geometry of the Universe's Hidden Dimensions* (Basic Books 2010) 125.

111   Barton Zwiebach, *A First Course in String Theory* (2nd edn, Cambridge Univ. Press 2012) 8.

112   Brad Lemley, 'Why is There Life?', *Discover Magazine* 1 November 2000, <http://discovermagazine.com/2000/nov/cover/> accessed 1 October 2020.

113   Richard Dawid, *String Theory and the Scientific Method* (Cambridge Univ. Press 2013) 92.

114   Stephen Hawking, *A Brief History of Time* (10th anniv. edn, Bantam Books 1998) 129.

115   Martin Rees, *Just Six Numbers: The Deep Forces that Shape the Universe* (Basic Books 2000).

116   Lemley (n 112).

117   Lee Smolin, *The Life of the Cosmos* (Oxford Univ. Press 1998) 45.

118   Stephen Bullivant and Michael Ruse (eds), *The Oxford Handbook of Atheism* (Oxford Univ. Press 2013) 31.

119   ibid.

120   Paul Davies, 'A Brief History of the Multiverse', 12 April 2003, *New York Times*, <www.nytimes.com/2003/04/12/opinion/a-brief-history-of-the-multiverse.html> accessed 1 October 2020.

121   Khalil Chamcham and others (eds), *The Philosophy of Cosmology* (Cambridge Univ. Press 2017) 29.

122   Peter Selby, 'Christianity in a world come of age', in John W. de Gruchy (ed), *The Cambridge Companion to Dietrich Bonhoeffer* (Cambridge Univ. Press 2002) 234.

123   William Lane Craig, *The Kalām Cosmological Argument* (Wipf and Stock 2000) 63.

124   ibid 150-51.

125   ibid 151.

126   David Mills, *Atheist Universe: The Thinking Person's Answer to Christian Fundamentalism* (Ulysses Press 2006) 74-75.

127   Peter E. Grimes, 'World-systems as dissipative structures: A new research agenda', in Salvatore J. Babones and Christopher Chase-Dunn (eds), *Routledge Handbook of World-System Analysis* (Routledge 2012) 140.

128   Raymond A. Serway and John W. Jewett, Jr., *Principles of Physics: A Calculus-Based Text*, vol 1 (fifth edn, Brooks/Cole 2013) 218.

129   Richard Dawkins, *The God Delusion* (First Mariner Books 2008) 188.

130   John Robert Ross, 'Constraints on Variables in Syntax', iv-v, September 1967 <http://hdl.handle.net/1721.1/15166> accessed 1 October 2020.

131   See (n 23).

132   See (n 32).

133   See (n 31).

134   Michael Yarus, *Life from an RNA World: The Ancestor Within* (Harvard Univ. Press 2010) 47.

135   Aristotle, *Aristotle's History of Animals in Ten Books* (Richard Cresswell tr, London 1862) 101.

136   John Tyndall, 'Spontaneous Generation', in W.H. Bidwell (ed), *The Eclectic Magazine of Foreign Literature, Science, and Art*, vol. 27 (New York 1878) 271.

137   *The Architecture of Marcus Vitruvius Pollio in Ten Books Translated from the Latin* (Joseph Gwilt tr, London 1860) 140.

138   Act II, Scene 7 in Henry N. Hudson, *Shakespeare's Antony and Cleopatra* (Boston 1881) 95.

139   Michael Windelspecht, *Groundbreaking Scientific Experiments, Inventions and Discoveries of the 17th Century* (Greenwood Press 2002) 8.

140   Francesco Redi, *Experiments on the Generation of Insects* (Mab Bigelow tr., Chicago 1909) 33.

141   Robert Fox, *The Savant and the State: Science and Cultural Politics in Nineteenth-Century France* (Johns Hopkins Univ. Press 2012) 156.

142   Anthony Carpi and Anne E. Egger, *The Process of Science* (rev. edn, Visionlearning 2011) 107-08.

143   Louise E. Robbins, *Louis Pasteur and the Hidden World of Microbes* (Oxford Univ. Press 2001) 48.

144   Fox (n 141).

145   ibid.

146   See Image No. 10308339 in the Science Museum's collection, available at <http://www.scienceandsociety.co.uk/results.asp?image=10308339&itemw=4&itemf=0001&itemstep=1&itemx=11> accessed 1 October 2020.

147   Charles Darwin, *On the Origin of Species by Means of Natural Selection, or the Preservation of Favoured Races in the Struggle for Life* (London 1860) 6.

148   'Letter of C. Darwin to J.D. Hooker, March 29, 1863', in Francis Darwin (ed), *The Life and Letters of Charles Darwin*, vol 2 (New York 1893) 203.

149   Thomas H. Huxley, 'Lecture VI: A Critical Examination of the Position of Mr. Darwin's Work, "On the Origin of Species," in Relation to the Complete Theory of the Causes of the Phenomena of Organic Nature', in *On the Origin of Species: or, The Causes of the Phenomena of Organic Nature* (New York 1890) 128 (emphasis added).

150   Wilhelm Bölsche, *Haeckel, His Life and Work* (Joseph McCabe tr, London 1906) 143.

151   Anonymous Author, 'The Germ Theory and Spontaneous Generation', in *The Contemporary Review*, vol. 29 (London 1877) 901-02.

152   Samuel Wainwright, 'Scientific Sophisms', in *The Humboldt Library of Popular Science Literature*, vol. 1 (New York 1881) 707.

153   Darwin (n 148) 202-03.

154   A.I. Oparin, *The Origin of Life* (Sergius Morgulis tr, Dover Publications 2003) 105-06.

155   See Pier Luigi Luisi, *The Emergence of Life: From Chemical Origins to Synthetic Biology* (2nd edn, Cambridge Univ. Press 2016) 39 and Oparin (n 153) 108-09.

156   Oparin (n 154) 106.

157   Luisi (n 155) 40.

158   George H. Shaw, *Earth's Early Atmosphere and Oceans, and The Origin of Life* (Springer 2016) 41-42.

159   J. Craig Venter, *Life at the Speed of Light: From the Double Helix to the Dawn of Digital Life*

(Penguin Books 2014) 132.

160   Reader's Digest, *Our Amazing World of Nature: Its Marvels and Mysteries* (Reader's Digest Association 1969) 287.

161   Dustin Trail, E. Bruce Watson, and Nicholas D. Tailby, 'The oxidation state of Hadean magmas and implications for early Earth's atmosphere', *Nature*, 30 November 2011 <https://www.nature.com/articles/nature10655> accessed 1 October 2020.

162   Daniella Scalice, 'Earth's Early Atmosphere: An Update', *Astrobiology at NASA*, 2 December 2011, <https://astrobiology.nasa.gov/news/earths-early-atmosphere-an-update/> accessed 1 October 2020.

163   Shuxun Cui, 'The Possible Roles of Water in the Prebiotic Chemical Evolution of DNA: An Approach by Single Molecule Studies', in Pierre Pontarotti (ed), *Evolutionary Biology: Exobiology and Evolutionary Mechanisms* (Springer 2013) 111.

164   Athena Coustenis and Thérèse Encrenaz, *Life Beyond Earth: The Search for Habitable Worlds in the Universe* (Cambridge Univ. Press 2013) 39.

165   See Kevin W. Plaxco and Michael Gross, *Astrobiology: A Brief Introduction* (2nd edn, Johns Hopkins Univ. Press, 2011) 85-86 and Scalice (n 161).

166   Martin Harwit, *Astrophysical Concepts* (3rd edn, Springer 2000) 565.

167   Karl Popper, *The Open Universe: An Argument for Indeterminism* (Routledge 2007) 147-149 (parenthetical quotation marks removed).

168   Lynn E.H. Trainor, *The Triplet Genetic Code: Key to Living Organisms* (World Scientific 2001) 46.

169   Martin Speight and Peter Henderson, *Marine Ecology: Concepts and Applications* (Wiley-Blackwell 2010) 9 and Matthew Levy and Stanley L. Miller, 'The stability of the RNA bases: Implications for the origin of life', in *Proceedings of the National Academy of Sciences of the United States of America*, 7 July 1998, <https://www.ncbi.nlm.nih.gov/pmc/articles/PMC20907/> accessed 1 October 2020.

170   ibid.

171   ibid.

172   ibid.

173   Levy and Miller (n 169).

174   L. Paul Knauth, 'Temperature and salinity history of the Precambrian ocean: implications for the course of microbial evolution' (2005) 219 Palaeogeography, Palaeoclimatology, Palaeoecology 53, 58.

175   Rosa Larralde and others, 'Rates of decomposition of ribose and other sugars: Implications for chemical evolution', (1995) 92 Proc. Natl. Acad. Sci. USA 8158, 8159.

176   ibid (emphasis added).

177   ibid.

178   Steven A. Benner and others, 'Setting the Stage: The History, Chemistry, and Geobiology behind RNA', in Raymond Gesteland and others (eds), *The RNA World* (3rd edn, Cold Spring Harbor Laboratory Press 2006) 16.

179   Donna G. Blackmond, 'The Origin of Biological Homochirality', Cold Spring Harb Perspect Biol. 2010 May; 2(5), <https://www.ncbi.nlm.nih.gov/pmc/articles/PMC2857173/> accessed 1 October 2020.

180   ibid.

181   Vladik Avetisov, 'Origin of Biomacromolecular Homochirality: in Search of Evolutional Dynamics' in Gyula Pályi and others (eds), *Progress in Biological Chirality* (Elzevier 2004) 3.

182   ibid.

183   ibid 4.

184   C.H. Lucas Patty and others, 'Remote Sensing of Homochirality: A Proxy for the Detection of Extraterrestrial Life' in Prasad L. Polavarapu (ed), *Chiral Analysis: Advances in Spectroscopy, Chromatography and Emerging Methods* (2nd edn, Elsevier 2018) 32.

185   Gyula Pályi and others, 'Dimensions of Biological Homochirality', in G. Pályi and others (eds), *Advances in BioChirality* (Elsevier 1999) 3.

186   Benner and others (n 178).

187   Phillip E. Johnson, *Defeating Darwinism by Opening Minds* (InterVarsity Press, 1997) 70.

188   To illustrate this, visit <https://www.mathisfun.com/combinatorics/combinations-permutations-calculator.html>, inserting '4' for the types to choose from field, and '70' for the number chosen, with the order important and repetition allowed. For a more manageable example, a chain of 2 nucleotides (4^2) would have sixteen possibilities—AA, AG, AU, AC, GA, GG, GU, GC, UA, UU, UG, UC, CA, GG, CU, and CC. A chain of three nucleotides would have 64 possibilities, a chain of 4 nucleotides would have 256 possibilities, a chain of 5 nucleotides would have 1,024 possibilities, and so forth.

189   David P. Clark and Nanette J. Pazdernik, *Molecular Biology* (2nd edn, Academic Press, 2013) 96, Nancy Irwin Maxwell, *Understanding Environmental Health: How We Live in the World* (2nd edn, Jones & Bartlett Learning 2014) 76, and David R. Harper, *Viruses: Biology, Applications, and Control* (Garland Science 2012) 52.

190   Uldis N. Streips and Ronald E. Yasbin (eds), *Modern Microbial Genetics* (2nd edn, Wiley-Liss 2002) 165.

191   Xinkun Wang, *Next-Generation Sequencing Data Analysis* (CRC Press 2016) 21.

192   Richard Dawkins, *The Blind Watchmaker: Why the Evidence of Evolution Reveals a Universe without Design* (W.W. Norton & Co. 1996) 317.

193   Fred Hoyle, 'The Universe: Past and Present Reflections', *Engineering & Science*, November 1981, 12 <http://calteches.library.caltech.edu/527/2/Hoyle.pdf> accessed 1 October 2020.

194   Voltaire, *A Philosophical Dictionary*, vol. 1 (Abner Kneeland tr, Boston 1852) 320.

195   Voltaire, *The Works of Voltaire: A Contemporary Version*, vol. 21 (William Fleming tr, New York 1901) 239-40.

196   Fred Hoyle, 'Evolution from Space', Omni Lecture, Royal Institution, 12 January 1982.

197   William Grimes, 'Antony Flew, Philosopher and Ex-Atheist, Dies at 87', 16 April 2010, *The New York Times* <https://www.nytimes.com/2010/04/17/arts/17flew.html> accessed 1 October 2020, and 'Letters', 26 December 2004, *The Sunday Telegraph* <https://www.telegraph.co.uk/comment/letters/3613812/The-Sunday-Telegraph-letters.html> accessed 1 October 2020.

198   See Richard Carrier, 'Antony Flew Considers God…Sort of', *The Secular Web* <https://infidels.org/kiosk/article/antony-flew-considers-godsort-of-369.html> accessed 1 October 2020 and Antony Flew and Roy Abraham Varghese, *There is a God: How the World's Most Notorious Atheist Changed His Mind* (HarperOne 2007) 124.

199   Eugene V. Koonin, 'The Cosmological Model of Eternal Inflation and the Transition from Chance to Biological Evolution in the History of Life', (2007) 2 Biology Direct 15 <https://www.ncbi.nlm.nih.gov/pmc/articles/PMC1892545/> accessed 1 October 2020.

200   ibid.

201   ibid.

202   James K. Feibleman, *Technology and Reality* (Martinus Nijhoff 1982) 28.

203   Elie A. Shneour and Eric A. Ottesen (eds), *Extraterrestrial Life: An Anthology and Bibliography* (National Academy of Sciences 1966) 273.

204   Trainor (n 168) 45.

205   Richard Carrier, 'Bad Science, Worse Philosophy: the Quackery and Logic-Chopping

of David Foster's The Philosophical Scientists (2000) - 9. The Odds of Life Evolving by Chance', <https://infidels.org/library/modern/richard_carrier/foster9.html> accessed 1 October 2020.

206   Oparin (n 154) 47.

207   See Wainwright (n 152), emphasis added.

208   A.I Oparin, *The Origin of Life on the Earth* (Ann Synge tr, Academic Press 1957) 38.

209   See Wainwright (n 152).

210   See (n 164).

211   See Koonin (n 199).

212   Davies (n 120).

213   Hoyle (n 193).

214   ibid.

215   Angus Stewart Woodburne, *The Relation Between Religion and Science: A Biological Approach* (Univ. Chicago Press 1920) 94.

216   See (n 31).

217   See (n 6) and (n 1).

218   Stephen Hawking and Leonard Mlodinow, *The Grand Design* (Random House 2010) 135.

Notes to Chapter 3 - True Religion

1   See Eugene V. Koonin, 'The Cosmological Model of Eternal Inflation and the Transition from Chance to Biological Evolution in the History of Life', (2007) 2 Biology Direct 15 <https://www.ncbi.nlm.nih.gov/pmc/articles/PMC1892545/> accessed 1 October 2020 and Lee Smolin, *The Life of the Cosmos* (Oxford Univ. Press 1998) 45.

2   Blaise Pascal, *Thoughts on Religion, and Other Subjects* (Edinburgh 1751) 145.

3   See (n 6) of the Introduction.

4   Renn D. Hampden, *An Essay on the Philosophical Evidence of Christianity* (London 1827) 32-33.

5   Philip Wilkinson, *Myths & Legends: An Illustrated Guide to their Origins and Meanings* (Penguin 2009) 92-93 and J. Edward Wright, *The Early History of Heaven* (Oxford Univ. Press 2000) 8.

6   A.A. Long (ed), *The Cambridge Companion to Early Greek Philosophy* (Cambridge Univ. Press 1999) 45 and William H. Stiebing Jr., *Ancient Near Eastern History and Culture* (2nd edn, Routledge 2016) 51.

7   207 US 463.

8   *Bramchari Sidheswar Shai & Ors. v State of West Bengal*, 1995 SCC (4) 646, decided 2 July 1995.

9   ibid.

10   See Alain Daniélou, *The Myths and Gods of India: The Classic Work on Hindu Polytheism* (Inner Traditions International 1991) 12, noting that 'The gods mentioned in the Vedas form only a small part of the Hindu pantheon, which gradually incorporated, and still is ready to incorporate, all the conceptions of divinity, all the gods, all the religious groups, all new "incarnations" or representations of the supernatural powers which pervade the universe.'

11   Helge Kragh, *Higher Speculations: Grand Theories and Failed Revolutions in Physics and Cosmology* (Oxford Univ. Press 2011) 199-200.

12   George Greenstein, *The Universe: An Inquiry Approach to Astronomy and the Nature of Scientific Research* (Cambridge Univ. Press, 2013) 545-47.

13   See John Olmsted III and Gregory M. Williams, *Chemistry: The Molecular Science* (2nd

edn, Wm. C. Brown Publishers 1997) 622 and Dilip Kondepudi and Ilya Prigogine, *Modern Thermodynamics: From Heat Engines to Dissipative Structures* (2nd edn, John Wiley & Sons 2015) 104.

14   Kragh (n 11) 200.

15   Steven Collins, *Aggañña Sutta: The Discourse on What is Primary (An Annotated Translation from Pali)*, (Sahitya Akademi 2001) 42.

16   P.D. Ryan, *Buddhism and the Natural World* (Windhorse Publications 1998) 77.

17   'The Buddhist World View in the Age of Science' in Francis Story (ed), *Dimensions of Buddhist Thought: Collected Essays*, vol. 3 (2nd edn, Buddhist Publication Society 2011) 129.

18   Book 1, Chapter 13, Section 33. Thomas Aquinas, *Summa Contra Gentiles*, <http://dhspriory.org/thomas/ContraGentiles.htm> accessed 28 November 2017.

19   Edward Conze, *Buddhism: Its Essence and Development* (Dover Publications 2003) 42-43.

20   ibid and Hirakawa Akira, *A History of Indian Buddhism: From Sākyamuni to Early Mahāyāna* (Paul Groner tr, Univ. Hawaii Press 1990), 170.

21   'Revelation given through Joseph Smith the Prophet, at Kirtland, Ohio, May 6, 1833', *The Doctrines and Covenants of The Church of Jesus Christ of Latter-day Saints*, 93:24-25 <https://www.lds.org/scriptures/dc-testament/dc/93?lang=eng> accessed 1 October 2020.

22   ibid 93:33 and Joseph Smith, 'Remarks, delivered before Aug. 8, 1839', in Andrew F. Ehat and Lyndon W. Cook (eds), *The Words of Joseph Smith: The Contemporary Accounts of the Nauvoo Discourses of the Prophet Joseph* (1980), 9.

23   Martin Meisel, *Chaos Imagined: Literature, Art, Science* (Columbia Univ. Press 2016) 386.

24   Keith E. Norman, 'Mormon Cosmology: Can it Survive the Big Bang?' (1985) 10 *Sunstone* no. 9, 20-23.

25   Diane Morgan, *Essential Buddhism: A Comprehensive Guide to Belief and Practice* (Praeger 2010) 70; Paul Dundas, *The Jains* (Routledge 2002) 90.

26   Luciano Floridi, *The Ethics of Information* (Oxford Univ. Press 2013) 180.

27   Nikky-Guninder Kaur Singh, *Sikhism: An Introduction* (I.B. Tauris 2011) 1.

28   W. Owen Cole and P.S. Sambhi, *Sikhism and Christianity: A Comparative Study* (Macmillan 1993) 42-43.

29   ibid 43.

30   Lucinda Mosher, *Personhood, Illness, and Death in America's Multifaith Neighborhoods* (Jessica Kingsley Publishers 2018) 52-53.

31   Hakim Singh Rahi, *Sri Guru Granth Sahib Discovered: A Reference Book of Quotations from the Adi Granth* (Motilal Banarsidass Publishers 1999) 63.

32   ibid 60-62.

33   See Stephen Little and others, *Taoism and the Arts of China* (Univ. California Press 2000) 262 and John Lagerwey, 'Evil and its Treatment in Early Taoism', in Jerald D. Gort and others (eds), *Probing the Depths of Evil and Good: Multireligious View and Case Studies* (Rodopi 2007) 74.

34   Lagerwey (n 33) 73.

35   Julian F. Pas, *The A to Z of Taoism* (Scarecrow Press 2006) 247.

36   Lagerwey (n 33) 75.

37   Yong Choon Kim, *Oriental Thought: An Introduction to the Philosophical and Religious Thought of Asia* (Littlefield 1973) Unpaginated Preface.

38   Ghorban Elmi and Mojtaba Zarvani, 'Problem of Evil in Taoism' (2016) 5 Religious Inquiries 35, 46.

39   ibid 41-42.

40   ibid 44.

41   A. E. Haigh, *The Tragic Drama of the Greeks* (Oxford 1896) 58.

42   Milton S. Terry, *The Shinto Cult: A Christian Study of the Ancient Religion of Japan* (Jennings and Graham 1910) 39.

43   ibid 40.

44   Lafcadio Hearn, *Kokoro: Hints and Echoes of Japanese Inner Life* (London 1905) 272-73.

45   ibid 273.

46   Ian S. Markham and Christy Lohr (eds), A World Religions Reader (3rd edn, Wiley-Blackwell 2009) 149.

47   ibid 148.

48   Wojciech Maria Zalewski, *The Crucible of Religion: Culture, Civilization, and Affirmation of Life* (Wipf & Stock 2012) 88.

49   Terry (n 42) 41-42, noting that 'How these evil deities originated is matter of myth, legend, and speculation'.

50   Wouter J. Hanegraaf, *New Age Religion and Western Culture: Esotericism in the Mirror of Secular Thought* (Brill 1996) 12.

51   George D. Chryssides, 'Defining the New Age', in Daren Kemp and James R. Lewis (eds), *Handbook of New Age* (Brill, 2007) 5-6.

52   ibid 19-20.

53   Bron R. Taylor and others (eds), *The Encyclopedia of Religion and Nature*, vol. 1 (Continuum 2008) 1194.

54   Chryssides (n 51) 6.

55   H.S. Olcott, *The Theosophist, a Magazine of Oriental Philosophy, Art, Literature & Occultism*, vol. 16 (Madras 1895) 152-54.

56   Ernest R. Hull, *Theosophy and Christianity* (London 1905) 57.

57   C.W. Leadbeater, *Some Glimpses of Occultism: Ancient and Modern* (2nd edn, Chicago 1909) 181.

58   ibid 387-88.

59   ibid 362.

60   Michael York, 'New Age and Magic' in Helen A. Berger (ed), *Witchcraft and Magic: Contemporary North America* (Univ. Pennsylvania Press 2005) 13.

61   ibid.

62   Michael L. Peterson, 'The Problem of Evil', in Stephen Bullivant and Michael Ruse (eds), *The Oxford Handbook of Atheism* (Oxford Univ. Press 2013) 71.

63   Greg M. Epstein, *Good Without God: What a Billion Nonreligious People Do Believe* (William Morrow 2009) ix.

64   Richard J. Bernstein, 'Rorty's Inspirational Liberalism', in Charles Guignon and David R. Hiley (eds), *Richard Rorty* (Cambridge Univ. Press 2003) 131.

65   ibid.

66   Marsha D. Fowler, 'Religion and Nursing', in Marsha D. Fowler and others (eds), *Religion, Religious Ethics, and Nursing* (Springer 2012) 3.

67   ibid.

68   J.L. Mackie, 'The Subjectivity of Values', in Russ Shafer-Landau (ed), *Ethical Theory: An Anthology* (Blackwell 2007) 31-32.

69   Michael Ruse, *Darwinism Defended: A Guide to the Evolution Controversies* (Addison-Wesley 1982) 275.

70   'Can atheists be moral?' Atheist Alliance International <https://www.atheistalliance. org/about-atheism/can-atheists-moral/#:~:text=Since%20atheists%2C%20reject%20 God%2C%20atheists,moral%20and%20what%20is%20not.> accessed 1 October 2020.

71   ibid.

72   ibid.

73   Louise Mabille, *Nietzsche and the Anglo-Saxon Tradition* (Continuum 2009) 133.

74   Ana Filipa Vrdoljak and Francesco Francioni, 'Introduction', in Ana Filipa Vrdoljak and Francesco Francioni (eds), *The Oxford Handbook of International Cultural Law* (Oxford Univ. Press 2020) 1.

75   George Thomson, *Evolution and Involution* (London 1880) 77 and Colin Heydt, 'Hume's Innovative Taxonomy of the Virtues', in Jacqueline Taylor (ed), *Reading Hume on the Principles of Morals* (Oxford Univ. Press 2020) 130.

76   Bernstein (n 64).

77   Using data from 2015, the Pew Research Center determined that 15.1% of the world's population were Hindu, 6.9% Buddhist, 5.7% followers of 'folk' religions (including Shinto, Jainism, Sikhism and Taoism), 31.2% Christian, 24.1% Muslim, and 0.2% Jewish. 16% of the world's population was unaffiliated with any religion, with the remaining .8% belong to 'other' religions. Conrad Hackett and David McClendon, 'Christians remain world's largest religious group, but they are declining in Europe', April 5, 2017 <https://www.pewresearch. org/fact-tank/2017/04/05/christians-remain-worlds-largest-religious-group-but-they-are-declining-in-europe/> accessed 1 October 2020.

78   Reuven Firestone, 'Abraham and Authenticity' in Adam J. Silverstein and others (eds), *The Oxford Handbook of the Abrahamic Religions* (Oxford Univ. Press 2015) 3-4.

79   Leviticus 11:44.

80   Deuteronomy 14:2.

81   Aaron W. Hughes, *Muslim Identities: An Introduction to Islam* (Columbia University Press, 2013) 80 and Cenap Çakmak (ed), *Islam: A Worldwide Encyclopedia*, vol. 1 (ABC-CLIO 2017) 1674.

82   Uriya Shavit, *Scientific and Political Freedom in Islam: A Critical Reading of the Modernist-Apologetic School* (Routledge 2017) 43. See also Christine Chism, 'Facing the Land of Darkness: Alexander, Islam, and the Quest for the Secrets of God', in Markus Stock (ed), *Alexander the Great in the Middle Ages: Transcultural Perspectives* (Univ. Toronto Press 2016) 51.

83   The founding of the city of Samaria has been dated to c. 887 BC, whilst the Exodus from Egypt is believed to have occurred sometime between 1400-1200 BC. K.A. Berney and others (eds), *International Dictionary of Historic Places*, vol. 4 (Fitzroy Dearborn 1996) 619.

84   See e.g. Muhammad Baqir Behbudi, *The Quran: A New Interpretation* (Colin Turner tr., Routledge 2013) 66, Oliver Leaman (ed), *The Qur'an: An Encyclopedia* (Routledge 2006) 396-97, and Muhammad M. Abu Laylah, *The Qur'an and the Gospels: A Comparative Study* (3rd edn, Al-Falah Foundation 2005) 123-24.

85   See e.g. Surah 3:54 at <https://quran.com/3/54-64>, <http://al-quran.info/#3> accessed 1 October 2020, and Mahmoud M. Ayoub, *The Qur'an and Its Interpreters*, vol. 2 – The House of Imran (State Univ. of New York Press, 1992) 154.

86   See the transliteration of Surah 3:54 <http://al-quran.info/#3> accessed 1 October 2020.

87   Edward William Lane, *An Arabic-English Lexicon*, part 7 (Beirut 1968) 2728.

88   ibid.

89   Per Surah 4:48, 'Indeed, Allah does not forgive association with Him, but He forgives what is less than that for whom He wills. And he who associates others with Allah has certainly fabricated a tremendous sin.' <https://quran.com/4/48-58> accessed 1 October 2020.

90   See Nabeel Qureshi's lecture, 'Jesus in Islam vs. Jesus in Christianity – Apologetics to Islam', delivered at Biola University on 21 April 2012 <https://youtu.be/QGR08BizLq8> accessed 1 October 2020, noting that 'To say that Jesus did not die on the cross, but it *looked* like He died on the cross, would explain why the disciples then went and started preaching

the risen Jesus; they thought He died, they saw Him alive, now they are preaching the risen Jesus ... but they are doing that because Allah tricked them. You have a deceptive god at this point. In other words, the Christian faith was started because Allah deceived the disciples. If Allah put somebody else's face on Jesus, or if Allah miraculously kept Jesus alive, the disciples who then went out and preached the risen Jesus were tricked by Allah—they were deceived. Are they to be blamed? Is it their fault? ... The deception has to be on Allah in this case ... Allah is responsible for Christianity. And if Christianity is *shirk*, the unforgiveable sin, then Allah is responsible for creating the religion which led the most people to Hell in all of history'.

Notes to Chapter 4 - The Creation of the Bible

1   Peter J. Williams, 'The Bible, the Septuagint, and the Apocrypha: A Consideration of their Singularity', in Geoffrey Khan and Diana Lipton (eds), *Studies on the Text and Versions of the Hebrew Bible in Honour of Robert Gordon* (Brill 2012) 169.

2   ibid.

3   Matt Stefon (ed), *Judaism: History, Belief, and Practice* (Britannica Educ. Publishing 2012) 96.

4   Konrad Schmid, *The Old Testament: A Literary History* (Linda M. Maloney tr, Fortress Press 2012) 16 and David Bridger and Samuel Wolk (eds), *The New Jewish Encyclopedia* (Behrman House 1976) 391.

5   Stefon (n 3).

6   Walter C. Kaiser Jr., *The Messiah in the Old Testament* (Zondervan 1995) 28-30.

7   Irving L. Jensen, *Jensen's Survey of the Old Testament* (Moody Publishers 1978) 19.

8   It is unlikely, for instance, that a man of Moses' modest character—even writing under the inspiration of God—would have described himself in Numbers 12:3 as 'very humble, more than all men who were on the face of the earth' or that he would have recorded the circumstances of his own death in Deuteronomy 34.

9   See e.g. D.M. Murdock, *Did Moses Exist? The Myth of the Israelite Lawgiver* (Stellar House 2014) 498 and Jacob Neusner, *The Four Stages of Rabbinic Judaism* (Routledge 2003) 7. As for arguments in support of the date of Mosaic authorship, see James K. Hoffmeier, *Israel in Egypt: The Evidence for the Authenticity of the Exodus Tradition* (Oxford Univ. Press 1999) 84-98; and Angel Sáenz-Badillos, *A History of the Hebrew Language* (John Elwolde tr, Cambridge Univ. Press 1996) 56-57. In addition to the arguments advanced by these sources, it is highly implausible that a priestly class writing after the Babylonian captivity would seek to invent 'founding fathers' who violated the religious laws they were trying to impose, such as Abraham's marriage to his half-sister (prohibited by Leviticus 18:9) or Jacob's marriage to his sister-in-law (prohibited by Leviticus 18:18).

10   Amnon Ben-Tor (ed), *The Archaeology of Ancient Israel* (Yale Univ. Press 1992) 303.

11   The evidence for the Torah's Mosaic authorship is too lengthy to be conveniently included in the chapter text without diverting the reader's attention, but broadly consists of a series of textual items that would either have been unknown to scribes who might have sought to fabricate them in later times or that would have not made sense for them to have included, such as (i) detailed geographic references to Egypt and the Sinai peninsula, but little familiarity with Canaan—and no mention of Jerusalem, (ii) cultural practices, (iii) descriptions of flora and fauna not native to the kingdoms of Israel and Judea, and (iv) divine commands that could not conceivably have been fulfilled in their era. By way of example, Numbers 13:22 refers to Hebron—a city that featured prominently in Israel's political interactions—having been built seven years before Zoan (later known as Tanis) in Egypt, a detail

that would have been impossible to know with certainty nearly 1,000 years after the time the Torah was alleged to have been written (if written by later scribes), and of no consequence to a post-exilic audience. The extensive descriptions of the Tabernacle's construction in Exodus also refer to the use of a type of wood from a tree—likely the *acacia nilotica*—that only grew around the Nile River and in Sinai (where the Israelites wandered), but not generally in the regions they would later inhabit, see William Smith (ed), *A Dictionary of the Bible, Comprising its Antiquities, Biography, Geography, and Natural History*, vol 3 (London 1863) 1295. The divine command to utterly destroy the idols, altars, and pagan cities in the region (see e.g. Deuteronomy 7) would also have been incongruous for a later writer to fabricate, given that Judah was a mere vassal state in a larger pagan empire and militarily incapable of effecting anything close to it.

12   Genesis 1:14-18.

13   See Stephen Quirke, *Exploring Religion in Ancient Egypt* (Wiley Blackwell 2015) 81 and S.G.F. Brandon, *Beliefs, Rituals, and Symbols of Ancient Egypt, Mesopotamia, and the Fertile Crescent* (Cavendish Square Publishing 2014) 40-42.

14   Genesis 3:15.

15   Genesis 12:3.

16   Watson E. Mills and others (eds), *Mercer Dictionary of the Bible* (Mercer Univ. Press 1990) 42.

17   Nadav Na'aman, *Ancient Israel and its Neighbors: Interaction and Counteraction*, vol 1 (Eisenbrauns 2005) 329.

18   See Katherine M. Stott, *Why Did They Write This Way? Reflections on References to Written Documents in the Hebrew Bible and Ancient Literature* (T & T Clark International 2008) 78 n 7.

19   Peter Adamson, *Philosophy in the Hellenistic and Roman Worlds: A History of Philosophy Without Any Gaps*, vol. 2 (Oxford Univ. Press 2015) 162.

20   Naomi Pasachoff and Robert J. Littman, *A Concise History of the Jewish People* (Rowman & Littlefield 2005) 39 and John Barton, *The Old Testament: Canon, Literature and Theology: Collected Essays of John Barton* (Ashgate 2007) 178.

21   Gregory W. Dawes, *Introduction to the Bible* (Liturgical Press 2007) 14.

22   ibid 14-15.

23   David Noel Freedman, *Pottery, Poetry, and Prophecy: Studies in Early Hebrew Poetry* (Eisenbrauns 1980) 131. See also Frank Moore Cross, Jr. and David Noel Freedman, *Studies in Ancient Yahwistic Poetry* (Wm. B. Eerdmans 1997) 3 and Graham Davies and Robert Gordon (eds), *Studies on the Language and Literature of the Bible: Selected Works of J.A. Emerton* (Brill 2015) 30.

24   Paul D. Wegner, *The Journey from Texts to Translations: The Origin and Development of the Bible* (Baker Academic 2004) 106.

25   Natalio Fernández Marcos, *The Septuagint in Context: Introduction to the Greek Version of the Bible* (Wilfred G.E. Watson tr, Brill 2000) 40.

26   Timothy Michael Law, *When God Spoke Greek: The Septuagint and the Making of the Christian Bible* (Oxford Univ. Press 2013) 35.

27   See Stephen M. Wylen, *The Seventy Faces of Torah: The Jewish Way of Reading the Sacred Scriptures* (Paulist Press 2005) 36; Barry L. Bandstra, *Reading the Old Testament: An Introduction to the Hebrew Bible* (4th edn, Cengage Learning 2009) 480 and B.H. McLean, *New Testament Greek: An Introduction* (Cambridge Univ. Press 2011) 2.

28   Daniel J. Elazar, *Covenant & Polity in Biblical Israel: Biblical Foundations & Jewish Expressions* (Transaction Publishers 1998) 97.

29   Flavius Josephus, *The Complete Works of Flavius Josephus, the Celebrated Historian* (William Whiston tr, Philadelphia 1895) 710.

30   See Galatians 1:13 and M. Eugene Boring, *An Introduction to the New Testament: History, Literature, Theology* (Westminster John Knox Press 2012) 209.

31   Boring (n 30) and 1 Thessalonians 2:14-15.

32   Romans 11:13.

33   Paul Barnett, *Jesus & the Rise of Early Christianity: A History of New Testament Times* (InterVarsity Press 1999) 417.

34   Henry Blackaby and others, *1 Corinthians: A Blackaby Bible Study Series* (Thomas Nelson 2008) 8.

35   See Galatians 2:10, 2 Corinthians 8:1-5 and 9:1-2, and Romans 15:25-28, for instance.

36   Alister E. McGrath, *Christianity: An Introduction* (2nd edn, Blackwell Publishing 2006) 84.

37   Keith F. Nickle, *The Synoptic Gospels: An Introduction* (2nd edn, Westminster John Knox Press 2001) 1-2 and Robert L. Thomas (ed), *Three Views on the Origins of the Synoptic Gospels* (Kregel Publications 2002) 8.

38   ibid.

39   John Beckwith, *Early Christian and Byzantine Art* (Yale Univ. Press 1993) 13 and Nathan Busenitz, *Reasons We Believe* (Crossway 2008) 135.

40   See Acts 1:1-3 and David G. Peterson, *The Acts of the Apostles* (Wm. B. Eerdmans 2009) 4-5.

41   Kenneth Schenck, *Understanding the Book of Hebrews: The Story Behind the Sermon* (Westminster John Knox Press 2003) 2.

42   Robert H. Mounce, *The Book of Revelation* (Rev. edn, Wm. B. Eerdmans 1998) 15.

43   Murray J. Smith, 'The Gospels in Early Christian Literature', in Mark Harding and Alanna Nobbs (eds), *The Content and the Setting of the Gospel Tradition* (Wm. B. Eerdmans 2010) 200 and Everett Ferguson (ed), *Encyclopedia of Early Christianity* (2nd edn, Routledge 1999) 264.

44   Tom Streeter, *The Church and Western Culture: An Introduction to Church History* (Booktango 2012) 50, Ian J. Elmer, 'The Pauline letters as community documents', in Bronwen Neil and Pauline Allen (eds), *Collecting Early Christian Letters: From the Apostle Paul to Late Antiquity* (Cambridge Univ. Press 2015) 45 and *The Genuine Epistles of the Apostolical Fathers* (William Wake tr, London 1893) 142.

45   Genuine Epistles (n 44) 142-43.

46   Elmer (n 44).

47   William A. Jurgens, *The Faith of the Early Fathers*, vol 1 (Liturgical Press 1970) 49.

48   Nigel Spivey and Michael Squire, *Panorama of the Classical World* (Thames and Hudson 2004) 206.

49   'Archaeological News' (1898) 2 American Journal of Archaeology 102.

50   ibid. See also Pat Southern, *The Roman Army: A Social and Institutional History* (Oxford Univ. Press 2007) 26, Sebastiana Nervegna, *Menander in Antiquity: The Contexts of Reception* (Cambridge Univ. Press 2013) 56, and Anne Rooney, *The History of Mathematics* (Rosen Publishing 2013) 80.

51   Rooney (n 50) and Lincoln H. Blumell, *Lettered Christians: Christians, Letters, and Late Antique Oxyrhynchus* (Brill 2012) 8.

52   Philip Comfort, *Encountering the Manuscripts: An Introduction to New Testament Paleography & Textual Criticism* (Broadman & Holman 2005) 156, 160.

53   ibid 139-43.

54   Robert M. Grant, *Second-Century Christianity: A Collection of Fragments* (2nd edn, Westminster John Knox Press 2003) 47-48.

55   ibid 48.

56 Grant (n 54) 47-48.

57 Jurgens (n 47) 55-56.

58 William Tooke, Lucian of Samosata, vol 1 (London 1820) 570.

59 Marvin R. Wilson, *Our Father Abraham: Jewish Roots of the Christian Faith* (Wm. B. Eerdmans 1989) 109.

60 ibid.

61 Harry Y. Gamble, 'Marcion and the "canon"', in Margaret M. Mitchell and Frances M. Young (eds), *The Cambridge History of Christianity: Origins to Constantine*, vol. 1 (Cambridge Univ. Press 2006) 202.

62 ibid 196.

63 Mills (n 16) 133 and Book 3, Chapter 11, Section 8 in Alexander Roberts and James Donaldson (eds), *Ante-Nicene Christian Library: Translations of the Writings of the Fathers down to A.D. 325*, vol 5 (Edinburgh 1884) 293.

64 Geoffrey Mark Hahneman, *The Muratorian Fragment and the Development of the Canon* (Clarendon Press, 1992) 5, Bruce M. Metzger, *The Canon of the New Testament: Its Origin, Development, and Significance* (Clarendon Press 1987) 305, and Michael D. Coogan (ed), *The Oxford Encyclopedia of the Books of the Bible* (Oxford Univ. Press 2011) 113.

65 Charles B. Puskas and C. Michael Robbins, *An Introduction to the New Testament* (2nd edn, Cascade 2011) 265.

66 ibid, and Tertullian, 'Of Baptism', in *A Library of Fathers of the Holy Catholic Church, Anterior to the Division of the East and West* (Oxford 1842) 275-76.

67 H.B. Swete, *The Gospel of Peter: The Text in Greek and English with Introduction, Notes, and Indices* (Wipf & Stock 2005) 27.

68 See Matthew 28:12-15.

69 Tertullian, 'On Prescription Against Heretics', in *A Library of Fathers of the Holy Catholic Church, Anterior to the Division of the East and West* (Oxford 1842) 463, noting that 'if Marcion separated the New Testament from the Old, he is later than that which he separated'.

70 Origen, *Homilies on Joshua* (Barbara J. Bruce tr, Catholic Univ. of America Press 2002) 13.

71 ibid 74-75.

72 Alexander Roberts and James Donaldson (eds), *Ante-Nicene Christian Library: Translations of the Writings of the Fathers down to A.D. 325*, vol 10 (Edinburgh 1895) 314-15.

73 See Thomas Paine, 'An Answer to a Friend', in Moncure Daniel Conway (ed), *The Writings of Thomas Paine*, vol 4 (London 1908) 196, arguing that "The Popish Councils of Nice and Laodicea, about 350 years after the time the person called Jesus Christ is said to have lived, voted the books that now compose what is called the New Testament to be the Word of God." See also Art Koroma, *Holy Axiom: Truth Exposed... The Bible is a Myth* (AuthorHouse, 2014) 58. With respect to the Edict of Milan, see Erwin Fahlbusch and others (eds), *The Encyclopedia of Christianity*, vol 5 (Wm. B. Eerdmans 2008) 189.

74 John Anthony McGuckin, *The Encyclopedia of Eastern Orthodox Christianity*, vol. 1 (Wiley-Blackwell 2011) 20.

75 Eusebius, *The Church History* (Paul L. Maier tr, Kregel Academic 2007) 261.

76 ibid.

77 Annemarie Luijendijk, 'Papyri from the Great Persecution: Roman and Christian Perspectives' (2008) 16:3 Journal of Early Christian Studies 341, 357.

78 George Kalantzis, *Caesar and the Lamb: Early Christian Attitudes on War and Military Service* (Cascade 2012) 176, Philip F. Esler (ed), *The Early Christian World*, vol 2 (Routledge 2000) 118, and Joyce E. Salisbury, *Encyclopedia of Women in the Ancient World* (ABC-CLIO 2001) 111-12.

79   Salisbury (n 78).

80   Dan Brown, *The Da Vinci Code* (Doubleday 2003) 231.

81   Robert F. Lay, *Readings in Historical Theology: Primary Sources of the Christian Faith* (Kregel Academic 2009) 136.

82   Eusebius, *The Ecclesiastical History of Eusebius Pamphilus, Bishop of Cesarea in Palestine* (Christian Frederick Crusé tr, 9th edn, New York 1850) 110.

83   ibid.

84   ibid.

85   Rein Fernhout, *Canonical Texts: Bearers of Absolute Authority* (Henry Jansen & Lucy Jansen-Hofland trs, Editions Rodopi 1994) 58, n 50.

86   See Canons 59 and 60 of the Council of Laodicea, which met in 364, in Louis Gaussen, *The Canon of the Holy Scriptures Examined in the Light of History* (Edward Kirk tr, Boston 1862) 86-87.

87   Craig D. Allert, *A High View of Scripture? The Authority of the Bible and the Formation of the New Testament Canon* (Baker Academic 2007) 140.

88   Thomas Hartwell Horne, *An Introduction to the Critical Study and Knowledge of the Holy Scriptures*, vol 1 (London 1828) 75.

89   Alec Gilmore, *A Dictionary of the English Bible and Its Origins* (Routledge 2013) 60.

Notes to Chapter 5 - The Transmission of the Bible

1   See e.g. *The Home and Foreign Record of the Presbyterian Church in the United States of America*, vol 3, (Philadelphia 1852) 22, David Newport, *Indices, Historical and Rational, to a Revision of the Scriptures* (Philadelphia 1871) 21, and Carl W. Ernst, *How to Read the Qur'an: A New Guide, with Select Translations* (Univ. North Carolina Press 2011) 55.

2   Robert B. Stewart (ed), *The Reliability of the New Testament: Bart D. Ehrman & Daniel B. Wallace in Dialogue* (Fortress Press 2011) 32-33.

3   Daniel B. Wallace (ed), *Revisiting the Corruption of the New Testament: Manuscript, Patristic, and Apocryphal Evidence* (Kregel Publications 2011) 43.

4   ibid 42.

5   See Genesis 31:47, Jeremiah 10:11, Daniel 2:4-7:28, and Ezra 4:8-6:18 and 7:12-26; A. Berkeley Mickelsen, *Interpreting the Bible* (Wm. B. Eerdmans 1972) 10.

6   Ziony Zevit, *What Really Happened in the Garden of Eden?* (Yale Univ. Press 2013) 37-38.

7   See the anachronistic reference to Dan in Genesis 14:14.

8   Zevit (n 6) 38.

9   John C. Pope, 'On the Date of Composition of Beowulf', in Colin Chase (ed), *The Dating of Beowulf* (Univ. Toronto Press 1997) 187.

10   Daniel B. Wallace, *Greek Grammar Beyond the Basics* (Zondervan 1996) 17.

11   ibid.

12   S.A. Nigosian, *From Ancient Writings to Sacred Texts: The Old Testament and Apocrypha* (Johns Hopkins Univ. Press 2004) 21.

13   Peter W. Martens, *Origen and Scripture: The Contours of the Exegetical Life* (Oxford Univ. Press 2012) 45.

14   ibid.

15   ibid 46.

16   ibid 47.

17   Robert J. Wilkinson, *Tetragrammaton: Western Christians and the Hebrew Name of God* (Brill 2015) 67.

18   See Polycarp's reference to the collection of Paul's letters at Philippi, c. 110 (Ch 4), Lu-

cian of Samosata's mention of the 'sacred books' c. 165 (Ch 4), and Speratus' possession of the 'epistles of Paul' c. 180 (Ch 4).

19   Philip Comfort, *Encountering the Manuscripts: An Introduction to New Testament Paleography & Textual Criticism* (Broadman & Holman 2005) 156, 160.

20   Nicholas P. Lunn, *The Original Ending of Mark: A New Case for the Authenticity of Mark 16:9-20* (James Clarke & Co. 2015) 27.

21   Jack Finegan, *Encountering New Testament Manuscripts: A Working Introduction to Textual Criticism* (Wm. B. Eerdmans 1980) 127.

22   David Parker, 'Ancient Scribes and Modern Encodings: The Digital Codex Sinaiticus', in Wido van Peursen and others (eds), *Text Comparison and Digital Creativity: The Production of Presence and Meaning in Digital Text Scholarship* (Brill 2010) 173.

23   Brenda Deen Schildgen, *Power and Prejudice: The Reception of the Gospel of Mark* (Wayne State Univ. Press 1999) 105 and Negussie Andre Domnic, *The Fetha Nagast and its Ecclesiology: Implications in Ethopian Catholic Church Today* (Peter Lang 2010) 191.

24   Janet W. Dyk and Percy S.F. van Keulen, *Language System, Translation Technique, and Textual Tradition in the Peshitta of Kings* (Brill 2013) 3 and Michael D. Coogan and others (eds), *The New Oxford Annotated Bible* (Aug. Third edn, Oxford Univ. Press 2007) 466.

25   Charles G. Herbermann and others (eds), *The Catholic Encyclopedia*, vol. 10 (The Encyclopedia Press 1913) 211.

26   ibid. See also (n 23).

27   As Augustine of Hippo wrote in Book 2, Chapter 11 of *On Christian Doctrine*, 'For the translations of the Scriptures from Hebrew into Greek can be counted, but the Latin translators are all out of number. For in the early days of the faith every person who happened to get his hands upon a Greek manuscript, and who thought he had any knowledge, were it ever so little, of the two languages, ventured upon the work of translation.' Martin McNamara, 'The Latin Gospels, with Special Reference to Irish Tradition', in Charles Horton (ed), *The Earliest Gospels: The Origins and Transmission of the Earliest Christian Gospels – The Contribution of the Chester Beatty Gospel Codex P[45]* (T&T Clark International 2004) 92.

28   William P. Brown (ed), *The Oxford Handbook of the Psalms* (Oxford Univ. Press 2014) 187.

29   Samuel IJsseling, *Rhetoric and Philosophy in Conflict: An Historical Survey* (Martinus Nijhoff 2012) 41.

30   Brown (n 28).

31   Martha Ann Kirk, *Women of Bible Lands: A Pilgrimage to Compassion and Wisdom* (Liturgical Press 2004) 152 and Brown (n 28) 188.

32   Brown (n 28) 188.

33   Bruce Corley and others (eds), *Biblical Hermeneutics: A Comprehensive Introduction to Interpreting Scripture* (2nd edn, Broadman & Holman 2002) 231.

34   Margaret Bald, *Banned Books: Literature Suppressed on Religious Grounds* (Rev. edn, Facts on File 2006) 21.

35   Richard Marsden, 'Old Latin Intervention in the Old English *Heptateuch*', in Michael Lapidge and others (eds), *Anglo-Saxon England*, vol. 23 (Cambridge Univ. Press 1994) 235 and Ronald F. Youngblood and others (eds), *Nelson's Illustrated Bible Dictionary: New and Enhanced Edition* (Thomas Nelson 2014) 178.

36   Félix Racine, 'Servius' Greek lessons', in Elizabeth P. Archibald and others (eds), *Learning Latin and Greek from Antiquity to the Present* (Cambridge Univ. Press 2015) 53.

37   Christopher Kelly, *The Roman Empire: A Very Short Introduction* (Oxford Univ. Press 2006) 1. In fairness to the Romans, the Empire's former territory now contains more than forty countries on three continents.

38   Alaric Watson, *Aurelian and the Third Century* (Routledge 2003) 23, Allen M. Ward and others, *A History of the Roman People* (6th edn, Routledge 2016) 429, and Lynn Hunt and others (eds), *The Making of the West: Peoples and Cultures* (4th edn, Bedford/St. Martin's 2012) 210.

39   Michael Frassetto, *Encyclopedia of Barbarian Europe: Society in Transformation* (ABC-CLIO 2003) 17.

40   Paula J. Rose, *A Commentary on Augustine's* De cura pro mortuis gerenda*: Rhetoric in Practice*, (Brill 2013) 128. In a letter to Principia recounting the attack on their 85-year-old friend Marcella, Jerome wrote 'When the soldiers entered she is said to have received them without any look of alarm; and when they asked her for gold she pointed to her coarse dress to shew them that she had no buried treasure. However they would not believe in her self-chosen poverty, but scourged her and beat her with cudgels. She is said to have felt no pain but to have thrown herself at their feet and to have pleaded with tears for you, that you might not be taken from her, or owing to your youth have to endure what she as an old woman had no occasion to fear. The barbarians conveyed both you and her to the basilica of the apostle Paul, that you might find there either a place of safety or, of not that, at least a tomb.' Henry Wace and Philip Schaff (eds), *A Select Library of Nicene and Post-Nicene Fathers of the Christian Church*, vol 7 (2nd series, Oxford 1893) 257.

41   Adrian Goldsworthy, *How Rome Fell* (Yale Univ. Press 2009) 11.

42   Justin McCarthy, *The Ottoman Turks: An Introductory History to 1923* (Routledge 2013) 18.

43   James Allan Evans, *The Power Game in Byzantium: Antonina and the Empress Theodora* (Continuum 2011) 27. Despite the passage of some 1,600 years, remnants of state control over the Eastern (now Greek Orthodox) Church still remain. When the Eastern Roman Empire was conquered by the Ottomans in 1453, imperial authority over the Church transitioned to the Ottoman Empire, which was succeeded by the Republic of Turkey in 1923. Today, Turkish law strictly regulates who can be elected Patriarch of Constantinople. See <http://www.cnn.com/2010/WORLD/europe/08/26/wus.patriarch/> accessed 1 October 2020.

44   George Mousourakis, *Roman Law and the Origins of the Civil Law Tradition* (Springer 2015) 254.

45   Craig R. Smith, *The Quest for Charisma: Christianity and Persuasion* (Praeger 2000) 125 and Michael Blodgett, 'Calming an Angry Enemy: Attila, Leo I, and the Diplomacy of Ambiguity, 452', in Robert M. Frakes and others (eds), *The Rhetoric of Power in Late Antiquity: Religion and Politics in Byzantium, Europe and the Early Islamic World* (Tauris Academic Studies 2010) 63.

46   Gilbert Highet, *The Classical Tradition: Greek & Roman Influences on Western Literature* (Oxford Univ. Press 2015) 6.

47   Bruce M. Metzger and Michael D. Coogan (eds), *The Oxford Guide to Ideas and Issues of the Bible* (Oxford Univ. Press 2001) 506.

48   Frans van Liere, *An Introduction to the Medieval Bible* (Cambridge Univ. Press 2014) 92.

49   ibid 93.

50   William Grange, *Historical Dictionary of German Literature to 1945* (Scarecrow Press 2011) xv.

51   Alexander Bergs and Laurel J. Brinton (eds), *English Historical Linguistics: An International Handbook*, vol. 1 (Walter de Gruyter 2012) 348.

52   See <http://www.bl.uk/manuscripts/FullDisplay.aspx?ref=Cotton_MS_Vespasian_A_I> accessed 1 October 2020. The British Library maintains an excellent collection of high-resolution digitised manuscripts which viewers can examine online.

53   John Blair, 'The Anglo-Saxon Period: (c.440-1066)', in Kenneth O. Morgan, *The Oxford History of Britain* (revised edn., Oxford Univ. Press 2001) 93.

54   Blair (n 53) 96-97.

55   Robert Stanton, *The Culture of Translation in Anglo-Saxon England* (D.S. Brewer 2002) 61.

56   Benjamin Thorpe, *Ancient Laws and Institutes of England*, vol. 1 (1840) 45 and Gabriele Diewald and others (eds), *Comparative Studies in Early Germanic Languages: With a focus on verbal categories* (John Benjamins 2013) 200.

57   See <http://www.bl.uk/manuscripts/FullDisplay.aspx?ref=Royal_MS_1_A_XIV> Folio 40r, accessed 1 October 2020. While the West Saxon Gospels were translated c. 990, the version held by the British Library and featured in this book dates from 1150-1200.

58   Benjamin Thorpe, *Ða halgan Godspel on Englisc* (London 1842) 11.

59   Charles Barber and others, *The English Language: A Historical Introduction* (2nd edn, Cambridge Univ. Press 2009) 144.

60   F.F. Bruce, *History of the Bible in English* (Lutterworth Press 2002) 9.

61   Christopher Daniell, *From Norman Conquest to Magna Carta: England 1066-1215* (Routledge 2003) 194 and Peter France (ed), *The Oxford Guide to Literature in English Translation* (Oxford Univ. Press 2001) 161.

62   Michael Costen, *The Cathars and the Albigensian Crusade* (Manchester Univ. Press 1997) 56.

63   Frans van Liere, *An Introduction to the Medieval Bible* (Cambridge Univ. Press 2014) 193.

64   ibid.

65   Emanuel Tov, *Textual Criticism of the Hebrew Bible* (3rd edn rev., Fortress Press 2012) 49.

66   Stephen M. Miller and Robert V. Huber, *The Bible: A History* (Lion Hudson 2015) 242 and Frans van Liere, 'Biblical Exegesis Through the Twelfth Century', in Susan Boynton and Diane J. Reilly (eds), *The Practice of the Bible in the Middle Ages: Production, Reception, and Performance in Western Christianity* (Columbia Univ. Press 2011) 172.

67   Tov (n 65) 50 and Greg Goswell, 'The Divisions of the Book of Daniel', in Raymond de Hoop and others (eds), *The Impact of Unit Delimitation on Exegesis* (Brill 2009) 92.

68   Malcom Barber, *The Cathars: Dualist Heretics in Languedoc in the High Middle Ages* (Routledge 2014) 7.

69   Christopher Tyerman, *God's War: A New History of the Crusades* (Harvard Univ. Press 2006) 570.

70   Jeffrey Richards, *Sex, Dissidence and Damnation: Minority Groups in the Middle Ages* (Routledge 2002) 33 and Tyerman (n 69).

71   Hugh B. Urban, *Magia Sexualis: Sex, Magic, and Liberation in Modern Western Esotericism* (Univ. California Press 2006) 34.

72   Tyerman (n 69) 577.

73   William M. Johnston (ed), *Encyclopedia of Monasticism*, vol. 1 (Fitzroy Dearborn 2000) 408.

74   Yuri Stoyanov, *The Other God: Dualist Religions from Antiquity to the Cathar Heresy* (Yale Univ. Press 2000) 205.

75   ibid.

76   Tyerman (n 69) 583.

77   William H. Brackney, *Historical Dictionary of Radical Christianity* (Scarecrow Press 2012) 78.

78   Emile de Bonnechose, *History of France*, vol 1 (London 1868) 180.

79   Tyerman (n 69) 596.

80   George Ripley and Charles A. Dana (eds), *The American Cyclopædia: A Popular Dictionary of General Knowledge*, vol 11 (New York 1883) 785.

81   Edward Peters (ed), *Heresy and Authority in Medieval Europe: Documents in Translation* (Univ. Pennsylvania Press 1980) 195.

82   E. Michael Gerli (ed), *Medieval Iberia: An Encyclopedia* (Routledge 2003) 169.

83   *A Controversial Correspondence Between The Rev. Paul Machlachlan, Roman Catholic Priest in Falkirk, and R.W. Kennard, Esq. of Grahamston, N.B., and Upper Thames Street, London* (Falkirk 1854) 60.

84   van Liere (n 66) 196.

85   Susan Hagood Lee, 'The Reformation', in John McGrath and Kathleen Callanan Martin (eds), *The Modernization of the Western World: A Society Transformed* (Routledge 2015) 50.

86   William C. Placher and Derek R. Nelson (eds), *Readings in the History of Christian Theology*, vol 1 (Revised edn, Westminster John Knox Press 2015) 166.

87   Kirsten Malmkjær, *Linguistics and the Language of Translation* (Edinburgh Univ. Press 2005) 4.

88   Philip W. Comfort, *The Essential Guide to Bible Versions* (Tyndale House Publishers 2000) 136.

89   Helen Barr, 'Wycliffite Representations of the Third Estate', in Fiona Somerset and others (eds), *Lollards and their Influence in Late Medieval England* (Boydell Press 2003) 197 and Mark Twinham Elvins, *Towards a People's Liturgy: The Importance of Language* (Gracewing 1994) 27.

90   See David Grummitt, *Henry VI* (Routledge, 2015) 26 and 2 Henry IV, c.15; Danby Pickering (ed), *The Statutes at Large, from the Fifteenth Year of King Edward III. to the Thirteenth Year of King Henry IV. inclusive*, vol 2 (Cambridge 1762) 415.

91   ibid 416-17.

92   ibid.

93   David Lawton, 'Englishing the Bible, 1066-1549', in David Wallace (ed), *The Cambridge History of Medieval English Literature* (Cambridge Univ. Press 1999) 459.

94   ibid.

95   Roger E. Olson, *The Story of Christian Theology: Twenty Centuries of Tradition & Reform* (InterVarsity Press 2009) 358.

96   Ben McCorkle, *Rhetorical Delivery as Technological Discourse: A Cross-Historical Study* (Southern Illinois Univ. Press 2012) 74.

97   Otto W. Fuhrmann, 'The Invention of Printing', in Paul A. Winckler (ed), *Reader in the History of Books and Printing* (Information Handling Services 1980) 267. Although it is difficult to quantify the present value of the loans Gutenberg received, the purchasing power of 800 guilders in the fifteenth century would have bought approximately eight substantial city houses, or eighty suburban houses with gardens.

98   David Deming, *Science and Technology in World History*, vol 3 (McFarland 2012) 33.

99   Jeffrey R. Wigelsworth, *Science and Technology in Medieval European Life* (Greenwood Press 2006) 69.

100   Fuhrmann (n 97).

101   Jan Luiten Van Zanden, *The Long Road to the Industrial Revolution: The European Economy in a Global Perspective, 1000-1800* (Brill 2009) 186.

102   Colin Imber, *The Ottoman Empire, 1300-1650: The Structure of Power* (2nd edn, Palgrave Macmillan 2009) 4.

103   W.A. Heurtley and others, *A Short History of Greece: From Early Times to 1964* (Cambridge Univ. Press 1967) 56.

104   Joel Cook, *The Mediterranean and its Borderlands*, vol 2 (John C. Winston Co. 1910) 213.

105   Arthur White, *Plague and Pleasure: The Renaissance World of Pius II* (Catholic Univ. of America Press, 2014) 99 and George Childs Kohn, *Dictionary of Wars* (Rev. edn, Routledge 2013) 126.

106   Steven Runciman, *The Fall of Constantinople 1453* (Cambridge Univ. Press 2012) 145-47

and Akbar Shah Najeebabadi, *The History of Islam*, vol 3 (Darussalam 2001) 418.

107   Michael Angold, *The Fall of Constantinople to the Ottomans: Context and Consequences* (Routledge 2014) 103 and Angus Mackay and David Ditchburn (eds), *Atlas of Medieval Europe* (Routledge 2003) 241.

108   Arthur Tilley, *The Dawn of the French Renaissance* (Cambridge Univ. Press 1918) 15 and Angold (n 107) 104.

109   Angold (n 107) 106.

110   F.L. Cross and E.A. Livingstone (eds), *The Oxford Dictionary of the Christian Church* (3rd edn revised, Oxford Univ. Press 2005) 375.

111   John Van Seters, *The Edited Bible: The Curious History of the "Editor" in Biblical Criticism* (Eisenbrauns 2006) 21.

112   William J. Bennett, *Tried by Fire: The Story of Christianity's First Thousand Years* (Nelson Books 2016) 322.

113   Marcia L. Colish, *Medieval Foundations of the Western Intellectual Tradition, 400-1400* (Yale Univ. Press 2002) 67 and John M. Najemy (ed), *Italy in the Age of the Renaissance: 1300-1550* (Oxford Univ. Press 2005) 75.

114   Jaroslav Pelikan and others (eds), *The Bible of the Reformation* (Yale Univ. Press 1996) 109.

115   Kevin Madigan, *Medieval Christianity: A New History* (Yale Univ. Press 2015) 416.

116   Alister E. McGrath, *Iustitia Dei: A History of the Christian Doctrine of Justification* (3rd edn, Cambridge Univ. Press 2005) 239.

117   David Daniell, *William Tyndale: A Biography* (Yale Univ. Press 2001) 61 and Robert M. Solomon, *The Enduring Word: The Authority and Reliability of the Bible* (Genesis Books 2011) 100.

118   Cornelis Augustijn, *Erasmus: His Life, Works, and Influence* (J.C. Grayson tr, Univ. Toronto Press 1995) 93 and George Thomas Kurian and Mark A. Lamport (eds), *Encyclopedia of Christian Education* (Rowman & Littlefield 2015) 476.

119   David S. New, *The Text of the Bible: Its Path Through History and to the People* (McFarland 2013) 110 and Augustijn (n 118).

120   Albert Rabil Jr., *Erasmus and the New Testament: The Mind of a Christian Humanist* (Univ. Press of America 1972) 92.

121   ibid.

122   Owen Chadwick, *The Early Reformation on the Continent* (Oxford Univ. Press 2003) 21.

123   Scott H. Hendrix, *Martin Luther: Visionary Reformer* (Yale Univ. Press 2015) 126 and Paul Arblaster, '"Totius Mundi Emporium": Antwerp as a Centre for Vernacular Bible Translations 1523-1545', in Arie-Jane Gelderblom and others (eds), *The Low Countries as a Crossroads of Religious Belief* (Brill 2004) 19.

124   Kerry M. Olitzky and Ronald H. Isaacs, *A Glossary of Jewish Life* (Jason Aronson 1992) 83.

125   Adele Berlin and Marc Zvi Brettler (eds), *The Jewish Study Bible* (Oxford Univ. Press 2004) 2141.

126   Isidore Singer and others (eds), *The Jewish Encyclopedia*, vol. 8 (Funk and Wagnalls 1912) 370.

127   I. Harris, 'The Rise and Development of the Massorah', in I. Abrahams and C.G. Montefiore (eds), *The Jewish Quarterly Review*, vol 1 (London 1889) 131.

128   ibid 131-32.

129   ibid.

130   Ralph W. Klein, 'Textual Criticism: Recovering and Preserving the Text of the Hebrew Bible', in Joel M. LeMon and Kent Harold Richards (eds), *Method Matters: Essays on the Inter-*

pretation of the Hebrew Bible in Honor of David L. Petersen (Soc. of Biblical Literature 2009) 77.

131 Singer (n 126) and Norman Roth (ed), *Medieval Jewish Civilization: An Encyclopedia* (Routledge 2003) 88.

132 H. Graetz, *Popular History of the Jews*, vol 4 (A.B. Rhine tr, Hebrew Publishing 1919) 324 and Peter Martyr Vermigli, *Commentary on the Lamentations of the Prophet Jeremiah*, (Daniel Shute tr, Truman State Univ. Press 2002) xxviii.

133 Robert Benedetto (ed), *The New Westminster Dictionary of Church History*, vol 1 (Westminster John Knox Press 2008) 475 and Ted Byfield (ed), *A Century of Giants, A.D. 1500 to 1600: In an Age of Spiritual Genius, Western Christendom Shatters* (Soc. to Explore and Record Christian History 2010) 51.

134 Peter J. Thuesen, *In Discordance with the Scriptures: American Protestant Battles over Translating the Bible* (Oxford Univ. Press 2002) 22.

135 Michael Farris, *From Tyndale to Madison: How the Death of an English Martyr Led to the American Bill of Rights* (B&H Publishing 2007) 6.

136 ibid 8.

137 Ralph S. Werrell, *The Roots of William Tyndale's Theology* (James Clarke & Co. 2013) 40 and Jocelyn Wogan-Browne and others (eds), *The Idea of the Vernacular: An Anthology of Middle English Literary Theory, 1280-1520* (Pennsylvania State Univ. Press 1999) 134.

138 Brad C. Pardue, *Printing, Power, and Piety: Appeals to the Public During the Early Years of the English Reformation* (Brill 2012) 84.

139 Andrew Atherstone, *Reformation: A World in Turmoil* (Lion Hudson 2015) 111.

140 While the Bishop of London claimed there were some 2,000 errors in Tyndale's translation, many of these had important theological implications which challenged the status quo: 'Tyndale rendered *presbuteros* as "elder" instead of "priest"; *ekklesia* as "congregation" instead of "church"; *agape* as "love" instead of "charity"; and *metanoeo* as "repent" instead of "do penance".' ibid.

141 Dorothy Auchter, *Dictionary of Literary and Dramatic Censorship in Tudor and Stuart England* (Greenwood Press 2001) 247.

142 ibid. See also James Raven, *The Business of Books: Booksellers and the English Book Trade 1450-1850* (Yale Univ. Press 2007) 62.

143 Gergely Juhász and Paul Arblaster, 'William Tyndale and the Falsification of Memory', in Johan Leemans (eds), *More than a Memory: The Discourse of Martyrdom and the Construction of Christian Identity in the History of Christianity* (Peeters 2005) 321.

144 David M. Whitford (ed), *The T&T Clark Companion to Reformation Theology* (T&T Clark 2012) 456 and Henry Walter, *A History of England, in Which it is Intended to Consider Men and Events on Christian Principles*, vol 3 (London 1832) 153.

145 John Anthony Nordstrom, *Stained with Blood: A One-Hundred Year History of the English Bible* (Westbow Press 2014) 106.

146 Joseph Lemuel Chester, *John Rogers: The Compiler of the First Authorised English Bible; The Pioneer of the English Reformation; and its First Martyr* (London 1861) 18.

147 John A. Wagner and Susan Walters Schmid (eds), *Encyclopedia of Tudor England*, vol 1 (ABC-CLIO 2012) 117.

148 Christopher Anderson, *The Annals of the English Bible*, vol 1 (London 1845) 577.

149 Roland H. Worth, Jr., *Church, Monarch and Bible in Sixteenth Century England: The Political Context of Biblical Translation* (McFarland 2000) 72.

150 Roger Lockyer, *Tudor and Stuart Britain: 1485-1714* (3rd edn, Routledge 2013) 67.

151 Jamie H. Ferguson, 'Miles Coverdale and the Claims of Paraphrase', in Linda Phyllis Austern and others (eds), *Psalms in the Early Modern World* (Ashgate 2011) 137.

152 James R. C. Perkin, '"…a thing begunne rather than fynnished…" William Tyndale

as Witness', in R. Glenn Wooden and others (eds), *You Will Be My Witnesses: A Festschrift in Honor of the Reverend Dr. Allison A. Trites on the Occasion of His Retirement* (Mercer Univ. Press 2003) 176.

153   Thomas Hartwell Horne, *A Manual of Biblical Bibliography* (London 1839) 72.

154   Allan K. Jenkins and Patrick Preston (eds), *Biblical Scholarship and the Church: A Sixteenth-Century Crisis of Authority* (Ashgate 2007) 228.

155   Jon Sweeney, *Verily, Verily: The KJV - 400 Years of Influence and Beauty* (Zondervan 2011) 70.

156   Femke Molekamp, "'Of the Incomparable treasure of the Holy Scriptures": The Geneva Bible in the Early Modern Household', in Matthew Dimmock and Andrew Hadfield (eds), *Literature and Popular Culture in Early Modern England* (Ashgate 2009) 121.

157   Robert L. Plummer, *The Story of Scripture: How We Got Our Bible and Why We Can Trust It* (Kregel Publications 2013) 24.

158   See (n 67).

159   David Scott Kastan (ed), *The Oxford Encyclopedia of British Literature*, vol 1 (Oxford Univ. Press 2006) 220 and Bruce (n 60) 91.

160   Bruce (n 60) 91 and John Strype, *The Life and Acts of Matthew Parker, the First Archbishop of Canterbury in the Reign of Queen Elizabeth* (London 1711) 207.

161   David Price and Charles C. Ryrie, *Let it Go Among Our People: An Illustrated History of the English Bible from John Wycliffe to the King James Version* (Lutterworth Press 2004) 94.

162   ibid. See also Bruce (n 60) 91.

163   Bruce (n 60) 92 and Crawford Gribben and David George Mullan (eds), *Literature and the Scottish Reformation* (Ashgate 2009) 12.

164   ibid.

165   Alister McGrath, *In the Beginning: The Story of the King James Bible and How It Changed a Nation, a Language, and a Culture* (Knopf Doubleday 2008) 141.

166   Michael D. Coogan (ed), *The Oxford Encyclopedia of the Books of the Bible* (Oxford Univ. Press 2011) 439.

167   John Saward and others (eds), *Firmly I Believe and Truly: The Spiritual Tradition of Catholic England* (Oxford Univ. Press 2013) 129.

168   Coogan (n 166).

169   Danby Pickering, *The Statutes at Large, From the First Year of Queen Mary, to the Thirty-fifth Year of Queen Elizabeth, inclusive*, vol 6 (Cambridge 1763) 333, *The Statutes at Large, From the First Year of King Edward the Fourth to the End of the Reign of Queen Elizabeth*, vol 2 (London 1763) 671 and Ceri Sullivan, *Dismembered Rhetoric: English Recusant Writing, 1580 to 1603* (Associated Univ. Presses 1995) 135.

170   Alan R. Young, 'The Phoenix Reborn: The Jacobean Appropriation of an Elizabethan Symbol', in Elizabeth H. Hageman and Katherine Conway (eds), *Resurrecting Elizabeth I in Seventeenth-Century England* (Fairleigh Dickinson Univ. Press 2007) 68.

171   *The Church of England in the Reigns of the Stuarts* (London 1851) 18.

172   ibid.

173   Edgar Taylor, *The Book of Rights: or, Constitutional Acts and Parliamentary Proceedings Affecting Civil and Religious Liberty in England, from Magna Charta to the Present Time* (London 1833) 157 and *Church of England* (n 171).

174   S. Mutchow Towers, *Control of Religious Printing in Early Stuart England* (Boydell Press 2003) 79.

175   ibid.

176   William Barlow, *The Summe and Substance of the Conference Which it pleased his Excellent Majestie to have with the Lords Bishops, and others of his Clergie (at which the most of the Lords of the*

Councill were present) in his Majesties Privie-Chamber, at Hampton Court Jan. 14. 1603 (London 1661).

177 ibid.

178 ibid.

179 ibid.

180 *The Primitive Church Magazine, Advocating the Constitution, Faith, and Practice of the Apostolic Churches*, vol 9 (London 1852) 170.

181 *The Cambridge Companion to the Bible* (Cambridge Univ. Press 1893) 86.

182 ibid.

183 Constance Harris, *The Way Jews Lived: Five Hundred Years of Printed Words and Images* (Mc-Farland & Co. 2009) 54 and David G. Burke and others (eds), *The King James Version at 400: Assessing its Genius as Bible Translation and Its Literary Influence* (Soc. of Biblical Literature 2013) 282.

184 Burke (n 183) 146.

185 Augustijn (n 118), George Hoffmann, 'Renaissance printing and the book trade', in Glyn P. Norton (ed), *The Cambridge History of Literary Criticism*, vol 3 (Cambridge Univ. Press 2001) 390, and Scott Mandelbrote, 'The authority of the Word: manuscript, print and the text of the Bible in seventeenth-century England', in Julia Crick and Alexandra Walsham (eds), *The Uses of Script and Print, 1300-1700* (Cambridge Univ. Press 2004) 143.

186 Simon Mills, 'Scripture and Heresy in the Biblical Studies of Nathaniel Lardner, Joseph Priestley, and Thomas Belsham', in Scott Mandelbrote and Michael Ledger-Lomas (eds), *Dissent and the Bible in Britain, c.1650-1950* (Oxford Univ. Press 2013) 92 and Robert F. Hull, Jr., *The Story of the New Testament Text: Movers, Materials, Motives, Methods, and Models* (Soc. of Biblical Literature 2010) 41.

187 Thomas Hartwell Horne, *An Introduction to the Critical Study and Knowledge of the Holy Scriptures*, vol. 2 (Fourth edition corrected, Philadelphia 1825) 249.

188 By one estimate, 63% of the text of the King James Version differs from the text of the Bishops' Bible. Naomi Tadmor, *The Social Universe of the English Bible: Scripture, Society, and Culture in Early Modern England* (Cambridge Univ. Press 2010) 8.

189 David Patrick (ed), *Chambers's Cyclopædia of English Literature*, vol. 1 (W. & R. Chambers 1901) 135.

190 Tadmor (n 188).

191 Lloyd E. Berry, 'Introduction to the Facsimile Edition', in *The Geneva Bible, 1560 Edition* (Hendrickson Publishers Marketing 2011) 19.

192 Peter White, *Predestination, Policy, and Polemic: Conflict and consensus in the English Church from the Reformation to the Civil War* (Cambridge Univ. Press 2002) 91.

193 Philip M. Pantana, Sr., *America—A Purpose-Driven Nation* (Pen Power 2007) ix and Alexander Leslie Klieforth and Robert John Munro, *The Scottish Invention of America, Democracy and Human Rights: A History of Liberty and Freedom from the Ancient Celts to the New Millennium* (Univ. Press of America 2004) 347.

194 Laura Arnold Leibman (ed), *Experience Mayhew's* Indian Converts: *A Cultural Edition* (Univ. Massachusetts Press 2008) 64.

195 David Norton, *The King James Bible: A Short History from Tyndale to Today* (Cambridge Univ. Press 2011) 134.

196 W.R. Owens (ed), *The Gospels: Authorized King James Version* (Oxford Univ. Press 2011) xlvi.

197 David Norton, *A Textual History of the King James Bible* (Cambridge Univ. Press 2005) 99.

198 Horne (n 187) 84.

199 ibid.

200 Paul C. Gutjahr, *An American Bible: A History of the Good Book in the United States, 1777-1880* (Stanford Univ. Press 1999) 21.

201 ibid.

202 *Journals of the American Congress: From 1774 to 1788*, vol 4 (Washington 1823) 76.

203 ibid.

204 Scott Mandelbrote, 'The English Bible and its Readers in the Eighteenth Century', in Isabel Rivers (ed), *Books and Their Readers in Eighteenth-Century England: New Essays* (Continuum 2003) 45.

205 Augustijn (n 118).

206 Allan D. Fitzgerald and others (eds), *Augustine Through the Ages: An Encyclopedia* (Wm. B. Eerdmans 1999) 529.

207 W. Andrew Smith, *A Study of the Gospels in Codex Alexandrinus: Codicology, Palaeography, and Scribal Hands* (Brill 2014) 8.

208 Juan Hernández Jr., *Scribal Habits and Theological Influences in the Apocalypse: The Singular Readings of Sinaiticus, Alexandrinus, and Ephraemi* (Mohr Siebeck, 2006) 100 and Smith (n 207) 10.

209 David S. Katz, *God's Last Words: Reading the English Bible from the Reformation to Fundamentalism* (Yale Univ. Press 2004) 182.

210 ibid.

211 Kurt Aland and Barbara Aland, *The Text of the New Testament: An Introduction to the Critical Editions and to the Theory and Practice of Modern Textual Criticism* (2nd edn, Erroll F. Rhodes tr, Wm. B. Eerdmans 1995) 7-9.

212 Eldon Jay Epp and Gordon D. Fee, *Studies in the Theory and Method of New Testament Textual Criticism* (Wm. B. Eerdmans 2000) 20.

213 ibid.

214 Bertil Albrektson (ed), *Text, Translation, Theology: Selected Essays on the Hebrew Bible* (Routledge 2016) 74.

215 Donald K. McKim (ed), *Historical Handbook of Major Biblical Interpreters* (InterVarsity Press 1998) 321.

216 Carl P. Cosaert, *The Text of the Gospels in Clement of Alexandria* (Soc. of Biblical Literature 2008) 50 and Brent Nongbri, 'Pauline Letter Manuscripts', in Mark Harding and Alanna Nobbs (eds), *All Things to All Cultures: Paul Among Jews, Greeks, and Romans* (Wm. B. Eerdmans 2013) 88.

217 Eldon Epp, 'Critical editions and the development of text-critical methods, part 2: from Lachmann (1831) to the present', in John Riches (ed), *The New Cambridge History of the Bible*, vol. 4 (Cambridge Univ. Press 2015) 14.

218 The phase 'Textus Receptus' owes its origin to the Elzevir edition of 1633, which noted in the preface that 'You now have the text which is accepted by all'. Kenneth Willis Clark, *The Gentle Bias and Other Essays* (Brill 1980) 120. See also Epp (n 218) 14-15.

219 See Kurian and Lamport (n 119), Epp (n 218) 15, and Thomas Hartwell Horne, *An Introduction to the Critical Study and Knowledge of the Holy Scriptures*, vol 4 (Cambridge Univ. Press 2013) 133.

220 Epp (n 217) 16.

221 Finegan (n 21) 133.

222 Stanley E. Porter, *Constantine Tischendorf: The Life and Works of a 19th Century Bible Hunter* (Bloomsbury 2015) 16-18.

223 Finegan (n 21) 133.

224 Johnston (n 73) 68 and George M. Eberhart (ed), *The Whole Library Handbook: Current*

Data, Professional Advice, and Curiosa about Libraries and Library Services (Amer. Library Assn 2013) 53.

225   Paul D. Wegner, *The Journey from Texts to Translations: The Origin and Development of the Bible* (Baker Academic 2004) 196.

226   ibid.

227   *A Full Collation of the Codex Sinaiticus with the Received Text of the New Testament: To Which is Prefixed a Critical Introduction by Frederick H. Scrivener, M.A.* (London 1864) xi.

228   Constantine Tischendorf, *The New Testament: The Authorised English Version; with Introduction, and Various Readings from the Three Most Celebrated Manuscripts of the Original Greek Text* (Tauchnitz edn, Leipzig 1869) xv.

229   ibid viii.

230   Hull (n 186) 71.

231   B.F. Westcott and F.J.A Hort, *The Greek New Testament* (Hendrickson Publishers 2007) xi.

232   Brooke Foss Westcott and Fenton John Anthony Hort, *The New Testament in the Original Greek: Introduction, Appendix* (London 1896) 2.

233   ibid 282-84.

234   Nigel Spivey and Michael Squire, *Panorama of the Classical World* (Thames & Hudson 2004) 206.

235   Comfort (n 19).

236   Eusebius, *The Church History* (Paul L. Maier tr, Kregel Academic 2007) 261 and Joseph M. Holden and Norman Geisler, *The Popular Handbook of Archaeology and the Bible* (Harvest House Publishers 2013) 380.

237   J.W. Rogerson and Judith M. Lieu (eds), *The Oxford Handbook of Biblical Studies* (Oxford Univ. Press 2006) 197.

238   Stanley E. Porter and Andrew W. Pitts, *Fundamentals of New Testament Textual Criticism* (Wm. B. Eerdmans 2015) 59.

239   British and Foreign Bible Society, *The Corrected English New Testament: A Revision of the "Authorised" Version* (Knickerbocker Press 1905) xxi.

240   Porter and Pitts (n 238) 142.

241   ibid.

242   See *The Twenty-Eighth Report of the British and Foreign Bible Society* (London 1832) lxxx-lxxxviii.

243   Philip C. Stine, *Let the Words be Written: The Lasting Influence of Eugene A. Nida* (Soc. of Biblical Literature 2004) 100.

244   ibid.

245   ibid.

246   ibid.

247   ibid.

248   Mildred L. Larson, 'Factors in Bible Translation', in Chan Sin-Wai and David E. Pollard (eds), *An Encyclopedia of Translation* (Chinese Univ. Press 2001) 53.

249   Frank Moore Cross, *The Ancient Library of Qumran* (3rd edn, Fortress Press 1995) 19.

250   Weston W. Fields, *The Dead Sea Scrolls: A Full History*, vol 1 (Brill 2009) 26.

251   Geoffrey W. Bromiley and others (eds), *The International Standard Bible Encyclopedia*, vol 1 (Wm. B. Eerdmans 1979) 883.

252   Peter W. Flint, *The Dead Sea Scrolls* (Abingdon Press 2013) 4.

253   Daniel A. Machiela, *The Dead Sea Genesis Apocryphon: A New Text and Translation with Introduction and Special Treatment of Columns 13-17* (Brill 2009) 21.

254   Flint (n 252) 5.

255 ibid.
256 Walter A. Elwell and Philip W. Comfort (eds), *Tyndale Bible Dictionary* (Tyndale House Publishers 2001) 181.
257 John J. Collins, *The Dead Sea Scrolls: A Biography* (Princeton Univ. Press 2013) 9-10.
258 C.D. Elledge, *The Bible and the Dead Sea Scrolls* (Soc. of Biblical Literature 2005) 5-8.
259 ibid 6.
260 Florentino García Martínez, *The Dead Sea Scrolls Translated: The Qumran Texts in English* (2nd edn, Wilfred G.E. Watson tr, Wm. B. Eerdmans 1996) lv.
261 Elledge (n 258) 94 and Lee Martin McDonald, *Forgotten Scriptures: The Selection and Rejection of Early Religious Writings* (Westminster John Knox Press 2009) 105.
262 McDonald (n 261) 108.
263 ibid 107.
264 Russell Fuller, 'Some Thoughts on How the Dead Sea Scrolls Have Changed Our Understanding of the Text of the Hebrew Bible and Its History and the Practice of Textual Criticism', in Nóra Dávid and others (eds), *The Hebrew Bible in Light of the Dead Sea Scrolls* (Vandenhoeck & Ruprecht 2012) 23.
265 Epp and Fee (n 212) 26.
266 'The Bible Societies' Greek New Testament', in Bruce Manning Metzger, *Reminiscences of an Octogenarian* (Baker Academic 2012), chapter 6, unpaginated.
267 ibid.
268 ibid.
269 ibid.
270 ibid.
271 ibid.
272 Gerd Mink, 'Problems of a highly contaminated tradition: the New Testament: Stemmata of variants as a source of a genealogy for witnesses', in Pieter van Reenan and others (eds), *Studies in Stemmatology II* (John Benjamins Publishing 2004) 17. See also <http://egora.uni-muenster.de/intf/index_en.shtml> accessed 1 October 2020.
273 See <http://ntvmr.uni-muenster.de/liste/> to explore the Institute's Virtual Manuscript Room, accessed 1 October 2020.
274 ibid.
275 ibid.
276 See <https://www.academic-bible.com/en/home/current-projects/editio-critica-maior-ecm/> accessed 1 October 2020.
277 Douglas Stuart, *Old Testament Exegesis, Fourth Edition: A Handbook for Students and Pastors* (Westminster John Knox Press 2009) 97-98.
278 David Ewert, *A General Introduction to the Bible: From Ancient Tablets to Modern Translations* (Zondervan 1990) 139.
279 Mark Juergensmeyer and Wade Clark Roof (eds), *Encyclopedia of Global Religion*, vol. 1 (SAGE 2012) 621.
280 Song Y. Yan, *Perfect, Amicable and Sociable Numbers: A Computational Approach* (World Scientific 1996) 3 and O. Neuberger, 'The History of Ancient Astronomy: Problems and Methods', in Otto Neuberger, *Astronomy and History Selected Essays* (Springer 1983) 60.
281 See Philip M. Miller, 'The Least Orthodox Reading is to be Preferred: A New Canon for New Testament Textual Criticism?', in Daniel B. Wallace (ed), *Revisiting the Corruption of the New Testament: Manuscript, Patristic, and Apocryphal Evidence* (Kregel Academic 2011) 63-64 and D.A. Carson, *The King James Version Debate: A Plea for Realism* (Baker 1979) 56.
282 *The Genuine Epistles of the Apostolical Fathers* (William Wake tr, London 1893) 142-43.

Notes to Chapter 6 - The Authenticity of the Bible

1   *The Encyclopædia Britannica*, vol. 12, (9th edn, Philadelphia 1881) 28.

2   Charles Burney, *Historical Dictionary of the Hittites* (2nd edn, Rowman & Littlefield 2018) 38.

3   See <www.soas.ac.uk/nme/languages/languages-of-the-near-middle-east-at-soas-hittite.html> accessed 1 October 2020.

4   Genesis 7:13.

5   See for example Luke Muehlhauser, 'Noah's Flood and its Predecessors', 5 June 2010 <http://commonsenseatheism.com/?p=8647> accessed 1 October 2020.

6   W.G. Lambert, 'Some new Babylonian wisdom literature', in John Day and others (eds), *Wisdom in Ancient Israel: Essays in Honour of J.A. Emerton* (Cambridge Univ. Press 1998) 37.

7   Andrew George (ed), *The Epic of Gilgamesh: The Babylonian Epic Poem and Other Texts in Akkadian and Sumerian* (Penguin Books 2003) 88.

8   ibid 89.

9   ibid 90.

10   ibid 92.

11   ibid 89-95.

12   ibid.

13   Russell E. Gmirkin, *Berossus and Genesis, Mantheo and Exodus: Hellenistic Histories and the Date of the Pentateuch* (T&T Clark 2006) 111.

14   Apollodorus, *The Library*, vol 1 (Sir James Frazer tr, London 1921) 53-55.

15   J. Muir, *Original Sanskrit Texts on the Origin and History of the People of India, their Religions and Institutions*, vol 1 (2nd edn, London 1868) 181-83.

16   John T. Short, *The North Americans of Antiquity: Their Origin, Migrations, and Type of Civilizations Considered* (2nd edn, New York 1880) 238.

17   See Sir James George Frazer, *Folk-Lore in the Old Testament: Studies in Comparative Religion, Legend, and Law*, vol 1 (Macmillan 1919).

18   Samuel Jenkins, *Letters on Welsh History* (Philadelphia 1852) 259-60.

19   ibid 261.

20   Frazer (n 17) 309.

21   ibid 310-11.

22   See e.g. Jenna Millman and others, 'Evidence Noah's Biblical Flood Happened, Says Robert Ballard', 10 December 2012 <https://abcnews.go.com/Technology/evidence-suggests-biblical-great-flood-noahs-time-happened/story?id=17884533>, Mark Strauss, 'Why Newton Believed a Comet Caused Noah's Flood', 30 December 2016 <www.nationalgeographic.com/news/2017/01/comet-new-years-eve-newton-flood-bible-gravity-science/> and Greg Neyman, 'Old Earth Creation Science: Where Was the Flood of Noah?' 12 May 2007 <http://www.oldearth.org/articles/flood_location.htm> accessed 1 October 2020.

23   For height calculations, see Francis Nimmo and others, 'Tidally Modulated Eruptions on Enceladus: Cassini ISS Observations and Models', *The Astronomical Journal*, 28 July 2014 <https://iopscience.iop.org/article/10.1088/0004-6256/148/3/46> accessed 1 October 2020.

24   See 'PIA11688: Bursting at the Seams: the Geyser Basin of Enceladus' <https://photojournal.jpl.nasa.gov/catalog/PIA11688> accessed 1 October 2020.

25   Hugh Rollinson, *Early Earth Systems: A Geochemical Approach* (Blackwell Publishing 2007) 178.

26   Tom Gleeson and others, 'The global volume and distribution of modern groundwater', Nature Geoscience, 16 November 2015 <https://www.nature.com/articles/ngeo2590.

epdf> accessed 1 October 2020.

27   John McClintock and James Strong (eds), *Cyclopædia of Biblical, Theological, and Ecclesiastical Literature*, vol. 10 (New York 1894) 465.

28   ibid.

29   Alfred John Church and William Jackson Brodribb, *The History of Tacitus Translated into English* (2nd edn, London 1873) 196.

30   Strabo, *The Geography of Strabo*, vol 3 (H.C. Hamilton and W. Falconer trs, London 1857) 183.

31   Numbers 22:5.

32   Edward Lipiński, *Studies in Aramaic Inscriptions and Onomastics*, vol 2 (Uitgeverij Peeters 1994) 103.

33   ibid 105-06.

34   J. Hoftijzer and G. Van Der Kooij (eds), *Aramaic Texts from Deir 'Alla* (Brill 1976) 179. For clarity, parenthetical marks have been removed from the text.

35   ibid 181.

36   ibid 269-71 (parenthetical references removed).

37   James Henry Breasted, *Ancient Records of Egypt: Historical Documents from the Earliest Times to the Persian Conquest*, vol 3 (Univ. Chicago Press 1906) 256.

38   ibid 263-64 (parenthetical linguistic marks removed).

39   Hywel Clifford and others (eds), *Companion to the Old Testament: Introduction, Interpretation, Application* (SCM Press 2016) 45.

40   Carol A. Redmount, 'Bitter Lives: Israel in and Out of Egypt', in Michael Coogin (ed), *The Oxford History of the Biblical World* (Oxford Univ. Press 2001) 72.

41   Michael G. Hasel, *Domination & Resistance: Egyptian Military Activity in the Southern Levant, 1300-1185 BC* (Brill 1998) 271 and Edward Mahler, 'The Exodus', in *The Journal of the Royal Asiatic Society of Great Britain and Ireland for 1901* (London 1901) 38.

42   Daniel E. Fleming, *The Legacy of Israel in Judah's Bible: History, Politics, and the Reinscribing of Tradition* (Cambridge Univ. Press 2012) 305.

43   Israel Finkelstein and Neil Asher Silberman, *The Bible Unearthed: Archaeology's New Vision of Ancient Israel and the Origin of Its Sacred Texts* (The Free Press 2001) 177.

44   Stephen C. Russell, *Images of Egypt in Early Biblical Literature: Cisjordan Israelite, Transjordan-Israelite, and Judahite Portrayals* (Walter de Gruyter 2009) 91-92.

45   See André Lemaire, '"House of David" Restored in Moabite Inscription' (1994) Biblical Archaeology Review 20:03, noting that 'Enough has been preserved at the end of line 31, however, to identify the new enemy of Moab against whom Mesha fought in the last half of the inscription: bt[d]wd , the House of David. Having described how he was victorious against Israel in the area controlled by it north of the Arnon, Mesha now turns to part of the area south of the Arnon which had been occupied by Judah, the House of David. In the tenth and first half of the ninth centuries B.C.E., the kingdom of Edom did not yet exist. The area southeast of the Dead Sea was apparently controlled by Judah. Thus, during Mesha's rebellion against the king of Israel (2 Kings 3:5), the king of Israel asks for assistance from the king of Judah, who agrees to provide the aid. The king of Israel instructs the king of Judah to attack the king of Moab by going through the "wilderness of Edom" (2 Kings 3:8) because apparently it was an area controlled by the kingdom of Judah. No doubt the missing part of the inscription described how Mesha also threw off the yoke of Judah and conquered the territory southeast of the Dead Sea controlled by the House of David.'

46   Bill T. Arnold and Bryan E. Beyer (eds), *Readings from the Ancient Near East: Primary Sources for Old Testament Study* (Baker Academic 2002) 165 (parenthetical marks removed).

47   Jeffrey Kah-Jin Kuan, *Neo-Assyrian Historical Inscriptions and Syria-Palestine: Israelite/*

Judean-Tyrian-Damascene Political and Commercial Relations in the Ninth-Eighth Centuries BCE (Wipf & Stock 2016) 31.

48   ibid.

49   ibid 63.

50   K. Lawson Younger, Jr, *Ancient Conquest Accounts: A Study in Ancient Near Eastern and Biblical History Writing* (Sheffield Academic Press 1990) 122.

51   2 Kings 17:3-4.

52   William R. Harper (ed), *The Biblical World*, vol 9 (Univ. Chicago Press 1897) 408.

53   Robert Williams Rogers (ed), *Cuneiform Parallels to the Old Testament* (Eaton & Mains 1912) 322.

54   2 Kings 20:20.

55   Joseph M. Holden and Norman Geisler, *The Popular Handbook of Archaeology and the Bible* (Harvest House 2013) 266.

56   Joan Aruz and others (eds), *Assyria to Iberia at the Dawn of the Classical Age* (Metropolitan Museum of Art/Yale Univ. Press, 2014) xxiv.

57   Austen H. Layard, *Discoveries Among the Ruins of Nineveh and Babylon* (New York 1853) 128.

58   Daniel David Luckenbill, *The Annals of Sennacherib* (Wipf & Stock 2005) 11.

59   See 'The Esarhaddon Prism/Library of Ashurbanipal', British Museum, <www.britishmuseum.org/research/collection_online/collection_object_details.aspx?objectId=291290&partId=1> accessed 1 October 2020.

60   Jane R. McIntosh, *Ancient Mesopotamia: New Perspectives* (ABC-CLIO 2005) 105-06.

61   David Diringer, *The Book Before Printing: Ancient, Medieval and Oriental* (Courier 2013) 109. See also Jeanette C. Fincke, *The Babylonian Texts of Nineveh: Report on the British Museum's Ashurbanipal Project* (2003) <http://oracc.museum.upenn.edu/saao/knpp/downloads/fincke_afo50.pdf> accessed 1 October 2020, and Sami Said Ahmed, *Southern Mesopotamia in the Time of Ashurbanipal* (Mouton 1968) 170.

62   Ed Hinson and Gary Yates (eds), *The Essence of the Old Testament: A Survey* (B&H Academic 2012) 417.

63   ibid.

64   John W. Betlyon, 'Neo-Babylonian Military Operations Other Than War in Judah and Jerusalem', in Oded Lipschits and Joseph Blenkinsopp (eds), *Judah and the Judeans in the Neo-Babylonian Period* (Eisenbrauns 2003) 264.

65   The New International Version of the Bible uses the name Nebo-Sarsekim, whilst other translations such as the New King James Version translation use 'Sarsechim'.

66   See the British Museum's inscription translation and curator's comments at <www.britishmuseum.org/research/collection_online/collection_object_details.aspx?objectId=1571630&partId=1&searchText=sarsekim&page=1> accessed 1 October 2020, noting that 'Nebusarsekim the chief eunuch' is the anglicised form of the Babylonian name, and 'The shortening of the name is due to the fact that the Hebrew text was originally written without all the vowels (as follows: N-b-w-sh-r-s-k-y-m). The vowels were filled in only much later, at a time when the full sound of the original name was no longer quite certain. The correspondence with the Babylonian form can therefore best be seen by comparing it with the Hebrew consonants only. The name represents an attempt to record a strange Babylonian name, where the details of the words were unfamiliar. The Hebrew scribe wrote –m at the end of the name instead of –n, perhaps because words ending in –ym were common in Hebrew. … The chief eunuch was one of the commanders of the Babylonian army and among the highest officials at the Babylonian court, as we know from contemporary cuneiform texts. Importantly, there was always only one man with this title at any given time.

Nabu-sharrussu-ukin and Nebusarsekim are clearly one and the same person.'

67   ibid.

68   Magnus Magnusson, *BC, the Archaeology of the Bible Lands* (BBC 1977) 203.

69   Jeremiah 52:34.

70   Thomas Newton, *Dissertations on the Prophecies, Which Have Remarkably Been Fulfilled, and at this Time are Fulfilling in the World* (London 1832).

71   ibid 2.

72   ibid 3.

73   George Rawlinson and others, *History of Herodotus*, vol 1 (3rd edn, London 1875) 423.

74   ibid 298-302.

75   See Isaiah 39:5-8 and Jeremiah 25:1-14.

76   William J. Doorly, *Isaiah of Jerusalem: An Introduction* (Paulist Press 1992) 92-94.

77   John Boardman and others (eds), *The Cambridge Ancient History*, vol 3 part 2 (2nd edn, Cambridge Univ. Press 2003) 109 and Barbara Nevling Porter, *Images, Power, and Politics: Figurative Aspects of Esarhaddon's Babylonian Policy* (American Philosophical Society 1993) 50.

78   J. Kenneth Kuntz, *The People of Ancient Israel: An Introduction to Old Testament Literature, History, and Thought* (Wipf & Stock 2009) 343.

79   Abba Eban, *Heritage: Civilization and the Jews* (Summit Books 1984) 62.

80   Xenophon, *The Cyropædia: or Institution of Cyrus* (J.S. Watson and H. Dale trs, London 1855) 221.

81   ibid 222.

82   ibid 147 and 221.

83   ibid 222.

84   ibid.

85   Daniel 5:1.

86   Daniel 5:2.

87   Daniel 5:5.

88   Daniel 5:5-9.

89   Daniel 5:13-16.

90   Daniel 5:26-28.

91   Xenophon (n 80) 223.

92   ibid.

93   ibid 224.

94   Jeremiah 51:30-57.

95   A. Kirk Grayson, *Assyrian and Babylonian Chronicles* (Eisenbrauns 2000) 21.

96   Benjamin R. Foster (ed), *Jean-Jacque Glassner's Mesopotamian Chronicles* (Brill 2005) 235.

97   British Museum, *A Guide to the Babylonian and Assyrian Antiquities* (2nd edn rev., Trustees of the British Museum 1908) 194.

98   Daniel 5:16.

99   M.A. Dandamaev, *A Political History of the Achaemenid Empire* (W.J. Vogelsang tr, Brill 1989) 48.

100   ibid.

101   Foster (n 96) 237 (emphasis added).

102   Pamela Dell and Debra Skelton, *Great Empires of the Past: Empire of Alexander the Great* (Facts on File 2005) 58.

103   K.A. Berney and others (eds), *International Dictionary of Historic Places*, vol 4 (Fitzroy Dearborn 1996) 104.

104   ibid.

105   ibid.

106 Strabo (n 30) 145.

107 Charles Rollin, *The Ancient History of the Egyptians, Carthaginians, Assyrians, Babylonians, Medes and Persians, Macedonians and Grecians*, vol 1 (New York 1879) 173.

108 Newton (n 70) 132.

109 ibid 133.

110 Rollin (n 107) 95 and Marvin A. Sweeney, *Isaiah 1-39: With An Introduction to Prophetic Literature* (Wm. B. Eerdmans 1996) 51-52.

111 Isaiah 13:20.

112 'Saddam Does Battle with Nebuchadnezzar' The Guardian (London, 4 January 1999) <https://www.theguardian.com/world/1999/jan/04/iraq1> accessed 1 October 2020.

113 See Leviticus 18:29.

114 See Surah 12:20.

115 See sections 116, 214, and 252, for instance, W.W. Davies, *The Codes of Hammurabi and Moses, with Copious Comments, Index, and Bible References* (New York 1905) 126.

116 K.A. Kitchen, *On the Reliability of the Old Testament* (William B. Eerdmans 2003) 345.

117 The New Testament, for instance, places soldiers at Jesus' tomb—a detail that, if fraudulent, would have been reckless to add. To account for the soldiers' public silence about the resurrection, Matthew 28:11-14 records that they were bribed and told to say they had fallen asleep whilst Jesus' body was stolen. For anyone remotely familiar with Roman discipline, this would have raised numerous suspicions. Notwithstanding the punishment for falling asleep on a watch being *fustuarium*, or being beaten to death by one's comrades, the idea that they could have slept through the movement of a heavy rock and the subsequent theft of a body defies logic. For writers seeking to convince an already sceptical audience that a man had risen from the dead, the mention of Roman soldiers guarding the tomb would have been a gratuitous obstacle to belief—no benefit could have come from its inclusion, whilst difficulty could have been avoided through its omission. It is the sort of detail too incredible to be mentioned unless it were true. Richard A. Gabriel, *Soldiers' Lives Through History: The Ancient World* (Greenwood Press 2007) 62.

118 Bruce W. Winter, *Roman Wives, Roman Widows: The Appearance of New Women and the Pauline Communities* (Wm. B. Eerdmans 2003) 176.

119 See Book 1, Section 190, T. Lambert Mears, *The Institutes of Gaius and Justinian, The Twelve Tables, and the CXVIIIth and CXXVIIth Novels* (London 1882) 301.

120 See Matthew 28:5-10, Mark 16:4-8, Luke 24:4-10, and John 20:10.

121 *The Fiftieth Annual Report of the American Missionary Association, and the Proceeding at the Annual Meeting Held in Boston, Mass.* (New York 1896) 106 and Jerome H. Neyrey, 'What's Wrong with This Picture? John 4, Cultural Stereotypes of Women, and Public and Private Space', in Amy-Jill Levine (ed), *A Feminist Companion to John*, vol. 1 (Sheffield Academic Press 2003) 98-99.

122 I am grateful to Lord Lyttleton's masterful arguments on this point, contained in a letter to Gilbert West in the latter's *Observations on the History and Evidences of the Resurrection of Jesus Christ* (4th edn, London 1749). The arguments contained in this chapter section follow his structure, with modifications as necessary to adapt vocabulary or include additional information.

123 Acts 7:58-8:1.

124 Acts 8:3.

125 Acts 22:3.

126 The time necessary to execute someone by stoning varied based upon the size and quantity of the rocks, the distance and aim of the throwers, and the physical constitution of the victim. The Bible does not record how long it took Stephen to die, but the process

historically took between ten and twenty minutes. See Mitchel P. Roth, *Crime and Punishment: A History of the Criminal Justice System* (2nd edn, Wadsworth 2011) 8.

127   Acts 9:1-2.

128   Acts 26:13.

129   Acts 26:14-15.

130   Acts 26:11.

131   Philippians 3:5-6.

132   1 Corinthians 4:11-12.

133   Acts 20:33-34.

134   1 Corinthians 4:13.

135   Richard Wolff, *The Popular Encyclopedia of World Religions* (Harvest House Publishers, 2007) 23 and Robert Bruce Flanders, *Nauvoo: Kingdom on the Mississippi* (Univ. Illinois Press 1975) 1.

136   Evan D. Murray and others, 'The Role of Psychotic Disorders in Religious History Considered' (2012) J. Neuropsychiatry Clin. Neurosci. 24:4, 410.

137   Frederick K. Goodwin and Kay Redfield Jamison, *Manic-Depressive Illness: Bipolar Disorders and Recurrent Depression* (2nd edn, Oxford Univ. Press 2007) 57.

138   Hani Raoul Khouzam and Fiza Singh, 'Religion, Spirituality and Psychiatry', in Sylvan D. Ambrose (ed), *Religion and Psychology: New Research* (Nova Science Publishers 2006) 137.

139   ibid.

140   George Frederic Nott, Religious Enthusiasm Considered: In Eight Sermons, Preached before the University of Oxford (Oxford Univ. Press 1803). See also Lyttleton's discussion of enthusiasm, n 122.

141   Leigh Dale, *Responses to Self Harm: An Historical Analysis of Medical, Religious, Military and Psychological Perspectives* (McFarland 2015) 50.

142   Acts 22:25.

143   Richard Belward Rackham, *The Acts of the Apostles: An Exposition* (London 1901) 73.

144   M. Bar-Ilan, 'Illiteracy in the Land of Israel in the First Centuries C.E.', in S. Fishbane, S. Schoenfeld and A. Goldschlaeger (eds), *Essays in the Social Scientific Study of Judaism and Jewish Society*, II, (Ktav 1992) 46-61.

145   Acts 17:28 (emphasis added).

146   See Acts 3:7 and 5:17.

147   See Acts 26:5.

148   See e.g. 'The Epistle of Ignatius to the Ephesians', in Alexander Roberts and James Donaldson (eds), *Ante-Nicene Library: Translations of the Writings of the Fathers Down to A.D. 325*, vol 1 (Edinburgh 1870) 160 and 'The First Epistle of Clement' in the same, at 11.

149   See William Smith (ed), *Dictionary of Greek and Roman Antiquities* (2nd edn, London 1853) 175 and 1189.

150   Warren Carter, *The Roman Empire and the New Testament: An Essential Guide* (Abingdon Press 2006) 64-73.

151   Runar M. Thorsteinsson, *Roman Christianity and Roman Stoicism: A Comparative Study of Ancient Morality* (Oxford Univ. Press 2010) 80.

152   William Paley, *A View of the Evidences of Christianity* (London 1829) 16.

153   See e.g. Luke 9:23 and Ephesians 4:22-24.

154   Acts 2:5-11.

155   Acts 3:7.

156   Acts 4:5-13.

157   John, Earl of Orrery, *The Letters of Pliny the Younger*, vol 2 (Dublin 1751) 437-39.

158   C. Stephen Evans, *A History of Western Philosophy: From the Pre-Socratics to Postmodernism*

(InterVarsity Press 2018) 101.

159   Peter Schäfer, *Jesus in the Talmud* (Princeton Univ. Press 2009) 68.

160   William Tooke, *Lucian of Samosata*, vol 1 (London 1820) 569-71.

161   James Bellamy, *Origen Against Celsus: Translated from the Original into English* (London 1710) 134 (Book I), 138 (Book II).

162   Willis Nevins, *The Arguments of the Emperor Julian against the Christians* (London 1873) 34-35.

163   James Boswell, *The Life of Samuel Johnson*, vol 3 (London 1824) 162.

164   John Jortin, *Discourses Concerning the Truth of the Christian Religion* (2nd edn, London 1747) 105.

165   Paley (n 152) 27.

166   Alfred John Church and William Jackson Brodribb, *Annals of Tacitus, Translated into English with Notes and Maps* (London, 1882) 304-05.

167   Christopher G. Boone and Ali Modarres, *City and Environment* (Temple Univ. Press 2006) 14.

168   Church and Brodribb (n 166).

169   William Wake, *The Genuine Epistles of the Apostolic Fathers* (7th edn, London 1840) 254.

170   J.H. Srawley, *The Epistles of St. Ignatius Bishop of Antioch* (SPCK 1919) 76-77.

Notes to Chapter 7 - The Great War

1   1 Peter 5:8.

2   John Milton, 'Paradise Lost', Book II, in *Milton's Poetical Works, with Life, Critical Dissertation, and Explanatory Notes by the Rev. George Gilfillan*, vol 1 (Edinburgh 1853) 40.

3   ibid.

4   See Matthew 25:41.

5   See Genesis 1:26-31.

6   See Romans 8:20 and Genesis 3:16-19.

7   Genesis 2:16-17.

8   Genesis 3:15.

9   Franz Delitzsch, *Messianic Prophecies in Historical Succession* (Samuel Ives Curtis tr, Wipf & Stock 1997) 34-36.

10   ibid 35.

11   Romans 15:4.

12   Charles Bray, *The Philosophy of Necessity* (2nd edn rev, London 1863) 41.

13   Exodus 34:6.

14   Psalm 33:5.

15   Les Murray, *New Selected Poems* (Farrar, Straus and Giroux 2014) 207.

16   Revelation 21:4.

17   1 John 4:16.

18   See e.g. Deuteronomy 7:13, Malachi 3:10, 2 Corinthians 9:8-9 and Leviticus 11:44, 19:2, 1 Peter 1:16, and Ephesians 4:11-16.

19   Daniel C. Dennett, *Elbow Room: The Varieties of Free Will Worth Wanting* (new edn, MIT Press 2015) 145.

20   See Genesis 1:12 and 2:8-9.

21   Genesis 2:17.

22   J.L. Mackie, 'Evil and Omnipotence', in Andrew Bailey (ed), *First Philosophy: Fundamental Problems and Readings in Philosophy* (2nd edn, Broadview Press 2011) 103.

23   Job 42:2

24   Alvin Plantinga, *The Nature of Necessity* (Oxford Univ. Press 1974) 189-90.

25   As Fred Berthold has noted, one problem is that Mackie and Plantiga appear to assign different meanings to the concept of 'free will', with the former insisting that an act that is completely determined (by God creating a world that constrains the choices that are 'possible' to eliminate those leading to evil) can still be free, whilst the latter argues—correctly, in my view—that free will relates to a person being able to perform an action or 'refrain from performing it; no antecedent conditions and/or causal laws determine that he will perform that action, or that he won't'. The issue appears to turn on a distinction between 'moral' free will and autonomy. Fred Berthold Jr, *God, Evil, and Human Learning: A Critique and Revision of the Free Will Defense in Theodicy* (State Univ. of New York Press 2004) 22-23.

26   Susan Neiman, *Evil in Modern Thought: An Alternative History of Philosophy* (Princeton Univ. Press 2015) 15.

27   C.S. Lewis, *Mere Christianity* (Samizdat, 2014) 30.

28   David Ray Griffin, *God, Power, and Evil: A Process Theodicy* (Westminster John Knox Press, 2004) 60.

29   ibid 60-61.

30   *The Works of Peter Pindar, Esq. to Which are Prefixed Memoirs of the Author's Life*, vol 2 (London 1812) 160.

31   Marcus Dods (ed), *The Works of Aurelius Augustine, Bishop of Hippo*, vol 1 (Edinburgh 1888) 197.

32   ibid.

33   Griffin (n 28) 61.

34   ibid.

35   Dods (n 31) 193.

36   Romans 8:21.

37   John 9:3.

38   Habakkuk 1:13.

39   Ephesians 2:3 and Isaiah 64:6.

40   Jonathan Edwards, *Sinners in the Hands of an Angry God* (Edinburgh 1745) 21.

41   Matthew 25:41.

42   See e.g. Matthew 25:41, Jude 5-6, and 2 Peter 2:4.

Notes to Chapter 8 - The Messiah

1   Shirley Lucass, *The Concept of the Messiah in the Scriptures of Judaism and Christianity* (T&T Clark 2011) 15.

2   ibid 13.

3   ibid 13-15.

4   Jacob Neusner, *Jews and Christians: The Myth of a Common Tradition* (Wipf & Stock 2003) 49.

5   Lucass (n 1) 4.

6   See Acts 3:25-26 and Galatians 3:8.

7   Abraham Gross, *Spirituality and Law: Courting Martyrdom in Christianity and Judaism* (Univ. Press of America, 2005) 84 and Isaiah HaLevi Horowitz, Shenei Luchot HaBerit Torah Shebikhtav, Vayera, Torah Ohr <https://www.sefaria.org/Shenei_Luchot_HaBerit%2C_Torah_Shebikhtav%2C_Vayera%2C_Torah_Ohr.51?ven=Shney_Luchot_Habrit_by_Rabbi_Eliyahu_Munk&lang=en&with=Chagigah&lang2=en> accessed 1 October 2020 (emphasis added).

8   Jacob Neusner, 'Defining Judaism', in Jacob Neusner and Alan J. Avery-Peck (eds),

The Blackwell Companion to Judaism (Blackwell 2003) 17. See the Jerusalem Talmud, Berakhot 17b <https://www.sefaria.org/Isaiah.11.1?lang=en&p2=Jerusalem_Talmud_Berakhot.17b&lang2=en> accessed 1 October 2020.

9   For His being born in Bethlehem, see Matthew 2:1 and Luke 2:4-7; for His being hailed as the 'Son of David', see Mark 10:48, Matthew 15:22, and Matthew 21:9; for his genealogy, see Matthew 1:1-16 and Luke 3:23-38.

10   James Bellamy, *Origen Against Celsus: Translated from the Original into English* (London 1710) 166-67.

11   'Apropos the Messiah, the Gemara asks: What is his name? The school of Rabbi Sheila says: Shiloh is his name, as it is stated: "Until when Shiloh shall come" (Genesis 49:10)'. Babylonian Talmud, Sanhedrin 98b, <https://www.sefaria.org/Sanhedrin.98b?lang=bi> accessed 1 October 2020.

12   Babylonian Talmud, Sanhedrin 5a <https://www.sefaria.org/Sanhedrin.5a.6?lang=en> accessed 1 October 2020.

13   ibid.

14   'Porphyry, as we learn from Jerome, denied its authenticity; but no other opponent is known, in Christian antiquity, who took the same course as he.' S.P. Tregelles, *Remarks on the Prophetic Visions in the Book of Daniel* (5th edn, London 1864) 294-95. See e.g. John J. Collins, *Daniel: with an Introduction to Apocalyptic Literature* (Eerdmans 1999) 103.

15   Lester L. Grabbe, 'Israel from the Rise of Hellenism to 70 CE', in J.W. Rogerson and Judith M. Lieu (eds), *The Oxford Handbook of Biblical Studies* (Oxford Univ. Press 2006) 291.

16   Peter W. Flint, 'The Shape of the "Bible" at Qumran', in Alan J. Avery-Peck and others (eds), *Judaism in Late Antiquity – Part 5*, vol. 2 (Brill 2001) 66.

17   See e.g. Rabbi Bentzion Kravitz, 'Daniel 9 – A True Biblical Interpretation', at <https://jewsforjudaism.org/knowledge/articles/daniel-9-a-true-biblical-interpretation/> accessed 1 October 2020, referencing 'King Agrippa the last King of Israel (Kings are considered anointed as it says in 1 Chronicles 11:3) who was killed during this time', and Rabbi David Rosenfeld, 'The Seventy Weeks of Daniel 9', <https://www.aish.com/atr/The-Seventy-Weeks-of-Daniel-9.html> accessed 1 October 2020, noting that 'Verse 26 describes what will happen at the time of the Second Temple's destruction. An "anointed one" will be cut off. This either refers to King Agrippa II, the Hasmonean King at the time of the destruction, the High Priest at that time, or the notion of priesthood in general. The Temple will be utterly destroyed by the Roman legions of Vespasian and Titus ("the people of the prince")'.

18   Avraham Grossman, 'The School of Literal Jewish Exegesis in Northern France', in Magne Sæbø (ed), *Hebrew Bible/Old Testament: The History of Its Interpretation*, vol. 1 part 2 (Vandenhoeck & Ruprecht 2015) 343-44.

19   See Rashi's commentary on Daniel 9:26, available at <https://www.chabad.org/library/bible_cdo/aid/16492/showrashi/true> accessed 1 October 2020.

20   Julia Wilker, 'Josephus, The Herodians, and the Jewish War', in Mladen Popović (ed), *The Jewish Revolt against Rome: Interdisciplinary Perspectives* (Brill 2011) 280-83.

21   Isidore Singer and others (eds), *The Jewish Encyclopedia: A Descriptive Record of the History, Religion, Literature, and Customs of the Jewish People from the Earliest Times to the Present Day*, vol 1 (Funk & Wagnalls 1916) 272, and Seth Schwartz, *Josephus and Judaean Politics* (Brill 1990) 151-52.

22   ibid.

23   James S. Jeffers, *The Greco-Roman World of the New Testament Era: Exploring the Background of Early Christianity* (InterVarsity Press 1999) 128.

24   The date of Herod's death is somewhat uncertain; most scholars place it in 4 BC, although some have argued for it occurring as late as 1 BC. Harold W. Hoehner, 'The Date of

the Death of Herod the Great', in Jerry Vardaman and Edwin M. Yamauchi (eds), *Chronos, Kairos, Christos: Nativity and Chronological Studies Presented to Jack Finegan* (Eisenbrauns 1989) 101.

25   Richard Alston, *Aspects of Roman History, AD 14-117* (Routledge 2005) 19.

26   Mark 13:2.

27   Franz Delitzsch, *Messianic Prophecies in Historical Succession* (Samuel Ives Curtis tr, Wipf & Stock 1997) 35.

28   See Rashi's commentary to Genesis 3:15 regarding the serpent wanting to kill Adam so that it could marry Eve, <https://www.chabad.org/library/bible_cdo/aid/8167/showrashi/true > accessed 1 October 2020.

29   Jacob Neusner, *A Theological Commentary to the Midrash*, vol. 2 (Univ. Press of America 2001) xxvii and Franz Delitzsch, 'Talmudic Notes on St. Paul's Epistle to the Romans', in M. Valentine and others (eds), *The Lutheran Quarterly*, vol. 11 (Gettysburg, 1881) 489 (emphasis added). Curiously, despite the majority of *Bereshit Rabbah* 23 being translated into English at <https://www.sefaria.org/Bereishit_Rabbah.23.5?lang=en&with=Midrash&lang2=en>, the passage relating to Genesis 4:25, in which Eve 'beheld that other see which was to come forth from another place, and who is that? It is the King Messiah' remains untranslated from the Hebrew. The words 'King Messiah' (חישמה דלמ) readily appear in a search of the text, however.

30   Jack P. Lewis, 'The Woman's Seed (Gen. 3:15)', Journal of the Evangelical Theological Society (September 1991), 299, 308.

31   ibid 308-09.

32   ibid 299.

33   ibid.

34   ibid.

35   Isaiah 7:1-2.

36   Isaiah 7:14.

37   See e.g. Rabbi Bentzion Kravitz, 'Isaiah 7:14 – A Virgin Birth?', Jews for Judaism <https://jewsforjudaism.org/knowledge/articles/isaiah-714-a-virgin-birth/>, <https://www.chabad.org/library/bible_cdo/aid/15938/showrashi/true>, and <https://www.sefaria.org/Isaiah.7?vhe=Tanach_with_Ta%27amei_Hamikra&lang=bi> accessed 1 October 2020.

38   Kravitz (n 37), noting that 'The Hebrew bible has a completely different word for virgin. The specific Hebrew word is (Betulah – הָלוּתְב). This word has no masculine form and indicates the physical sexual status of a woman. It is always translated as "virgin." For example: "the girl was very beautiful, a virgin (הָלוּתְב), and no man had had any relations with her" Genesis 24:16'.

39   See Rashi's commentary to Isaiah 7:14, claiming that the *almah* referred to Isaiah's wife <https://www.chabad.org/library/bible_cdo/aid/15938/showrashi/true> accessed 1 October 2020.

40   Kravitz (n 37).

41   Jonathan D.H. Norton, *Contours in the Text: Textual Variation in the Writings of Paul, Josephus, and the Yahad* (T&T Clark 2011) 39 and Timothy Michael Law, *When God Spoke Greek: The Septuagint and the Making of the Christian Bible* (Oxford Univ. Press 2013) 96.

42   As noted in the Jewish Encyclopedia's entry for the Peshitta, 'The Peshitta was translated directly from the Hebrew, in accordance with the Jewish tradition current in Palestine', 'the proofs which show the Peshitta to have been a Jewish work are numerous', and 'there are other incontestable proofs that the Peshitta was the work of Jews', Isidore Singer and others (eds), *The Jewish Encyclopedia: A Descriptive Record of the History, Religion, Literature, and*

Customs of the Jewish People from the Earliest Times to the Present Day, vol. 9 (Funk & Wagnalls 1907) 653-54. See also M.P. Weitzman, *The Syriac Version of the Old Testament: An Introduction* (Cambridge Univ. Press 2005) 206-10. For a discussion of the translation of 'virgin', see 'Critical Notes – The Authorship of the Peshitta', in John Merlin Powis Smith and others (eds), *The American Journal of Semitic Languages and Literature*, vol. 35 (Univ. Chicago Press 1919) 218.

43   Singer (n 42) 654.

44   See e.g. Lawrence Lincoln, 'An Analysis of the Use of *Hebel* as a Metaphorical and Symbolic Device as Interpreted in LXX Ecclesiastes', in Johann Cook and Hermann-Josef Stipp (eds), *Text-Critical and Hermeneutical Studies in the Septuagint* (Brill 2012) 166 noting that 'It is not known if there had been an earlier version than Aquila's first edition'; R.C. Foster, *Studies in the Life of Christ* (College Press Printing 2000) 252-53; and Geoffrey W. Bromiley and others (eds), *The International Standard Bible Encyclopedia*, vol. 4 (Wm. B. Eerdmans 1988) 404.

45   William F. Beck, a noted Biblical scholar and translator, wrote how he had 'searched exhaustively for instances in which *almah* might mean a non-virgin or a married woman. There is no passage where *almah* is not a virgin. Nowhere in the Bible or elsewhere does *almah* mean anything but a virgin.' William F. Beck, 'What Does Almah Mean?' 3 March 1970 <https://essays.wls.wels.net/bitstream/handle/123456789/301/BeckAlmah.pdf?sequence=1&isAllowed=y> accessed 1 October 2020.

46   ibid.

47   Tremper Longman III and David E. Garland (eds), *The Expositor's Bible Commentary: Proverbs - Isaiah* (rev. edn, Zondervan 2008) 520.

48   Beck (n 46).

49   See 'Judaism: Weekly Torah Readings' for Ki Tavo and Nitzavim, <https://www.jewishvirtuallibrary.org/weekly-torah-readings> accessed 1 October 2020.

50   See Rashi's commentary for verse 5, noting that the ears would be unstopped of those 'Who did not hearken to the voice of the prophets until now', <https://www.chabad.org/library/bible_cdo/aid/15966/showrashi/true>. As for Isaiah 61:1, Rashi commented that 'This anointing is nothing but an expression of nobility and greatness', <https://www.chabad.org/library/bible_cdo/aid/15992/showrashi/true> accessed 1 October 2020.

51   Lidija Novakovic, '4Q521: The Works of the Messiah or Signs of the Messianic Time?' in Michael Thomas Davis and Brent A. Strawn (eds), *Qumran Studies: New Approaches, New Questions* (Wm. B. Eerdmans 2007) 210.

52   John J. Collins, 'Jesus, Messianism and the Dead Sea Scrolls', in James H. Charlesworth and others (eds), *Qumran-Messianism: Studies on the Messianic Expectations in the Dead Sea Scrolls* (Mohr Siebeck 1998) 113.

53   Although the dating of the Gospel of Matthew is somewhat uncertain, a consensus places its composition between AD 80-90, with the community at Qumran being abandoned—and the scrolls necessarily having been hidden beforehand—around the destruction of Jerusalem in AD 70. Matthew A. Collins, *The Use of Sobriquets in the Qumran Dead Sea Scrolls* (T&T Clark 2009) 7.

54   With respect to the arguments of some that Zechariah 9 forms part of a later work from chapters 1-8, Eugene H. Merrill has written that 'Though the arguments for divided authorship are quite substantial … they are not insuperable and, in fact, even at the level of vocabulary, style, motifs, and themes a strong case can be made for the contrary and traditional persuasion that the entire book originated from the pen of one man, its attributive author, and from the last quarter of the sixth century'. Eugene H. Merrill, *Haggai, Zecharia, Malachi: An Exegetical Commentary* (Biblical Studies Press 2003) 75.

55   See Rashi's commentary to Zechariah 9:9, noting that with respect to the phrase 'Behold! Your king shall come to you', it 'is impossible to interpret this except as referring to the King Messiah', <https://www.chabad.org/library/bible_cdo/aid/16213/showrashi/true> accessed 1 October 2020.

56   Babylonian Talmud, Sanhedrin 98a:13, <https://www.sefaria.org/Sanhedrin.98a?lang=bi> accessed 1 October 2020.

57   See e.g. C.G. Montefiore and H.M.J. Loewe (eds), *A Rabbinic Anthology* (Cambridge Univ. Press 2012) 544; Rabbi Stuart Federow, *Judaism and Christianity: A Contrast* (iUniverse 2012) 186; and Mark S. Kinzer and Jennifer M. Rosner, *Israel's Messiah and the People of God: A Vision for Messianic Jewish Covenant Fidelity* (Lutterworth Press 2012) 109.

58   See Rashi's commentary on Isaiah 53:2-3, reflecting the application of the passage to Israel <https://www.chabad.org/library/bible_cdo/aid/15984/showrashi/true> accessed 1 October 2020.

59   See Bellamy (n 10) 175, Tovia Singer, 'Who is God's Suffering Servant? The Rabbinic Interpretation of Isaiah 53', Outreach Judaism <https://outreachjudaism.org/gods-suffering-servant-isaiah-53/> and Gerald Sigal, 'Is it true that Jews interpreted Isaiah 53 as referring to the Messiah before Rashi?', Jews for Judaism <https://jewsforjudaism.org/knowledge/articles/is-it-true-that-jews-interpreted-isaiah-53-as-referring-to-the-messiah-before-rashi>, accessed 1 October 2020.

60   Babylonian Talmud, Sanhedrin 98b, <https://www.sefaria.org/Sanhedrin.98b?lang=bi> accessed 1 October 2020.

61   Sol Scharfstein, *Torah and Commentary: The Five Books of Moses* (Ktav 2008) 533.

62   Martin Sicker, *An Introduction to Judaic Thought and Rabbinic Literature* (Praeger 2007) 71.

63   Jacob Neusner, *The Classics of Judaism: A Textbook and Reader* (Westminster John Knox Press 1995) 95.

64   Ruth Rabba 4, <https://www.sefaria.org/Ruth_Rabbah.4?lang=en> accessed 1 October 2020.

65   Ilana Sasson, *The Arabic Translation and Commentary of Yefet ben 'Eli on the Book of Proverbs*, vol 1 (Brill 2016) 3.

66   S.R. Driver and A. Neubauer, *The Fifty-Third Chapter of Isaiah According to the Jewish Interpreters* (James Parker 1877) 19-24.

67   Arthur Green, *A Guide to the Zohar* (Stanford Univ. Press 2004) 87.

68   Driver and Neubaur (n 66) 14-15.

69   Babylonian Talmud (n 60).

70   Origen also recognised the persuasiveness of this argument. Bellamy (n 10) 176-77.

71   Mark 6:3.

72   Luke 22:28.

73   Matthew 8:16-17.

74   Mark 10:45.

75   Luke 23:9.

76   Luke 23:32-53 and Matthew 27:57.

77   1 John 2:2 and Luke 24.

78   See Rashi's commentary to Zechariah 11:12-13, <https://www.chabad.org/library/bible_cdo/aid/16215/showrashi/true> and Babylonian Talmud, Chullin 92a <https://www.sefaria.org/Chullin.92a?lang=en> accessed 1 October 2020.

79   It is unclear what the precise monetary value of this silver was, particularly in terms of its purchasing power in the ancient world. Assuming that Judas was paid with Tyrian shekels—valued by the Temple authorities for their higher silver content—thirty pieces would have had an approximate silver content of 430 grams, valuing them in 2019 prices at $240.

Isidore Singer and others (eds), *The Jewish Encyclopedia*, vol 12 (Funk & Wagnalls 1906) 485.

80   This field became known as *Akeldama*, or the Field of Blood, and served as a burial ground until the Middle Ages. Simon Sebag Montefiore, *Jerusalem: The Biography* (Knopf 2011) 114.

81   It must be acknowledged that some translations render the word 'potter' as 'treasury' based upon the use of this in the Syriac Peshitta, but this 'cannot be sustained. This is opposed by the critical maxim that the more difficult reading is to be preferred. How a potter came to be in the house of the Lord is hard to say, and this may well have suggested the emendation "treasury". But why should any one have changed "treasury" to "potter?" Again the preponderance of textual authority is against is. Only one Hebrew manuscript, the Peshito-Syriac version, and (possibly) one Targum, give or suggest this reading. The reading "treasury" is no less opposed by the internal evidence. For the whole object of the context is to stamp this valuation of the prophet as contemptible and iniquitous. This idea is strikingly emphasized by the command that the wages of the Lord's servant should be given, *not* into the Lord's treasury, where it would naturally have belonged, but to the potter, as money made unclean and unfit for the Lord's use by the wickedness which was expressed in giving it. To this line of thought the sense given by the word "treasury" is wholly foreign.' S.H. Kellog, 'Matthew and Zechariah', in Joseph Sanderson (ed), *The Pulpit Treasury*, vol 2 (New York 1885) 424-25.

82   Matthew 27:35.

83   This section of the Babylonian Talmud attributes his manner of execution to stoning instead of crucifixion, but preserves the key elements of his death on Passover Eve. Sanhedrin 43A, <https://www.sefaria.org/Sanhedrin.43a.20?ven=William_Davidson_Edition_-_English&lang=en> accessed 1 October 2020.

84   Michael L. Satow, *Creating Judaism: History, Tradition, Practice* (Columbia Univ. Press 2006) 226. See Maimonides' *Iggeret Teiman*, written in reply to a letter from R. Jacob of Yemen, <https://www.sefaria.org/Iggerot_HaRambam%2C_Iggeret_Teiman?ven=Iggeret_Teiman&lang=en> accessed 1 October 2020.

85   'A key issue is raised in the text—namely, the involvement of lawless persons from among Daniel's people who join the forces of Antiochus and/or support him (11:14, 16). The writer notes the reason for this—to fulfill the vision of rebellion that was depicted in 8:13 and in Gabriel's answer (9:24). This did not succeed because the appointed end had not arrived—that would occur under Antiochus IV, his younger son.' Philip W. Comfort (ed), *Cornerstone Biblical Commentary*, vol 9 (Tyndale House 2010) 445. See also George Wesley Buchanan, *The Book of Daniel* (Wipf & Stock 2005) 421-22 and Dov Gera, *Judaea and Mediterranean Politics: 219 to 161 B.C.E.* (Brill 1998) 28.

86   See *Bava Metzia 105a*, Babylonian Talmud <https://www.sefaria.org/Bava_Metzia.105a.13?lang=en> and Rashi's commentary on Daniel 11:14, <https://www.chabad.org/library/bible_cdo/aid/16494/showrashi/true> accessed 1 October 2020.

87   Maimonides, *Mishna Torah*, Laws of Kings and Wars 11:3 <https://www.sefaria.org/Mishneh_Torah%2C_Kings_and_Wars.11.3?ven=Laws_of_Kings_and_Wars._trans._Reuven_Brauner,_2012&lang=en> accessed 1 October 2020.

88   Horowitz (n 7).

89   2 Samuel 7:16.

90   Genesis 3:15 and 2 Samuel 7:16.

91   Isaiah 35:3-6, 61:1, and 7:14.

92   Zechariah 9:9.

93   Isaiah 53:11.

94   Isaiah 53:8-9.

95   Isaiah 50:5-6, Psalm 22:18, and Psalm 22:6-8.

96   Zechariah 11:12-13.

97   John MacArthur, *The MacArthur New Testament Commentary: Matthew 24-28* (Moody Press 1989) 144.

98   John 1:29.

99   Rabbi Michael Skobac, 'Why Don't Jews See Jesus in The Scriptures?', Jews for Judaism <https://jewsforjudaism.org/knowledge/articles/why-dont-jews-see-jesus-in-the-scriptures> accessed 1 October 2020.

100   See e.g. 'The King Messiah will in some future time come, restore the kingdom of David to its former power, build the Temple, bring together the scattered of Israel, and all the ancient laws will again be in force.' 'Jewish Belief in Messiah and the Messianic Age', Jews for Judaism <https://jewsforjudaism.org/knowledge/articles/jewish-belief-in-messiah-and-the-messianic-age> accessed 1 October 2020.

101   Skobac (n 99).

102   'The ninth king is King Messiah, who, in the future, will rule from one end of the world to the other, as it is said, "He shall have dominion also from sea to sea" (Psalm 72:8); and another Scripture text stays, "And the stone that smote the image became a great mountain, and filled the whole earth" (Daniel 2:35)'. See Pirke de-Rabbi Eliezer 11:19 <https://www.sefaria.org/Pirkei_DeRabbi_Eliezer.11.19?lang=en> accessed 1 October 2020.

103   Babylonian Talmud, Sanhedrin 98a:13, <https://www.sefaria.org/Sanhedrin.98a?lang=bi> accessed 1 October 2020.

104   ibid.

105   Emphasis added.

106   'Zechariah's king is peaceful, humble and gentle, and thus riding a donkey shows that Jesus comes as Prince of Peace. The donkey was also the animal used by merchants, businessmen, and men of peace. Had Jesus come as a conqueror or warrior he would have used a war horse'. Andrew C. Brunson, *Psalm 118 in the Gospel of John: An Intertextual Study on the New Exodus Pattern in the Theology of John* (Mohr Siebeck 2003) 266-67.

107   Isaiah 53:6.

108   See Philippians 2:10-11, Romans 14:11, and Isaiah 45:23.

109   Romans 3:23.

110   Romans 6:23.

111   Emphasis added.

112   Emphasis added.

113   Emphasis added.

114   See Rashi's commentary to Daniel 2:44, noting that 'And in the days of these kings' meant 'in the days of these kings, when the kingdom of Rome is still in existence', <https://www.chabad.org/library/bible_cdo/aid/16485/showrashi/true> accessed 1 October 2020 (emphasis added).

Notes to Chapter 9 - The Rational Faith

1   Michael L. Kennedy, *The Jacobin Clubs in the French Revolution, 1793-1795* (Berghahn Books 2005) 155, 158.

2   Anselm of Canterbury, *Monologion - Chapter 1*, <https://sourcebooks.fordham.edu/basis/anselm-monologium.asp#CHAPTER%20I> accessed 1 October 2020; Brian Davies and Brian Leftow (eds), *The Cambridge Companion to Anselm* (Cambridge Univ. Press 2004) 11

3   Michael R. Slater, *William James on Ethics and Faith* (Cambridge Univ. Press 2009) 42.

4   Thomas Nagel, *The Last Word* (Oxford Univ. Press 1997) 130 (emphasis added).

5   Blaise Pascal, *Thoughts on Religion, and Other Subjects* (Edinburgh 1751) 2.

6   Aldous Huxley, *Ends and Means: An Inquiry into the Nature of Ideals* (Transaction Publishers 2012) 315.

7   Psalm 19:1.

8   Richard Dawid, *String Theory and the Scientific Method* (Cambridge Univ. Press 2013) 92

9   See Chapter 2, nn 191-94.

10   Charles Drelincourt, *The Christian's Defence Against the Fears of Death, with Seasonable Directions How to Prepare Ourselves to Die Well* (Marius D'Assigny tr, London 1825) 3.

11   1 Corinthians 15:22.

12   See n 4 of the Introduction.

13   Thomas Chalmers, *The Evidence and Authority of the Christian Revelation* (4th edn, Edinburgh 1817) 216.

14   M.A. Thiers, *The History of the French Revolution* (London 1845) 374.

15   Numbers 23:19.

16   See e.g. 'Watchtower False Prophecies', Apologia Online Academy, <http://www.apologiaonlineacademy.com/files/128915684.pdf > accessed 1 October 2020 and John Dart, 'Jehovah's Witnesses Abandon Key Doctrine: Sect has quietly retreated from prediction that those alive in 1914 would see end of world', 4 November 1995 <https://www.latimes.com/archives/la-xpm-1995-11-04-me-64883-story.html> accessed 1 October 2020.

17   See 1 Peter 5:2 and John 10:11.

18   It is described as a type of zizania then common throughout the area which 'grows among corn: the reapers do not separate the plant, but, after threshing, they reject the seeds by means of a fan or sieve. … Its leaves resemble those of wheat or barley, but spring up rougher.' *Extracts from the Works of Travellers, Illustrative of Various Passages in Holy Scripture* (Society for Promoting Christian Knowledge 1841) 163-64.

19   Richard Cecil, *Memoirs of the Rev. John Newton* (London 1839) 32 and John Newton, *Olney Hymns, in Three Books* (New York, 1810) 59.

20   Baron Albrecht von Haller, *Letters from Baron Haller to His Daughter, on the Truths of the Christian Religion* (London 1803) 145-46.

21   St. Augustine, *The Confessions* (Hendrickson Publishers 2004) 90.

22   Samuel IJsseling, *Rhetoric and Philosophy in Conflict: An Historical Survey* (Martinus Nijhoff 2012) 41.

23   Stephen Bullivant, 'Europe's Young Adults and Religion: Findings from the European Social Survey (2014-16) to inform the 2018 Synod of Bishops', 21 March 2018, Benedict XVI Centre for Religion and Society, <www.stmarys.ac.uk/research/centres/benedict-xvi/docs/2018-mar-europe-young-people-report-eng.pdf> accessed 1 October 2020.

24   S.P. Tregelles, *Remarks on the Prophetic Visions in the Book of Daniel* (London 1864) 296.

25   George A. Akerlof and others, 'An Analysis of Out-of-Wedlock Childbearing in the United States', May 1996, The Quarterly Journal of Economics, 277.

26   Maxine Eichner, *The Free-Market Family: How the Market Crushed the American Dream (and How It Can Be Restored)* (Oxford Univ. Press 2020) 83, noting that 'these suicides are related to family status: In 2005, single middle-aged women were almost three times as likely to commit suicide as married women. And single men were three-and-a-half times more likely than married men to take their own lives'.

27   See 'The Majority of Children Live With Two Parents, Census Bureau Reports', 17 November 2016 <www.census.gov/newsroom/press-releases/2016/cb16-192.html> accessed 1 October 2020 and Sam Tyano and others (eds), *Parenthood and Mental Health: A Bridge Between Infant and Adult Psychiatry* (Wiley-Blackwell 2010) 36.

28 As of 2019, the global pornography industry's revenues were estimated to be approximately $100 billion, Catharine A. MacKinnon, *Butterfly Politics* (Harvard Univ. Press 2017) 411. Per the International Monetary Fund's listing of countries by GDP, Kenya's 2019 estimated GDP was $98.6 billion.

29 Arvind Singhal and others, 'Risk of self-harm and suicide in people with specific psychiatric and physical disorders: comparisons between disorders using English national record linkage', Journal of the Royal Society of Medicine (May 2014) <www.ncbi.nlm.nih.gov/pmc/articles/PMC4023515/> accessed 1 October 2020.

30 Mark Olfson and others, 'National trends in hospital-treated self-harm events among middle-aged adults', General Hospital Psychiatry (December 2015) <www.sciencedirect.com/science/article/abs/pii/S0163834315001954> accessed 1 October 2020.

31 See Table HH4. Households by Size: 1960 to Present, < www.census.gov/data/tables/time-series/demo/families/households.html> accessed 1 October 2020. In 1960, 6,917 households out of a total of 52,799 consisted of one person. In 2019, the figures had changed to 36,479 out of 128,579. For the UK, see 'Families and Households in the UK: 2019' Figure 4 <www.ons.gov.uk/peoplepopulationandcommunity/birthsdeathsandmarriages/families/bulletins/familiesandhouseholds/2019> accessed 1 October 2020.

32 Sachin Jain, 'A Treatment for Loneliness: Can a physician write a prescription for friendship?' *Harvard Medicine* <https://hms.harvard.edu/magazine/imaging/treatment-loneliness> accessed 1 October 2020.

33 William Wilberforce, *A Practical View of the Prevailing Religious System of Professed Christians, in the Higher and Middle Classes in this Country, Contrasted with Real Christianity* (4th edn, Glasgow 1833) 446-48.

34 George Elliot, *Middlemarch* (Gregory Maertz ed., Broadview 2004) 640.

35 'While We're at It', *First Things* October 2020 69, quoting Fr. Gerald Murray.

36 Penn Jillette, *God, No! Signs You May Already Be an Atheist and Other Magical Tales* (Simon & Schuster 2012) 59-62.

37 Romans 10:17.

38 2 Timothy 4:2.

39 William J. Wright, *Martin Luther's Understanding of God's Two Kingdoms: A Response to the Challenge of Skepticism* (Baker Academic 2010) 106.

40 Warren Mosher (ed), *The Catholic Reading Circle Review*, vol. 12 (Youngstown 1898) 14.

41 Tertullian of Carthage, *Apology of Tertullian* (S. Thelwall tr, Dalcassian 2017) 30 (emphasis added).

42 Eric Francis Osborn, *Justin Martyr* (Mohr 1973) 77.

43 See Marcus Dods (ed), *The Works of Aurelius Augustine, Bishop of Hippo*, vol. 1 (Edinburgh 1871) 80 and 78.

44 ibid 192.

45 John Marenbon (ed) *The Oxford Handbook of Medieval Philosophy* (Oxford Univ. Press 2012) 49.

46 Isaac Newton, *The Mathematical Principles of Natural Philosophy*, Book III (Andrew Motte, tr., New York 1848) 504-05.

47 Helge Kragh, *Matter and Spirit in the Universe: Scientific and Religious Preludes to Modern Cosmology* (Imperial College Press 2004) 143.

48 Joseph Butler, *The Analogy of Religion, Natural and Revealed* (Oxford Univ. Press 1849).

49 Herbert Schlossberg, 'How Great Awakenings Happen', First Things (October 2000) <www.firstthings.com/article/2000/10/how-great-awakenings-happen> accessed 1 October 2020.

50 ibid.

51   ibid.

52   ibid.

53   ibid.

54   See e.g. Acts 2:46, Acts 5:42, Acts 20:20, 1 Corinthians 16:19, Colossians 4:15, and Romans 16:1-27.

55   Ephraim Radner, 'Theology After the Virus', *First Things*, August 11, 2020 <https://www.firstthings.com/web-exclusives/2020/08/theology-after-the-virus> accessed 1 October 2020.

56   Romans 8:31.

57   Romans 1:16.

Made in the USA
Monee, IL
11 September 2021